Genesis

INTERPRETATION
A Bible Commentary for Teaching and Preaching

INTERPRETATION
A BIBLE COMMENTARY FOR TEACHING AND PREACHING

James Luther Mays, *Editor*
Patrick D. Miller, Jr., *Old Testament Editor*
Paul J. Acthemeier, *New Testament Editor*

Walter Brueggemann

Genesis

A Bible Commentary for
Teaching and Preaching

John Knox Press
ATLANTA

Library of Congress Cataloging in Publication Data

Brueggemann, Walter.
  Genesis : in Bible commentary for teaching and preaching.

  (Interpretation, a Bible commentary for teaching and preaching)
  Bibliography: p.
  1. Bible. O.T. Genesis—Commentaries.
I. Title. II. Series.
BS1235.3.B78   222′.1107   81-82355
ISBN 0-8042-3101-X   AACR2

© copyright John Knox Press 1982
10 9 8 7 6 5 4 3 2 1
Printed in the United States of America
John Knox Press
Atlanta, Georgia 30365

SERIES PREFACE

This series of commentaries offers an interpretation of the books of the Bible. It is designed to meet the need of students, teachers, ministers, and priests for a contemporary expository commentary. These volumes will not replace the historical critical commentary or homiletical aids to preaching. The purpose of this series is rather to provide a third kind of resource, a commentary which presents the integrated result of historical and theological work with the biblical text.

An interpretation in the full sense of the term involves a text, an interpreter, and someone for whom the interpretation is made. Here, the text is what stands written in the Bible in its full identity as literature from the time of "the prophets and apostles," the literature which is read to inform, inspire, and guide the life of faith. The interpreters are scholars who seek to create an interpretation which is both faithful to the text and useful to the church. The series is written for those who teach, preach, and study the Bible in the community of faith.

The comment generally takes the form of expository essays. It is planned and written in the light of the needs and questions which arise in the use of the Bible as Holy Scripture. The insights and results of contemporary scholarly research are used for the sake of the exposition. The commentators write as exegetes and theologians. The task which they undertake is both to deal with what the texts say and to discern their meaning for faith and life. The exposition is the unified work of one interpreter.

The text on which the comment is based is the Revised Standard Version of the Bible. The general availability of this translation makes the printing of a translation unnecessary and saves the space for comment. The text is divided into sections appropriate to the particular book; comment deals with passages as a whole, rather than proceeding word by word, or verse by verse.

Writers have planned their volumes in light of the requirements set by the exposition of the book assigned to them. Biblical books differ in character, content, and arrangement. They also differ in the way they have been and are used in the liturgy, thought, and devotion of the church. The distinctiveness and use of particular books have been taken into account in decisions about the approach, emphasis, and use of space in the commentaries. The goal has been to allow writers to develop the format which provides for the best presentation of their interpretation.

The result, writers and editors hope, is a commentary which both explains and applies, an interpretation which deals with both the meaning and the significance of biblical texts. Each commentary reflects, of course, the writer's own approach and perception of the church and world. It could and should not be otherwise. Every interpretation of any kind is individual in that sense; it is one reading of the text. But all who work at the interpretation of Scripture in the church need the help and stimulation of a colleague's reading and understanding of the text. If these volumes serve and encourage interpretation in that way, their preparation and publication will realize their purpose.

The Editors

PREFACE

The intent of this commentary (and indeed of this entire series) requires and evokes interpretive moves that go beyond the conventions of a commentary. This commentary, of course, makes much use of the rich tradition of commentaries. And that tradition is richer in Genesis than almost anywhere else in Old Testament studies. It has not been the purpose of this effort to advance beyond these commentaries, either in terms of method or in terms of historical-critical understandings. The primary task of this commentary has been to bring the text and its claims closer to the faith and ministry of the church.

And that is a responsibility requiring boldness, imagination, and some risk. The farther one moves away from "then" toward "now," the more the risks increase. On the one hand, that is because we have no methodological consensus about how to move from "then" to "now," or even if it is legitimate to make the move. On the other hand, the move very much depends on the interpreter's judgment about the needs and prospects of the present situation, a judgment inevitably personal. But the intent of the commentary has not permitted caution or reserve about those moves. Thus the commentary has been required to take some interpretive chances which may be questionable. The purpose of such chances is not to arrive at a "final judgment" on a question, but to invite the reader to the same hazardous process of moving in the interpretive space between "then" and "now." The juggling act is to speak with immediacy and contemporaneity over a longer period. That is no mean task, but one which is attempted here.

On the difficult question of language for God (i.e., masculine and feminine metaphors and pronouns), the best that can be done is to acknowledge the problem and claim to have been as responsible as possible. Phyllis Trible (*God and the Rhetoric of Sexuality,* 1978, p. 23, n.5), who has thought long about this question, has attempted to deal with the problem by avoiding pronouns. Norman Gottwald (*The Tribes of Yahweh,* 1979, pp. 685–89 and especially n. 628) from whom I have learned so much, has proceeded by putting masculine pronouns in quotes. Both suggestions help, but neither is sufficient, as both Trible and Gottwald know. Here I have managed the process as best I could, by avoiding pronouns as much as possible, but where necessary, using them because I have not known what else to do. But such use reflects no lack of awareness of the danger of such use, no sense of having done the best thing, no failure to recognize the high stakes in the question. I can only resolve to continue reflection on the matter.

It remains to thank a community of support which makes such scholarship not only possible but worthwhile. That community includes Eden Seminary and our President Robert T. Fauth, for a generous sabbatical leave, and hospitable Old Testament colleagues in Cambridge University who accommodated me in every way. I am grateful to the editors of the series, Professors James L. Mays and Patrick D. Miller, Jr., for their steadfast support, their firm insistence on quality, and their tenacity for the vision of the series. They have been patient and attentive to detail in most important ways. My colleague, Professor M. Douglas Meeks, continues to be my dialogue partner and teacher in most important ways. Most concrete thanks goes to four people who have stayed "in the trenches" with the manuscript to ready it for publication, Jane Hoffman, Arlene Jones, Joan Smith and, especially, Mary Waters, my secretary, who presides over my work with unlimited patience and unfailing good judgment. But finally my thanks is to the processive community of students, colleagues, pastors (especially my wife, Mary), and church people (only some of whom I know by name) who assure me regularly that such expository work matters. More than that, one does not need to know.

Walter Brueggemann
Eden Theological Seminary
Maundy Thursday, in the midst
of Passover, 1980

CONTENTS

Abbreviations used in citations

AB   Anchor Bible

BZAW Beihefte zur Zeitschrift für die alttestamentliche
      Wissenschaft

CBQ   Catholic Biblical Quaterly

CTM   Currents in Theology and Mission

JBL   Journal of Biblical Literature

JSOT   Journal for the Study of the Old Testament

VT   Vetus Testamentum

VTS   Supplement to Vetus Testamentum

ZAW   Zeitschrift für die Alttestamentliche Wissenschaft

ZTK   Zeitschrift für Theologie und Kirche

INTRODUCTION

This exposition of Genesis comes out of the church and is addressed to the church. For that reason, we may structure our interpretation according to the structure of the Statement of Faith of the United Church of Christ, the church of which the author is a member. That Statement is organized around two calls from God:

> God calls the worlds into being . . .
> God calls us into the church . . .

The two calls must be taken together. Neither may be taken alone nor subsumed under the other. The two calls together affirm that God has formed *the world* to be his world and *a special community* to be his witness. It is the same God who calls the world and who calls the special community. Both creations, world and community of faith, spring "fresh from the word"; both have been evoked by the speech of this God.

Genesis is structured around the same calls: *(a)* Gen. 1—11 concerns the affirmation that God calls the world into being to be his faithful world. *(b)* Gen. 12—50 concerns the affirmation that God calls a special people to be faithfully his people. Genesis is a reflection upon and witness to these two calls. It is concerned with the *gifts* given in these calls, the *demands* announced in them, and the various *responses* evoked by them.

The Call as an Interpretive Center

To focus on the call as the center of our exposition has important implications. The call announces the special character of God as the one who calls. It announces a special vocation for creation and for Israel as the ones called and the ones who must answer. In the faith of the Bible, creation and Israel are distinct, two objects of God's call. While this is an ambiguous statement, we may treat the objects together as the partner of the God who calls. In terms of God's call, they have the same function, yet they are not confused with each other. The call announces that the peculiar connection between God and world/Israel is that of calling and answering.

1. *The substance of the call in Genesis is the promise.* This exposition follows a long theological tradition in presenting

1

promise as the theological focus of Genesis. The narrative concerns the promise God has made to Israel to give it land and to be their peculiar God. *Promise* weaves in and out of the narrative. At times it is explicit and intrinsic to the texts. At other times, it is imposed on the text in a secondary way. At still other times, it is only implicit and not stated at all. But in all three cases, primary, secondary, and implicit, the persistent claim is that God has promised to stay with his called partner until his way is accomplished. The partner—creation/Israel—is called to rely only on God's promise.

The theological interest of the text concerns the way in which the two partners (God and creation/Israel) deal with the promise. The one making the promise is sovereign and will have that promise taken seriously. God is gracious, for he makes his promise even to the unqualified. And God perhaps is faithful, watching over his promise to fulfillment. The one to whom the promise is given is summoned to be obedient, responsive, and perhaps faithful. Notice: for both the caller and the called —*perhaps* faithful. That is the issue of Genesis. It is not fully known whether Yahweh, the God of Israel and Lord of creation, will be faithful. And it is not known whether creation or Israel will be faithful. Each text is an invitation to faithfulness and an exploration of the risks and temptations that accompany faithfulness.

2. *The material by which Genesis presents the issue of call consists of diverse narratives which have become the canon of the community.* (There are some few materials other than narrative in Genesis, such as poems and genealogies, but they are marginal for our study.) The narratives come from many times and places and are couched in various literary genres.

The peculiar character of the various materials must be respected. Our exposition must not level the texts nor treat them uniformly. This is a temptation for theologians. But we will do better to recognize the distinctive angularity of the texts and the world from which they come.

At the same time, we do not simply deal with materials which have been appropriated from the larger repertoire of the Near East. As we deal with the material of the call, we are always somewhat in transit. These are materials *from the ancient world* which are *becoming the canon* of the church. Our exposition must face the whole range of possibilities in that process of becoming. While the material has been declared canon, in a more functional way it becomes canon in the time when we take it normatively. Yet in becoming canon, it does not cease to be material shaped by and cast in the ways of the Near East. A theological interest in canonical material neither permits nor requires us to abandon what we know about the world in which the material was shaped.

The movement of the material from ancient Near Eastern literature to canon is the route of our exposition. The decisive ingredient in the move from one function to another is the increasing relation of the material to the substance of promise. Not all of the material is related to promise in the beginning. Indeed, some of it is quite remote. Even in our Bibles some of it continues to stand at a distance from promise. But as the texts are drawn closer to promise, either by redaction, traditioning, or exposition, they come more fully to be the normative literature to which we attend.

So we must deal with the diverse origins of the narrative and with the movement of the texts in becoming canon. But our primary concern is with the material as the canon of the church. To take the text seriously as canon is not a decision we have made simply for the purposes of this exposition. An old and deep decision made by the community of faith evokes and justifies this commentary. The matter of canonical authority is not something peripheral or extraneous to our exposition. Nor is it a matter of woodenly asserting the "truth" or "validity" of a text.

Rather, the canonical character of the material is important in two respects. First, it requires that the texts be taken seriously on the assumption that when we listen faithfully they may yield to us important disclosures about our life and faith. The disclosures of God may not be forced and we must leave some texts unsatisfied; but we begin with the presupposition that the texts bear burdens which are important to us.

Second, the canonical character of the text indicates the kinds of expectations we may have and the kinds of questions we may ask. It affirms that we are not primarily interested in historical questions, though they must be considered where appropriate. Nor are we primarily interested in literary questions, though they must be faced when it is useful. But our main purpose in this exposition is to try to hear in the text what there

3

is of the gospel as it bears upon the life of the community of faith. To identify the material as canon is to recognize the importance and legitimacy of theological exposition.

3. *The mode of the call is story-telling.* Genesis is a process of story telling in which there are important transactions between listener and teller. That is why, in our exposition, we have referred to "the listening community." The stories do not exist by themselves nor for themselves. They exist as they are told and valued, transmitted and remembered by a community which is seriously engaged in a life and ministry of faith.

The faith that Israel transmits here is not about a *structure* of reality (as in myth) nor a *chronicle* of events (as in history). Rather, it is about a memory that is transformed, criticized, and extended each time it is told. It is a tradition in which there are no objective controls but only the perception and passion, imagination and discipline, of those who care for the memory. It is a memory of gifts and surprises, of discontinuities and incongruities. For such a community, the *mode of the story* matches the *substance of promise* in a peculiar way and is important in Israel's self-understanding. Story is not interested in "deep structures," in "abiding truths," nor in "exact proofs." It does not trade in "eternal realities." Thus our exposition must avoid all the *solidity* which appeals to myth and all the *proof* which rests on history. Story offers nothing that is absolutely certain, either by historical certification or by universal affirmation. It lives, rather, by the *scandal* of concreteness, by the *freedom* of imagination, and by the *passion* of hearing. It is *concrete* in telling about real people in a specific time and place who engaged in irreversible events. It is freely *imaginative.* The story can be told in more than one way. It has more than one meaning, depending on the way it is told and the way it is heard. The hearing must be done with *passion.* The listening community knows that the events now being presented may matter as much to "us" as to the original participants. These stories are not timeless, but there is a coincidence so that the events of another time may loom with authority in the present time. Thus, the old concrete events may intrude upon and transform the present situation.

4

Story is concrete and particular, as is every good promise. But stories are also open-ended. They do not linger in the first moment of the promise-making. They have a career and can follow the promise. Stories can tell promises toward fulfillment.

And when the story is finished, both the teller and the listener are faced with possibilities, with the freedom that the promise may take more than one form of fulfillment.

The Intent and Method of the Commentary

It is the purpose of this exposition to consider the texts as they address the community of faith in its present context. In that regard, this commentary does not seek to do what critical commentaries have done, though it relies on them. Of these, we have found the older exposition of Luther and Calvin particularly suggestive. Of the more recent critical commentaries, reliance has been on the work of Gunkel, Von Rad and Westermann. (In the use of these commentaries, reference is made only to the text discussed.)

Though our exposition depends on careful exegesis, it does not seek either to reiterate that fund of learning nor to advance the frontiers of exegetical method. It has a much more modest though specific aim. That aim has resulted in an unevenness of discussion. Some passages have been given disproportionate attention to the neglect of others. Further, exposition of this kind has required some interpretive risks. Perhaps some of the risks run beyond the evidence of the text and will be found doubtful. But we have judged those risks justifiable, given the task of the exposition. For the church is not permitted simply to repeat the "old truths." It must listen for and take a chance that from time to time the normative word is breaking through in new ways. The purpose of this commentary has required some other decisions related to method and presentation:

1. By and large, historical questions have not been given major attention in this commentary. That is appropriate for two reasons:

First, the recent scholarly consensus concerning the history of the patriarchal period is now very much under attack. Until recently, it was assumed that the patriarchs could be securely placed in the Middle Bronze (and some said Late Bronze) period and correlated to the language, movements, and customs of other peoples. Especially because of the work of John van Seters (*Abraham in History and Tradition,* 1975) and Thomas Thompson (*The Historicality of the Patriarchal Narratives,* 1974), this consensus is now in doubt. Therefore, it seemed prudent not to rely on such unsettled opinion.

Second, because of our aim, those questions of historical

5

location have not required settlement. That is not because historical issues are unimportant, nor are the materials treated as history-less; but with some few exceptions, it has seemed sufficient to deal with the claims of the text itself and the presuppositions of the story-teller.

2. In a similar way, literary questions have been treated sparsely. The term "literary criticism" is used in Old Testament study in two distinct ways. In current use, literary criticism describes attention to the form, structure, and rhetoric of the text. This method attempts to deal with the text on its own terms and is to be sharply distinguished from the older source analysis, even though the same term is used for both. In this sense, we have tried to be attentive to literary-critical matters. Particular consideration has been given to matters of structure, style, and movement in the narrative, for these provide hints about the way of story telling.

The older usage referred to the identification of literary sources or "documents." This author accepts in a general way the "documentary hypothesis" and certainly affirms a concern for the historical dynamic which lies behind the hypothesis. But it has not been necessary in most places to appeal to the separation of sources for our exposition. This decision, like the one concerning historical issues, is founded on reasons of scholarly upheaval and the intent of this commentary.

First, the older consensus about the sources is now under attack, especially from H. H. Schmidt (*Der Sogenannte Jahwist,* 1976), Rolf Rendtorff (*Die Überlieferungsgeschichtliche Problem des Pentateuch,* 1977) and Van Seters. This scholarly criticism is not from those who conventionally resist source analysis. It is rather from those who believe either that the question of sources is the wrong question (Rendtorff) or that the sources must be dated later (Schmidt, Van Seters). Since matters are that precarious, it seemed unwise to pursue those issues here.

Second, because we have tried to handle the material as canon, we have tried to take it as presented. There are few places in which source analysis might have changed things greatly, though we have simply not dealt with some of the matters of duplication and overlap which have evoked the hypothesis. In two ways, we have relied on source analysis in a limited way. Since the consensus on the priestly materials remains stable, and since those materials are in any case distinctive, we have accepted assignment of materials to P. In han-

6

dling the Joseph narrative, we have appealed to Von Rad's placement of the narrative in the tenth century. Von Rad's hypothesis is presently in dispute, but we hope our exposition will stand on its own merit.

3. The language used in the commentary has required us to be candid about its Christian orientation. This decision has not been made lightly or easily. But it has seemed unavoidable, given the purposes of the commentary. This has necessarily followed from the decision to treat the material as the canon of the community. But this candid confessional language should not be misunderstood.

a. There are no claims or presumptions here that the New Testament is "the resolution" of the Old Testament. There is no imperial notion here which claims that the church is the "fulfillment" of "unfulfilled" Israel. The best faith that can be kept with Jewish brothers and sisters is to be honest and candid about our presuppositions and to hold them in the presence of those brothers and sisters. Thus, we have engaged in no euphemisms about "Hebrew Scripture," for serious Jews know what we Christians are up to in that regard in any case. In doing serious theological exposition, it is essential to refer to the community of faith which functions as a confessional point of reference. Theological exposition must be intensely contextual in that regard. This exposition explores what happens when the text is brought to our faith in Jesus of Nazareth as the Christ. It is not claimed that this perception is the true or only or best reading. But it is the one we can make responsibly in relation to the canon of the church which insists on a linkage between New and Old Testaments.

This expositor is suspicious of attempts to use less than candid language about confessional orientation in an effort to arrive at interpretations which are "common." That appears to be a deception which detracts from the sharpness needed in interpretation. This effort, then, is offered not in a polemical way, but as a gesture of fidelity to Jewish friends, hopeful that this gesture of faith may serve our common pilgrimage. We speak here of promise, believing that fulfillment runs in more than one direction. And so we have used the vocabulary of the Christian faith community, eager that Jewish brothers and sisters will make the translations of that language to their own particular idiom. In Genesis, if anywhere, we may affirm our common inheritance as children of Abraham and Sarah.

b. Throughout the commentary, we have used the phrase, "the listening community." By that, we refer to the community to whom the text and the exposition are addressed. In the first instance, this means the church. But derivatively, it refers to any person or group seriously engaged with the text. That is, perhaps, an important difference between critical exegesis and the task undertaken here. Exposition of this kind is addressed to someone. The exposition, like the text, addresses those prepared to engage with, respond to, and be impacted by the text and its exposition. The work to be done in this kind of exposition is in dialogue. It expects that the reader/listener has as much work to do as the expositor. And it expects that the expositor is impacted by the texts as much as the reader/listener may be.

c. This expository intention has led to one other decision. We have freely alluded to New Testament passages at various points. It has not seemed proper to withhold such reference until the end of a discussion, as though the New Testament reference were simply an addendum. Rather, the premise of this exposition is that the relation between the two Testaments is a mutual one in which each may aid in the interpretation of the other. This reflects no desire to "Christianize" the Old Testament nor to import into the Old Testament alien matters. But it is to recognize that the New Testament in some ways is for us the normative interpretation of the Old Testament. We are not required to follow that interpretation in every respect. But it can be a useful point of reference which aids in seeing things we might have missed or in discerning nuances proper to our theological tradition. It is intended that this way of relating the two Testaments takes account of a special expository tradition and fully respects the text of Genesis itself.

The Plan of the Commentary

1. The commentary is presented in four sections, following traditional and obvious divisions. For each of these, a more specific introduction is offered. Then there follows exposition which gives proportionate attention to texts thought to be most useful for the life and faith of the church.

a. *Genesis 1:1—11:29. "The Sovereign Call of God."* The pre-history of Gen. 1:1—11:29 focuses on the narratives of creation, garden, Cain and Abel, the flood, and the tower. (Scant attention has been given here to the genealogies of 5; 10—11.) We have interpreted this unit in terms of "The Sovereign Call

8

of God." By appeal to Eph. 1:9–10, we have urged that the entire narrative is concerned with the tension between God's will for and call to creation and the mixed way in which creation heeds that will and answers that call. Informed by 8:20–22 and 9:8–17, we have found that the pathos of God is a clue to the movement of the flood narrative. In terms of the structure of the narrative, it is clear that 8:20–22 and 9:8–17 form a decisive turn in the total narrative. The materials in 9:18—11:29, then, form a transition in which the main dramatic tension no longer seems to prevail.

b. *Genesis 11:30—25:18. "The Embraced Call of God."* In the Abraham materials of Gen. 11:30—25:18, we have been guided especially by the exposition of Heb. 11:8–19. We have focused on the issues of faith, of trusting in the promise of the land, and of the heir. We have placed this material under the rubric of "The Embraced Call of God." With some occasions of resistance, Abraham is the one who embraces the call. The primary dramatic movement stretches from the initial promise in 12:1–3 to the testing of 22:1–14, with the reassertion of the promise in 22:15–18. Major attention is given to the theological issues of 12:1–4; 15:1–6; 18:1–15; 16–32; and 22:1–14. The materials of 22:19—25:18 appear to be mostly transitional and occur after the main issue has been settled.

c. *Genesis 25:19—36:43. "The Conflicted Call of God."* In the Jacob texts of Gen. 25:19—36:43, we have been led by I Cor. 1:27–29 to regard Jacob as one of the "lesser ones" called by God. Because of the pervasive conflicts in the life of Jacob, we have treated this narrative in terms of the "Conflicted Call." The call from God seems to have created unending problems for Jacob. It is our conclusion that the content of the oracle of 25:23 is the source of conflict for Jacob. "Will the younger rule the older?" is the question of the governing motif which comes to its resolution in 33:1–17. The materials in 33:18—36:43 are miscellaneous and serve primarily to give closure to the section.

d. *Genesis 37:1—50:26. "The Hidden Call of God."* The Joseph narrative is tightly unified (with the exclusion of chapters 38, 49, which we have treated briefly). Because the theme is God's providential leadership to work his own purposes, we have appealed to Rom. 8:28–30 and treated this under the rubric of "God's Hidden Call." In this narrative, the dream of 37:5–9 announces the dominant motif of Joseph's call. The "hidden call" controls the flow and suspense of the narrative

9

thereafter. It is difficult to determine the conclusion. We have provisionally regarded 47:27, when Jacob and his family are safely settled in Goshen, as the ending of the narrative. (Cf. George W. Coats, *From Canaan to Egypt,* 1976, 8, pp. 48–54.) This suggests that 47:28—50:26 are again materials placed after the resolution of the central issue. Special consideration is given to the explicit theological assertions of 45:5–8 and 50:19–20. Thus, as an overview, the following may be useful:

1:1—11:29 "The Sovereign Call of God" (Eph. 1:9–10):
    Will God bring his creation to the unity he intends?

11:30—25:18 "The Embraced Call of God" (Heb. 11:8, 11, 17, 19):
    Will Abraham live by faith?

25:19—36:43 "The Conflicted Call of God" (I Cor. 1:27–29):
    Will the younger rule the older?

37:1—50:26 "The Hidden Call of God" (Rom. 8:28–30):
    Will the dreamer keep his dream?

2. No single rubric has been employed with each text. It has not seemed wise, prudent, or possible to deal with every text in a uniform way. Thus, we have attempted to deal with different texts according to the issues which surfaced in each. In general, we have attempted to *(a)* locate the key theological issue, *(b)* deal with any important exegetical issues or problems, *(c)* pursue the structure and the movement of the passage with expository comment, and *(d)* reflect on the connections toward the Christian faith.

For all the critical and detailed expository issues dealt with, the main issue should not be lost. The text before us is a *Genesis.* It affirms a *beginning* for the world and for Israel. It stands as unqualified and unexplained good news. This God is so free and unencumbered that he can form a newness which derives neither from the *chaos* of the old creation (1:2) nor from the *barrenness* of the old family (11:30). From that remarkable faith in God, everything else here follows. It is no wonder that an early expositor heard this text affirming that "God was able to raise men even from the dead" (Heb. 11:19).

PART ONE

The "Pre-History": The Sovereign Call of God

GENESIS 1:1 — 11:29

For [as] he has made known to us in all wisdom and insight the mystery of his will, according to his purpose which he set forth in Christ as a plan for the fullness of time, to unite all things in him, things in heaven and things on earth (Eph. 1:9–10).

The first eleven chapters of Genesis are among the most ✓ important in Scripture. They are among the best known (in a stereotyped way). And they are frequently the most misunderstood. Misunderstandings of substance likely occur because the style and character of the literature is misunderstood. A faithful understanding of these materials requires that interpreters be clear about the nature of the material presented and the relationship it has to the remainder of Scripture.

In these texts, there is almost no historical particularity. Other than the reference to specific peoples in chapters 10—11, there is no concrete identification of historical persons, groups, movements, or institutions. Creation is treated as a unity. And where individual persons are cited, they are treated as representatives of all creation, the part for the whole. The only distinction made is that between human and non-human creatures. In various texts, the interrelation of human and non-human creation is presented in three ways: *(a)* It is treated together without differentiation. All stand before God in the same way, as the single reality of creature *vis à vis* creator (9:9–10). *(b)* Human creation is treated as superior and non-human as subordinate (1:25–30; 2:15): human creatures are designated to *order, rule, and care for* the other creatures;

11

creatures are to *obey and to be responsive to* the human creatures. *(c)* At other times texts are highly anthropocentric (11:1–9), concerned only with human creatures, disregarding the rest of creation. Obviously, these three ways of speaking of creation have some tension among them. It is not obvious that one can speak of human creatures *together with* the other creatures and at the same time of human creatures *over* the others. Because of the different ways of speaking, it is not easy to generalize about "creation." For theological purposes, it is important to distinguish the three modes. Each of them is employed when the tradition addresses a different issue or dimension of reality. On balance, speech here about creation tends to be anthropocentric. The text cares foremost about the human creature. And when the rest of creation is mentioned, there is a tendency to be interested in how the other creatures relate to this human creature. The central concern is with the large issue of the relation of creator and "creature" (which here refers to: [*a*] the undifferentiated creation, [*b*] human and non-human creatures in differentiated relation, and [*c*] human creatures alone).

These chapters embody a peculiar and perceptive intellectual tradition. This intellectual tradition has discerned that all other philosophical and political questions (i.e., issues of meaning and power) are subordinated to this fundamental issue of the relation of the creator and creation. Upon that issue everything else hinges, including human *authority, power,* and the reality of *order* and *freedom* in human life. It is likely that the work of these chapters is linked to the royal court which sponsored scientific and philosophical investigation of the mystery of life (cf. Prov. 25:2–3), for such investigations are closely related to the use and the legitimation of human power.

The theologians of Israel, in these texts, face the basic mystery of life upon which all social well-being depends. The texts appropriate materials from the common traditions of the Near East. But they handle and utilize them in a peculiarly theological way. On the one hand, they break with the "mythological" perception of reality which assumes that all the real action is with the gods and creation in and of itself has no significant value. On the other hand, they resist a "scientific" view of creation which assumes that the world contains its own mysteries and can be understood in terms of itself without any transcendent referent. The theologians who work in a distinctively Israelite way in Gen. 1—11 want to affirm at the same time *(a)* that the ultimate meaning of creation is to be found in the heart and

12

purpose of the creator (cf. 6:5–7; 8:21) and *(b)* that the world has been positively valued by God for itself. It must be valued by the creatures to whom it has been provisionally entrusted (1:31).

This delicate statement is neither mythological (confining meaning to the world of the gods) nor scientific (giving creation its own intrinsic meaning). The affirmations of Israel are dialectical. They affirm two realities in tension with each other, neither of which is true by itself. We have no adequate word for this dialectical affirmation about creation which is peculiarly Israelite. It is probably best to use the word "covenantal," as Barth has urged (*Church Dogmatics,* III 1 #41; IV 1 #57). That word affirms that the creator and the creation have to do with each other decisively. And neither can be understood apart from the other. (The word "covenantal" needs to be taken in that general sense, as in Gen. 9:8–12, and not in the more precise ways that have been employed in some recent scholarly discussion, for example, relating to treaty formulae. These perceptions lead to two overriding theological affirmations.

First, the creator has a purpose and a will for creation. The creation exists only because of that will. The creator continues to address the creation, calling it to faithful response and glad obedience to his will. The creation has not been turned loose on its own. It has not been abandoned. Nor has it been given free rein for its own inclinations. But the purposes of the creator are not implemented in a coercive way nor imposed as a tyrant might. The creator loves and respects the creation. The freedom of creation is taken seriously by the creator. Therefore, his sovereign rule is expressed in terms of faithfulness, patience, and anguish.

Second, the creation, which exists only because of and for the sake of the creator's purpose, has freedom to respond to the creator in various ways. As the texts indicate, the response of creation to creator is a mixture of faithful obedience and recalcitrant self-assertion. Both are present, though the negative response tends to dominate the narrative.

These theological affirmations, then, set the main issues and the dramatic tensions of the text: the faithful, anguished, respectful purpose of the creator and creation's mixed response of obedience and recalcitrance.

We are so familiar with these texts that we have reduced them to cliches. But we should not miss the *bold intellectual effort* that is offered here, nor the *believing passion* which informs that intellectual effort. Israel is thinking a new thought. In the use of their faithful imagination, Israel's theologians have

13

articulated a new world in which to live. The shapers of the text are believers. They are concerned with theological reality. But they are not obscurantists. They employ the best intellectual data of the time. And they force the data to yield fresh insight. Their faith is genuinely "faith seeking understanding." Their gift to us is an alternative way of discerning reality. It is a way which neither abdicates in "mythology" nor usurps in autonomy. It is a way in which obedience is known to be the mode of the world willed by God. But this is not obedience which is required or demanded. It is a grateful obedience embodied as doxology. These texts ask if this world of mixed response can become a creation of doxology (cf. Rev. 11:15–19).

Critical Issues

1. More than any other part of the Bible, this material has important links to parallel literature in the ancient Near East. Not only are there parallel creation stories and flood stories, as has long been recognized, there are also parallels in which *creation and flood* are joined together in one large complex. Thus our material relates to an old tradition even in its present shaping. Having acknowledged that, no special attention is given in our exposition either to comparison or contrast. This exposition has no more stake in stressing the *uniqueness* of the material than in showing the *parallels*. Rather, our concern is to hear what the text has to say in its present canonical form. Our task is to enter into this remarkable intellectual achievement of faith seeking understanding.

2. More than anywhere else in Genesis, one is aware here of the problem of literary sources. It is conventional (and accepted) that these chapters are of two different traditions, commonly J and P. The J material in Gen. 2—3, 4; 11: 1–9, and in some parts of the flood narrative and the genealogies, is usually taken to be earlier. It may be a critique of royal autonomy (perhaps Solomonic) and thus a polemic against the rebellious pride of the creature who will not live in relation to the creator but craves autonomy (cf. 3:5; 11:6). The P source is commonly dated to the exile. It deals with the problem of despair and hopelessness. This tradition is found in Gen. 1:1—2:4a, parts of the flood narrative and elements of the genealogies. While the former tradition is concerned with prideful self-assertion, the latter deals with despair. Against despair, it asserts not only humanness in the image of God (1:26) but that this image is enduring after the expulsion (5:1) and after the flood (9:6).

14

The two literary strands and their two theological agenda live in uneasy tension. That tension is never completely resolved. But the traditions are shrewdly held together in the canon. The expositor is not free to choose one at the expense of the other. It is required that our presentation should be faithfully dialectical. It must deal with *(a)* the human *refusal* and God's response, as well as *(b)* human *faithfulness* and God's affirmation. Thus, the sources commonly found here need not be viewed as a problem. They may be seen as a way of understanding the richness of material that is offered for theological interpretation.

3. After the two literary sources have been identified, theological exposition must seek the unity of Gen. 1—11, a unity surely intended by the present form of the text. Thus after *sources,* we must investigate the *structure* of the text. As we shall see, the structure of the entire unit is difficult and admits of more than one interpretation.

a. It is possible to see the material in several "clusters." Malcolm Clark ("The Flood and the Structure of the Pre-Patriarchal History," ZAW 83:204–10 [1971]) follows Rolf Rendtorff ("Genesis 8:21 und die Urgeschichte des Jahwisten," *Kerygma und Dogma* 7:69–78 [1961]) and suggests two great cycles. We may speak of the "Adam cycle" of Gen. 1—4 (5) which asserts God's intent for the creation. Here there is an affirmation and then a pattern of indictment and sentence (3—4). This cycle is completed in chapter 5 with the genealogy of the generations.

The second "Noah cycle" (6—9) begins with the curious statement of 6:1–4 and ends with the equally odd narrative of 9:21–28. This cycle presents the sorry picture of old creation and the beginning of new creation. This cycle is structured in the reverse order from the "Adam cycle." That cycle began with affirmation and ended in indictment. This cycle begins in indictment in 6:5–8 and is resolved in 8:20–22. The decision to destroy in 6:11–13 is resolved in 9:1–17. In this construction it is the assertion of 8:20–22 which inverts the action and marks the decisive end of the pre-history.

In this interpretation, the remaining materials of chapters 10—11 occupy a transitional position in a third grouping. They make a shift from *primeval history* to *world history.* Both genealogy and narrative move closer to political reality.

b. The foregoing hypothesis of Clark and Rendtorff regards 8:20–22 as the real end of the narrative, and the remainder of Chapters 1—11 is only transition. Against that, David Clines

15

pays more attention to the post-flood materials to show that even in those narratives and genealogies God is still at work to have creation on his own terms and yet receives a continuing mixed response of resistance and compliance on the part of creation (*The Themes of the Pentateuch*, JSOT Supp. 10, Chap. 7). Seen in that way, 8:20–22 marks no decisive turn. The unresolved issues in and before the flood continue after the flood.

The difference between the two hypotheses is one of accent. Taken either way, the discussion makes clear that the theological issue is the troubled relation of creator and creation. Further, it is clear that read in terms of such clusters of narrative, material from both the J and P sources are essential to presenting the full anguish and persistence of the troubled relationship. Thus, even in the face of *literary dissection, a theological coherence* is evident which may control our exposition.

4. Comment needs to be made on the matter of creation, world-beginnings and attempts to correlate creation narratives with modern scientific hypotheses. No special attention is given to this issue here because it is judged as not pertinent to our purpose. The expositor must move knowingly between two temptations. On the one hand, there is the temptation to treat this material as historical, as a report of what happened. This will be pursued by those who regard science as a threat and want to protect the peculiar claims of the text. If these materials are regarded as historical, then a collision with scientific theories is predictable. On the other hand, there is the temptation to treat these materials as myth, as statements which announce what has always been and will always be true of the world. This will be pursued by those who want to harmonize the text with scientific perceptions and who seek to make the texts rationally acceptable.

Our exposition will insist that these texts be taken neither as history nor as myth. Rather, we insist that the text is a *proclamation* of God's decisive dealing with his creation. The word "creation" is controlling for such a view. The whole cluster of words—creator/creation/create/creature—are confessional words freighted with peculiar meaning. Terms such as "cosmos" and "nature" should never be carelessly used as equivalents, for these words do not touch the theocentric, covenantal relational affirmation being made.

The word "creation" belongs inevitably with its counter word "creator." The grammar of these chapters presumes that

16

there is a *Subject* (creator), a *transitive verb* (create) and an *object* (creature/creation). The single sentence, *"Creator creates creation,"* is decisive for everything. It is not subject to inversion. The sentence asserts that God does something and continues to care about what he does. The pathos and involvement of God is implicit in all these texts, even though it is most explicit in 6:5–8; 8:21. The subject of the sentence, then, is never separated from the object; and the object is surely never separated from the subject. Finally, the verb that links them is irreversible. While it may be used synonymously with "make" or "form," the verb "create" is in fact without analogy. It refers to the special action by God and to the special relation which binds these two parties together. Creator creates creation. Subject, verb, object: This governing sentence affirms that the creator is not disinterested and the creation is not autonomous. This is the peculiar "grammar of creation" in Israel.

The text, then, is a *proclamation of covenanting* as the shape of reality. The claim of this tradition is opposed both to a materialism which regards the world (nature, cosmos) as autonomous and to a transcendentalism which regards the world as of the same stuff as God. The term "create" asserts distance and belonging to. It is affirmed that the world has *distance* from God and a life of its own. At the same time, it is confessed that the world *belongs to* God and has no life without reference to God. Both characterize the relation of creator and creation. This idiom of covenant applies not only to the creation stories of Gen. 1—2, but to all of the materials of Gen. 1—11. The whole is a narrative about God's insistence that the creation should be nothing other than his creation. Such a view leaves ample room for every responsible scientific investigation. But it yields not at all on the issue of the fundamental character of reality as *derived from* and *belonging to this sovereign, gracious God* who will seek to have his own way. This *theological* affirmation permits every scientific view that is genuinely scientific and not a theological claim in disguise.

Theological Affirmations and Possibilities

1. The assertion, "Creator creates creation," articulates the main issues before us. It affirms that God has a powerful purpose for his creation. Creation is not a careless, casual, or accidental matter. We suggest that as an entry into God's intention for creation, reference be made to Eph. 1:9–10. While we have not

17

pursued the christological element stated by Paul, the text affirms that the creator intends the creation to embody an obedient unity (cf. Gen. 1:31; 8:22). The statement of Eph. 1:9–10 makes several claims. First, it affirms that the purpose of creation is already decided. It is not to be decided in the future. It is not an optional matter for creation. The creatures do not have a vote in the matter. Second, that purpose is unity. The statement of 1:31 understands this unity to be aesthetic as well as ethical. The world is to be "beautiful" as well as "obedient." God does not call the world to be chaotic, fragmented or in conflict (cf. Isa. 45: 18–19). And he stays with it until it becomes as he wills it.

2. It is by speaking and hearing that the interaction of the creator and creation takes place. In Genesis chapter 1 God creates by speaking. Creation is to listen and answer. Language is decisive for the being of the world. For that reason, it is exegetically correct that "God calls the worlds into being" (cf. Rom. 4:17). That call is given with passion and yearning. It is telling that in the final narrative of 11:1–9 the last state of pre-Israelite humanity is *lo'-shema'*, "they did not listen" (Gen. 11:7). And when creation does not listen, it cannot respond as God's creature. Nonetheless, the caller still calls, urging the world to answer.

3. This speech of God is a sovereign call. It is not subject to debate. It is sure to have its own way. Clearly, the creation will be God's creation. Yet, in these narratives, the sovereign call is unheeded. We are dealing here with a peculiar kind of sovereignty. This sovereign speech is not coercive but evocative. It invites but it does not compel. It hopes rather than requires. Thus, it may be resisted and unheeded. But the call of the creator is not thereby voided.

By reference to Eph. 1:9–10, we do, of course, suggest a christological reading of the creation account. But in doing so, we do not misuse the text. The same claim, that the creator overcomes recalcitrance by embracing it, would be made in other language by Jewish interpreters. From both perspectives, a break is required from mechanistic notions of creation. Our exposition concludes that God does not create in the sense of a manufacturer. He does not "make" so that an object is simply "there." Rather, he creates by speaking in ways that finally will be heard. His word has the authority of suffering compassion. The creation, then, is not an object built by a carpenter. It is a vulnerable partner whose life is impacted by the voice of one who cares in tender but firm ways.

18

4. Creation, the object of our governing sentence, is presented by our text as a special treasure of God. Yet, the creature is stridently disobedient, proud, and alienated. That is clear of the first man and woman (3:1–7), of Cain (4:1–16), of the world in the flood narrative (6:5–13), and of the nations in the tower narrative (11:1–9). But it is not unmitigatedly so. There are hints of an alternative reality as well. Our exposition must be attentive to those hints. Too much interpretation of these chapters has focused on the sin to the neglect of obedient creatureliness.

The hints of an alternative reality include the creator at rest because creation is "good" (2:1–4), the orders of life guaranteed (8:21–22), the world embraced and guaranteed (9:8–17). And of course, Noah is the new man, the new king who will relieve the world of its fruitless efforts (5:29). Noah stands as an alternative to disobedient Adam and perhaps to disobedient Solomon. As is well known, the P tradition summarizes this positive note in the model, "image of God." But the most staggering claim is not in P, where it might be expected, but in J, in 4:7: ". . . Sin is couching at the door; its desire is for you, but you must master it." If that statement is taken optatively, it is a promise, a hope and a permit: "You may." That promise is an appropriate counterpart to God's persistent, evocative speech. God will be sovereign. Creation may be whole.

5. The theme of this entire section may be stated in various ways. David Clines (*The Theme of the Pentateuch*, 1978, pp. 61–79) has summarized three contemporary thematic proposals: *(a)* Claus Westermann has argued that the drama moves from *sin* to God's *mitigation* and finally to *punishment* ("Types of Narrative in Genesis," *The Promises to the Fathers*, 1964, pp. 47–58). *(b)* Gerhard von Rad has traced the theme of the *spread of sin* and the counter theme of the *spread of grace* (*Genesis*, 1972, pp. 152f.). *(c)* Joseph Blenkinsopp has seen the narrative as shaped in terms of *creation/uncreation/recreation* (*The Pentateuch*, 1971, pp. 46f.).

While there are important differences, these three proposals are variations on the same theme, the troubled relation of creator/creation and God's enduring resolve to have creation on his terms. The unit of Gen. 1—11 makes an assertion about the situation of the world into which God will make the second call to his special people, Israel (12:1–3). It is a world in which fundamental issues are still to be resolved. Still to be settled is the way in which the world will come to terms with the purposes of God, willingly assenting to be God's good creation. Still

19

to be resolved is the way in which God will stay with the world in its resistance. To see the issues in this way is an important affirmation, no matter how they will be settled. Barth has seen this well (*Church Dogmatics* III 2, 1960, pp. 28–36). There is sin; this is how the world is marked. There is grace; this is how God presents himself. But the grace of God is the very premise for sin. "Thus the grace of God itself is the presupposition of man's sin" (Barth, 35). Sin is only and always a resistance to God's gracious will. It is the compassion of God which makes sin possible. As the narrative advances, we move between these two important recognitions. In one sense, the issues between creator and creation are unresolved in Gen. 1—11. It is unknown how it will be between the partners. Yet in another sense, the issues are resolved because the governing sentence remains: "Creator creates creation." The accent is finally on the subject. And the object must yield, not to force, but to faithful passion. Both the *strange resistance of the world* and the *deep resolve of the creator* persist in the text. The expositor must not relax the tension in either direction. To conclude only that the world is "fallen" is to miss the point. But to conclude that God will prevail is perhaps to claim too much. The narrative leaves the issue open. What is proclaimed is that God is God. Nothing in the narrative alters that reality by a cubit.

6. Because the issues are unresolved and the relationship unsettled, the message here is one of promise. The stories must not be taken in isolation from each other. On the whole, it is clear that the purpose of God will not leave the world alone. God is patient (cf. Rom. 3:25-26) and will wait. But God will never abandon the world, as evidenced even in 11:1-9. That was good news to exiles who felt abandoned (cf. Isa. 49:14). It was good news to a bewildered community of faith (Matt. 28: 20). It continues to be good news to those who believe the world is autonomous and must make its own way, and it is good news to those who know about sin but who do not know that creatureliness is bound to a determined, pathos-filled creator.

God's sovereignty is not yet fully visible. Creation is not yet fully obedient. The text of Gen. 1—11 leaves the issues open. In these troubled stories are the hints that later are discerned as the abiding promises. But the narrative lives in hope. At the end of this section (Gen. 1—11) in 11:1-9, we make a canonical move to the new life given in Acts 2:1-13. The angry but persistent creator of 11:1-9 now moves with a fresh surge of life-giving power. The community yearned for is now granted. In

20

even larger sweep, we move from the unresolved tensions of Gen. 1—11 to the great hymnic vision of chapter 11 in Revelation, in which the issues of our text are resolved: "The kingdom of the world has become the kingdom of our Lord and of his Christ, and he shall reign for ever and ever" (v. 15). The ones who could not listen in Gen. 11:7 now have become the ones who hear (Rev. 2:11) and therefore praise (Rev. 11:16–18). The later faith tradition in our texts makes incredibly large claims. Perhaps they are understated. Perhaps they could only be seen in the light of the fulfillments. But once discerned, these claims loom large for biblical faith. It is the task of exposition to make visible these large claims for the world. At the same time, exposition seeks to let that grand vision touch individual creatures, ones who are valued and called in this "grammar of creation." It is the intent of these texts that the hearer may respond in this way:

> The text *asks,* What is your only comfort in life and in death? The creature may *answer,* That I belong, body and soul, in life and in death, not to myself but to my faithful saviour, Jesus Christ, who at the cost of his own blood has fully paid for all my sins and completely freed me from all the dominion of the devil; that he protects me so well that without the will of my Father in heaven, not a hair can fall from my head; indeed, everything must fit his purpose for my salvation. Therefore, by his Holy Spirit, he also assures me of eternal life, and makes me wholeheartedly willing and ready from now on to live for him. (*Heidelberg Catechism,* question and answer 1).

The intent of the sovereign Lord is that creation's only comfort is in his care and promise. It is important to observe that the comfort of the gospel announced in the catechism is anticipated by the New Man, Noah (Gen. 5:29). There is enough in the stories (Gen. 1—11) to assert that this claim of comfort is true not only for individual believers, but for the whole of creation, object of this incredible verb "create," partner of this amazing subject, "creator."

A Schema for Exposition

The chart of chapters 1 through 11 of Genesis entitled "The History of Creation," suggests the points of accent and emphasis in the exposition that follows. The carefully structured flood narrative stands at the center and has as its major counterpoint the creation of the world in chapter 1. These two together provide the main dynamic of creation/uncreation/new crea-

21

tion. Specifically, the first verse of chapter 8 is a turning point, not only for the flood narrative, but for the entire presentation.

As the flood narrative is the center of the tradition, we may note the following correlations:

There are two basic creation accounts: pre-flood (1:1—2:24) and post-flood (9:1–17).

There are two stories of disobedience: pre-flood (6:1–4) and post-flood (9:18–28).

There are two genealogies of continuity: pre-flood (5) and post-flood (10:1–32; 11:10–29).

There are two major traditions of sin and judgment: pre-flood (3—4) and post-flood (11:1–9).

If the point were pressed to complete the symmetry, we should juxtapose 12:1–4 as the counterpart of chapter 1. As it is presently shaped, the tradition of 1:1—11:29 ends without resolution. God's will for his creation is not in doubt. He has pledged to stand by his creation (8:21–22; 9:8–17). Now there is a waiting and a groaning (cf. Rom. 8:19–23). Those who value these texts are those who "wait with patience" (Rom. 8:25) and with "eager longing" (Rom. 8:19).

Genesis 1:1—2:4

This text is a poetic narrative that likely was formed for liturgical usage. It is commonly assigned to the Priestly tradition, which means that it is addressed to a community of exiles. Its large scope moves in dramatic fashion from God's basic confrontation with chaos (1:2) to the serene and joyous rule of God over a universe able to be at rest (2:1–4a).

Introduction

The main theme of the text is this: God and God's creation are bound together in a distinctive and delicate way. This is the presupposition for everything that follows in the Bible. It is the deepest premise from which good news is possible. God and his creation are bound together by the powerful, gracious move-

22

GENESIS 1:1—11:29: THE "PRE-HISTORY"

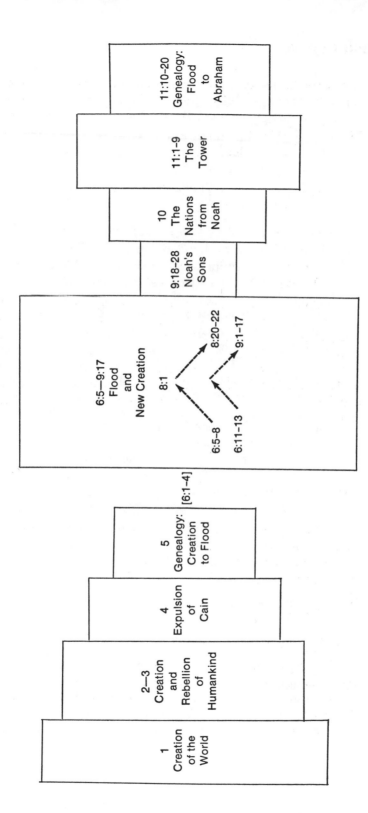

ment of God towards that creation. The binding which is established by God is inscrutable. It will not be explained or analyzed. It can only be affirmed and confessed. This text announces the deepest mystery: God wills and will have a faithful relation with earth. The text invites the listening community to celebrate that reality. The binding is irreversible. God has decided it. The connection cannot be nullified.

The mode of that binding is speech. The text five times uses the remarkable word "create" (vv. 1, 21, 27). It also employs the more primitive word "make" (vv. 7, 16, 25, 26, 31). But God's characteristic action is *to speak* (vv. 3, 5, 6, 8, 9, 10, 11, 14, 20, 22, 24, 26, 28, 29). It is by God's speech that the relation with his creation is determined. God "calls the worlds into being" (cf. Rom. 4:17; II Pet. 3:5). By God's speech that which did not exist comes into being. The way of God with his world is the way of language. God speaks something new that never was before.

As God's "speech-creature," the world is evoked by this summoning God who will have his way. Creation by such speech shows God's authority. God authors life, but there is no hint of authoritarianism. Every part and moment of this creation is like the freshness of the morning, like the blackbird which has sprung "fresh from the Word." God's speaking initiates a relationship for the fullness of time when all things will be united and gratefully in his care (Eph. 1:10). Movement towards a unity of harmony, trust, and gratitude is underway in this poetry. Against every other way of discerning the world, this liturgy affirms that we are fully and gladly the creation of God. It is a grateful response to lordly speech which promises and gives well-being beyond our imagining (cf. Eph. 3:20).

Critical Considerations

Gen. 1:1—2:4 has had more than its share of attention, even though the power of the text transcends every interpretation. Here we shall summarize some important aspects of interpretation which may aid in our hearing of the text.

1. There is no doubt that the text *utilizes older materials.* It reflects creation stories and cosmologies of Egypt and Mesopotamia. However, the text before us transforms these older materials to serve a quite new purpose, a purpose most intimately related to Israel's covenantal experience. The external parallels are helpful, but they are not the primary clue to the claim of the text.

2. The text is likely dated to the sixth century B.C. and

24

addressed to exiles. It served as a refutation of Babylonian theological claims. The Babylonian gods seemed to control the future. They had, it appeared, defeated the dreams of the God of Israel. Against such claims, it is here asserted that Yahweh is still God, one who watches over his creation and will bring it to well-being. While our interpretation should not be limited to a situation of exile, that context should not be neglected because it enhances the force and vitality of the claims made for the God of Israel. To despairing exiles, it is declared that the God of Israel is the Lord of all of life.

Such a judgment means that this text is not an abstract statement about the origin of the universe. Rather, it is a theological and pastoral statement addressed to a real historical problem. The problem is to find a ground for faith in this God when the experience of sixth century Babylon seems to deny the rule of this God. This liturgy cuts underneath the Babylonian experience and grounds the rule of the God of Israel in a more fundamental claim, that of creation. The use of this text is not for general ruminations about the world. It continues to be a ground for faith in this God when more immediate historical experience is against it. Its affirmation is: this God can be trusted, even against contemporary data. The refutation of contemporary data may include sickness, poverty, unemployment, loneliness, that is, every human experience of abandonment.

a. At the outset, we must see that this text is not a scientific description but a theological affirmation. It makes a faith statement. As much as any part of the Bible, this text has been caught in the unfortunate battle of "modernism," so that "literalists" and "rationalists" have acted like the two mothers of I Kings 3:16–28, nearly ready to have the text destroyed in order to control it. Our exposition must reject both such views. On the one hand, it has been urged that this is a historically descriptive account of what "happened." But that kind of scientific, descriptive reporting is alien to the text and to the world of the Bible. In any case, believers have no stake in biblical literalism, but only in hearing the gospel. On the other hand, largely by way of comparative study, the text has been understood as "myth" about the enduring structure of reality. But such a statement about what always was and will be is equally alien. Such an interpretation has been attractive because it leaves the impression of being faithful to the text, but in fact, it is safe and conventional without any discontinuity from the "reasonableness" of modern perspectives. But this text does not announce an abiding structure any more than it describes a historical happening.

Rather, it makes the theological claim that a word has been spoken which transforms reality. The word of God which shapes creation is an action which alters reality. The claim made is not a historical claim but a theological one about the character of God who is bound to his world and about the world which is bound to God. The literalists and rationalists have each been right in one dimension of their argument but doubtful in what they affirm. Literalists have correctly insisted upon the scandal of the text which rationalism wants to tone down. Yet, the antidote of literalism is no way out. Rationalists have rightly insisted that the literalists are unnecessarily obscurantists. However, the alternative about cosmic structure fails to meet the claim of the text.

b. In interpreting this text, the listening community must speak its own language of confession and praise, which is not the language of "scientific history" nor the language of "mythology and rationalism." These tempting epistemologies reflect modern controversies and attest to a closed universe. Neither holds promise for hearing this text. Against both, our exposition must recognize that what we have in the text is *proclamation*. The poem does not narrate "how it happened," as though Israel were interested in the *method* of how the world became God's world. Such a way of treating the grand theme of creation is like reducing the marvel of any moving artistic experience to explorations in technique. Israel is concerned with *God's lordly intent*, not his *technique*. Conversely, the text does not present us with what has always been and will always be: an unchanging structure of world. Rather, the text proclaims a newness which places the world in a situation which did not previously exist. It is *news* about a transaction which redefines the world. The known world, either of chaos or of management, now becomes a new world surging with the mystery of God's gracious, empowering speech. For that reason, it is important to hear this text as a declaration of the gospel. Our interpretation must reject the seductions of literalism and rationalism to hear the news announced to exiles. The good news is that life in God's well-ordered world can be joyous and grateful response.

26

When the text is heard as news in a theological idiom, it leaves open all scientific theories about the origin of the world. The Bible takes no stand on any of these. The faith of the church has no vested interest in any of the alternative scientific hypotheses. The text is none other than the voice of the evangel proclaiming good news.

3. If the form is proclamation, then we may ask about *the substance of the proclamation.* The news is that God and God's creation are bound in a relation that is assured but at the same time is delicate and precarious.

a. The relation is grounded in a mystery of faithful commitment. Everything else depends on that commitment. This affirmation requires the abandonment of two false assumptions which are alive in the church. First, the relation of creator and creation is often understood in terms of coercion and necessity because of the power of mechanistic models of reality and tyranical notions of God. But the relation of creator and creation-creature in Gen. 1:1—2:4 is not one of coercion. It is, rather, one of free, gracious commitment and invitation. The linkage is one of full trust rather than of requirement or obligation. Second, there is a common inclination to confine the matter of God's grace to individual, guilt-related issues of morality. But this text affirms graciousness on the part of God as his transforming disposition towards his whole world. Creation faith is the church's confession that all of life is characterized by graciousness. Well-being is a gift which forms the context for our life of obedience and thanksgiving.

Our exposition may be freed, then, from mechanistic notions of reality and from restrictive ideas of God's grace. As a result, our entire world can be received and celebrated as a dimension of God's graceful way with us.

b. The text further proclaims that creation is a source of rejoicing and delight for creator and creature. All of creation is like Leviathan, which God has created for his enjoyment (Ps. 104:26). All of creation is characterized by God's delight:

I was daily his *delight,*
  rejoicing before him always,
rejoicing in his inhabited world
  and *delighting* in the sons of men (Prov. 8:30-31).

Delight is here understood as structured into the character of reality. The wisdom which rejoices belongs to createdness. (On God's delight, see Isa. 5:7; Jer. 31:20, where the same term reports his attitude toward Israel.)

The creature's proper mode of speech about creation is not

27

description but lyric, not argumentation but poetry. The texts most closely paralleled to Gen. 1:1—2:4a are not scientific explorations but the Psalms which speak of God's generosity and the world's grateful response. Thus, the morning and evening shout for joy (Ps. 65:8). God waters, enriches, blesses, and crowns (vv. 9–11); and as a result, the hills are wrapped in joy (v. 12) and sing and shout for joy (v. 13). God's movement toward creation is unceasing generosity. The response of creation is extended doxology (Job 38:7; Ps. 19:1).

c. The substance of the proclamation of this text is that *between creator and creature there is closeness and distance.* The *closeness* of the two parties concerns God's abiding attentiveness to his creation day by day (cf. Deut. 11:12) and creation's ready response. Thus the "be fruitful" of God is immediately answered (v. 24) not because of coercion but because creation delights to do the will of the creator.

Yet in the very closeness of trust, there is *a distance* which allows the creation its own freedom of action. The creation is not overpowered by the creator. The creator not only cherishes his creation but honors and respects it according to its own way in the relationship.

Faithful exposition must be genuinely dialectical to express both the closeness and distance that belong to this announcement. The closeness affirms that creator and creation must come to terms with each other. But at the same time, the two stand distinct from each other. Each has its own way in the relationship. The one will not be nullified by the other. The grace of God is that the creature whom he has *caused* to be, he now *lets* be.

This same dialectic of closeness/distance is evident in the way of Jesus in his work of renewing creation. Jesus functioned with lordly power. But his invitation to embrace the new creation is invitation, not demand (cf. Mark 2:11; 3:5; 5:41; 10:21, 52). He is not weak, timid, or limited; his power is grace-filled power. We are inclined to shift the dialectic either to (1) the extreme of closeness which is expressed as coercive or smothering control or (2) to the extreme of distance expressed as indifference and autonomy. But our text is clear about the kind of power which can genuinely create. In contrast to the Babylonian gods and every other form of oppressive power, the news is that only God's gracious power can create. This is another kind of power, but no less lordly (cf. Mark 10:42–44). This God

28

speaks not of "must be," but of "let be." Life in its fullness is therefore possible.

The Way of the Liturgy: A Detailed Study

The liturgy moves from a primal assertion of God's rule (1:1) to the serene completion of God's work (2:1–4*a*).

1. Chapter 1, verses 1–2, contain the premise of all of biblical faith. But the two verses also offer a number of interpretive problems.

a. The familiar statement of verse 1 admits of more than one rendering. The conventional translation (supported by Isa. 46:10) makes an absolute claim for creation as a decisive act of God. But the verse may be a dependent temporal clause, "when God began to create. . . ." It then relates closely to what follows. And creation is understood as an ongoing work which God has begun and continues. The evidence of the grammar is not decisive, and either rendering is possible.

b. Verse 2 appeals to traditional imagery and is informed by the common notion that creation is an ordering out of an already existing chaos. Conventionally, it has been held that Genesis 1 is creation by God out of nothing. But this verse denies that. If our text is linked to the exile, then the historical experience of exile may be the "formless and void" about which this verse speaks and from which God works his creative purpose.

c. The relation of verses 1 and 2 is not obvious. Verse 1 suggests God began with nothing. Verse 2 makes clear there was an existing chaos. It is likely that verse is a more primitive, traditional notion, whereas 1 is more reflective about its theological claim. By the time of the New Testament, it was affirmed that God created out of nothing (cf. Rom. 4:17; Heb. 11:3). Though that goes beyond the actual statement of our verses, it likely understands the intent of the poem. But we should not lose sight of the experiential factor in the notion of creation from chaos. The lives of many people are chaotic (cf. Mark 1:32–34). In such a context, the text claims that even the chaos of our historical life can be claimed by God for his grand purposes.

The very ambiguity of *creation from nothing* and *creation from chaos* is a rich expository possibility. We need not choose between them, even as the text does not. Both permit important theological affirmation. The former asserts the majestic and

29

exclusive power of God. The latter lets us affirm that even the way life is can be claimed by God (cf. Isa. 45:18–19). Perhaps for good reason, this text refuses to decide between them. By the double focus on the power of God and on the use made of chaos, the text affirms the difference between God and creature and the binding that also marks them (cf. John 1:1–5).

2. The long section of the liturgy in 1:3–25 covers five days of creation.

a. The structure of these verses is important, for it bears a part of the message:

1) The structure is remarkably *symmetrical*. It moves in a careful sequence:

time: "there was evening and morning . . ."
command: "God said, 'Let there be . . .' "
execution: "And it was so."
assessment: "God saw that it was good."
time: "there was evening and morning . . ."

The time pattern of this liturgy itself comments upon the good order of the created world under the serene rule of God.

2) The rhetorical pattern has as its central element the movement of *command and execution*. God summons. It happens exactly as he commands. The design of the world is not autonomous or accidental. It is based upon the will of God. The narrative form matches the content. The shape of reality can only be understood as the purpose of God. Creation is in principle obedient to the intent of God. This is affirmed even to exiles who have doubted if the world is at all in the purview of God. Creation is what it is because God commands it. But the command is not authoritarian. It is, rather, "let be." God gives permission for creation to be. The appearance of creation is a glad act of embrace of this permit. Clearly, creation could not be, for all its wanting to be, except by this lordly permit.

3) As liturgy, this poetry invites the congregation to *confess and celebrate* the world as God has intended it. Thus, the rhetoric and rhythm of command/execution/assessment permit appropriate antiphons and responses. Giving voice to the poem is itself a line of defense against the press of chaos. It is a way of experiencing the good order of life in the face of the disorder.

30

b. In their symmetry and comprehensiveness, these verses affirm that God is the God of all creation. Though expository attention tends to concentrate on the subsequent verses 26–31, verses 3–25 protest against an exclusively anthropocentric view of the world. The creator God is not totally preoccupied with human creatures. God has his own relation with the rest of creation. The others are also his faithful, valued, and obedient creatures (cf. Matt. 6:26–29; 8:20; 10:29–31).

c. A repeated verdict is pronounced over the creation. It is "good." And in verse 22, the creatures are blessed. The first blessing of the liturgy (and of the Bible) is not for humankind, but for the other creatures who have their own relation to God.

3. Major expository attention, of course, must be given to *verses 26–31.*

a. While careful regard is given to the rest of creation in verses 3–25, the special clustering of the word "create" in verse 27 suggests that the text wishes to *focus on the creation of humankind.* The liturgy celebrates the creation of humankind. This text makes a decisive assertion about humankind. The dialectic of *closeness/distance* applies especially to humankind in relation to God. Human persons are honored, respected, and enjoyed by the one who calls them to be. And this gives human persons their inalienable identity.

1) It is important that of all the creatures of God's eight creative acts, God speaks directly only to human creatures. The others have no speech directed toward them at all. By contrast, in 1:28, God speaks *to the human creatures,* and in verse 29, he twice addresses them directly, "you." This creature has a different, intimate relation with the creator. This is the speech-creature *par excellence.* This is the one to whom God has made a peculiarly intense commitment (by speaking) and to whom marvelous freedom has been granted (in responding).

2) While the terminology for image is not the same in both instances, the statement about the image of God (vv. 26–27) must be understood in juxtaposition to Israel's resistance to any image of God (cf. Exod. 20:4; Deut. 5:8). During the exile (the time of our text), Israel resisted every effort to image God. Because of the temptation of Babylonian religion, Israel resisted every notion that things in the world resembled God. Israel was at pains to affirm the otherness and transcendence of God (cf. Isa. 40:17–26). It was concerned to announce God's freedom from Israel and from the world. It was the *freedom of God* which gave exiles hope against the massive power of the empires around them. Therefore, God must not be seen as imaged in any of them. (Cf. Deut. 4:15–18, in which imaging is linked to creation.)

31

Within that critique of every religious temptation to idolatry, our text makes a surprising counter-assertion. There is one way in which God is imaged in the world and only one: humanness! This is the only creature, the only part of creation, which discloses to us something about the reality of God. This God is not known through any cast or molten image. God is known peculiarly through this creature who exists in the realm of free history, where power is received, decisions are made, and commitments are honored. God is not imaged in anything fixed but in the freedom of human persons to be faithful and gracious. The contrast between *fixed images* which are prohibited and *human image* which is affirmed represents a striking proclamation about God and about humanness.

3) It is now generally agreed that the image of God reflected in human persons is after the manner of a king who establishes statues of himself to assert his sovereign rule where the king himself cannot be present. (We may draw on this analogy only while recognizing its inadequacy, such plastic or sculpture is "fixed.") The human creature attests to the Godness of God by exercising *freedom with* and *authority over* all the other creatures entrusted to its care. The image of God in the human person is a mandate of power and responsibility. But it is power exercised as God exercises power. The image images the creative use of power which invites, evokes, and permits. There is nothing here of coercive or tyrannical power, either for God or for humankind. The power-laden image is further attested in the words "subdue . . . and have dominion" (v. 28).

a) In the now popular indictment of the biblical tradition the notion of human "subjugation" of earth is blamed for the abuse of nature by way of technology (cf. Lynn White, "The Historical Roots of Our Ecological Crisis," *Science* 155:1203–07 [1967]). It is doubtful, however, if that indictment is appropriate. The "dominion" here mandated is with reference to the animals. The dominance is that of a shepherd who cares for, tends, and feeds the animals. Or, if transferred to the political arena, the image is that of a shepherd king (cf. Ezek. 34). Thus the task of "dominion" does not have to do with exploitation and abuse. It has to do with securing the well-being of every other creature and bringing the promise of each to full fruition. (In contrast, Ezek. 34:1–6 offers a caricature of the human shepherd who has misused the imperative of the creator.)

Moreover, a Christian understanding of dominion must be

32

discerned in the way of Jesus of Nazareth (cf. Mark 10:43–44). The one who rules is the one who serves. Lordship means servanthood. It is the task of the shepherd not to control but to lay down his life for the sheep (John 10:11). The human person is ordained over the remainder of creation but for its profit, well-being, and enhancement. The role of the human person is to see to it that the creation becomes fully the creation willed by God.

In the very center of our text (vv. 26–29), the liturgy makes a bold confession. Amidst the polemics of the sixth century, this poem discloses that the peculiar affinity of God and humankind helps us understand both parties in new ways. The creator is "humanized" as the one who cares in costly ways for the world (cf. Karl Barth, *The Humanity of God*). The creature is seen as the one who is entrusted with power and authority to rule. The text is revolutionary. It presents an inverted view of God, not as the one who reigns by fiat and remoteness, but as the one who governs by gracious self-giving. It also presents an inverted view of humanness. This man and woman are not the chattel and servants of God, but the agents of God to whom much is given and from whom much is expected (cf. Luke 12:48). The creation will be misunderstood if we hold to old and conventional religious notions of God and of humankind. The miracle and celebration is in the disclosure of a quite new understanding of both.

b) The human person is ordained by God to be male and female (cf. 27). While this is not a major stress of the text, these observations may be made:

(1) Sexuality is good and is ordained by God as part of creation.

(2) Sexual identity is part of creation, but it is not part of the creator. This text provides no warrant for any notion of the masculinity or feminity or androgyny of God. Sexuality, sexual identity, and sexual function belong not to *God's person* but to *God's will* for creation. Because humankind is an image, a modeling, an analogy of God, sexual metaphors are useful for speaking of the mystery of God. But they are ways of reference and not descriptions. The slippage between God and image of God is apparent in sexual language here and elsewhere in the Bible. Sexuality is ordained by God, but it does not characterize God. It belongs to the goodness God intends for creation.

33

(3) The statement of verse 27 is not an easy one. But it is worth noting that humankind is spoken of as *singular* ("he

created him") and *plural* ("he created them"). This peculiar formula makes an important affirmation. On the one hand, humankind is a single entity. All human persons stand in solidarity before God. But on the other hand, humankind is a community, male and female. And none is the full image of God alone. Only in community of humankind is God reflected. God is, according to this bold affirmation, not mirrored as an individual but as a community.

c) Christian interpretation will hear this text in terms of Jesus of Nazareth, who is confessed as "the image of God" (II Cor. 4:4; Col. 1:15). It is beyond our purpose to explore fully the person of Jesus in this connection. But his identity as God's image on earth is evident in his readiness to turn from himself toward creation and toward his fellow creatures. Specifically, attention may be given to Phil. 2:1–11, which speaks of the *form* rather than the *image*. It is on the basis of Jesus' "form of God" that Paul appeals for unity and fidelity in the church:

> So if there is any encouragement in Christ, any incentive of love, any participation in the Spirit, any affection and sympathy. . . . Let each of you look not only to his own interests, but also to·the interests of others. Have this mind among yourselves, which is yours in Christ Jesus, who, though he was in the form of God, did not count equality with God a thing to be grasped, . . .

Apparently, the key mark of Jesus in the image/form of God is that he did not grasp after equality with God but became obedient. God is the one who does not grasp. And human persons in his image are those who do not grasp. Grasping power cannot create. Grasping power cannot enhance creation. As we shall see in Gen. 2—3, grasping brings death.

In Jesus Christ, we are offered a new discernment of who God is and of who humankind is called to be. The striking feature of Jesus is that he did not look after his own interests but always after the interests of others. That is an echo of God's act of creation. Creation is God's decision not to look after himself but to focus his energies and purposes on the creation.

And as Jesus models *a new disclosure of God,* so he embodies *a call for a new human community.* Paul urges an abandonment of the old life for an embrace of the new: "Put off your old nature which belongs to your former manner of life and is corrupt through deceitful lusts, . . . put on the new nature, created after the *likeness of God* in true righteousness and holiness" (Eph. 4:22–24). The idea of the "image of God" in

34

Gen. 1:26–29 and in Jesus of Nazareth is not an idea which lives in a cosmological vacuum. It is an explicit call to form a new kind of human community in which the members, after the manner of the gracious God, are attentive in calling each other to full being in fellowship.

d) It is plausible that the language of Gen. 1:26–31 reflects an old rubric for enthronement. In such monarchic societies, it is the ruler who images God. But in the Christian tradition, every person is the "new creature" (II Cor. 5:17), crowned king/queen, entrusted with self-giving rule for the sake of others. The rule of the queen/king is to practice gracious freedom toward others which lets them be, even as the creator does toward us.

4. The text culminates in 2:1–4a with the *institution of the sabbath*, that is, the practice of a weekly cessation of work. The original sabbath in Israel was not a day of worship but a day of rest. In the exilic period, the observance of the sabbath had special significance for exiled Israelites. It was an act which announced their faith in this God and a rejection of all other gods, religions, and world-views. The celebration of a day of rest was, then, the announcement of trust in this God who is confident enough to rest. It was then and is now an assertion that life does not depend upon our feverish activity of self-securing, but that there can be a pause in which life is given to us simply as a gift.

a. The sabbath discloses something *about the God of Israel*. The creator does not spend his six days of work in coercion but in faithful invitation. God does not spend the seventh day in exhaustion but in serenity and peace. In contrast to the gods of Babylon, this God is not anxious about his creation but is at ease with the well-being of his rule.

b. The sabbath is a kerygmatic statement *about the world*. It announces that the world is safely in God's hands. The world will not disintegrate if we stop our efforts. The world relies on God's promises and not on our efforts. The observance of sabbath rest is a break with every effort to achieve, to secure ourselves, and to make the world into our image according to our purposes.

c. The sabbath is a sociological expression of *a new humanity* willed by God. Sabbath is the end of grasping and therefore the end of exploitation. Sabbath is a day of revolutionary equality in society. On that day all rest equally, regardless of wealth or

35

power or need (Exod. 20:8–11). Of course, the world is not now ordered according to the well-being and equality of sabbath rest. But the keeping of sabbath, in heaven and on earth, is a foretaste and anticipation of how the creation will be when God's way is fully established. Sabbath is an unspoken prayer for the coming of a new sanity shaped by the power and graciousness of God:

> Dear Lord and Father of mankind,
>   Forgive our foolish ways;
> Reclothe us in our rightful mind,
>   In purer lives Thy service find, find,
>   In deeper reverence praise.
>
> O Sabbath rest by Galilee,
>   O calm of hills above . . .
> Take from our lives the strain and stress,
>   And let our ordered lives confess
>   The beauty of Thy peace.
>   (John G. Whittier, 1807–1892)

d. The sabbath of Gen. 2:1–*a* is about the rest of God. But because humankind is in the image of God, the rest of God is a promised rest for humankind (cf. Matt. 11:28–30). The rest to be granted is not a sleep which escapes history. It is the freedom and well-being of a new kind of history. As it is kept by the faithful week by week, sabbath is a disciplined reminder of how creation is intended. Sabbath as rest for God is the ground of a sweeping humanism. It exists for the well-being of humankind (Mark 2:27). That Jesus is the Lord of the sabbath (Mark 2:28) means a break with the old world of dehumanizing exploitation (cf. Amos 8:4–6). In a second priestly statement about sabbath (Exod. 31:12–17), it is affirmed that keeping sabbath, that is, breaking with the world of frantic self-securing, is a way to know God and his commitment to his world. The rest of God is an invitation to form a new kind of human community.

A Theology of Blessing

The creation narrative is a statement about *the blessing God has ordained into the processes of human life.* Three times the term "blessing" is used: of living creatures (v. 22), of human creatures (v. 28), and of the sabbath (2:3). God's action is sometimes regarded as extrinsic to life, essentially alien to it, and even in some tension with it. There is a tendency in some theological traditions to articulate a deep gulf between the goodness of God and the unhealthiness of the world. Sometimes

36

the "otherness" of God is linked to the depravity of the world. Curiously, this is articulated both in some forms of Reformation thought and in Gnostic traditions. But here that gulf is denied. The world itself is a vehicle for the blessings God has ordained in it as an abiding characteristic.

Westermann has shown that a theology of blessing (quite distinct from the salvation theology commonly taught in the church) refers to the generative power of life, fertility, and well-being that God has ordained within the normal flow and mystery of life (*Blessing in the Bible and the Life of the Church,* 1978). God's life-giving work is not extrinsic to creation as though it must always intrude. Rather, it characterizes the world. Creation is itself life-giving in the image of the God who gives all of life.

Blessing theology defines reality in an artistic and aesthetic way. Throughout the narrative, God judges the results of his work "good" (1:10, 12, 18, 21, 25), and in verse 31, he pronounces the whole "very good" (v. 31). The "good" used here does not refer primarily to a moral quality, but to an aesthetic quality. It might better be translated "lovely, pleasing, beautiful" (cf. Eccles. 3:11). The shift from the sixth day to the seventh is perhaps, then, not just that time has run its course, but that God knows satisfaction and delight in what he has wrought. He rests not because the week ends, but because there is a satisfying, finished quality in his creation.

Recently, Samuel Terrien has urged that we might usefully distinguish the *ethical* and the *aesthetic* in the faith of Israel (*The Elusive Presence,* 1979). By this, he suggests that the ethical (which is expressed especially in the tradition of Moses and the prophets) tends to urge obedience and to be structured as an intense over-againstness between God and world. In distinction, this aesthetic sense pursues wholeness. God stands not over against but alongside and in friendly continuity with the world. In the aesthetic perspective, the distinction of God from God's creature is not nullified. But the friendly disposition of God toward the world is affirmed. God is satisfied that the world he has evoked in love is attuned to his purposes. The blessed world is indeed the world that God intended. Delighting in the creation, God will neither abandon it nor withdraw its permit of freedom.

This theology of blessing is not derived from ancient Near Eastern texts. It has emerged out of the faith of Israel. As it was

37

offered as a principle of survival and sanity for the exiles of Babylon, so it may be offered as ground for sanity and survival in our time. This liturgy affirms and enacts a blessing in the world that the world cannot reject or refute. It voices a protest against alternative ideologies of our day.

i. The declaration of news about our situation is addressed to literalists and rationalists who believe the world is settled, fixed, and without news. This liturgy affirms that God is at work to bring creation to his purpose.

ii. The dialectic of nearness (embodying fidelity) and distance (embodying freedom) is offered against every escape into a religious womb of transcendentalism and every escape from the hard obligations of freedom. It is further offered against the deception that we are on our own and can avoid answering this giver of life.

iii. The calling of human persons in the vocation of shepherd is offered against an ideology of grasping exploitation and against retreat into irresponsible self-indulgence. It invites a new modeling of humanness after "The Good Shepherd" who does not grasp.

iv. The articulation of sabbath as the goal of life is affirmed against all efforts to justify and secure in the name of competence.

v. The delight in the goodness and blessing of life is asserted against the view that life is neutral or hostile and that God is an outsider to it all.

From Proclamation to Doxology

The creation liturgy of Gen. 1—2:4a refutes false religions and false anti-religions. It provides alternative ground for a conviction about the faithfulness of the world derived from the faithfulness of God. This text is a point of entry into "the strange new world of the Bible." From the beginning, we are on notice that we cannot penetrate here with our conventional presuppositions. There is here a call to repentance concerning our most elemental suspicions about life. In keeping with the mood of the text itself, this call to repentance is not harsh or abrasive. It is the friendly offer of an alternative that permits us to understand who we really are, perhaps for the first time.

The good news found here is that there are beginnings. There are not simply repetitions, moving pieces around, or

38

copying. There are beginnings, and they are wrought by the speech of God which evokes among us a new world. The church has discerned this good news in Jesus of Nazareth (Luke 7:22; II Cor. 5:17). Through him, God's powerful speech is still being spoken. God's powerful wind is still blowing.

As God has spoken this text of blessing to us, so we may say it back to God. We must listen to the text, but it does not stay in our ears. It leaps to our lips. The proclamation becomes a doxology. The text invites us to join the doxology of the throng in the throne room of this king who will never coerce but only invite, evoke, and hope:

> Then I looked, and I heard around the throne and the living creatures and the elders the voice of many angels, numbering myriads of myriads and thousands of thousands, saying . . . "Worthy is the Lamb who was slain, to receive power and wealth and wisdom and might and honor and glory and blessing!" And I heard every creature in heaven and on earth and under the earth and in the sea, and all therein, saying, "To him who sits upon the throne and to the Lamb be blessing and honor and glory and might for ever and ever!" And the four living creatures said, "Amen!" and the elders fell down and worshiped (Rev. 5:11–14).

Perhaps there will not be such eloquent speech about creation in most traditional settings where this text is used. The point of entry for this *"proclamation-become-doxology"* is more likely to occur at table grace. These are brief sabbaths when we live by gift and know that we are strangely sustained, nurtured, and nourished. It will be worthwhile to make visible links between the *overpowering miracle of creation* and the daily *reality of food.* So Israel prayed from its creation faith:

> These all look to thee,
> to give them their food in due season.
> When thou givest to them, they gather it up;
> when thou openest thy hand, they are filled with good
> things....
> When thou sendest forth thy Spirit, they are created;
> and thou renewest the face of the ground (Ps. 104:27-30; cf.
> 145:15-16).

It has been more than a cliché, then, when the church has prayed through the generations:

> Come dear Lord Jesus, be our guest, and may these gifts to us be blessed.

Genesis 2:4b—3:24

Various traditional elements are utilized in this narrative. This narrative offers a sophisticated, sustained, and intentional reflection on human destiny. It is not correct to divide the garden narrative of chapter 2 from the disobedience narrative of chapter 3, for they have dramatic coherence. Nor is it correct to view the narrative as a parallel to the creation liturgy of 1:1—2:4a. The narrative is commonly assigned to Israel's early theological tradition. It perhaps is concerned with the new emergence in Israel of a royal consciousness of human destiny, for which the main issues are power and freedom.

Introduction: The Theme of Human Destiny

After the cosmic assertion of 1:1—2:4a, this text focuses on human persons as the glory and central problem of creation. These are the children of *The Eighth Day* (Thornton Wilder). Delightful creation is finished. Sabbath is celebrated as a sign of the new life. Now human destiny in that world must be faced. The destiny of the human creature is *to live in God's world,* not a world of his/her own making. The human creation is to live *with God's other creatures,* some of which are dangerous, but all of which are to be ruled and cared for. The destiny of the human creation is to live in God's world, with God's other creatures, *on God's terms.*

Immediately after the majestic statement of 1:1—2:4a, we face now a quite different human reality. Whereas 1:1—2:4a is about world creation and issues in *doxology,* our present text concerns the crisis of humankind, which results in *alienation.* Whatever may be concluded about literary history, theologically this text is best understood in its canonical context. We should not speak of a second, parallel story of creation. Rather, this is a more intense reflection upon the implications of creation for the destiny of humanity.

Preliminary Considerations

1. No text in Genesis (or likely in the entire Bible) has been more used, interpreted, and misunderstood than this text. This applies to careless, popular theology as well as to the doctrine of the church. The text has received from the dogmatic tradition such an overlay of messages that the first and perhaps most important task of interpretation is to distinguish between the statement of the text and the superstructure laid upon it. We may distinguish five large misunderstandings that need to be cleared away as a beginning in our interpretation:

a. It has been assumed that this is a decisive text for the Bible and that it states the premise for all that follows. In fact, this is an exceedingly marginal text. No clear subsequent reference to it is made in the Old Testament, though there are perhaps links in Ezek. 28. And even in the New Testament the linkage developed in the Augustinian tradition of anthropology is based on the argument of Paul in the early chapters of Romans. Even Paul does not make general appeal to this text. The Bible is not under any tyranny to this text. A beginning in exposition is to see the text in its actual role in the Bible. That role is limited. Paul's exposition is not unimportant, but it must be seen in perspective.

b. The text is commonly treated as the account of *"the fall."* Nothing could be more remote from the narrative itself. This is one story which needs to be set alongside many others in the Old Testament. In general, the Old Testament does not assume such a "fall." Deut. 30:11–14 is more characteristic in its assumption that humankind can indeed obey the purposes of God. The Genesis text makes no general claim about the human prospect. If one were to locate such a pessimistic view of human nature in the Old Testament, one might better look to the tradition of Hosea, Jeremiah, and Ezekiel than here.

c. Frequently, this text is treated as though it were an explanation of *how evil came into the world.* But the Old Testament is never interested in such an abstract issue. In fact, the narrative gives no explanation for evil. There is no hint that the serpent is the embodiment of principle of evil. The Old Testament characteristically is more existential. It is not concerned with origins but with faithful responses and effective coping. The Bible offers no theoretical statement about the origin of evil. And, indeed, where the question of theodicy surfaces, it is

41

handled pastorally and not speculatively (cf., for example, Habakkuk).

d. Similarly, the narrative is taken as an account of the *origin of death* in the world. That assumption is in turn based on the mechanistic connection of sin and death. But again, the Bible does not reflect on such a question in any sustained way. A variety of responses to the reality of death are offered, most often assuming that while certain forms of death may be punishment, death in and of itself belongs properly to the human life God wills for humankind. It is especially worth noting that no one dies in this text. This is not a reflection on death but on troubled, anxiety-ridden life. That is a greater problem than death, both in our own context and in the world of this narrative.

e. Popular tradition concerning fall, "apples and snakes," is prone to focus this narrative around questions of sex and the evil wrought by sex. It is possible that in the pre-history of this text the serpent is derived from a phallic symbol and that "knowing good and evil" refers to sexual knowledge. And there is also the mention of nakedness (2:25; 3:7). But to find in this any focus on sex or any linkage between sex and sin is not faithful to the narrative. Insofar as the text reflects on the relation of the sexes, its concern is with the political dynamics of power, control, and autonomy.

2. That, of course, leaves for Christian interpretation the whole issue of Pauline theology, which is decisive for much of the church. There is a divergence between an exposition of the text offered here and the dominant dogmatic tradition shaped by Paul. This divergence offers a rich interpretive possibility. On the one hand, we must try to hear the text as it stands. On the other hand, Paul has offered what must be regarded as the normative exposition for much of the church. This raises important questions about the relation of fresh exposition and normative exposition, for which there is no easy resolution. Detailed consideration of Pauline exegesis lies beyond the scope of this study. But at the very least, four matters can be insisted upon:

a. Paul draws judgments that are not based in the text as such (cf. esp. Rom. 5:12–21). Paul's exegesis reflects later theological developments especially evident in IV Ezra. This suggests that our reading of the text may provide a fresh, critical approach to the Pauline texts.

b. Paul's argument concerning Gen. 2—3 is not every-

42

where decisive for Paul. He has many other things to say. Much dogmatic theology has made Paul's exposition of these chapters much more controlling than Paul himself did.

c. Paul deals with a specific problem of the early church in Rome and is not providing a dogmatics for the church even in his most sophisticated work in the letter to the Romans, and even our understanding of that historical problem may require some reconsideration (cf. Krister Stendahl, *Paul among Jews and Gentiles* 1976, pp. 78–96).

d. Paul's argument is not concerned with an analysis of the *origin* of evil, sin, or death, but with the proclamation of good news. In Paul's work, Gen. 2—3 is not used for the presentation of a problem, but for proclamation of the gospel. Thus, even on the usually assumed Pauline grounds, our text needs to be approached for its evangelical assertion and not for a reasoned description of how the world is.

3. Two principles may serve as guidelines for interpreting the text in light of our theological tradition.

a. The text is not interested in theoretical or abstract questions of sin/death/evil/fall. The usual abstract questions of the world (e.g., origin of death and sin, meaning of the "fall") are likely to be false, escapist questions. Such questions are no part of biblical testimony and are of no interest to genuine faith. The real issues of the text may not be posed by seeking theoretical origins. The Bible is not an answer book to all of the curious questions we may ask. Of very many such questions, we may, along with the Bible, be prepared to say, "We do not know." There is much that we do not need to know and have not been given to know. We may rather focus on what has been entrusted to us in the gospel. The Heidelberg Catechism, question three, nicely puts the issue: "How many things must you know that you may live and die in the blessedness of this comfort?" And the answer is: "Three." Exposition may focus on what is given us to know.

b. What has happened in this overlay of theology, both popular and dogmatic, is that issues of evil/fall/sin/death/sex have been objectified and seen as things in themselves. In the popular mind, they have taken on a life of their own separated from the faith issues that are properly in question. But when the issues of evil/death/sex are related to the gospel, they properly concern the *purposes of God* and the *trust of humankind*. The categories in which this story is conventionally interpreted

43

need to be drawn back into the fabric of evangelical reality. Like the people in this narrative, our concern is not finally the danger of sex, the origin of evil, the appearance of death, or the power of the fall. It is, rather, the summons of this calling God for us to be his creatures, to live in his world on his terms.

Because the narrative is concerned with the reality of God, it is more than a hopeless analysis of the "human predicament." It is an arena in which the gospel may be discerned. Thus, the text is linked in the lectionary with Mark 3:20–35 and II Cor. 4:13—5:1. Both New Testament texts affirm God's powerful resolve to overcome the alienation. Special note may be taken of the assertion of Paul: "Though our outer nature is wasting away, our inner nature is being renewed every day" (II Cor. 4:16). Our text leaves us with the hope that the creator is at work *renewing every day.* The text requires us to ask about the reality of God and his resolve for life in a world on its way to death.

The Drama in Four Scenes

It will be well to begin with the recognition that this is a shrewdly stated story which moves knowingly through plot development, suspense, and resolution. The interpreter may do best to strike a bargain with his/her listeners by simply telling the story and nothing more. The words are laden with rich suggestion so that it is likely that any interpretive attempt will detract from rather than enhance the artistry of the narrative. The themes and tones of the story move in so many different dimensions that it diminishes what is given when we press the story too far toward any single meaning or intent. In that regard, this narrative is contrasted with 1:1—2:4. As we have seen, that text is not really a story, for there is no action or development. Whereas 1:1—2:4a permits a summary of its teaching, this narrative resists such summarizing. It prefers to be told according to its own flow and pace. The telling of the story will permit the play of imagination and impression.

It is clear that the narrative is carefully structured and designed, as is evident in the subtle analyses of Phyllis Trible (*God and the Rhetoric of Sexuality,* chapter 4) and Jerome Walsh ("Genesis 2:4b–3:24: A Synchronic Approach," JBL 96: 161–77 [1977]). Though more developed analyses are quite plausible, here we shall consider the story in four scenes:

I. 2:4*b*–17 (omitting vv. 10–14) the placement of the
man in the garden

44

    II. 2:18–25   the formation of a "helper"
   III. 3:1–7   the disruption of the garden
   IV. 3:8–24   judgment and expulsion

Of the four scenes, clearly I and IV belong together in terms of movement into and out of the garden. Scenes II and III similarly belong together concerning the establishment of community and the violation of community. Thus, the garden (scene I) exists for community (II). When the community is violated (III), the goodness of the garden is lost (IV).

    1. *In Scene I (2:4b–17),* the action develops quickly in terms of *(a)* formation from clay of a creature totally dependent upon god, *(b)* planting of a garden as a good place for the creature, and *(c)* identification of the two trees. The presence of human creature/garden/trees gives the setting and the potential dynamics for the story. The garden is an act of utter graciousness. But the trees disclose the character of that graciousness. There is no cheap grace here. The story-teller is terse. We are not told why the trees are as they are. One might wish for a garden without such dangerous trees. But that is not given to us. And if it were so, it obviously would be a garden which evoked no story, that is, one which offered no history.

    The *tree of life* is a motif which may once have belonged to a royal ideology in which the task assigned the king by the gods is to guard and nurture the mystery of life. While the metaphor undoubtedly has mythological origins, in the Book of Proverbs it is used to refer to anything which enhances and celebrates life. Thus, it is related to righteousness (Prov. 11:30), desire fulfilled (13:12), and a gentle tongue (15:4). The particular identity of the tree is not pressed in our narrative. Its presence by name suggests an earlier story, royal in intent. In Rev. 2:7, the tree of life refers to fellowship with God.

    Even less is known of the *tree of knowledge.* It is found nowhere else in Scripture. While it is true that this is the prohibited tree (Gen. 2:17), nothing is made of that. It seems incidental that there are two trees. Clark may be correct in concluding that for the purpose of the story, there is one tree, "the tree of command" (Clark, "A Legal Background to the Yahwist's Use of 'Good and Evil' in Genesis 2–3," JBL 88:278 [1969]). In any case, the story is not interested in the character of the tree. The trees are incidental to the main point that God's command is a serious one.

    Chapter 2, verses 10–14, telling of the four rivers, is commonly regarded as an intrusion in the text. The statement means to assert that the gift of life for all creation comes from the garden, only as gift of God. Though the reference to the rivers plays no part in the Genesis narrative, the motif is used in Ezek. 47:1–12 as a hope for food and healing. In the dramatic vision of Rev. 22:1–2, the rivers are a source of food and healing for the nations. Thus, the figure attests to the gift of life which may overcome every fracture.

But all that is preparatory to verses 15–17, which state the warrant for being in the garden at all and the condition for plot development:

a. There is a *vocation* (v. 15). The human creature is to care for and tend the garden. The word pair, "till and keep," may suggest a gardener or a shepherd. In either case, work belongs to the garden. Work is good, surely, to enhance the garden. From the beginning of human destiny, God is prepared to entrust the garden to this special creature. From the beginning, the human creature is called, given a vocation, and expected to share in God's work.

b. There is a *permit* (v. 16). Everything is permitted (cf. I Cor. 6:12; 10:23). In the context of both Pauline references, the concern, as here, is food. Interestingly, in I Cor. 10:26, there is a quotation from Ps. 24:1 celebrating the goodness of God's creation. Reference may be made to 1:1—2:4*a*, in which thanksgiving for food is seen as an acknowledgment of creation. The permit of creation is for elemental sustenance.

c. There is a *prohibition* (v. 17). Nothing is explained. The story has no interest in the character of the tree. What counts is the fact of the prohibition, the authority of the one who speaks and the unqualified expectation of obedience.

These three verses together provide a remarkable statement of anthropology. Human beings before God are characterized by *vocation, permission,* and *prohibition.* The primary human task is to find a way to hold the three facets of divine purpose together. Any two of them without the third is surely to pervert life. It is telling and ironic that in the popular understanding of this story, little attention is given the mandate of *vocation* or the gift of *permission.* The divine will for vocation and freedom has been lost. The God of the garden is chiefly remembered as the one who *prohibits.* But the prohibition makes sense only in terms of the other two. The balance and juxtaposition of the three indicates that there is a subtle discernment of human destiny here.

46

2. *Scene II (2:18–25)* develops the plot by presenting a second creation, related to, but quite distinct from the first. In this scene, we may note first that God engages in a sharp secularization of the human creature. God does not intend to be the *man's* helper. (Elsewhere, e.g., Ps. 121:1; Isa. 41:10, God is helper. But not in this quite secularized presentation.) The "help" the man needs and must have will be found among the "earthlings." That the helper must be creature not creator shows to what extent creation is left to its own resources and expected to honor its vocation, explore its freedom, and respect the prohibition.

But even of the earth, not just anything will do. First, it is not good to be alone (2:18). Second, the other creatures will not do (2:19–20). The narrative moves systematically: not God/not alone/not other creatures. None of the known elements will suffice. There must be a newness. The good news of the episode is that the well-being of the man requires a fresh creative act of God. The emergence of woman is as stunning and unpredicted as the previous surprising emergence of the man. The woman is also God's free creation. Now the two creatures of surprise belong together. The place of the garden is for this covenanted human community of solidarity, trust, and well-being. They are *one!* That is, in covenant (2:24). The garden exists as a context for the human community.

3. *Scene III (3:1–7)* moves quickly into a new agenda. In its beginning, the scene appeals to the prohibition of 2:17. In its conclusion, it looks to the shamelessness of 2:25. The scene serves to invert the realities ordained by God at the end of Scene I and at the end of Scene II. The serpent is a device to introduce the new agenda. The serpent has been excessively interpreted. Whatever the serpent may have meant in earlier versions of the story, in the present narrative it has no independent significance. It is a technique to move the plot of the story. It is not a phallic symbol or satan or a principle of evil or death. It is a player in the dramatic presentation. This is the first theological talk in the narrative. The new mode of discourse here warns that theological talk which seeks to analyze and objectify matters of faithfulness is dangerous enterprise.

a. The prohibition which seemed a *given* is now scrutinized as though it were not a given but an *option.* The serpent engages in a bit of sociology of law in order to relativize even the

47

rule of God. Theological-ethical talk here is not to serve but to avoid the claims of God.

b. God is treated as a third person. God is not a party to the discussion but is the involved object of the discussion. This is not speech *to* God or *with* God, but *about* God. God has been objectified. The serpent is the first in the Bible to seem knowing and critical about God and to practice *theology* in the place of *obedience*.

c. The matter of death had been mentioned in 2:17 by God. But it had not been the main point. It was not a threat but a candid acknowledgment of a boundary to life. But the *boundary* is now altered to become a *threat*. It is transformed into a terror which puts everything in question. It is not God, but the serpent who has made death a primary human agenda.

d. This subtle theological talk is a distortion of the realities. The serpent says back God's speech in just enough of a twist to miss the point. The serpent grossly misrepresents God in 3:1 and is corrected by the woman in verses 2–3. But by then the misquotation has opened up to consciousness the possibility of an alternative to the way of God. From that point on, things become distorted.

The rhetoric of fidelity has given way to analysis and calculation. The givenness of God's rule is no longer the boundary of a safe place. God is now a barrier to be circumvented. The scene moves quickly to its sorry resolution. The first of "the working theologians" has done his work: "and she ate . . . and he ate. . . ." The couple stands exposed beyond the safe parameters of vocation/permission/prohibition, now having taken life into their own hands. The *prohibition* of 2:17 is violated. The *permission* of verse 16 is perverted. The *vocation* of verse 15 is neglected. There is no more mention of tending and feeding. They have no energy for that. Their interest has focused completely on self, on their new freedom and the terror that comes with it.

What had been a story of trust and obedience (chapter 2) now becomes an account of *crime and punishment* (3:1–7). In brief limits, the dynamics are not unlike those of Dostoevski. There is a strange slippage between the crime and the punishment. The torture of Raskolnikov is in seeing what is not there, in hearing voices and imagining threats. The power of guilt takes on its own life. It works its own destruction. Death comes, not by way of external imposition, but of its own weight. So the nakedness of 3:7 and the hiding of 3:8 already manifest the power of death, even before the Lord of the garden takes any action. Serpentine distortion has set before the earthlings a destiny not envisioned by the Lord of the garden.

4. Scene IV (3:8–24) moves the plot to its focus in verses 9–10. After these verses, the scene moves to its inevitable end. They had wanted knowledge rather than trust. And now they have it. They now know more than they could have wanted to know. And there is no place to run.

a. But the Gardener cares for his garden. Everything hinges on that. The lordly voice of God presides over the entire garden and will not yield the garden, even to the most subtle of creatures. The serpent had a silly notion of outflanking the prohibition. He thought it was only a rule. But it turned out to be the wise passion of the Gardener. There is no escape from that wise passion. The rule might be overcome, but the Gardener is not so easily nullified. He finally must be answered, even by those so foolish.

b. The scene becomes a trial. The Gardener becomes a questioner. The pitiful answer must be given: "I was afraid" (3:10). It is the same answer that will be given by Abraham (20:11) and then by Isaac (26:9) and by all who cannot trust the goodness of God and submit to his wise passion. The speech of the indicted couple is revealing, for it is all "I." Therein lies the primal offense: "I heard . . . , I was afraid . . . , I was naked; I hid. . . . I ate. . . . I ate" (3:10–13). Their own speech indicts them. It makes clear that their preoccupation with the Gardener, with his vocation, his permission, his prohibition, has been given up. Now the preoccupation is "I." The fear and the hiding helped no more than the eating. Life is turned back on self. (Hans Walter Wolff has discerned how the same thing happens in the speech of Jonah when he is alienated from Yahweh in Jonah 4:1–3 ["Jonah-The Messenger Who Grumbled," CTM 3:142–43 (1976)].

c. The sentence (3:8–19) and the final action (3:20–24) still hold surprise. Guilt is not in question. The situation is clear. Since chapter 2 (v.17) everyone has known that death follows guilt that violates the boundary. Perhaps the sentence of 3:8–19 is heavy. But it is less than promised, less than legitimate. The miracle is not that they are punished, but that they live. Graciousness in this narrative is not just in verse 21, after the sentence. God's grace is given in the very sentence itself. Perhaps

49

"by one man came death" (Rom. 5:12). But the news is that life comes by this one God (cf. John 6:68–69). The sentence is life apart from the goodness of the garden, life in conflict filled with pain, with sweat, and most interestingly, with the distortion of desire (3:16). But it is nonetheless life when death is clearly indicated. This is not a simple story of human disobedience and divine displeasure. It is rather a story about the struggle God has in responding to the facts of human life. When the facts warrant death, God insists on life for his creatures.

Thus the last scene contains a surprise. The cursed ones are protected. The one who *tests* is the one who finally *provides* (3:21; cf. 22:1–14). With the sentence given, God does (3:21) for the couple what they cannot do for themselves (3:7). They cannot deal with their shame. But God can, will, and does. To be clothed is to be given life (cf. Gen. 37:3, 23, 32; II Cor. 5:4). But the creatures cannot clothe themselves, nor finally each other.

The situation moves from the *forming* by God (2:7, 22) to the *driving out* by God (3:23–24). Between there is the *hiding* of humankind (3:8–10) and the *walking* of God (3:8). The human creatures, in or out of the garden, still finally must live on God's terms.

The story is not explained. It is simply left there with the listening community free to take what can be heard. There is, of course, talk here of sin and evil and death. But it is understated talk. The stakes are too high for reduction to propositions. The story does not want to aid our theologizing. It wants, rather, to catch us in our living. It will permit no escape into theology.

Agendas in the Drama

We may identify a near agenda and a far agenda.

1. The near agenda (by which is meant the one we are likely to notice because it is our agenda) is the relation between the man and the woman. It is not likely that this was any conscious agenda of the narrator. But we may be attentive to what is said on the subject, even if it is not very intentional. Like so much other disservice drawn from this text, the narrative has been used to justify the subordination of women, first because the woman is created derivatively (it is argued) and second, because she is the temptress of the man (it is argued). Such exegesis betrays the text and is a good example of the ways our values and presuppositions control our exegesis.

Trible points out that the creation of woman is a second full creation story which is necessary to the completion of creation (*God and the Rhetoric of Sexuality,* 1978, Chap. 4). Woman is the crowning event in the narrative and the fulfillment of humanity. Moreover, there is mutuality in the second scene (2:18–25). It is only in the fourth scene (3:8–24), the sentencing of distorted human community, where there is trouble and inequity between the two earthlings. In that scene, there is distorted desire (3:16) and a gesture by which man controls woman in pronouncing her name (3:20). But none of that is urged by the narrator as normative. The contrast between *the faithful work of God* in Scene II and *the result of human distrust* in Scene IV is an eloquent comment on the relation of the man and the woman. In God's garden, as God wills it, there is *mutuality and equity.* In God's garden now, permeated by distrust, there is *control and distortion.* But that distortion is not for one moment accepted as the will of the Gardener.

2. The far agenda (by which is meant the one that is likely intended by the narrator) is how to live with the creation in God's world on God's terms. The narrative appears to be a reflection on what knowledge does to human community. The story is not a counsel to obscurantism, as though knowing nothing is an act of fidelity. But it is an assertion that the recognition and honoring of boundaries leads to well-being. Likely, this narrative reflects the influence of wisdom teachers who are preoccupied with understanding life and probing its mysteries (cf. George Mendenhall, "The Shady Side of Wisdom: The Date and Purpose of Genesis 3," *A Light unto My Path,* H. N. Bream and others, eds., pp. 319–34). It may be that this text reflects concern for the Solomonic effort to overcome every mystery and to manufacture new knowledge, because knowledge is power. Knowledge leads to freedom to act and the capacity to control. This text may be a reflection on the role of *wisdom,* perhaps in an aggressive *royal* context. It probes the question: Are there modes of knowledge that come at too high a cost? (cf. Prov. 25:2–3.) It asks if there are boundaries before which one must bow, even if one could know more. It probes the extent to which one may order one's life autonomously, without reference to any limit or prohibition.

This is an enduring problem in the Old Testament: *(a)* The text may be seen in relation to the story of David and Bathsheba (II Sam. 11—12), in which the king knows enough to rearrange his world for his own ends. In doing so, he brings death. *(b)* Isaiah indicts the king of Assyria who has, by his own wisdom,

51

removed the boundaries of the peoples, and plundered their treasures (Isa. 10:13–14). *(c)* Special ties are evident in the indictment of the king of Tyre in Ezek. 28, who said, "I am a god" (vv. 2, 9). He is indicted because he considers himself "wise as a god" (v. 6) and is therefore sentenced to death (v. 10).

Our text is congenial to this whole cluster of texts concerning royal assertion. They all deal with the problem of *human autonomy* and the ways in which such autonomy leads to alienation and death, for self and for others. The Genesis narrative understands that autonomous thinking, albeit theological autonomous thinking as embodied in the serpent, dares to assert that God is a paper tiger, an idle threat, a literary hypothesis. It insists, to the contrary, that the *freedom* of human persons to enjoy and exploit life and the *vocation* of human persons to manage creation are set in the context of the *prohibition* of God.

This story affirms that the reality of God exceeds our literary ability to properly cast him. Particularly if we are dealing with a wisdom tradition (and even if not), the God announced in this story is not a petty god who jealously guards holy secrets or who eagerly punishes the disobedient. This story is, rather, the anguished discernment that there is something about life which remains hidden and inscrutable and which will not be trampled upon by human power or knowledge. There are secrets about the human heart and the human community which must be honored, bowed before, and not exposed. That is because the gift of life in the human heart and in the human community is a mystery retained by God for himself. It has not been put at the disposal of human ingenuity and human imagination.

So what is urged, if not knowledge? Ignorance? No, not ignorance, but trust. It is illuminating to exchange the *knowledge/obedience* dialectic for the antithesis of *wisdom and foolishness.* Wisdom (of the royal sort) would be to eat all the fruit, for it appears to be at human disposal. Foolishness would be to settle for a command which is unexplained and untested. Like those who shaped our narrative, Paul understood about wisdom and foolishness. He knew that wisdom taken into human hands may bring death. But the other half of his proclamation is indeed news: The foolish trust of God and the foolish care of neighbor bring life (I Cor. 1:18–25).

52   3. We may reflect on the inner connection between what we have called the far agenda (the vertical issue) and the near agenda (the horizontal). Perhaps the two agenda are pieces of the same issue. The issues which likely concern us are horizon-

tal issues, problems of human and social relations. Yet, the primary thrust of the story is vertical, trying to decide about the rule of God and the shape of human destiny. Clearly, our *horizontal propensity* and the *vertical agenda* of the story belong together. The happy covenanting of Scene II (2:18–25) is premised in acceptance of God's vocation, permission, and prohibition. That is the context for the covenanting of "bone of my bones, flesh of my flesh." But as we have seen, the distortions in human community in Scene IV (3:8–24) have come from a fundamental disobedience of the prohibition. The warning about taking the mysteries of God (life, knowledge) in our own hands is directly related to oppressive social relationships and to authoritarian and hierarchical ways of organizing life.

The holding of these two agenda, far and near, vertical and horizontal together, has warrant in the New Testament: *(a)* The two commandments of love of God and love of neighbor are not the same, but they cannot be separated (Matt. 22:36–40). *(b)* The Johannine reflection is surely pertinent for our interpretation: "There is no fear in love, but perfect love casts out fear. For fear has to do with punishment and he who fears is not perfected in love. . . . he who does not love his brother whom he has seen, cannot love God whom he has not seen" (I John 4:18–20). Perfect love casts out fear. But the man and the woman in our narrative learned another thing. Perfect fear casts out love and leaves only desire (cf. Gen. 3:10). *(c)* Paul also held the vertical and horizontal together: In Christ, God was reconciling the world to himself, . . . and he gave to us the ministry of reconciliation (II Cor. 5:18–19). The discernment of a new solidarity of man and woman in this story is a necessary way of understanding the vocation, permission, and prohibition entrusted us by God.

4. The story is a theological critique of anxiety. It presents a prism through which the root cause of anxiety can be understood. The man and woman are controlled by their anxiety (3:1). They seek to escape anxiety by attempting to circumvent the reality of God (3:5), for the reality of God and the reality of anxiety are related to each other. Overcoming of God is thought to lead to the nullification of anxiety about self. But the story teaches otherwise. It is only God, the one who calls, permits and prohibits, who can deal with the anxiety among us. This text may be brought to comment upon the power of anxiety among us: *(a)* The causes for anxiety among us are wrongly discerned. This text fixes the issue in terms of accepting the realities of our life with

53

God. Our mistake is to pursue *autonomous* freedom. Freedom which does not discern the boundaries of human life leaves us anxious. *(b)* The attempts to resolve anxiety in our culture are largely psychological, economic, cosmetic. They are bound to fail because they do not approach the causes. *(c)* Our public life is largely premised on an exploitation of our common anxiety. The advertising of consumerism and the drives of the acquisitive society, like the serpent, seduce into believing there are securities apart from the reality of God. Hermann Gunkel has a marvelous phrase for interpreting our text and our cultural situation. He says the man and woman seek to have "Vernunft ohne Pathos," "reason without pathos." They seek masterful discernment of all, without the capacity to suffer and be vulnerable. The assertion of this text is that every embrace of reason must live with the power of pathos. Every attempt to control by knowing must reckon with the anxiety-producing reality of God.

Perhaps this text runs especially to Jesus' understanding of anxiety (Matt. 6:25–33). Anxiety comes from doubting God's providence, from rejecting his care and seeking to secure our own well-being. Failure to trust God with our lives is death. To trust God with our lives is to turn from the autonomous "I" to the covenanting "Thou," from our invented well-being to God's overriding purposes and gifts. This shrewd narrative does not believe there are many alternatives.

Genesis 4:1–16

This text is commonly assigned to Israel's early theological tradition. Like 2:4*b*—3:24, it may address a situation of grasping royal power in which sustained human aggression damages the human community. But even if it is so placed, it nonetheless also addresses a perennial problem of human life: human relations in which the hidden will of God and the strange power of death are at work. The text moves from a situation of stable family (v. 1) to unresolved alienation (v. 16). The narrative stands at the beginning of an extended biblical struggle with the reality of the "brother"* as a troubled but crucial part of human

54

---

*Throughout we will use the term "brother," faithful to the narrative. But the term refers to every other human person and surely includes "sisters" as well as "brothers" in its theological implication.

destiny. This narrative foreshadows the interaction of Jacob and Esau (cf. 25:19–34; 27:1–45) and the career of Joseph with his brothers (37:1–35).

The Theme: Human Destiny and the Brother Problem

To live in God's world on God's terms is enough of a problem, a problem the man and woman of 2:4*b*—3:24 could not face. But to live with God's other creatures, specifically human creatures (the brother), is more of a dilemma. The move from the travesty of 3:1–24 to the scandal of 4:1–16, the move from a vertical crisis to a horizontal temptation, shows that a crucial human agenda is the brother-problem. It is bad enough to be children of *The Eighth Day,* when everything is ambiguous in the garden. It is worse to face that eighth day *East of Eden* (John Steinbeck), no longer protected (4:14).

It is conventional to read Genesis 4:1–16 as linked to Genesis 3. The genealogical link making Cain the son of the man and woman intends us to read it so. But we must take the story by itself. It is yet another perception of our fractured human world.

This story, too, is so well-known that we must take care not to let it be routine. The world knows that the murder of a brother is a scandalous, unacceptable act. It does not require the Bible to announce that unchallenged norm. Thus, our interpretation must not trivialize the story by treating it in terms of morality. Rather, we shall follow the contours of the text closely so that we may move behind any moralizing. The murder itself is handled quickly. What interests the story-teller (and therefore us) is the destiny of the murderer, a destiny haunted by a skewed relation with God. And that relation is skewed because a brother has been violated.

The Drama of Cain in the Triangle of Brother/God/Sin

This story, as the enigmatic one before it, must be told rather than explained. It contains so many layers of meaning that attempted explanations are likely to hinder and miscommunicate rather than illuminate. Thus, the telling of it must respect the listener and permit the listener to be attentive to the disclosures that come in his/her own life. Our best approach is to follow where the story takes us, to retell rather than explain.

1. Verses 1–2 simply offer stage setting. Worth nothing is that Cain is first-born. As with Isaac and Ishmael, Jacob and Esau yet to come, the first-born does not fare well in Genesis. The story-teller prepares us for the dominance of Cain. We

55

expect the older to dominate. But the next verses contain a surprise for all parties.

a. There is no doubt that in some stage of the story, it dealt with the conflict and relation between farmers and shepherds, including their relation to God. Worth nothing is that the "keeper of sheep" and the "tiller of the ground" (v. 2) divide the work assigned to the man in 2:15 (though one of the terms is different). The vocation of 2:15 anticipates this sociological reality and conflict. Now, however, the story has no interest in such differences. It focuses on the individual persons. And of these, only one brother has any significant part to play. The struggle of the brothers is only backdrop. The real action concerns Cain and God, who must relate over the cries from the dear brother.

b. The names are suggestive. "Cain" derives from *qanah*, "to get, to create." The name is given as praise to God. Cain is celebrated and well thought of. As first-born, he embodies future possibility. Abel's name is "vapor, nothingness," without the possibility of life. In the text, Abel is dismissed while Cain is an embodiment of vitality. By the time of the New Testament, matters are reversed. Abel is a man of faith (Heb. 11:4) whereas Cain is reckoned as a form of evil (I John 3:12; Jude 11).

2. Verses 3–5 set the story and define the plot. The worship of Yahweh is presumed (v. 26 notwithstanding). Both brothers do what is appropriate. Both bring their best. Both had reason to anticipate acceptance. There is nothing to indicate that God must discriminate or prefer one to the other. There is no hint of rivalry or hostility. This is simply a family at worship.

The trouble comes not from Cain, but from Yahweh, the strange God of Israel. Inexplicably, Yahweh chooses—accepts and rejects. Conventional interpretation is too hard on Cain and too easy on Yahweh. It is Yahweh who transforms a normal report into a life/death story for us and about us. Essential to the plot is the capricious freedom of Yahweh. Like the narrator, we must resist every effort to explain it. There is nothing here of Yahweh preferring cowboys to farmers. There is nothing here to disqualify Cain. Calvin and others after him malign Cain and give reason for his rejection, thus introducing a moral dimension into the incident. But when Calvin does so, he knows more than the text. The rejection of Cain is not reasoned but is a necessary premise for the story. Life is unfair. God is free. There is ample ground here for the deathly urgings that move among us.

56

Life is not a garden party (cf. 2:16) but a harsh fellowship among watchful siblings, made harsher by the heavy ways of God. The family would perhaps have gotten along better without this God. But he is there. All through the Genesis narratives, Yahweh is there to disrupt, to create tensions, and to evoke the shadowy side of reality. Here the interpreter may pause to acknowledge that our lives are filled with disruptions, tensions, and shadows. And we must either credit the abrasion to God, as does this story, or offer an alternative account. Either way, it causes our face to fall (v. 5). We respond either with the urge to kill or in deep depression. But through verse 5, we have not yet come to the focus of our narrative.

3. Only when we come to verse 6 are we prepared to take up the action. The most interesting element of the narrative is the curious speech of Yahweh (vv. 6–7). It consists of three questions: "Why/why/will you not?" and two if-clauses, "If you do well/if you do not do well." The questions suggest Yahweh is not quite acting in good faith, for Yahweh himself is the cause of Cain's anger and depression. Obviously, the two questions of verse 6 are a ploy on Yahweh's part. He already knows the answer. Indeed, he knows the answer better than does Cain. So he does not linger for an answer but hurries to the statement of choice in verse 7. The two choices are not stated symmetrically. The first is a question to which Cain knows the answer. The second is presented as a warning, if not a threat. Or is it, perhaps, an invitation?

By his seemingly capricious rejection of Cain, Yahweh has created a crisis. He poses the crisis to Cain and insists that Cain resolve it. The first alternative, "to do well," is instructive. It suggests that a post-Genesis 3 man can do well (cf. Amos 5:15). He is not "fallen." He is not the victim of any original sin. He can choose and act for the good. Such an affirmation by the narrator suggests that chapter 3 must not be permitted to control chapter 4. Cain in this story is free and capable of faithful living.

But the second alternative of verse 7 is stated with peculiar vividness and power. It may be seen in three parts:

(*a*) Sin is waiting like a hungry lion ready to leap (v. 7). (Cf. the same figure in another context in Jer. 5:6.) Sin is not a breaking of rules. Rather, sin is an aggressive force ready to ambush Cain. Sin is larger than Cain and takes on a life of its own (cf. Rom. 7:17). Sin is lethal. God's human creations must

57

be on guard for themselves. There is danger to the life of Cain in how he handles his rage and depression. The looming figure of sin suggests something important about human persons. The stakes are high in our handling of disorders among siblings. Whereas we are inclined to justify rage and depression in subjective psychological categories, this story-teller lets them be objective enough to portray their awesome power (cf. Eph. 6:12).

(*b*) Sin has a desire for Cain. Sin lusts after Cain with an animal hunger. The term "desire" is telling here. It is the same word used in 3:16 to describe the perverted inclination of the woman for the man in the disordered affair of the garden. This desire is not a normal human yearning. It is the dark side of life under perversion. The only other biblical use of the term is in Song of Sol. 7:10 (11) where the "desire" is healthy and unperverted. Trible has explored the ways in which the Song of Solomon stands juxtaposed to the Genesis narratives as positive to negative, as celebration contrasted to exploitation (*God and the Rhetoric of Sexuality,* 1978, Chap. 5). In 4:1–16, everything is exploitation which has taken on a power of its own. In the world of Cain and Yahweh, there is an animal yearning for destructiveness that will destroy both the victim and the perpetrator. Freud may have first named it "id." But he did not first discern it. This story-teller already knows about the power of sin that drives, even to death. Led by the metaphor of the ambushing animal, we know we may be torn apart by that power at work in our lives.

(*c*) Yahweh threatens and tantalizes. And yet, having clarified the danger, there is this marvelously positive assurance. The animal lusting for death need not have its way. It can be ruled! These early chapters of Genesis offer a degenerative play on the theme of "rule." In Gen. 1:28, the human pair is to have dominion over plants and creation, even as the great lights are to govern (1:16–18). In the disordered, oppressive world of 3:16, it was the man ruling the woman. Now, it is this pitifully rejected man taking responsibility for himself. He has the capacity to tame the beast at the door. (Perhaps the story of 37:5–9 expresses a dream about the same possibility of ruling.)

58

John Steinbeck has constructed the major themes of *East of Eden* (1952) around this phrase, "you may rule" (from the Hebrew *timšel*). Our interpretation would do well to consider

Steinbeck's handling of the theme as a way of entering the text. His introduction of the theme merits extensive quotation:

> There was only one place that bothered me. The King James Version says this—it is when Jehovah has asked Cain why he is angry. Jehovah says, "If thou doest well, shalt thou not be accepted? And if thou doest not well, sin lieth at the door. And unto thee shall be his desire, and *thou shalt* rule over him." It was the "thou shalt" that struck me, because it was a promise that Cain would conquer sin. . . . Then I got a copy of the American Standard Bible. It was very new then. And it was different in this passage. It says. *"Do thou* rule over him." Now this is very different. This is not a promise, it is an order. And I began to stew about it. I wondered what the original word of the original writer had been. . . . (p. 301)
>
> . . . It is easy out of laziness, out of weakness, to throw oneself onto the lap of the deity, saying, "I couldn't help it; the way was set." But think of the glory of the choice! That makes a man a man. A cat has no choice, a bee must make honey. There's no godliness there. And do you know, those old gentlemen who were sliding gently down to death are too interested to die now. . . .
>
> . . . These old men believe a true story, and they know a true story when they hear it. They are critics of truth. They know that these sixteen verses are a history of mankind in any age or culture or race. They do not believe a man writes fifteen and three-quarter verses of truth and tells a lie with one verb. . . .—this is a ladder to climb to the stars. . . . You can never lose that. It cuts the feet from under weakness and cowardliness and laziness. . . . I feel that I am a man. And I feel that a man is a very important thing—maybe more important than a star. This is not theology. I have no bent towards gods. But I have a new love for that glittering instrument, the human soul. It is a lovely and unique thing in the universe. It is always attacked and never destroyed—because "Thou mayest." (pp. 301, 304, chapter 24, 2).

Steinbeck ends his novel this way, with the very sick Adam Trask straining his numbed speech to give a blessing:

> Adam looked up with sick weariness. His lips parted and failed and tried again. Then his lungs filled. He expelled the air and his lips combed the rushing sigh. His whispered word seemed to hang in the air. "Timshel!" His eyes closed and he slept.

Steinbeck has seen that much hangs on this strange word to Cain. It is invitation, challenge, promise. The different translations indicate the ambiguity of the verbal form. It is a statement which admits of more than one rendering. But any way it is taken, the interaction between Cain and the destructive power at work on him has been redefined.

59

It may well be asked if God is a gamesman, setting such dangerous alternatives and playing with this elder son whom he has so easily rejected. Yes, says the story. The story brings to expression the haunting presence of God, known to every enraged brother or sister. God presents himself not quite enemy, surely not friend, certainly not advocate, finally leaving it fully "up to us."

4. After such a paced taunting, the second element is Cain's resolution, handled tersely by the narrative (v. 8). It is over and done and nothing need be said. Waiting sin has had its dangerous way. Cain has not ruled but has been ruled, overcome by the lust that lies in ambush.

5. The remainder of the narrative (vv. 9–16) is a lawsuit. Yahweh tries Cain for his life. The narrative has close parallels to the lawsuit of Gen. 3:9ff. as the drama moves through investigation (vv. 9–10), sentence (vv. 11–12) and, finally, to banishment (v. 16). In the initial exchange, Cain's angry counterquestion (v. 9) is very like the rhetorical questions of Jacob (30:2) and Joseph (50:19). Their questions mean to dismiss the point raised and limit the scope of responsibility. Here, Cain refuses brotherly responsibility. He wants release from the empowerment of verse 7. (In 28:15, it is God and no human agent who is a "keeper.") (See pp. 245–246.)

The crucial element is the exchange between the offender and the judge (vv. 13–15). The sentence is that he be a fugitive, consigned to keep farming land that has no life in it (vv. 11–12; cf. 3:17–19; 4:2). But the pause in the action is when Cain seeks mercy. The killer now fears to be killed (vv. 13–14). The killer has no resources of his own but must cast himself upon the mercy of the life-giver. And such a mercy: a mark asserting both guilt and grace. God's mark over Cain (v. 15) has evoked endless speculation. There is no consensus on its meaning. While it may originally have referred to a visible mark as a tattoo, it must now be understood in terms of its function in the narrative. That function is two-edged. On the one hand, it announces the guilt of Cain. On the other, it marks Cain as safe in God's protection. In such a simple way, the narrative articulates the two-sidedness of human life, in jeopardy for disobedience and yet kept safe. The acknowledgment of *guilt* and the reality of *grace* come together in this presentation.

60

The drama has moved quickly from Yahweh's invitation to responsibility (vv. 6–7), through Cain's refusal (v. 8) to the settlement (vv. 9–16). But the settlement is a troubled one. Danger of death is mitigated. But the future of the crime is not terminated. Cain had a choice of embracing a brother preferred over him. But he yielded to the waiting rage. He picked his destiny for time to come. He is protected, but far from home and without prospect of homecoming.

The settlement may be as troubled for Yahweh as it is for Cain. The story turns neither on the murder by Cain nor on the punishment by Yahweh but upon the pathos of Cain (v. 14) and the movement of Yahweh in response to that pathos (v. 15). Guilt has been met with judgment. But even the guilty one is met with surprising grace.

Derivative Reflections on the Brother Theme

Our interpretation must take care that this not be handled as a story about murder, nor as an appeal for self-control. Rather, it is a statement about the awesome choices daily before us and the high stakes for which we take daily risks. The context for those risks includes the active power of sin which can just barely be tamed, plus the unexplained arbitrariness of God who evoked the crisis. Sibling choices are not made in a vacuum but in the most dangerous of contexts, in the presence of a God who appears arbitrary and may be an enemy.

The narrative is not for moral instruction. It enables us to reflect upon the enigmatic situation in which we are set. Every person is willy-nilly set between a sister/brother with whom we compete and a God who acts toward us in seemingly capricious ways. It is not only the problem of the brother, for Cain had quickly resolved that. Nor is it only the problem of God. It is the *brother and God together* that create conflict for Cain and finally lead to his unbearable destiny. We try as best we can to separate "the human predicament" from the God question. Things are then bearable. But this narrative insists that they converge and cannot be separated. Yahweh's attentiveness to the murdered brother means that Cain's destiny must echo the cries (v. 10) and yet deal with God. The story would have Cain discover that life with the brother is not lived in a void but in relation to God. Whoever violates the brother must face the riddle of God.

1. Israel lives in hope of brothers together:

> Behold, how good and pleasant it is
>   when brothers dwell in unity!

61

It is like the precious oil upon the head,
running down upon the beard,
upon the beard of Aaron,
running down on the collar of his robes!
It is like the dew of Hermon,
which falls on the mountains of Zion!
For there the LORD has commanded the blessing,
life for evermore (Ps. 133).

The psalm affirms we are not fated to fracture and alienation. There is an alternative, perhaps envisioned in verse 7 of our text. Our experience moves between the promise of Ps. 133 and the grimness of Gen. 4. Israel knows most about the grief to which brothers come, for example, Jacob and Esau, Ammon and Absalom (II Sam. 13—14). (Note especially the story of II Sam. 14:6–7 which surely has contact with our text.)

2. In the New Testament, the setting between brother and God is acknowledged. It is hinted at in Luke 15:11–32. Why must a certain man always have two sons? Why not only one? Why not only me? But two sons are essential to the reality of the plot. In Jesus' story of the prodigal, the older brother is not quite a murderer. But he senses the same realities. He smells the blood. And the father knows. Like Cain, the older brother is "in the field" (Luke 15:25), an exile away from the house, from security and joy, away from the father, unprotected. (Note in Gen. 25:27, Esau is also a "man of the field.") For that brother also, sin waited in lust. The story of Gen. 4 is reenacted in Luke 15. Only the father deals differently. But the older is nonetheless left in exile.

3. The terror of having a brother and being a brother is explicit in Jesus' teaching in Matt. 5:21–26. This exposition of our narrative prevents Genesis 4 from being a moralistic lesson about murder. Jesus' comment begins with an acknowledgment of the prohibition, "You shall not kill." The killing by the brother violates God's command. But Jesus moves underneath the prohibition and comes very close to our narrative. Anger in and of itself leads to judgment. The indictment is clear: "Whoever insults . . . whoever says . . ." Such anger appears even at the altar. At the time when we face the Lord of life, the juices of death flow in our body. As for Cain, so in Matt. 5: at the moment of religious sacrifice, Jesus turns our attention to the brother. It is required that we turn from the things of God to get the brother matters settled first. Until that happens, there will be a paying of the last penny (v. 26). Cain paid the last

penny. And paid and paid. Our lives are pressed to the last penny. The only alternative is reconciliation. That surely is the meaning of Gen. 4:7, "If you do well." If you turn to your brother and be reconciled (Matt. 5:24) . . . But Cain chose not to do well. He killed. And his life is forever skewed.

4. Our narrative yields two insights which the expositor can pursue.

a. Life is perpetually skewed when the one thing required of us seems too much. It seems too much to turn from the things of God to the things of the brother, too much to give up our anger and be freed in reconciliation. The story brings to objective expression the fearfulness that stalks the unreconciled. There is pathos in such a future. The burden is too heavy (Gen. 4:13). The haunted fear of Cain is a perfect match to the offense. The murderer fears being murdered. How much energy is used guarding the awful hidden burden of anger? How much life is bottled up because reconciliation would mean the end of grasping and the act of emptying (Phil. 2:4–7)? Neither the God of Gen. 4 nor the teacher of Matt. 5 asks much. Only everything, for yielding to the primacy of the brother in the face of God is everything. The good news of Gen. 4 is that such yielding is possible.

b. God does not let go of the unreconciled one. The God who calls the worlds into being does not stop calling, even this chaotic brother. He marks him with a mark signifying both shame and security. The mystery of God is that God's protection extends now even to the land of Nod (v. 16), to the place thought beyond protection, the place that seemed beyond humanness. God's face is still toward the brother, after he is banished from the face of the earth (v. 14). Perhaps it is especially the haunted fugitive who can join the Pauline doxology:

> I am sure that neither death, nor life, nor angels, nor principalities, nor things present, nor things to come, nor powers, nor height, nor depth, nor anything else in all creation, will be able to separate us from the love of God in Christ Jesus our Lord (Rom. 8:38–39).

Biblical faith is clear: Violation of the brother is a deathly act. Yet, God's will for life is at work with the one under death sentence. By verse 11, Cain is a dead man. The protective mark of verse 15 is less than resurrection for this dead man. But it is an anticipation of resurrection. It announces that God has not lost interest in the murderer nor given up on him. The comment of I John 3:11–18 presses the point. The daily estrangement of brother and brother has come to seem ordinary, routine, and accepted. Estrangement seems to be "our common lot." And the world wants to keep it so. The world hates those who practice otherwise (I John 3:13). But that conventional estrangement is turned into the ultimate issue of life and death in the context of the gospel. By joining *brother-love to resurrection* ("We know that we have passed out of death into *life,* because we love the brethren" [I John 3:14]) and by linking *brother-hate to death* ("He who does not love remains in *death* [I John 3:14]), the issue of the brother is made the ultimate theological crisis. The brother issue is saved from trivialization. The question of resurrection is rescued from unreality.

The miracle of new life, the wonder of resurrection, is linked to brotherly reconciliation. That is what passing from death to life is about (I John 3:14). But life with the brother is so ominous because of the "waiting one." Most days, we would choose death (cf. Deut. 30:19) rather than to face the brother. But the gospel is uncompromising. The promises are linked to the brother and will be had no other way. It is a mystery that the gift of new life is so close at hand, present in the neighbor. So close at hand but so resisted. We do not readily embrace such a mystery. Perhaps that is the reason sin waits so eagerly.

Genesis 4:17—6:4

In tracing the main theological elements in Genesis, it is usual to move directly from the Cain story in 4:1–16 to the flood story beginning in 6:5, with some minor attention to 6:1–4. The materials which concern us here fall between the Cain narrative and the flood account and may be treated with relative brevity. They are comprised of three elements which have no direct relation to each other. They may, therefore, be treated separately.

The Genealogy of Cain

64   4:17–26, like the other genealogies in Genesis, is used to tie stories together which originally had no connection. This abbreviated genealogy has peculiar overlaps with the more ex-

tended and stylized one that follows in chapter 5. Likely the two genealogies developed separately but in part drew from the same sources. The genealogy of this section is of interest, (*a*) because it comes from Cain (Cain, the exiled murderer of 4:1–16 is blessed with the gift of life and family. The curse is not operative here except in the poetry of verses 23–24) and (*b*) the genealogy includes seven generations, perhaps expressive of completion and a sense of totality about this family, again a statement unrelated to the preceding account of curse. Scattered in the midst of the genealogy, five other matters may be noted.

1. This is the first and one of the few explicit references in the Old Testament to the arts as legitimate and recognized enterprises (vv. 21–22). The arts referred to are music and metal work now set alongside shepherding. Nothing should be deduced from this about the actual history of culture. But as the story stands, the appearance of art in human history is linked to the vitality of the murderer, or at least to the one willing to engage in self-assertion. In addition to the three closely related sons of Lamech—Jabal, Jubal, Tubal-cain—(all names perhaps derived from *yabal,* which may mean "productive"), there is the curious mention of one daughter, Na'amah—"pleasant, lovely." The four names together suggest a celebration of life.

2. Closely related to the emergence of the arts is the appearance of the first city, built by Cain (v. 17). It is likely the case that the material of verses 17–25 is linked to the narrative of 1–16 only by the genealogy of Cain. But another more substantive link may be suggested in the relation between the "desire" (v. 7) and arts and city (vv. 17, 21–22). Freud has fully explored the relation between *desire and culture.* He has seen that on the one hand there would be no culture without desire. On the other hand, there will be no culture unless desire is channeled and controlled. Thus behind the arts and city of verses 17, 21–22 is the desire of verse 7. Perhaps the narrative suggests that the family of Cain has now begun to "master" (cf. v. 7). The "mastery" leading to culture is never an untainted one; it brings together desire and control. Together they make arts, city, and culture possible.

3. In the midst of the genealogy is the primitive song of vengeance by Lamech (vv. 23–24). The song may suggest that in the family of the undisciplined murderer, vengeance runs rampant, uncontrolled, and without limits. It fits the general

65

theme of Gen. 3—11. Creation is not unified as willed by God. It is increasingly scattered, alienated, and hostile. Probably Jesus' teaching of forgiveness "seventy times seven" (Matt. 18: 21–22; Luke 17:3–4) is a direct response to Lamech and means to refute the practice of unbridled vengeance. Jesus embodies the inversion of the world, a world set on a course to death by the family of Cain.

The free rein given to human vengeance here is contrasted with Israel's recognition that vengeance belongs only to God. That is, when Yahweh can be entrusted to avenge wrong, the offended party is neither obligated nor free to take vengeance into his own hands. This is most eloquently stated in Ps. 94:1:

> O LORD, thou God of vengeance,
> thou God of vengeance, shine forth!

The entire psalm (cf. Deut. 32:39; Rom. 12:19) sounds strangely like a cry Abel might make against Cain and his family. Thus the song of Lamech may be the *voice of the offending party* who must defend itself, whereas Ps. 94 is the *voice of the offended party* who can and must rely upon another intervener (cf. Job 19:25). The management of vengeance is an important theological matter. But in the context of the building of a city, it is also a concrete political, sociological matter. The containment of vengeance is necessary to the ordering of a stable society. The cry of Lamech militates against the city of Cain. The son reflects the conflicted state of this family, not yet able to handle the question of the brother. And if the question of the brother is not handled, there will be no peaceable city. Culture depends on desire; but the city of culture is perennially troubled by the unresolved issue of the brother.

4. The genealogy of Cain is often linked to the tribes of the Kenites. Moreover, it appears that in some pre-Israelite settings, these Kenites were the first worshipers of Yahweh, thus the precursors of the religion of Israel. While such a connection is of interest to the history of religion, it is of no special value for understanding the text nor the faith of Israel.

5. At the end of our section (vv. 25–26), the narrative suggests an alternative history, beginning with Seth, now a substitute for the murdered Abel (cf. Acts 1:15–26). After this time, the family of humankind is not traced from the deathly Cain, whose genealogy ends with Lamech. Now it is the legacy of Seth. In subsequent tradition (outside the Bible) there has

66

grown around the figure of Seth a considerable mythology. But in the confines of the Bible, he is only a link among generations (cf. Luke 3:38). With the beginning of the new life, there is reference to the beginning of reliance on Yahweh (4:26; cf. 12:8; 13:4; 26:25). The God to whom Cain turned in despair is the God the new family now embraces.

Taken all together, Gen. 4 is a telling juxtaposition of themes. It asserts the peculiar appearance of *(a)* radical sin (vv. 8–11), *(b)* high culture (vv. 17, 21–22) and *(c)* confessional religion (v. 26). The three seem to come together in an uneasy combination which reflects our common life.

From Creation to the Flood

5:1–32 presents the first of two extended genealogies in the pre-Israelite material of Gen. 1—11, the other one being 11: 10–29 (cf. 10:1–32). The two are symmetrical, this one tracing humankind from creation to flood, the second from flood to Abraham. Genealogies are notoriously difficult to interpret. We can never be sure of the intent of the tradition. It is likely that this genealogy of ten generations is primarily for purposes of continuity, to show the linkage of humankind from its wholesome beginning to its shameful arrival at the flood. The fact of ten generations is a way the tradition suggests completion. That is, this eon of human life has run its full course. If we knew more, we would likely discover that the genealogy is an index of extended traditional materials about each of these names. But by the time of the genealogy, the names seem largely to have lost their specific traditional content and are only ciphers, the key to which is largely missing.

It is generally agreed that this listing belongs to the Priestly tradition and resumes the structured account of 1:1—2:4*a*. Thus the "book of generations of Adam" (5:1) continues the "book of generations of heaven and earth" (2:4*a*). Clearly, the narrative material of 2:4*b*—4:26 is from a different (earlier) hand and has been inserted between these stylized accounts. The Priestly material contains no account of man-woman, the garden, or of Cain. But as the material stands we must try to see it in sequence, as the final form of the tradition has shaped it.

We may divide our brief comments into two parts:

1. First, this text will evoke questions and wonderments of a *historical* kind, mostly related to the enormous numbers in the chapter. At the outset, we must concede we do not know

67

the intended meaning of the numbers. They may have precise, perhaps astronomical function, but this is uncertain. In general, they seem to suggest a view that in pre-flood time there was much longer life than now. It is noteworthy, however, that this account follows Gen. 2—4 in the present tradition. Thus, longevity cannot now be attributed to the "absence of sin."

In responding to such matters of curiosity, two responses may be useful.

a. The materials should be seen in comparison with and in contrast with other materials, especially the Mesopotamian King List which exists in variant forms and is quite old. The comparison suggests there may have been a stock tradition of ten generations with very long years. Compared to that list, the interesting feature of Gen. 5 is not the long years but that the years are quite shortened from the parallels. Thus, chapter 5 may reflect a sobering toward historical reality in contrast to neighboring cultures, though no critical commentator takes the numbers as historically valid.

b. Verse 3 contains an odd ambiguous statement about Seth, the father of humankind. It is not said he is in the image of God, but in the image of Adam, who is in the image of God. Thus, he is one step removed. This might mean he continues the image of God, for the image of God is granted not only to the first human but to all humans. But such an assertion is hedged, for the image of Adam is something less, and marred (cf. Gen. 3). Thus, the text may realistically recognize that Seth and his heirs are a strange, unresolved mixture of the *regal* image of God and the *threatened* image of Adam. Such a double statement recognizes the ambivalence of humankind, even as Paul later experienced it (cf. Rom. 7:15–23).

c. The special notations on Enoch (vv. 22–23) are brief, highly isolated, and so not very useful. The special formula "walked with God," is used only of Enoch and Noah (6:9) though Abraham walked "before God" (17:1; 24:40). While this formula of special intimacy is often understood in terms of moral uprightness and obedience (cf. Heb. 11:5–6; Jude 14–15), the main reading in the tradition does not concern obedience (which is presumed) but privileged entry into the secrets of God. Thus, Enoch subsequently became a clustering point for apocalyptic traditions. See the extended book bearing his name in the apocrypha, summarizing God's secrets revealed to him about the end of history. Obviously, such a later development is only remotely derived from our verses. The mode of his life-ending, "God took him," could suggest something other than death, and that is likely the root of much later speculation. But as this phrase stands in isolation, nothing can be made of it. Even in this terse form, it reflects that Enoch represents some role in overcoming the utter discontinuity of God and humankind. This is the basis for the special revelations of apocalyptic traditions in which such special persons (seers) penetrate God's mysteries denied to humankind generally. It will be well for our interpretation to be as restrained here as is the text. The "secrets of God" in the New Testament are not the bizarre visions of apocalyptic and of later Gnosticism, but the good news of the gospel (cf. I Cor. 4:1–2).

d. Worth noting is the attitude and presentation of Lamech here (vv. 28–31), quite a contrast to the vengeful man of 4:23–24. While the contrasting presentations of the same man may be explained on grounds of different sources, it is important that this two-sidedness is preserved in the tradition. Lamech prefigures the tendency we all know of trying to serve two masters (Matt. 6:24); in his case, self-security (4:23–24) and the vision of uncursed earth (5:29).

e. Most important in the chapter is Lamech's anticipation of Noah (v. 29). While this verse is commonly regarded as an intrusion in the chapter (because of the name used for God), it offers the most inviting expository possibility in the chapter:

1) The anticipated help will come from the ground cursed by God (cf. 3:17; 4:11). The statement is obviously a careful theological link with those earlier narratives. It asserts on the one hand that God has not abandoned his intentions for the cursed earth. On the other hand, help must come from that very ground, and not as spirit or from heaven. The salvific promise shows how earthy and earthly the Bible is. Indeed, this is a hint of incarnational faith. The affirmation that *relief* comes from *cursed ground* reflects a way of thinking that easily runs toward crucifixion and resurrection in the New Testament. As help comes from the place of curse, so life comes from the reality of death (cf. Gal. 3:13–14).

2) The Hebrew name "Noah" probably means *rest,* that is, serenity in God's safe world. But the name "Noah-rest" cannot be linked to the verb "relief" as is claimed in the RSV rendering of Gen. 5:29. The Hebrew word rendered "relief" (*nḥm*) in the RSV is continually rendered "comfort" elsewhere (cf. Ps. 23:4;

69

71:21; 86:17, Isa. 49:13; 66:13). Most familiarly, the word is used in Isa. 40:1 to announce the end of exile and the inversion of the fortunes of Israel. That rendering is more appropriate here. Linked to the consequences of Gen. 2—4, it is the task of Noah to end the banishment of the man and woman (3:24) and of Cain (4:16). He is to invert the sorry situation and cause a homecoming. Thus, Noah is to do for humanity just what Second Isaiah announced for Israel then in exile (cf. Isa. 54:9–17). These connections are not remote if Gen. 5 (with or without v. 29) is Priestly and therefore exilic. (The text would then date as a near contemporary of II Isaiah.)

This anticipation of the work of Noah, placed in the mouth of Lamech, is a gospel announcement. Noah is a gift of the "God of all comfort" (II Cor. 1:3–7) and is already a way in which God sends his comforter (cf. John 14:26; 15:26; 16:7). The motif of comfort appears in various texts of Genesis, each time at a break point between life and death (24:67; 27:42; 37:35; 38:12; 50:21). In a way more intentional than most of these, our verse places Noah at the turn from death to life.

3) The comfort promised by Noah (v. 29) is to reverse the destiny of living with the consequences of sin. As we have suggested, the RSV translation is a poor one because it sounds like rest from work. But that is doubtful, for work as such is a proper vocation of humankind, as we have seen in Gen. 1—2. Rather, what is anticipated is deliverance from the sorry situation which human ingenuity has wrought. Thus, while Israel may pray for the "work of our hands" to be established (Ps. 90:17), there must also be prayers for deliverance from the work of our hands.

In these ways, this chapter provides links between the hopes of *creation* and the reality of human *sin*. Noah holds promise of a new beginning in which the hopes of creation are not qualified by the realities of human choice. The words of Lamech are good news, daring to hope for a break in the sequence. That break comes, by the power of God, in human form.

Sons of God and Daughters of Men

6:1–4 has no connection with chapter 5 or any of the preceding material. This text may provide a prelude to the flood story as an example of the "great wickedness" of 6:5. The brief narrative is a most curious one. It participates as fully in the common mythological tradition of the ancient Near East as any Old Testament text. The meaning of the text is disputed and likely the effort taken in understanding it will not be matched by gains for exposition in the listening community.

These preliminary observations may clear the way for interpretation:

(*a*) The narrative has etiological motifs. At some stage in its development, it was told to explain the "giants" in the earth (cf. Num. 13:33). That, however, is not its present function.

(*b*) The story clearly belongs with parallel stories of hero characters who live somewhere in the middle zone between human and divine. Reality discerned in this way lies beyond the perceptual field of Israel's faith. This way of overcoming the distance of God and humanity is in contrast to the salvific anticipation of 5:29.

(*c*) The "sons of God" (v. 2) refers to lesser gods in a polytheistic understanding of the world. Luther, against such a consensus of interpretation, refers the phrase to the pious of Israel. But that is scarcely possible.

(*d*) The text ill fits with the main flow of biblical faith. Its presence in the tradition, however, provides a basis for religious speculation in non-canonical literature (cf. I Enoch 6:1–2; 7:2).

1. The structure of the passage will help us to engage this difficult text. The first two verses seem clear enough about the interaction of the world of God and human creatures. There is no criticism implied in these verses. Verse 4 would seem to continue that picture by drawing an etiological conclusion. It is generally agreed that verse 3 represents a break in that sequence and is, of course, the place where Yahweh asserts his sovereignty. The relation of verse 3 to verses 1–2 and 4 represents a confrontation between the religious world around Israel and an assertion of Yahweh's uncompromising sovereignty over that world, a sovereignty not easily accommodated to those religious perspectives. That interface between *religious speculation* and *Yahweh's sovereignty* may provide an issue for exposition.

We have seen that God calls the worlds into being, wills them ordered and purposeful in a harmony. He created the *heavens of mystery* and the *earth of responsibility*. Both are important. God presides over both for his purposes. But this text (cf. v. 3) reports a "perversion of the order appointed by God" (Calvin). This disruption tries to overcome the separation fixed

71

between heaven and earth (cf. Gen. 1:6–10). The limitation of human years by Yahweh parallels his concern for limit in 2:17 (cf. 15:5) and 11:6. Thus, the New Testament reads this story as a dangerous disordering of God's creation (II Pet. 2:4; Jude 6). It is an extravagant way in which the powers of heaven (the sons of God) and of earth, all creatures of the Creator, attempt to seize the mystery of life for their own.

2. But the structure of the text asserts that the great cleavage is not between heaven and earth. It is, rather, between God on the one hand and the powers of both heaven and earth on the other. All of "heaven and earth" stand over against God and are responsive to him. The perversion wrought by the sons of God and the daughters of men is another example of the attempt to "be like God." And so the intervention of God (v. 3) is for the sake of his sovereignty. That intervention contains a judgment and an assurance.

a. The judgment is that God will not endlessly and forever permit his life-giving spirit to enliven those who disorder his world. The breath of life (Gen. 2:7; Ps. 104:29–30) remains his to give and his to recall. He has not finally entrusted it to any other. The judgment of verse 3 asserts the sovereignty of Yahweh, who presides over the gift of life.

b. At the same time, the verse contains what appears to be a promise, albeit limited, that life, even life in rebellion, is vouchsafed for one hundred and twenty years. This is, of course, a limitation after the numbers of Gen. 5. But it is, nonetheless, an assurance of long life (cf. Isa. 65:20; Ps. 90:9–10). Could it be that the rescue from the "work of our hands" in 5:29 and the discussion of longevity in 6:3 come together in a reflection of Ps. 90? Both themes are there:

> The years of our life are *threescore and ten,*
> or even by reason of strength *fourscore;*
> yet their span is but toil and trouble;
> they are soon gone, and we fly away. . . .
> Let the favor of the Lord our God be upon us,
> and establish thou the work of our hands upon us,
> yea, the *work of our hands* establish thou it (vv. 10, 17).

The psalm suggests that the motifs of Gen. 5:29 and 6:3 together are a reflection on the placement of human life before the sovereign mystery of the creator.

3. The narrative must not be pressed too far because we do not understand it. But it seems to assert that in heaven and on

earth, in good order and in disorder, God still is the only giver of life. He gives life to all his creatures. Only by his gift do they live. No attempted usurpation changes that.

Such a restrained theological reading of the text will not satisfy those who want to penetrate deeper into the mythological aspects of the text. For that, it will be important to observe how marginal these motifs are in biblical faith.

These three elements concerning the family of Cain (4:17–26), the family of Seth (5:1–32) and he strange giants (6:1–4) provide a transition. Now the opening vision of harmony and unity (1:1—2:4b) is thoroughly shattered. The creator is not indifferent. It remains to be seen whether the son of Lamech (cf. 5:29) can indeed comfort creation and provide rescue from what creaturely ingenuity has wrought. God's purpose for his world is now fully at issue.

Genesis 6:5—9:17

The flood story is among the best-known biblical narratives. It is undoubtedly borrowed from a common religious tradition of flood accounts. However, in this text the flood narrative has been claimed to express the peculiar theological affirmations of Israel's faith. Our exposition will indicate that the theological intent of the story as shaped in Israel has significantly altered it from the purposes of earlier traditions. As Israel moved beyond popular understandings, a serious exposition of the text today requires an abandonment of the stereotypes of the account held in most current popular understandings. In contrast to those understandings, we will suggest that the focus of the story is not on the flood but upon the change wrought in God which makes possible a new beginning for creation.

The Theme: The Incongruity of Creator and Creation

The flood narrative faces a basic incongruity of human life. On the one hand, God has called the world into being to be his faithful covenant partner. He has willed unity, harmony, and goodness. With quite different textures, the poetic liturgy of 1:1—2:4a and the narrative of 2:4b–25 have sought to model such an intent. But on the other hand, it has not happened that

73

way. God willed a creation ordered by Sabbath rest. But it is a
recalcitrant creation resistant to the purposes of the very one
by whom and for whom the world exists. The incongruity is
asserted about creation. It is also true of Israel, the paradigm of
creation. God has such *high hopes* for Israel:

> "I thought
>> how I would set you among my sons,
> and give you a pleasant land,
>> a heritage most beauteous of all nations.
> And I thought you would call me, My Father,
>> and would not turn from following me" (Jer. 3:19).

But *Israel refuses* the destiny envisioned by God:

> "Surely, as a faithless wife leaves her husband,
>> so have you been faithless to me,
>> O house of Israel, says the LORD" (Jer. 3:20).

It is the same with creation. The creation has refused to be
God's creation. That essential fracture between creator and
creation is the premise and agenda of the flood narrative. This
text provides a way to reflect on the meaning and cost of that
fracture and upon the future that is yet in prospect between
God and God's world.

The Text and the Task Before Us

1. The beginning point is to be clear on the character of the
text before us. As with Gen. 1:1—2:4a, we do not have before
us history, that is, a detailed account of what happened. No
doubt, there are various historical reminiscences here of flood
experiences which must be deep in various cultural memories.
But our interpretation will be distracted if there is insistence on
finding data to prove that this is a "historical" narrative. Whatever historical memory lies behind the narrative likely cannot
be recovered. The finding of the ark on Mt. Ararat is a doubtful
enterprise and not likely to succeed. Even if such data could be
recovered, it would not in any serious way affect our exposition.
This story is not concerned with historical data but with the
strange things which happen in the heart of God that decisively
affect God's creation.

74   With equal firmness, we must deny that this is a "myth"
expressed in Israel just as it is in every other ancient culture.
Such comparative literary study may appeal to our rational
inclination with such a story. But that approach takes the text

as a universal statement about the nature of the cosmos as fractured and threatened. Such a perspective misses the claim of the text. The Genesis narrative is not a universal statement but a peculiarly Israelite statement in the categories of covenant. And it is not a statement about the world but about the God of Israel and his peculiar way in transforming the world.

What meets us here is *proclamation,* the announcement of what God has done about the fractured world. The text goes on to say that what God has done has decisively changed the situation of all creatures. The proclamation is one of *warning.* It announces that God has powerful ways to bring the world to his vision of unity and harmony and order. Attention to that proclamation requires our exposition to bracket the curious questions which could claim our energies. We need attend neither to issues of *historical uniqueness* nor to issues of *literary comparisons.* Rather, our focus is on the disclosure of God in this text and the ways in which that disclosure recharacterizes the world.

2. One other question as well must be bracketed. It is beyond dispute that this text conflates two strands of tradition, commonly designated J and P, or at least designated as Israel's early and later theological traditions. Most interpretation addresses these separately. However, there is currently an interest among critical scholars to move past such dissections to deal with the text as it now stands. That will be our approach here. Without denying or minimizing the importance of traditional source analysis, we must hear the whole text. To be sure, one can detect differences in style and nuance. But our exposition indicates that the early and late elements of the tradition express the same convictions. In the end, they share the same affirmation of the gospel.

The Beginning, the End, and the Crucial Turn

We may begin by being particularly attentive to the story style of the text. Two features are worth noting. Bernhard Anderson ("From Analysis to Synthesis: The Interpretation of Genesis 1–11," JBL 97:31–39 [1978]), has shown how the text is set into discrete frames and scenes which make dramatic storytelling effective. There is a deliberate pace and structure to the account which means to carry the listener. In more detail, Sean McEvenue has shown how the story combines a freedom and spontaneity with sober discipline that likens it to a story de-

75

signed for children *(The Narrative Style of the Priestly Writer,* ANALECTA BIBLICA 50, pp. 12–18). The stylized sober discipline that likens it to a story designed for children. The stylized transitions, the pace and repetitions present a marvelous statement which builds tension and then resolves it. The skill of the narrator is not an end in itself. Its purpose is to carry the listening community to a new discernment about the character of the world and its locus in relation to God.

Our exposition will approach the text by observing where the narrative begins, where it ends, and where there is a turn which advances the story. The narrative does not progress gradually. There is a decisive turn which abruptly reshapes the world.

1. The beginning of the narrative is the unit *6:5—7:12.* Our focus will be first on the affirmation of 6:5–8 (J) and its counterpart 6:11–13 (P). The two elements are agreed in their main point.

a. God has concluded that the world has betrayed his intent. The noble decisions of God have been treated shabbily. God deals with that reality with great seriousness. The terms for the perversion are various: wickedness (v. 5), evil (v. 5), corrupt (vv. 11, 12), filled with violence (vv. 11, 13). No special or specific content is given to any of these terms. But the preceding narratives of man-woman (2:4*b*—3:24), Cain (4:1–16), Lamech (4:23–24) and the sons of God (6:1–4) all suggest that what is wrong is that creation has refused to be God's creation, refused to honor God as God. Both the world and God have been denied their real character. In various ways "creation has exchanged the truth about God for a lie, worshiping and serving the creature rather than the Creator" (Rom. 1:25; cf. Jer. 2:11; Hos. 4:7). The indictment is as harsh as any from Israel's prophets. It means the death of the whole world. The flood story begins in a harsh criticism which is theological (and not moral) in character.

b. The indictment is followed by an uncompromising resolve on the part of God to destroy the creation which has refused to be his faithful, obedient creation. Thus:

I will blot out (6:7; cf. 7:4, 23).

I will destroy (6:13).

I will bring a flood . . . to destroy (6:17).

The end is coming. The prophetic judgment of Amos 8:2 is here made cosmic in scope. The "very good" of 1:31 has become, "I will blot out."

As Claus Westermann has seen, the structure of the beginning of the narrative follows the normal prophetic speech of judgment, structured as indictment and sentence ("Types of Narratives in Genesis," *The Promises to the Fathers*, 1964, pp. 48–56). The text does not concern itself with amounts of water or pairs of animals or rainbows, but with the way God deals with his creation. The narrative begins by bringing us face to face with the God of Israel. This God takes with uncompromising seriousness his own purposes for creation. And he is impatient when those purposes are resisted. God holds an expectation for his world. He will not abandon it.

c. If the beginning of the flood narrative claimed only that, the text would be flat and one-dimensional. But there are two other matters here that enrich and greatly complicate the beginnings. First, with amazing boldness the narrative invites the listening community to penetrate into the heart of God (vv. 6–7). What we find there is not an angry tyrant, but a troubled ✓ parent who grieves over the alienation. He is growingly aware that the "imagination of the thoughts" of the human heart are unrelievedly hostile (v. 5). The conjuring, day dreams, and self-perceptions of the world are all tilted against God's purpose. God is aware that something is deeply amiss in creation, so that God's own dream has no prospect of fulfillment. With that perverted imagination, God's world has begun to conjure its own future quite apart from the future willed by God (cf. 11:6).

As a result, verse 6 shows us the deep pathos of God. God ✓ is not angered but grieved. He is not enraged but saddened. ✓ God does not stand over against but with his creation. Tellingly, ✓ the pain he bequeathed to the woman in 3:16 is now felt by God. Ironically, the word for "grieve" *('asav)* is not only the same as the sentence on the woman ("pain" 3:16), but it is also used for the state of toil from which Noah will deliver humanity (5:29). The evil *heart of humankind* (v. 5) troubles the *heart of God* (v. 6). This is indeed "heart to heart" between humankind and God. How it is between humankind and God touches both parties. As Ernst Würthwein suggests, it is God who must say, "I am undone" (cf. Isa. 6:5; *Wort und Existenz*, 1970, pp. 313).

d. Two kinds of pastoral questions are likely to arise here.

1) Could God bring an end to his world? And to that a pastoral (not an ontological) answer must be given. We know about the collapse of the world. We are acquainted with the disintegration and demise of our precious life-world. We know

77

we live jeopardized lives. While it is not clear that our faithfulness will guarantee our world, it is beyond doubt that our infidelity diminishes our lives and all of life around us. The answer to such a dreaded cosmic question can be made out of the experience of our own shattered lives. Worlds do disintegrate. Yes, the world, even under God's rule, can end. And Israel affirms it is God's will.

2) Can God change his mind? Can he abandon the world which he has so joyously created? That is a central question for Israel. Many people hold a view of God as unchanging and indifferent to anything going on in the world, as though God were a plastic, fixed entity. But Israel's God is fully a person who hurts and celebrates, responds and acts in remarkable freedom. God is not captive of old resolves. God is as fresh and new in relation to creation as he calls us to be with him. He can change his mind, so that he can abandon what he has made; and he can rescue that which he has condemned.

With this in mind, the agenda for our narrative has quickly shifted. We are confronted in this text not with a flood, but with a heavy, painful crisis in the dealings of God with creation. It is popularly thought that the crisis of the flood is to place the world in jeopardy. But a close reading indicates that it is the heart and person of God which are placed in crisis. The crisis is not the much water, which now has become only a dramatic setting. Rather, the crisis comes because of the resistant character of the world which evokes hurt and grief in the heart of God. Franz Delitzsch has seen that the depth of pathos of God expressed here is matched by the extraordinary statement of Hosea 11:8–9 (*A New Commentary on Genesis I*, 1888, pp. 233–34; cf. also Hos. 6:4). The narrative is centered in the grief of God, whose heart knows about our hearts (cf. I Chron. 28:9; Jer. 17:10; Ps. 139:23; Rom. 8:27). This daring assertion about God is problematic in every static theology which wants God always acting the same and predictably. But the text affirms that God is decisively impacted by the suffering, hurt, and circumstance of his creation. God enters into the world's "common lot."

In our discussion of 1:1—2:4*a*, we have seen that God's creative power was not coercive and authoritarian. Rather, it is invitational and permit-granting. While God wills creation to be turned toward him, he does not commandeer it. So in this

78

narrative, bringing the world to trust and obedience is not done by God's fiat. Rather, it is done by the anguish and grief of God, who enters into the pain and fracture of the world. The world is brought to the rule of God, but only by the pathos and vulnerability of the creator. The story is not about the world assaulted and a God who stands remote. It is about the hurt God endures because of and for the sake of his wayward creation. The *new creation* is wrought with the same costly engagement and waiting as is the *first creation.*

The first part of our narrative moves in much the same way as does the entire unit of Hos. 11:1–9. Hos. 11:1–9 begins in verses 1–7 with a *speech of judgment.* Then in verses 8–9 it makes a break from the judgment speech to express the *passion of God.* The same break is suggested in this text. The conflict between *judgment* and *pathos* in the heart of God (with which Hosea struggled) is important for the presentation of the flood narrative.

e. A further enhancing feature of this "beginning" of the narrative (6:5—7:12) is the figure of Noah. Noah does not fit the scheme of indictment and sentence. He is the bearer of an alternative possibility. Though he had been anticipated (5:29), he appears here abruptly. He is first mentioned with the the statement that God is positively inclined toward him (6:8).

The narrative has held off as long as possible in permitting Noah entrance into the drama. When he appears, we know nothing about him. But God and the narrator know enough. Noah is righteous and blameless. He walks with God (vv. 6:9; 7:1; cf. 5:22). In this dismal story of pain, there is one who embodies a new possibility.

The narrator presents him against the main flow of the story. There is the announcement of flood, destruction, and death. Then, J has it, "But Noah found favor . . ." (v. 8); P has it, "But I will establish my covenant . . ." (v. 18). The narrator wants the listening community to turn to Noah, to consider that in this troubled exchange between creator and creation there is the prospect of fresh alternative. Something new is at work in creation. Noah is the new being (II Cor. 5:17) for whom none of the other data applies. He is the fully responsive man who accepts creatureliness and lets God be God. So the presentation of faithful Noah is rather like a refrain:

79

> He . . . did all that God commanded him (6:22).
> Noah did all that the Lord had commanded him (7:5).
> . . . as God had commanded Noah (7:9).

Noah regards God's commands as promises of life (cf. John 12:50). He is a model of faith such as has not yet appeared in biblical narrative (except perhaps the truncated reference to Enoch). It is ironic that at the moment of pathos and impending death, embodied faith first appears in the world. The narrative announces a minority view. Faithfulness is possible even in this world.

So the narrative has its beginnings. But its beginnings are not unambiguous. Along with (1) the *law-suit* (judgment speech), there is also (2) the *grief of God* and (3) the new creation in *Noah.* The speech of judgment announces what everyone knows about the flood story: God gets angry with his world and causes a flood to punish. But there are other more decisive factors when the narrative is seen through the eyes of faith. The narrative concerns the *grief of God* and the *emergence of new humanity* in the midst of the old judged humanity. These dimensions of the narrative change our reading of God's well-known anger and redirect our exposition.

2. When we turn to the ending of the story (8:20—9:17), it is not hard to see that the grief of God and the new creature have overridden the force of the law-suit. The flood ends. Life begins again. The resolve to destroy has been mitigated. The issue of the narrative's beginning is resolved, but not in terms of destruction as we might have expected. The resolution is not by God's indulgence of his anger. Nor is it by indulgence of the hostile creation or by some change in creation. Rather, the resolution comes by the resolve of God's heart to fashion a newness.

a. The conclusion may be divided into three parts, 8:20–22; 9:1–7 and 8–17. The first of these (8:20–22) (J) begins a new history with an altar, making a fresh announcement that God is genuinely acknowledged as God (8:20). But the substance of this unit is the speech of God (vv. 21–22). God speaks "in his heart"—in the same place where he first struggled in 6:6. By reference to God's heart, the narrator makes a clear connection between 6:5–8 and 8:20–22. God now reaches two conclusions:

80   1) Humankind is hopeless. Creation has not changed. It is deeply set against God's purposes. The imagination of the heart first recognized as evil in 6:5 is still imagination of the heart which is evil in 8:21. All the terror of the waters has not changed

that. Hope for the future is not premised on possibility thinking
or human actualization. Hope will depend on a move from God.

2) The second conclusion of God is a fresh decision cast as
a royal decree. This resolve gathers up the curse of 3:17, the
sentence of Cain in 4:11, and the anticipation of 5:29. God
resolves that he will stay with, endure, and sustain his world,
notwithstanding the sorry state of humankind. He will not let
the rebellion of humankind sway him from his grand dream for
creation. He will stay with his decision for a harmonious, obedient, creation. This decision of God is not unlike God's self-
perception in Hos. 11:9. He is God. He takes as his vocation not
judgment but the resilient work of affirmation on behalf of the
death-creature. The flood has effected no change in humankind. But it has effected an irreversible change in God, who now
will approach his creation with an unlimited patience and for-
bearance. To be sure, God has been committed to his creation
from the beginning. But this narrative traces a new decision on
the part of God. Now the commitment is intensified. For the
first time, it is marked by grief, the hurt of betrayal. It is now
clear that such a commitment on God's part is costly. The God-
world relation is not simply that of strong God and needy world.
Now it is a tortured relation between a grieved God and a
resistant world. And of the two, the real changes are in God.
This is a key insight of the gospel against every notion that God
stands outside of the hurt as a judge. (Cf. Rom. 3:25 in which
God's righteousness comes not as judgment, but as incredible
compassion.)

The new resolution in the heart of God to stay with his
creation has affinity with the salvation oracle spoken through
Second Isaiah to the hopeless exiles. What God there speaks to
Israel he here speaks to his *world:*

> "Fear not, for I am with you,
>   be not dismayed, for I am your God (Isa. 41:10)
>
> Fear not, for I have redeemed you;
>   I have called you by name, you are mine.
> When you pass through . . . the rivers, they shall not overwhelm
>   you; . . ." (Isa. 43:1–2).

The promises are parallel. The faith of the Bible moves in a
double focus, with promises to Israel and to the world. The
linkage between the decree of the flood narrative and that of
II Isaiah is suggested (*a*) by the contemporaneity of the Priestly
tradition with the poetry of II Isaiah in exile, and (*b*) by the

81

explicit analogy suggested in Isa. 54:9–11. As Israel is not abandoned in exile, creation is not abandoned to the chaos of its disobedience.

b. The narrative has a dim view of the human heart. The question is not whether people are "good-hearted" in the sense we call "nice," but whether in the deep places of life, human persons and the human community are capable of saving themselves. Can human persons transcend calculated self-interest which inevitably leads to death? Is the source of new life ordained in our bodies? Or is humankind dependent upon a gift of grace which we cannot give to ourselves nor even to each other? Our answers to these questions have largely been self-deceiving. Freud has understood about our capacity for self-deception. Marx has seen clearly our fascination with our own interests. This narrative permits the believing community to create an island of candor in a "flood" of self-deception. The candid vantage point permits a glimpse of the human imagination as it actually is.

The heavy discernment about humankind in 8:21 does not stand alone. The statement about humankind is kept in close connection to the passion and responsive grief of God. What distinguishes God in this narrative from every other god and from every creature is God's deep grief. That grief enables God to move past his own interest and to embrace his creature-partner in new ways. In the self-abandoning of God (cf. Phil. 2:5–11) comes the basis for a new world called now into being. So the Reformer could say of this juxtaposition of *humankind's evil heart* and *God's troubled heart*:

> Our hope is in no other save in Thee;
> Our faith is built upon Thy promise free;
> Lord, give us peace, and make us calm and sure,
> That in Thy strength we evermore endure
> (John Calvin, "I Greet Thee Who My Sure Redeemer Art").

c. The second element of the conclusion is 9:1–7 (P). This regal speech announces that the intent and mandates of creation (cf. 1:1—2:4a) are operative in this new creation. The benediction of 1:28 is restated in 9:1 and 7. The vocation in "God's image" from 1:26–27 is claimed again in 9:6. Post-flood humankind is in God's image, responsible for and capable of rule. The human creature of 2:4b—3:24 who refused not only the prohibition of God (2:17) but also the vocation (2:15) and the permit of God (2:16) now is able to embrace all three. The power of this decree in 9:1–7 is better heard when set over against the dismal assessment of 8:21. Though the two statements are from separate sources, they should be held together in our exposition. Only together do they say what must be said. The one in God's image (9:1–6) is the same one who troubles God's heart (8:20–22). The one whose imagination is evil is the one who is, nonetheless, created in God's image, formed in order to preside over creation.

The ruling human is entrusted with a fresh rule (9:1–7). In Gen. 1:26, the human creature was to rule over fish, birds, and animals. This meant to bring the other creatures to fullness. But now the New Being is to preside over humankind in order to enhance, celebrate, and dignify it. God yields no ground on his purpose for creation. If anything, this is an even more exalted view of human reality. The statement about blood (v. 4) is not now an isolated statement. Though it may originally have been a cultic rule, it now stands as part of a formidable barrier against dehumanization. An old statement on blood has now been transformed into an affirmation about human life and human worth. This decree urges human enhancement and the valuing of human persons. In this post-flood decree of creation, the sanctity of human life is established against every ideology and every force which would cheapen or diminish life. "God deems himself violated in the violation of these persons" (Calvin). In this decree is ground for Karl Barth's thesis of the *Humanity of God.* God unqualifiedly aligns himself with every human person as of ultimate value to him (cf. Matt. 6:32). The heavenly father is faithful. The ultimate valuing of every human person is echoed in the statement of Jesus, "Even the hairs of your head are all numbered. Fear not; you are of more value than many sparrows" (Luke 12:7).

d. The third piece of the conclusion is 9:8–17 (P). This majestic statement about covenant includes not only humankind but the whole creation. God makes an irreversible commitment that the post-flood, post-chaos situation is decisively different. In extraordinary resolve, God now says, "never again" (v. 11). What has changed is not anything about humankind or creation or waters or floods. What has changed is God. God has made a decision about the grief and trouble of his own heart.

The "never again" of God is an important point for pastoral exposition. Certainly, the question may legitimately be raised: Can there be no further destruction? Specific questions of theodicy may be raised about the holocaust, in which it seems

83

that God again released the flood waters. But all those who regard such events as punishment for sin have failed to understand the change in God. We have seen that in 6:5—7:10 there is a simple structure of indictment-sentence in which God resolves to punish the guilty. But that has now been changed. The one-to-one connection of guilt and punishment is broken. God is postured differently. From the perspective of this narrative, there may be death and destruction. Evil has not been eradicated from creation. But we are now assured that these are not rooted in the anger or rejection of God. The relation of creator to creature is no longer in a scheme of retribution. Because of a revolution in the heart of God, that relation is now based in unqualified grace. As God ordained reliability in creation (8:22) and as he requires the valuing of human life as an absolute (9:5–6), so now God values creation and stands for it. The "never again" spoken to creation has its parallel in the same "never again" he has spoken to his people Israel:

> I will not take my steadfast love from him, as I took it from Saul, whom I put away from before you. And your house and your kingdom shall be made sure for ever before me; your throne shall be established for ever (II Sam. 7:15–16).

And that "never again" of God is taken by the church (albeit often in excessively individualized ways) as the ultimate guarantee of his being with and being for his creatures:

> When through the deep waters I call thee to go,
> The rivers of sorrow shall not overflow;
> For I will be near thee, thy troubles to bless,
> And sanctify to thee thy deepest distress,
> And sanctify to thee thy deepest distress.
> ("How Firm a Foundation")

On the basis of God's "never again," the rainbow sign is established (vv. 12–16). The bow is a promise to creation. It is at the same time a reminder to God of a vow he will honor (9:16). In exploring the meaning of the bow, George Mendenhall regards it not only as bow as a weapon, but as an *undrawn* bow, that is, the creator has won his victory, over the chaos and perhaps also over his inclination to punish (*The Tenth Generation,* 1973, pp. 38–48). God is no longer in pursuit of an enemy. The promise of God is that he will not again be provoked to use his weapon, no matter how provocative his creation becomes. The bow at rest thus forms a parallel to the sabbath in 2:1–4a at the resolve of creation. The first creation (1:1—2:4a) ends

84

with the serene rest of God. The recreation (8:20—9:17) ends
with God resting his weapon. God's creation is for all time
protected from God's impatience.

Attention to the beginning and ending of the narrative tells
of a movement in God's posture toward creation:

from 6:5–8	to	8:20–22 (J)
from 6:11–13	to	9:1–17 (P)
from judgment	to	assurance
from destructive anger	to	promissory vow
from law-suit speech	to	salvation oracle.

3. The telling of the story must focus on that surprising and
irreversible turn. That is the substance of the gospel. The God
who rules over us has turned toward us in a new way.

a. But the telling of the narrative must be for the sake of
raising the crucial question: How is it that this move happened?
What is it that evokes God's turn toward his creation? Bernhard
Anderson has shown how that turn is. It is put this way:

> God remembered Noah and all the beasts and all the cattle that
> were with him in the ark (8:1).

God remembered Noah. God remembered. (Cf. Ps. 105:5; Luke
1:54–55).

This God is not timeless and immune to the flow of human
events. It was regularly the query of Israel in complaint
whether God had forgotten his people (cf. Pss. 10:11; 13:1; 42:9;
Isa. 49:14; Lam. 5:20). The issue of being forgotten is a genuine
pastoral issue. Every person knows times of the dark night of
being forgotten. In this narrative, the whole creation comes to
that time of being forgotten by God as the waters surge.

But the gospel of this God is that he remembers. The only
thing the waters of chaos and death do not cut through (though
they cut through everything else) is the commitment of God to
creation. His remembering is an act of gracious engagement
with his covenant partner, an act of committed compassion. It
asserts that God is not preoccupied with himself but with his
covenant partner, creation. It is the remembering of God, and
only that, which gives hope and makes new life possible (cf. I
Sam. 1:11, 19; Judg. 16:28; Ps. 8:4; 10:12; 74:1–3; Jer. 15:15).
Above all, Job 14:13 articulates the conviction that God's memory is the last ground of hope in the realm of death. Job pleads: 85

> Oh that thou wouldest hide me in Sheol,
>   that thou wouldest conceal me until thy wrath be past,
>   that thou wouldest appoint me a set time, and *remember me!*

Thus Paul Tillich has rightly discerned (albeit with his perspective of idealism) this theme in the face of death: "Is there anything that can keep us from being forgotten? That we were known from eternity and will be remembered in eternity is the only certainty that can save us from being forgotten forever. We cannot be forgotten, because we are known eternally, beyond past and future (*The Eternal Now*, 1963, pp. 25). The flood not only has no memory. It means to destroy memory (cf. Ps. 6:5) and set us in a world of utter amnesia. But the flood will not have its way. Yahweh will not be "brain-washed" by the flood.

The experience of chaos and death lets one conclude that everything is broken off, that everything in creation is ended. But this God stands free from and not controlled by creation. His commitments are not subject to such circumstances. And that is the ground of the gospel in this narrative. The world rests on a graciousness not subject to the waxing and waning of historical initiatives, or even to the rising and falling of waters.

b. Thus 8:1 stands at the center of the middle section (7:17–8:9). In the section before 8:1 (7:11–24), there is death and destruction until there is "only Noah" (7:23). But immediately upon remembering Noah, the waters begin to subside, until in 8:18–19, there is an exodus. Noah and all creatures enter a liberated earth. The shift from beginning to end, from judgment speech to promise of assurance, is because of God's commitment to this new man. (It is not difficult to discern why Noah became a type for Jesus of Nazareth in subsequent interpretation.) The flood story may now be seen in this way:

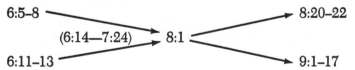

| The beginning in hostility | The remembering of forgotten creation by God | The end in commitment |

It is *remembering* which changes the situation of the world from *hostility* to *commitment*.

Here as much as anywhere in Scripture, people are likely to ask the wrong questions. Curiosity raises questions about water and anger and rainbows. But behind all such questions, this narrative is a statement about our common human pilgrimage and the way in which our common lot is decisively changed by the change wrought in God.

The On-going Experience of Chaos and Deliverance

The reality of chaos is not an ancient memory of peoples too primitive to think otherwise. It is as contemporary as human experience today. The community of faith is invited to partici- pate in the story and to be identified with the new humanity which will preside over the new creation. It is important to recall that it was the experience of Israel's exile that made the flood an existential reality. Exile is indeed the collapse of the known world. The Priestly tradition (which moves from 6: 11–13 to 9:1–17) is commonly dated to the exile. Our exposition, therefore, will be illuminated by two texts that belong to the same context of crisis.

1. Ezekiel is peculiarly linked to the flood tradition. In 14:12–20, the crisis of Israel is so deep that not even Noah could make a difference. But Ezekiel appeals to the same God attest- ed by the flood story. As in our narrative, the prophet is clear that there is no longer anything about Israel that is worth sav- ing. God acts not for Israel, but for his own sake, the sake of his reputation (cf. 20:9, 14, 22, 44; 36:22). The source of hope is singularly God and not Israel. Ezekiel's analysis of the situation is much like that of the flood narrative. He understands that Israel has a heart of stone (11:19; 36:26), a whorish heart (6:9), and therefore it cannot change. This is in agreement with Gen. 8:21. But of his own free power, God will grant a new heart (11:19; 36:26) which makes faithfulness possible. When the Genesis and Ezekiel texts are placed together, we are granted a remarkable insight. In Ezekiel, God acts *for himself.* In the Genesis text, God acts not for himself but *for his troubled crea- tion.* The good news is that because of his person, this God acts most fully for himself when he acts for the world he created and loves.

2. More directly, Second Isaiah (also in exile) is concerned with the problem of chaos (45:18–19). In Isa. 49:14, Israel com- plains of being forgotten in exile. The resolution of the crisis of exile and abandonment makes direct appeal to the flood narra- tive, urging that the commitment of God to Israel is more reli- able than creation itself (Isa. 54:9–17).

87

3. The New Testament makes only limited direct use of this tradition. In I Pet. 3:17–21, the flood is linked with baptism. In

II Pet. 3:6–7, it is affirmed that even in the waters we may rely on the word which stands over against and free of the waters.

Obviously, interpretation may move in different directions. In any case, it is clear that chaos is not the last word. The last word is retained by the One who stands outside of and presides over the flood (cf. Ps. 29:10–11). And his last word is, "I will remember my covenant" (Gen. 9:15). At the beginning of the narrative, one would not have suspected God would ever be so fully inclined toward his creation. But something has happened to God. As a consequence, life is radically changed for all his creatures. Noah embodies a newness in human history.

Genesis 9:18—10:32; 11:10–29

In the present unit, we will deal with the remainder of the "pre-history" of Gen. 1—11, with the exception of 11:1–9 which will be given separate discussion. These materials provide continuity from the resolution of the flood to the call of Abraham and the beginning of the saving history of Israel. They include one narrative (9:18–28), a "map" of the nations (10:1–32) and a genealogy (11:10–29). The narrative concerns the sons of Noah. The "map" symmetrically considers all three sons (10:1–32). The genealogy focuses on the line of Shem, the oldest son of Noah, which leads to the family of Abraham (11:10–29). Each of these segments will be considered individually.

After the resolution of the flood, a new beginning has been made. With Noah, a new man has been identified who will beget a new family. A significant turn in the relation between creator and creation has been expressed in 8:20–22. But we have not yet come to the decisive turn, which is the calling of Abraham. The material between 9:17 and 12:1 constitutes an in-between period in which the new creation is underway but Israel's pilgrimage has not yet begun.

The materials placed between the blessing of Noah (9:1–17) and the call of Abraham (12:1–3) function in a dual way. On the one hand, this material insists on *continuity* so that Israel is properly placed among the nations. This is affirmed by the genealogy from Shem, son of Noah, begetter of Israel (10:21–31; 11:10–29). On the other hand, these texts also show the need and context for the sharp *discontinuity* which is Israel. This is asserted in the barrenness of Sarah (11:30). Israel's calling by God lives always in the strange ambivalence of continuity and discontinuity with the nations. Israel derives from them and yet stands over against them for the sake of a new promise. The new beginning "after the flood" (cf. 11:10) suggests new power for blessing and the removal of some of the poison of the pre-flood perspectives. Longevity is still granted. And yet the blessed earth and humankind still go their recalcitrant way, as 8:21 had anticipated. The two narratives of 9:20–27 and 11:1–9 stand in some tension with the map (10:1–32) and the genealogy (11:10–29). The map and the genealogy attest to the power of life which God has granted in creation. The blessing is simply tabulated. But the narratives do not flinch from the realities of disobedience still among humankind. While the *blessing* may simply be summarized, the *disobedience* requires a more detailed presentation.

Noah and His Sons

In 9:18–29 the strange narrative of the three sons (9:20–27) is told in the midst of the Noah genealogy (vv. 18–19, 28–29). Both the steadfastness of God and the evil imagination are presumed in the text. Verses 20–21 provide a context for what follows. Almost in passing, verse 20 identifies Noah as the one who cares for the earth. While this may be a note on cultural history paralleling 4:17–22, it also suggests that Noah fulfills the mandate given the first man (1:28) and the vocation refused in the garden (2:15). He rules the earth so that it fulfills its productive function. Verse 21 cannot be interpreted as a negative comment on drinking, alcohol, or drunkenness. Indeed, the Old Testament is not preoccupied with such a "moral" issue. It is aware of the potential destructiveness of excess, but Lev. 10:9 is an exception to the general acceptance of wine. The drunkenness of Noah is only presented as a context for what follows.

1. The real concern here is the contrast of the brothers, Shem, Japheth, and Ham-Canaan. The identification of the brothers is not obvious. Undoubtedly, Shem represents the Semites and anticipates Israel. Thus, a concern for Israel appears early in the narrative in a cryptic fashion. Japheth is impossible to identify, though as an ally of Israel against Canaan, he is often thought to be Philistine. That he will "dwell in the tents of Shem" (v. 27) suggests sharing the land. This makes a Philistine identity possible. In any case, the narrative has no special interest in the third son.

89

INTERPRETATION

The narrative is clearly concerned with Canaan. As a result of the narrator's polemical interest in Canaan, a rival of Israel is imposed on a symmetrical family genealogy originally unrelated to Canaan. Ham is the third son of Noah in the genealogies (9:18; 10:6–20). And he is the key actor in this narrative. But the poetic curse of verses 25–27 ignores Ham and centers on Canaan. It is clear that the means of a *family narrative* is used to characterize *political realities* at some point in Israel's history.

2. Relations with the father set the stage for blessing and curse. There are two obedient sons who honor their father and one who blatantly dishonors his father.

a. The text sets in juxtaposition the *commandment* to honor parent (Exod. 20:12, Deut. 5:16) and the *prohibition* of Lev. 18:7–8. It is probable that the prohibition against "uncovering" in Leviticus 18 means to have sexual intercourse. Thus, the "uncovering of the father" may be to have intercourse with the mother. (Or, conversely, the affront of Canaan is considered by some to be homosexuality.) But even with such a concrete prohibition, the danger and temptation to dishonor may be taken more symbolically. It may mean to penetrate the ultimate personal mystery of the parents by probing their most vulnerable action or condition.

Perhaps this prohibition which protects the dignity and mystery of the parent is paralleled to that of Gen. 2:17, which prohibits the tree of knowledge. Like the prohibition of the tree, the prohibition of our narrative seeks to maintain the mystery of the other person. Like the "tree of knowledge," this prohibition and this narrative of violation may reflect both, at the same time, *a concrete sexual agenda* and also be concerned with the much broader implications of the *mystery of life.*

b. The text, then, is not overly concerned about the specific offense of Canaan. It is more concerned with the far-reaching political and theological implications of the act. The focus is on the blessing of Shem-Japheth (Israel?) and the corresponding curse of Canaan. This narrative is an opportunity to root in pre-history the power relations between Israel and Canaan and to justify it on theological grounds. Political relations are here determined by God's power to bless and to curse. This is an early form of the same approach which subsequently fixes the relation between Isaac-Ishmael, Jacob-Esau, and Ephraim-Manasseh.

Beyond providing political foundations, the larger intent of Lev. 18 and our text is to sharpen the theological contrast between Israel and Canaan. The prohibitions of sexual violation and indignity embody a rejection of Canaanite ways of life and self-securing. Israel understands that life is premised on grace and not on the manipulation of the powers of life and well-being. In such a polemical contrast, Canaan is not to be understood as an ethnic grouping but as a characterization of all those who practice alternatives to obeying the sovereignty and trusting the graciousness of Yahweh. The indictment of Canaan in our text is a rejection of a whole way of life which presumes the mystery of life can be taken into human hands and managed. Shem and Japheth are presented as honoring not only father but the mystery of life embodied in the father. Even though the text has a more specific historical referent, it is continuous with the violation of the creator-creature relation of the earlier narratives. Canaan is presented as the concrete expression of an essential disorder which leads to dehumanization even in the new post-flood creation.

c. Certainly our exposition cannot fail to note that the disorders between father and son are given sexual expression. The story anticipates the insights of Freud concerning the sexual rootage of social disorder. However, the text should not be pushed excessively in that direction. The proper counterpart in Freud is not to be found in any narrow focus on sexuality but on Freud's larger understanding of society, which he critiqued as essentially disordered and therefore oppressive.

This curious narrative appeals to old tribal and familial traditions which are used in new ways. It is likely that we do not understand what was intended by the shaping of this text. In any case, it is an example of how historical reminiscences may be reused for quite different purposes. In this case, the old memories are used for a very different political agenda. Thus, the past is made "usable" for the present.

The Family of Nations

10:1–32 is commonly seen as a verbal "map" of the world. It pays attention to territorial and political realities. Most probably, it reflects the political world of the Solomonic period.

1. The chapter is organized around Noah's three sons. Thus, the world is viewed according to a familial symmetry already introduced in 9:18. This basic structure is supplemented by other materials. The whole represents a summary of the known world, urging that the known world has a fundamental unity to it. The basic principle of organization is not racial, ethnic, lin-

91

guistic, or territorial, but *political.* It reflects networks of relations at a given time. These features may be observed:

a. The family of Japheth is least developed (vv. 2–5). We may presume that the tradition lacked information, or more likely, interest in this element.

b. In the family of Ham (vv. 6–20), Canaan receives a major block of attention (vv. 15–19), breaking the symmetry. As we have already seen in 9:18–28, the tradition has a peculiar interest in Canaan, indeed more so than with the remainder of the Ham connection. As in 9:18–28, Canaan here seems curiously placed in the family of Ham. But that is for the *political* reason that Palestine was regarded as being in the Egyptian sphere of influence. Thus, the map is primarily a political rather than an ethnological statement. It does not speak of racial groups. Rather, it comments on present *political* realities in terms of Israel's friends and enemies.

c. The Shem connection points directly and intentionally toward Abraham (vv. 21–31). Nonetheless, no special regard is given of Israel. This line is treated here simply as a part of the family of humankind. Special attention to the line of Shem is deferred until 11:10–29.

d. The only major departure from the stylized narrative is the treatment of Nimrod (vv. 8–9). In a structural way, the peculiar digression on Nimrod is parallel to that of Enoch in 5:22–24. The difference is that Enoch is assessed theologically whereas Nimrod is celebrated politically. This is what might be expected as the narrative moves closer to identifiable historical reality. Two factors are noted about Nimrod:

1) He is the first "mighty man," the first to possess the power and authority to assert leadership; hence, the first empire builder. (On the "mighty men" as kings, cf. Isa. 9:6). The treatment of Nimrod is commonly connected to the empire of Assyria, even though in verse 22 Asshur occurs again in the line of Shem.

2) Nimrod is a mighty hunter. This may reflect the fact that the rulers of Mesopotamia were especially celebrated for their prowess in hunting. Thus on both counts, this list seems to take special note of imperial power in Mesopotamia and perhaps more specifically in Assyria. It is possible that the name Nimrod derives from the verb, *mrd,* "to rebel." If anything can be made of that derivation, it suggests empire-building is regarded here as a rebellion against Yahweh's intent of unity. The links to

Mesopotamia may also anticipate the narrative of 11:1–9, which also has its setting here.

2. While the text is not likely to be much utilized in contemporary exposition, the following points are worth noting:

a. The "map" offers an unparalleled ecumenical vision of human reality. In a sweeping scope, the text insists that there is a network of interrelatedness among all peoples. They belong to each other. As ecumenists are fond of saying, we have to do not with a unity to be achieved, but with a unity already given among us.

b. The political organization of the material (and especially the Nimrod element) makes clear that the world is understood politically. A major break is made from mythological views of reality. In the closest Near Eastern parallels, it is claimed that human politics and kingship are given by God and wrought in heaven, that is, political institutions have ontological reality and are immune to criticism. In contrast, this text suggests that human relationships are a result of human power and human decision. As a consequence, they can be changed and are subject to criticism. Thus, human affairs have taken place in the arena of freedom and not in the changeless world of necessity.

c. It is important that Israel is absent in this map, especially in light of Canaan's extended coverage. Israel belongs to and is derived from the nations but comes late in the history of humankind. Israel makes no claim and has no claim of being a party of the ontological structure of reality. Israel, like Isaac, comes late as a child of God's surprise.

d. The ecumenical and political reality of this text affirms that all nations derive their historical existence from the life-giving power of God and are called to be responsive to him:

> And he made from one every nation of men to live on all the face of the earth, having determined allotted periods and the boundaries of their habitation, that they should seek God, in the hope that they might feel after him and find him. Yet he is not far from each one of us, for
> "In him we live and move and have our being" (Acts 17: 26–28).

No nation or people is given ground or reason for being other than this one God who has formed all creatures.

e. The multiplication of nations is here regarded as a fulfillment of creation (cf. v. 32). The nations are indeed blessed,

93

being fruitful and multiplying. In the map of chapter 10, the well-being promised and envisioned in chapter 1 becomes visible.

The Line of Election

11:10–29 resumes the listing of nations given in chapter 10.* This listing, which singularly points to Israel, has ten generations from Shem to Abraham. In that regard, it neatly parallels the generations from Adam to Noah in chapter 5, again suggesting a kind of symmetry and completion. Without being tendentious, this genealogy shows how the history of *all creation* is moving toward the history of *this one people and this one man* for the sake of the one promise. Of necessity, this genealogy has parallels with the Shem account of 10:21–31, though in chapter 10 the account presents the fullness of the family, whereas here the tracing is to the single line of Abraham. This is the canonical listing also reiterated in Luke 3:34–38 linking the generations from Jesus to the new creation of Noah and hence back to "Adam, the son of God."

This listing is noticeably single-minded. Its purpose seems to counter that of chapter 10, even with the parallels it presents. Whereas chapter 10 reports the *multiplication,* spread and vastness of humankind, leading to the Tower of Babel story, this listing *narrows, restricts, and confines* interest to this single family. Thus, a symmetry can be observed in which each listing makes a distinctive narrative statement:

Gen. 10 ⟶ Tower (11:1–9)   God and the nations

Gen. 11:10–29 ⟶ Abraham (12:1–3)   God and Israel

There is a tension between the universal sovereignty (and *providence*) of God, who cares for and presides over all nations (10:1–32) and the *election* of God, who focuses on this distinctive people (11:10–29). Proper interpretation requires maintaining this tension, refusing to relax in either direction.

In this listing of 11:10–29, we may observe three points which may lead to fruitful interpretation:

1. The object of the whole recital is Israel. This genealogy establishes the peculiar connection between *creation* and *Is-*

94

*For a separate discussion of 11:1-9, see below. This sequence of exposition is only for purposes of convenience and proposes no shift in sequence of texts.

rael, between the first call and the second call. The text insists that *(a)* creation can and must be understood historically and *(b)* Israel can and must be interpreted cosmically. The text (and therefore our exposition) must be dialectical, holding to the connection between *providence for all* and *election for Israel.* Genesis does not simply attach an account of creation before the history of Israel, nor does it cast creation as finally running to history. Rather, it confesses creation which looks to new creation. This genealogy is the hinge at the point of tension between judgment and hope. It has to do with *judgment over a creation* shrouded in curse and with *hope for a new creation* marked by obedience and blessing. With Israel as its goal, this genealogy affirms that creation cannot be understood in the Old Testament as an act that stands unto itself. It is always an expectation, awaiting the appearance of the full, faithful creation of God (I John 3:2). The call to and existence of Israel keeps creation from having notions of autonomy and from being understood either mythologically, naturalistically, or scientifically. The first call listens eagerly for the second call (Rom. 8:19).

2. Though the point of it all is Israel, the road to Israel is unexceptional. That is, there is nothing special, sacred, or religious about the appearance of Israel. Israel is a free act of God's grace. But apart from that always surprising grace, there is no preparation that leads us to expect it. Israel appears as a surprise among and from the nations. With reference to Amos 9:7 and Ezek. 16:3, Delitzsch comments, "If the factor of grace is deducted, Israel is . . . in its origin and composition a nation like any other" (*A New Commentary on Genesis I,* 1888, pp. 376). That Israel is the proximate goal of creation is rooted unambiguously in the will of God and not in Israel. Israel will not enter history without this genealogy. But Israel's entry through this genealogy is not a hereditary accident. It is an act of God's peculiar graciousness.

3. The unexpected result of this creation tradition comes in 11:30: Sarah is barren! This innocent little verse is too carefully placed and too cryptic to be regarded simply as a historical observation. It is, in fact, a quite intentional theological notice. The blessing, mandate, and promise was to "Be fruitful and multiply" (Gen. 1:28; 9:1). And now barrenness! The incongruity between what is intended and what happens is overwhelming. The tale could be nuanced differently if ended in

95

verse 32. But the narrative refuses to end with the nations. It insists on ending with Israel. Its object has been Israel. But quite clearly Israel is a major disappointment in terms of the purposes of creation.

The Ending Waits for a Beginning

Thus far, the creation has turned out quite against the dreams of the creator. According to an Israelite reading of reality, creation has not been responsive to God's purposes. In the beginning, we understood Gen. 1 not to be coercive. It was an inviting summons to creation which could be gladly embraced but could also be resisted. The data of response is mixed. There is some embracing. But there is also much resistance. Thus "creation-time" is not remembered as the good days in Israel. The resistance of creature to creator has been "evil *from his youth*" (Gen. 8:21). The verdict of this Israelite tradition upon creation parallels one made upon the disobedient history of Israel:

> For we have sinned against the LORD our God, we and our fathers, *from our youth* even to this day; and we have not obeyed the voice of the LORD our God (Jer. 3:25).

> For the sons of Israel and the sons of Judah have done nothing but evil in my sight *from their youth* (Jer. 32:30).

(Other, less negative readings of the history of Israel are also offered, as in Jer. 2:2–3. But that is not the reading of creation offered in the main thrust of Gen. 1—11. The most negative reading of *Israel's history* parallels the way *creation* is here assessed.)

At this point in the text, precisely at 11:30, there is a waiting. The waiting is not for a development, a "passage," or an extension of what has been. The waiting is for new life, "fresh from the word." When it is spoken, it must be a word as powerful, summoning, and uncoercive as the first word. It must be a word spoken by the same voice with the same intent, that all things may be new.

Waiting Israel believes that new word will fashion its own new object:

96

> It is a word that creates worlds (II Pet. 3:5).

> It is a word that calls into existence what does not exist (Rom. 4:17).

It is a word that can raise up a new people (Matt. 3:9).

At the end of chapter 11, it is a word yet to be spoken. The first call of God has created a context in which a second call now needs to be issued. The first call was spoken over the *void*. When it is given, the second word will be spoken over a creation gone *barren*.

Genesis 11:1–9

This last narrative of the "pre-history" is well-known. Its message seems evident. However, our exposition will suggest that it must be assessed much more delicately than has often been the case, for its intent is expressed with some subtlety. The narrative belongs to the oldest theological tradition of the Book of Genesis. It presents the crisis in which creation is now found at the end of this "history of the first call." This narrative poses important issues about the practice and function of language. It suggests that all human language has become a language of disobedience.

An Entry into the Narrative

By way of genealogy, the post-flood texts trace the continuity and interrelatedness of all peoples as children of Noah. God wills the multiplication and spread of peoples over the earth and claims them all as his own. They do so by his blessing and according to his mandate (Gen. 1:28). But as they spread and multiply, they are still to be one interrelated people, faithful to his purposes. The well-being of all peoples is assured *(a)* by God's resolve never again to destroy (8:21–22; 9:8–17) and *(b)* by God's unqualified covenant with "all flesh" (9:8–11). Because of the post-flood promises, we expect well-being for all creation. In such a context, this narrative of the tower is a surprise.

1. At the outset, we must set aside several history-of-religion questions which need not concern us:

a. At some point, the narrative was no doubt an etiology for the diversity of languages. At some other point, it served as a polemical etiology for the city of Babylon, even though the etymology claimed in verse 9 is false.

97

b. The theme of the tower may have referred originally to a Babylonian ziggurat, a temple-tower presented as an imperial embodiment of pride and self-sufficiency (cf. 28:12). But that specific connection to the Babylonian factor is here subdued.

c. The story appears to be a polemic against the growth of urban culture as an expression of pride. But as we shall see, the narrative requires a more dialectical treatment. The interpreter need not linger with these more historical points of reference, for these earlier functions have been superseded.

2. The narrative is as symmetrically structured as any since chapter 1 of Genesis. Its beginning with "whole earth" and "one language" (v. 1) is nicely balanced in verse 9 with "all the earth" and "the language of all the earth." These verses form an envelope for the narrative. In between verses 1 and 9, 3–4 provide a statement about human words and actions balanced in verses 6–7 with the actions of Yahweh. Each in turn is marked by "come let us," in verse 4 by humankind and in verse 7 by Yahweh in counterpoint. The structure of the narrative shows that the resolve of humankind is in conflict with the resolve of God. The action of Yahweh responds to and correlates deliberately with the actions of humanity though the two parts are presented as sin and judgment.

The Dialectic of Unity and Scattering

The common element of the human proposal (v. 4), of Yahweh's action (v. 8), and the conclusion (v. 9), is the use of the verb "scatter" *(puṣ)*. Humankind fears scattering and takes action to prevent it. Then, against their will, Yahweh scatters. Now there is no doubt that in some contexts "scatter" refers to exile and is a negative term (Ezek. 11:17; 20:34, 41; 28:25). But here another denotation must be considered. Especially in chapter 10, we have seen that "spreading abroad" (v. 32) is blessed, sanctioned, and willed by Yahweh. It is part of God's plan for creation and the fulfillment of the mandate of 1:28. It is not necessary that 11:1–9 should be treated together with chapter 10, except for the remarkable statement in 10:18 in which our term *puṣ* is used: "Afterwards the families of the Canaanites spread abroad [*puṣ*]." The idea of "scatter/spread abroad" (*puṣ*), at least in this context, is not negative nor concerned with punishment. It can be argued that in this context (10:18) the intent of creation finally comes to fulfillment (1:28).

98

1. Seen from this perspective, the fear of scattering expressed in 11:4 is resistance to God's purpose for creation. The peoples do not wish to spread abroad but want to stay in their own safe mode of homogeneity. Thus the tower and city are attempts at self-serving unity which resists God's scattering activity. Note the curious expository possibility and complication in such a conclusion. Characteristically, unity is regarded as God's purpose and scattering is viewed as God's punishment. And indeed, by appeal to Eph. 1:9–10, we have argued and presumed that the unity of creation is the purpose of the creator.

This subtle point suggests that there are two kinds of unity. On the one hand, God wills a unity which permits and encourages scattering. The *unity willed by God* is that all of humankind shall be in covenant with him (9:8–11) and with him only, responding to his purposes, relying on his life-giving power. The *scattering God wills* is that life should be peopled everywhere by his regents, who are attentive to all parts of creation, working in his image to enhance the whole creation, to bring "each in its kind" to full fruition and productivity. This unity-scattered dialectic does not presume that different families, tongues, lands, and nations are bad or disobedient. They are a part of his will. And the reason God allows for that kind of differential is that all parts of humanity look to and respond to God in unity.

It is conventional to read this text as a simple either/or proposition: the disobedient unity of the peoples based in *pride* or the scattering done by God as *punishment.* But our exposition requires not a two-sided tension but a *three-factored* possibility: *(a)* the unity desired by the peoples in resistance against God, *(b)* the scattering feared by the peoples and carried out by God as punishment, but also *(c)* a *unity* willed by God based only on loyalty to him. Here that unity is expressed as a *dispersion* all over the earth. The purpose of God is neither *self-securing homogeneity* as though God is not Lord, nor a *scattering of autonomous parts* as though the elements of humanity did not belong to each other.

Thus the scattering feared in this narrative and scattering wrought by God may be two-edged. It is surely presented in the narrative as a judgment upon the peoples. But it is also a way in which God accomplishes his purpose for creation, as anticipated in 1:28 and hinted at in 10:18. Our interpretation must

99

not be simplistic about the purposes of God. The issue of God's will for unity and for scattering is much more delicately stated.

This subtle balancing of motifs has been illuminated by the daring proposal of Juan Luis Segundo (*Our Idea of God,* 1974, p. 65). He suggests God's will for humanity can be understood on the basis of the dogmatic formulation of the Trinity in which the Godhead is "neither confused nor divided." So God's will is that humanity should not be *confused,* that is, with parts inappropriately combined, nor *divided,* with parts treated as autonomous. But the human community as both scattered and gathered is like the character of God who is confessed as three in one and one in three. Thus what may be discerned in our text as the judgment of God may also be another way of forming a community genuinely loyal to the creator and dependent upon God's gifts and purposes. In such a community there may be different languages attending to distinctive needs, yet the community is not divided in its primary loyalty.

2. This text suggests a different kind of unity sought by fearful humanity organized against the purposes of God. This unity attempts to establish a cultural, human oneness without reference to the threats, promises, or mandates of God. This is a self-made unity in which humanity has a "fortress mentality." It seeks to survive by its own resources. It seeks to construct a world free of the danger of the holy and immune from the terrors of God in history. It is a unity grounded in fear and characterized by coercion. A human unity without the vision of God's will is likely to be ordered in oppressive conformity. And it will finally be "in vain" (Ps. 49:10–20; 127:1–2).

It may not need to be presumed that the Babel proposition is an anti-religious proposal, for religion can provide exactly that kind of unity and certify social oppression. In such a world, the tower can participate in religiosity as a symbol of unity. Thus the text need not be taken simply as a critique of imperialism, of Promethean tendencies, nor as an attack upon technology as it is often taken to be. It may as well be a protest against religious efforts to establish conformities or to construct a "sacred canopy" which consolidates human freedom. The narrative then is a protest against every effort at oneness derived from human self-sufficiency and autonomy.

3. The issue is not simply scattering, for we have seen that scattering may be either an act of punishment or the plan of salvation. Nor is the issue oneness, which may be the purpose of God or an act of human resistance. Either unity or scat-

100

teredness has the possibility of being either obedient or disobedient. The issue is whether the world shall be organized for God's purposes of joy, delight, freedom, doxology, and caring. Such a world must partake of *the unity God wills* and *the scattering God envisions.* Any one-dimensional understanding of scattering denies God's vision for unity responsive to him. Any one-dimensional view of unity denies God's intent for the whole world as peopled by his many different peoples.

Modeling a Faithful Community, Unified and Scattered

On the basis of that judgment, these comments follow:

1. The narrative is often taken as a polemic against urban culture (cf. 4:17ff.). Our interpretation suggests this is not necessarily so. One may ask whether a massive urban culture can reflect the purposes of God or whether it is inevitably autonomous and therefore inhumane. And in that context, one may ask about *pax americana,* which has difficulty practicing any criticism of itself. A dialectic interpretation of Babel suggests that the city or the empire in and of itself is not condemned. But if Babylon is a symbol of a self-securing, imperial consciousness, then our text has close connections to Isa. 47. On the other hand, Isa. 1:21–26 envisions a transformation of urban reality. Thus, our text may be a critique of urban reality. The critique is not one in principle but only of urban realities which persist in a certain orientation.

2. The modeling of an alternative city of trustful obedience may be the task of the faithful community. We may cite two models of an alternative city in the Isaiah tradition. In 2:2–4 (cf. Mic. 4:1–4) there is a vision of a unified city which is characterized by a glad pilgrimage, an embrace of torah, and a program of disarmament. Clearly, autonomy is rejected. The embrace of torah is viewed in the Bible as the only secure ground of humanness. In Isa. 19:18–25, there is an amazing ecumenical vision of the political world of the Near East. There is no hint of giving up different national identities. But there is an overriding common allegiance to Yahweh, the practice of worship of Yahweh, establishment of free interaction among the participants, and most strikingly, a hint (v. 18) of a common language. This is surely the healing of the nations (v. 22) which in Gen. 11:1–9 have been fractured (cf. Rev. 22:2).

3. While the text appears primarily to address social and political questions, the same issues may be used to address personal and interpersonal questions. The matter of unity/

101

scattering has as much to do with personal fragmentation/integration as with public issues. A human person may be a scattered person whose "members are at war with each other" (Rom. 7:23; cf. Mark 5:9; James 4:1; I Pet. 2:11). Or there may be a unified personhood which is a false unity founded on competence, discipline, or self-sufficiency (Luke 12:15–19). Against either (falsely scattered persons or falsely unified persons), this text envisions persons who practice openness based on trust and integrity based on knowing the true language of the faithful Speaker. This text is not concerned with just any unified personality anymore than it is concerned with just any unified society. It hopes for a unity based on the gospel of God's sovereign call.

The Gift and Task of Language

The text encourages reflection upon language as a peculiarly important human activity. It raises important questions about how we speak and how we listen and answer. It asks about the quality of human communication and the function of language. The faithful community exists (among other things) to maintain a faithful universe of discourse against the languages around us which may coerce, deceive, manipulate, or mystify.

1. Language is decisive for the shape and quality of human community. More than anything else, language determines the way in which human persons care for each other. Language shapes the ways in which human communities conduct their business and arrange power. Language is the way we bestow upon each other the gifts of life and death (James 3:10).

a. In a positivistic society, language is conventionally understood simply as descriptive of what is. When language only describes what is, it inevitably becomes conservative. It tends to become ideological, giving permanence to the way things presently are. But language in serious community need not be only descriptive of what is. It can be evocative and creative, calling into being things that do not exist. Such language is the way of promise and of hope. And because such speech calls into existence things that do not exist, it is dangerous and subversive speech. It stands characteristically over against things as they are. This text invites reflection on the possibility of language and on the dangers of language misused.

b. Language not only reports but shapes power relations. Language can be coercive. Or it can liberate those who speak and those who listen. It is apparent that Jesus' speech was liberating. But those who did not want the world changed and power redistributed rightly viewed his speech as a subversion (cf. Mark 2:9; 15:29f.).

2. In that context, we may note what God did to interrupt the tower-building in our narrative. While verse 7 is conventionally translated "that they may understand," the word in the text is *shema'*. It permits the rendering, "that they do not listen to each other." If the word is rendered "understand," it may reflect only a verbal, semantic problem. But if translated as "listen," the text may pose a covenantal, theological issue. We may usefully reflect on what makes it possible for persons to listen to each other and what makes listening difficult or impossible. The capacity to listen in ways which transform depends upon trust in the speaker, readiness to be impacted, and willingness to have newness come into one's life. Such speaking and listening is the intended mode of speech in the Bible from the first chapter of Genesis. But the Bible offers many evidences of listening failures not grounded in trust or readiness for newness. While many texts may be cited, we may consider Gen. 42:21 in which the brothers admit "not listening" to Joseph. They did not listen because they feared, resented, and hated. Failed speech is linked to the disappearance of trust. Not listening is related to death in a relationship. To fail to listen means to declare the other party null and void. A society which suffers failed speech, as in our text, not only cannot build towers, it cannot believe promises, cannot trust God, cannot be human. The consignment of humanity to "not listening" subsequently becomes an indictment against Israel (cf. Jer. 5:21; 7:13; 11:10; 13:10, 11; 22:5; 29:19).

The Possibility of a New Language Community

So what may be hoped for from this passage? It is conventional to link the grim conclusion of this text to Acts 2, wherein there is new hope. That text concerns the new surge of the spirit which makes communication possible.

1. The usual connection of Gen. 11:1–9 and Acts 2 is "speaking in tongues." But the accent of Acts 2 would seem to lie not on *speaking*, but on *hearing:*

> . . . each one *heard* them speaking in his own language (v. 6).
>
> how is it that we *hear*, each one of us in his own native language (v. 8)?
>
> . . . we *hear* them telling in our own tongues the mighty works of God (v. 11).
>
> . . . give *ear* to my words (v. 14).
>
> Now when they *heard* this, they were cut to the heart (v. 37).

103

Perhaps the miracle of Pentecost concerns a new gift of speech. But we should not miss the hint of the text. The newness concerns *a fresh capacity to listen* because the word of God blows over the chaos one more time. Perhaps the promise of Acts 2 (to which our text is the counterpart) is that when God blows his wind over the "emptiness and void," what is freshly given is a new speech situation. In Pentecost, when the ideal speech situation emerges, we are granted both ears to hear and tongues to speak. The new language-situation of the faithful community is when, "Although their language may differ in sound, they all speak the same thing, while they cry, 'Abba, Father' " (Calvin).

2. The Pentecost text is, of course, placed at the beginning of Acts. The history of the church begins in a new language community where human speech is possible. On the one hand, the new community in Acts 2 regarded its differences of language as no threat or danger, in contrast to the fear of Gen. 11:4. On the other hand, it sought no phony, autonomous unity. It was content with the unity willed by God without overcoming all the marks of scatteredness. And so a new eon begins.

Our Genesis text ends with a scattering. There is not listening. But there is a populating of the earth, as God willed from the beginning (1:28). And then there is a waiting—a waiting for a new word, a new call which will evoke a new community. The whole creation waits to see if Abraham will listen and trust, if Sarah (cf. 11:30) will laugh, if Isaac will be born. Then there will be another "spreading abroad" in that family, a spreading of blessing and not of fear or anger (cf. Gen. 28:14). After 11:1–9, humanity lives in a deep crisis of language. There is no hint here of resolution. But along the way we may observe that in 50:21 Joseph is able to practice "new speech" with his brothers. They come in fear, but he speaks "to their heart." And their lives are transformed. In the scope of Genesis, the tower narrative looks back to Gen. 1 when there was faithful speech and obedient hearing. It looks forward to the new speech of Joseph that can create a community. But the community of trust given in chapter 50 is only provisional. The breaking of language at Babel is deep. There will not be restoration of genuine speech and listening until the spirit is given (Acts 2) like the first wind that blew to give life (Gen. 1:2).

PART TWO

The Abraham Narrative: The Embraced Call of God

GENESIS 11:30 — 25:18

> By faith Abraham obeyed when he was called to go out to a place which he was to receive as an inheritance; . . . (Heb. 11:8).
>
> By faith Sarah herself received power to conceive, even when she was past the age, since she considered him faithful who had promised. . . . (Heb. 11:11)
>
> By faith Abraham, when he was tested, offered up Isaac, and he who had received the promises was ready to offer up his only son, . . . He considered that God was able to raise men even from the dead; . . . (Heb. 11:17, 19).

The one who calls the worlds into being now makes a second call. This call is specific. Its object is identifiable in history. The call is addressed to aged Abraham and to barren Sarah. The purpose of the call is to fashion an alternative community in creation gone awry, to embody in human history the power of the blessing. It is the hope of God that in this new family all human history can be brought to the unity and harmony intended by the one who calls.

In its canonical form, Genesis is clear about two things. First, the God who forms the world is the same God who creates Israel. It is the same God who calls creation and who calls the community of faith. This same God works his powerful, creative purpose and intervenes in surprising, redemptive ways. The call to Sarah and Abraham has to do not simply with the forming of Israel but with the re-forming of creation, the transforming of the nations. The stories of this family are

105

not ends in themselves but point to God's larger purposes. Thus Gen. 11:35—25:18 must be read in the context of Gen. 1:1—11:29.

Second, it is clear that Abraham and Sarah, in contrast to the resistant, mistrustful world presented in Gen. 1—11 (with the important exceptions of creation in chapter 1 and Noah) are responsive and receptive. They fully embrace the call of God. It is speculative to ask if this is the only family God has called in this way (cf. Amos 9:7). But it is unambiguous that this family has responded in a peculiar and faithful way. In this narrative, there is a striking correspondence between God's call and the response of Abraham and Sarah. It is that correlation that offers to us the theme of *promise and faith* around which the narrative revolves. In their present form, regardless of their earlier history, each of the texts must be considered in relation to the issues of promise and faith. *Promise* is God's mode of presence in these narratives. The promise is God's power and will to create a new future sharply discontinuous with the past and the present. The promise is God's resolve to form a new community wrought only by miracle and reliant only on God's faithfulness. *Faith* as response is the capacity to embrace that announced future with such passion that the present can be relinquished for the sake of that future.

Critical Issues

The critical issues in the Abraham-Sarah narrative must be acknowledged even though they cannot all be solved.

1. It is clear that the literature of Gen. 11:30–25:18 is the result of a complex development of tradition. The completed narrative is made up of various elements gathered around several distinct themes. Scholars have grouped and analyzed the materials in a variety of ways. They include the following elements:
   a. Materials related to the *family of Abraham:*
      1) *Sarah* materials:
         (a) Sarah as the endangered wife (12:10–20; 20)
         (b) Sarah and her two sons (16; 18:1–15; 21)
         (c) Sarah's death (23)
      2) *Lot* materials:
         (a) Lot and the land (13)
         (b) Sodom and Gomorrah (19:1–29)
         (c) Lot and his daughters (19:30–38)

    3) *Isaac* materials:
      a) The sacrifice (22) (See below, d. 4, on this narrative as a theological statement.)
      b) A wife for Isaac (24)
    4) The *Genealogy* of Abraham (25:1–18)
  b. Materials related to God's *covenant* with Abraham:
    1) The older tradition (15:7–21)
    2) The later tradition (17)
  c. A narrative of public events (14)
  d. Theological affirmations:
    1) The initial promise (12:1–9)
    2) The faith of Abraham (15:1–6)
    3) The new righteousness (18:16–32)
    4) The testing of Abraham (22).

The materials are not easily contained in any scheme, and this arrangement should not be considered authoritative. What we have is a collection of narratives. It is in the nature of narrative to be distinctive and peculiar. For that reason, no pattern should be suggested which diminishes the particular character of the materials.

2. The common judgment among scholars is that these texts include very old materials, even though the historical rootage of old materials cannot be recovered. (This judgment has recently been challenged, especially by John van Seters, *Abraham in History and Tradition,* 1975. However, the earlier consensus remains predominant.) Coupled with these older materials, which do not have great theological intentionality, there are more reflective materials which do make intentional theological affirmations.

As we have them, the texts are a combination of the two kinds of materials. Exposition must attempt to let these two perspectives interact with each other. This means that the early *traditional materials* must be dealt with as they are, with their own power. But at the same time, they must be seen through the lens of the later *theological affirmations* which transform them. As a result, the older materials become vehicles for affirmations they did not originally claim.

Finally, we must try to hear the texts in their present completed form as they have been brought together in the unity of the canon. When all of the materials are thus brought together, they become a statement about the overriding promise of God and the way of that promise in the faith and life of this family.

Our exposition will focus on each individual text. But our interpretation must take into account the place and role of the text in the larger statement of promise and faith.

3. The historical questions are as complicated and difficult as the literary questions though they do not need to detain us for very long. Until recently, there was a consensus established (on the basis of archaeology) that the Abraham stories could be located in the Middle Bronze Period, having been correlated with non-biblical evidence. This evidence related especially to the occurrence of parallel names and the utilization of social practices attested elsewhere. More recently, that consensus has been sharply challenged, especially by Van Seters (*Abraham in History and Tradition,* 1975) and Thompson (*The Historicity of the Patriarchal Narratives,* 1974). As a result, it is now unclear whether these materials can be located in any identifiable historical setting. A still more radical judgment questions that the stories have any historical point of reference at all. This latter view returns to the scholarly skepticism of an older generation, working before recent archaeological gains. For the purpose of our exposition, it is not necessary to enter into these disputed questions, for we have attempted to stay with the text in its canonical form. While the historical issues are important, our present concern is to hear the theological claim of the text as it has come to us.

4. Following Westermann, we may identify four theological statements which can usefully provide the focus of exposition ("Types of Narratives in Genesis," *The Promises to the Fathers,* 1964, pp. 71–73).

a. *12:1–9.* The basic theme of radical newness is announced. This unit presents the primary summons of God, the ready answer of Abraham, and the derivative blessing to the nations. As Wolff ("The Kerygma of the Yahwist," *Interpretation* [1966]) has observed, that blessing may be seen as an organizing principle relating Abraham to a variety of peoples, including Pharaoh (12:10–21), Melchizedek (14:17–24), Ishmael (21:9–21) and Moab and Ammon (19:30–38).

b. *15:1–6.* This text provides a singular statement on the meaning of faith (cf. v. 6). It is this theme that provides a clue to the coherence of the Abraham tradition. The faith of Abraham has become a programmatic element for Paul's exegesis of Abraham in Romans and Galatians and for the subsequent Reformation tradition of justification by grace through faith.

c. *18:16–33.* This narrative has not received the attention it merits. The faithfulness of Abraham here is manifested in his bold posture as God's "theological teacher." He urges God to a new notion of righteousness. As our exposition will seek to show, this text represents one of the most daring theological explorations in the entire narrative.

d. *22:1–9.* Concerning the God of Israel, this text boldly affirms the dialectic but crucial unity of God. God is the one who tests (and takes from his people) and the one who provides (and gives what is needed for a future). The placement of this text in the lectionary with the transfiguration narrative of Mark 9:1–9 and with Rom. 8:31–39 is suggestive. In the Genesis narrative there is also a transfiguration, the appearance of a "new form of God," quite as radical as the "metamorphosis" of the Marcan narrative. It is the unity of *testing/providing* which makes the proximity with Rom. 8:31–39 appropriate. It is God's staggering surprise in 22:13 which makes it certain that there is no ultimate separation from him.

Theological Affirmations and Possibilities

The long traditioning process behind these materials was not especially concerned about making a coherent theological statement. These materials were a treasured memory which served to construct and maintain the ethos of this people. However, it is reasonable to conclude that over a long period, by means of a shrewd and knowing reshaping, the materials did become a coherent theological statement. They became an earthen vessel for a treasure of faith. It is to that treasure of faith that our exposition addresses itself.

1. In its present form, the governing promise concerns the *land.* The issues are whether God can keep that promise and whether Abraham can live from that promise. But within the frame of the land promise, the promise of *an heir* takes on increasing importance. There can be no fulfillment of the land promise unless there is an heir. The promise of the heir is always in the service of the land promise. In the narrative itself, the promise of an heir receives major attention and gives the narrative its primary dynamic.

These diverse narrations have been shaped into a staggering and suspenseful theological statement. The basic plot moves from profound tension to unexpected resolution. That movement occurs principally between the promise of 12:1–3 and the reiteration of that promise in 22:15–18. The initial struggle is for

109

an heir to receive the land. The heir is finally granted in 21:1–7. Immediately in 22:1–13, the heir is placed in jeopardy. When the heir is risked, the promise is confirmed and afterwards, the suspense is largely gone from the narrative. Chapters 23:1—25:18 are primarily materials of transition which lie outside the main artful presentation. Altogether, the narrative affirms that God will keep his promise and that Abraham and Sarah will trust the promise.

2. The main emphases of the theological affirmation in the transition materials are articulated in the text from Hebrews 11 (cited at the beginning of this section.) That indicates three dimensions of theological concern.

a. *Heb. 11:8–10. The promise of a land* is made to a landless people. It does not matter if Abraham is thought to be a nomad, a merchant prince, or a caravaner. All of these are recent scholarly suggestions. In any case, he has no place of his own. The "outlandishness"of the promise should not be missed.

b. *Heb. 11:11–12. The promise of an heir* is made to a barren, hopeless couple. The first promise of land depends on the fulfillment of the second, on the reality of a second generation. The narrative presses that issue until the birth in chapter 21. The central text is 18:1–15, in which the promise of a son is shown to be scandalous and impossible. The question of the narrative is the question of all faithful people: "Is anything too hard for the Lord?" (18:14). It is an enduring question for all of biblical faith (cf. Mark 10:23–31).

c. *Heb. 11:17–19.* Abraham is tested by the *command to offer Isaac.* In the total narrative this might seem a subordinate point. And yet the movement of the promise from chapter 12:1–3 to chapter 22:15–18 shows (supported by Heb. 11) that this event is as crucial for the total tradition as are the promises of land and son. It is this event that places everything in jeopardy. The faithfulness of God is called into question. And the responding faithfulness of Abraham is deeply tested. A popular question out of that narrative may be whether God *tests* in such a way. But an even more difficult question is whether God *provides.* The narrative leads the writer of Hebrews, addressing a community in persecution, to a proclamation of the resurrection. The resurrection is seen as the way in which God incredibly keeps promises against all the data.

The three issues together, *(a)* believing a land will be

110

given, *(b)* believing an heir will be born, *(c)* believing God can provide beyond testing, all press the listening community to the issue of faith.

The tradition affirms Abraham as a "knight of faith" who does trust. But the evidence of the individual texts is more mixed than that. To be sure, the moments of faith are profound. He immediately departs to answer the call (12:4). He leaves early with his son (22:3). And between the two obedient departures, he trusts the promise (15:6). The trust of Abraham is the main claim of the narrative. It is stated at the beginning (12:3), in the middle (15:6), and at the end (22:1–13).

But Abraham's believing does not occur in a vacuum. He must live in history. And so he is not always sure. Thus there is his deception to save his skin (12:10–20; 20:1–18). There is his alternative wife, just in case (16:1–16). There is his clinging to Ishmael when God has Isaac in mind (17:18). These texts guard against any inclination to interpret Abraham's faith as having been easy or without anguish.

3. The faith to which Abraham is called and for which he is celebrated means the acknowledgment of a particular God. He trusts in a God who can violate religious conventions (cf. 18:16–32), shatter normal definitions of reality (18:14), and bring about newness (21:1–7). Isaac—long anticipated, finally given, and then demanded back—is the embodiment of the newness God can bring about in this family of barrenness. There are in the Bible three primary ways of speaking of such radical, unextrapolated newness: *(a)* creation out of nothing, *(b)* resurrection of the dead, and *(c)* justification by grace through faith (cf. Rom. 4:17). In the Abrahamic narrative, it is the birth of Isaac which points to all three. We have before us a God for whom there is no analogy or parallel. The narrative raises questions about and protests against a world that is fixed on what is safe, predictable, and controllable. This text affirms that there is a discontinuity between what is and what is promised by God. The newness which God has promised will not be wrought from the things that are but will be given freshly by God in his powerful faithfulness. This faith, as Abraham understands so well in chapter 22, places in question everything that is. God has issued a call and made a promise against the barrenness and landlessness of this family. And he forms a minority community, "the Abrahamic minority," based on nothing more reliable than

111

the laugh of Sarah (21:6) which anticipates the "Easter laugh" of the community around Jesus.

4. It does not surprise us that the New Testament has found the Abraham narratives especially freighted. They express the "gospel beforehand" (Gal. 3:8). The main themes of the gospel are either stated or anticipated here. This is evident in the reflections of Heb. 11. It is equally clear in the Pauline treatment of faith in Rom. 4; Gal. 3—4. Of course, the contrast of Isaac and Ishmael and the allegorical pairing of Sarah/Hagar, Zion/Sinai in Gal. 4 is beyond the Genesis narrative itself. But Paul has surely understood the narrative faithfully on the main point of the children of promise born to freedom (Gal. 4:31—5:1).

Special mention may be made of the cryptic and threatening statement of John the Baptist in Matt. 3:9:

> "Do not presume to say to yourselves, 'We have Abraham as our father'; for I tell you, God is able from these stones to raise up children to Abraham."

The news of the gospel and the reality of new life depend only upon the will of God. The statement of John and the entire Abrahamic narrative speak a judgment against those who cling to their anti-promise ways of identity.

5. The Abrahamic narrative offers rich opportunity for exposition. The narrative sets itself against every world-view and ideology which regards the world as settled and fixed. It is ironic and troubling that the modern world which so celebrates freedom also tends to believe that present life is closed and self-contained. It is an assumption of the modern world (in which our exposition must be done) that there will be no genuine newness, no really independent gift yet to be given. Such ideologies press persons either *(a)* to *inordinate pride* which imagines the world has been completely entrusted to us and that we may construct our own future out of the present, or *(b)* to *deep despair* which believes the present world of inequity and oppression is forever and that there is no power in heaven or on earth that can make real change. Both the ideology of pride and the ideology of despair presume that the world is essentially a human artifact, that all possibilities are comprehended in human capacities for good or for ill.

Against such judgments, the Abraham narrative proposes an alternative reality which rescues from both pride and de-

112

spair. The narrative affirms that the world has not been entrusted to humanity. In inscrutable graciousness, God has retained the amazing gift of life.

The "gospel beforehand" (cf. Gal. 3:8) is good news to those who despair. It announces that what the world has thought impossible is possible by the power of God (cf. Gen. 18:14; Mark 10:27). It is possible by the promise of God to be delivered from the barren world of oppression, injustice, and hopelessness. If the despairing ones listen to these texts, they will be able to join in the "Easter laugh" of Sarah (Gen. 21:6).

The "gospel beforehand" is shattering to those who come to the world in strident pride. This narrative is the assertion that our best laid plans are called into question. It affirms that not all our deceptions (cf. 12:10-20; 20:1-18) or alternative arrangements (16; 17:18) can resist God's odd ordering of things. This narrative calls life into question in ways that are good news and bad news. Some are given new hope by the narrative. Others are shattered by the same narrative, but it is hoped, on the way to newness.

6. Such an understanding of the Abraham and Sarah narratives permits us to discern afresh what Jesus, son of Abraham, is about. For Jesus of Nazareth, "Kingdom of God" (cf. Mark 1:14-15) is the cipher for the newness that is given by the promise of God. It is the Kingdom that gives new life to the barren ones (Luke 7:22). That is a scandal whenever it is given (v. 23). It is the Kingdom which comes as a disruptive newness to give life back to the dead. Predictably, it evokes resistance (cf. Mark 3:5-6). It is the disruption of the kingdom of this age by healing (Mark 5:17).

The threat and the possibility articulated in the narrative of Abraham and Sarah put a crisis before humanity. It is the crisis of deciding to live either *for the promise,* and so disengaging from the present barren way of things, or to live *against the promise,* holding on grimly to the present ordering of life. Luke's summary about Jesus is a conclusion we might expect in response to the news of our narrative: *(a)* Some *resist the promise,* "The chief priests and the scribes and the principal men of the people sought to destroy him" (Luke 19:47). *(b)* Some *welcome the promise,* ". . . all the people hung upon his words" (Luke 19:48). 113 Faith in God's promise is a possibility which the world sees as scandalous. The world will do what it can to eliminate the promise and to crush the "impossible possibility" with ideologies of conformity, oppression, "the good life," self-realization. The promise jeopardizes everything the world holds dear. But for all of that, Sarah and the community of Abraham have the last laugh (Gen. 21:6; Luke 6:21; John 16:20; Heb. 11:12). It is that laugh which is the ground for this ludicrous story-telling which is both our deepest threat and our best hope.

A Schema for Exposition

The chart suggests the points of emphasis in the exposition which follows. The two major points of interpretation are the initial promise of 12:1–9 and the testing of 22:1–13. These two narratives reiterate the main promises and provide the parameters of the story. Between these are stressed the faith statement of chapter 15 and the theological reflection of 18:16–33, which also presents a stylized wording of the promise (18:18). The narratives of 16; 17; 18:1–15 (though of quite diverse materials) are treated together as anticipations of the child. The chart indicates that the third of these, 18:1–15, is the most crucial for the movement of the narrative. The episodes of 12:10–20 and chapter 13 are treated as parallels, modeling Abraham as a man of unfaith and of faith. Rather unexpectedly, the narrative of the actual birth (21:1–8) is understated. Our treatment here honors that understatement. The concluding chapters of 23:1—25:18 stand outside the main plot, and chapter 14 seems unrelated to the rest.

By the end of the narrative, the promise (12:1–9) has not only been kept alive and intact. It is matured theologically by the exploration of faith (15:1–6), by the affirmation of new righteousness (18:16–33), and by the disclosure of the God who tests and provides (22:1–14). In a rather independent way, chapter 24 offers a reprise on the theme that God practices *loyalty* (vv. 12, 14, 27), causes *prosperity* (vv. 21, 40, 42, 46) and leads his people (vv. 27, 48). God does all this for the barren, landless ones. God can be trusted by them!

Genesis 11:30—12:9

This text is pivotal in Genesis. It links the traditions of God's *providential care* for the world and God's *electing call* of Israel. It also presents a primary model for the promise-making word

GENESIS 11:30—25:18: THE ABRAHAM NARRATIVE

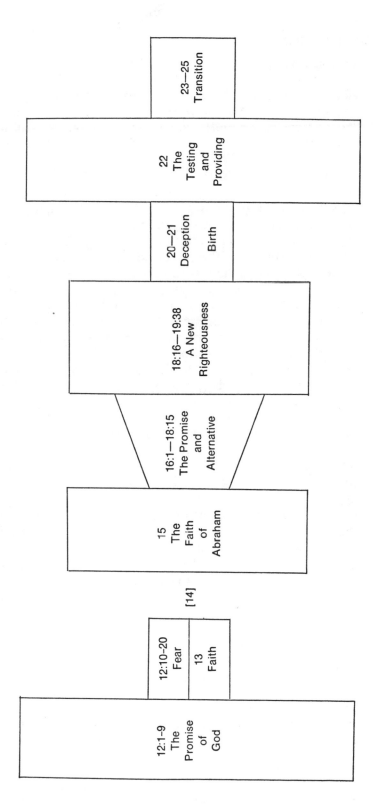

of God which begins the history of Israel and the responding faith of Israel in the person of Moses. Our exposition will consider *(a)* the situation of Israel addressed by the call of God, *(b)* the intrusive word of God which makes a Genesis for this family, and *(c)* the beginnings in Abraham's risky life of faith.

The Interface of Barrenness and Speech

There is no doubt that in the construction of Genesis, a major break in the narrative is intended between 11:32 and 12:1. Indeed, it is perhaps the most important structural break in the Old Testament and certainly in Genesis. It distinguishes between the history of humankind and the history of Israel, or between the history of the curse and the history of the blessing. Some explanation is then required for our treating these verses, 11:30—12:9, as a unity across this break. The reason for this arrangement is that God does not begin the history of Israel *ex nihilo.* The history of promise does not emerge in a vacuum. Rather, the new history emerging from God's call in 12:1–3 is wrought by the power of God from the stuff of 11:30–32. The connection of 11:30–32 and 12:1–9 is proposed here for the purpose of understanding the new beginning worked by the power of God's word.

1. Here we stand before the most incredible announcement in the tradition of Israel. The family of Abraham has derived naturally from historic antecedents, as indicated in the genealogies of Gen. 10—11. But that natural derivation now results in nothing. It ends in barrenness (11:30). The reference is cryptic and seems to be only descriptive. There is no reflection on the cause. There is no suggestion of punishment or curse. It is simply reported that this family (and with it the whole family of Gen. 1—11) has played out its future and has nowhere else to go. Barrenness is the way of human history. It is an effective metaphor for hopelessness. There is no foreseeable future. There is no human power to invent a future.

But barrenness is not only the condition of hopeless humanity. The marvel of biblical faith is that barrenness is the arena of God's life-giving action. Barrenness is no stranger to this new family of promise. After Sarah, Rebekah (25:21), Rachel (29:31), and Hannah (I Sam. 1:2) were barren. So also was Israel in exile (Isa. 54:1f.). A proper hearing of the Abraham-Sarah texts depends upon the vitality of the metaphor of barrenness. It announces that this family begins its life in a situation of irreparable hopelessness.

2. Then comes 12:1. If it had been our task to begin a new history, we would have done so in a more hopeful context. But not this God. Inexplicably, this God speaks his powerful word directly into a situation of barrenness. That is the ground of the good news. This God does not depend on any potentiality in the one addressed. Abraham and Sarah were quite without potential. The speech of God presumes nothing from the one addressed but carries in itself all that is necessary to begin a new people in history. The power of this summoning word is without analogy. It is a word about the future spoken to this family without any hope of a future. The juxtaposition of the *barrenness of Israel* and the *speech of God* is definitional for Israel. "Barrenness" marks the deep futility of Israel. "Speech of God" asserts the freedom and power of God to work his will among the hopeless. The remainder of the text is simply the announcement that the speech of God overcomes and overpowers the barrenness of human reality.

3. The speech of God has its way over the barrenness: *The Lord said* (12:1). The speech of this God is at the same time imperative and promise, summons and assurance. The barren one is moved and comes to life. And so we dare say that this text is a paradigm for the resurrection. This resurrection is the calling of the barren one(s) to pilgrimage. The speech of this God brings people to a faithful response, people who heretofore had no capacity for any response.

Paul urges this understanding of resurrection when he speaks of the God in whom Abraham believed, as the one "... who gives life to the dead and calls into existence the things that do not exist" (Rom. 4:17). What did not exist and now does exist is Israel, a people formed by God's word to bear his promise and do his purposes. In the time of Abraham, in the time of Paul, and in our own time, the world fears that word. In its fear, the world settles for silence, ideology, or propaganda. In its doubt, the world listens for less powerful words. But, says our text, God's word breaks all these resistances.

The Promise and Response

1. The first call of God is in calling the worlds into being, the work of creation. In this second call (as "God calls us into the Church," UCC Statement of Faith), God calls an alternative

117

community, an alternative to the cold, barren ones who have ceased to listen and have therefore ceased to live and ceased to hope. God calls the hopeless ones into a community with a future. He calls the fixed ones into pilgrimage.

The speech of God to this barren family, then, is a call to abandonment, renunciation, and relinquishment. It is a call for a dangerous departure from the presumed world of norms and security. The command is terse and peremptory, asking Abraham and Sarah to go "with closed eyes . . . until having renounced thy country, thou shalt have given thyself wholly to me" (Calvin). Such renunciation, of course, is exceedingly difficult to speak of in our culture which focuses on self-indulgence because "you owe yourself this." But notice, the summons is not law or discipline, but promise. The narrative knows that such departure from securities is the only way out of barrenness. The whole of the Abrahamic narrative is premised on this seeming contradiction: to stay in safety is to remain barren; to leave in risk is to have hope.

That lordly call is, of course, echoed in the invitation of Jesus: "For whoever would save his life will lose it; and whoever loses his life for my sake and the gospel's will save it" (Mark 8:35). This speech requires its listeners to ask now, as it did then: Do we genuinely want to be out of the barrenness? Perhaps renunciation is too great a cost. The theme of renunciation and departure to promise governs much of the gospel tradition. It is reflected in the tradition of discipleship and the call to follow Jesus (Mark 1:16–20; 10:28). With Jesus, as with Abraham, the call is dangerously open-ended. As with Jesus' summons, the call to Abraham is an imperative. But it is an imperative like the one we have found in Gen. 1:1—2:4a. The imperative is an invitation. It is a permit to move out of a life of *barrenness* as out of a world of *chaos*.

2. The imperative is followed by the promise, presented in five first-person statements (vv. 2–3a): (1) I will make of you, (2) I will bless you, (3) I will magnify your name, (4) I will bless those who bless you, (5) I will curse those who curse you. I/I/I/I/I! (The self-assertion of Yahweh here is nicely contrasted to the destructive self-assertion of the first man and woman in Gen. 3:10–13.) The future now to be received by Israel is no accomplishment or achievement by Israel. It is a gift by the one who is able to give good gifts (Matt. 7:11). That will be strange to those who believe the claims of our managed world. Could we

118

imagine that we live in a world ordered by gifts? It is much like the dilemma of speech. If we could believe we are seriously addressed by one who calls us into being, then the *speaker* could possibly be taken as the *gift-giver*. But we are suspicious of serious speech and anyone bearing gifts.

The gifts of the promise are worth reflecting on. They are an index of what we crave: well-being, security, prosperity, prominence (cf. Mark 10:30). The situation envisioned in 12:2 is drastically contrasted with that of 11:30. Well-being cannot be conjured by Abraham and Sarah. It can only be given. But the giving depends upon receiving, upon Israel's conceding that the initiative for life is held by this other one. It requires a break with the ideology of modernity which assumes there is only us. There is no promise without a promise-maker. There is no real Genesis, no new beginning for barren people, apart from the reality of this God. It is thus not the command, but the promise, which puts the hard issue to Israel. It is the promise which requires a decision and a radical repentance. It is the promise which requires a rejection of all posturing, a recognition that the world revolves around and is powered by this other one who will be trusted and praised.

3. There is a long-standing tradition that these promises are fulfilled in David and Solomon. Perhaps this text was written in the time of the great kings (cf. I Kings 1:47). That is, the particular expression of the promises may be in light of the kings and their well-being. The context of royal success is one possible location of the promises. The promise provides exactly what the people of Babel (11:4) tried to form for themselves and could not. It is an offer of preeminence which even the disciples envision in their misunderstanding of the gospel (Mark 10:35–37). The promise, as apt for David and Solomon as for the disciples of Jesus, moves in and out of all of the history of this community. This people is always the same, yearning for what it is not competent to create, needing to wait while wanting to grasp.

4. The promise is concluded with what seems to be a commissioning (v. 3*b*). The well-being of Israel carried potential for the well-being of other nations. Israel is never permitted to live in a vacuum. It must always live with, for, and among the others. The barren ones are now mandated for the needs of the others. This text hints at what subsequently became the mission of the church in the world. As Wolff ("The Kerygma of the

119

Yahwist," 1966) has seen, "by you all the families of the earth shall bless themselves" becomes programmatic for Israel. It is utilized in 18:18; 22:18; 26:4; 28:14 and then by Paul (in Gal. 3:8), who regards it as "the gospel beforehand." The good news beforehand is that God wills life for all peoples. God freely gives it and none must "qualify." Most likely the meaning of the phrase is not that Israel has a direct responsibility to do something for the others, but that the life of Israel under the promise will energize and model a way for the other nations also to receive a blessing from this God.

The same text is used in the sermon of Peter (Acts 3:25), this time as a warrant for an appeal to "men of Israel" that they embrace the gospel of Jesus. Its use in Acts so soon after the Pentecost narrative of chapter 2 may be investigated further. It suggests that the juxtaposition of Acts 2 and 3 is parallel to the structure of Gen. 11:1–9 (alluded to in Acts 2) and Gen. 12:1–4 (quoted in Acts 3). Interestingly, the address in Acts 2 concerns all the nations, while the appeal in Acts 3 is especially to the Jews. Thus, the juxtaposition of *providence* and *election* in Genesis 11—12 is reiterated in Acts 2—3.

5. The connection between Abraham and the outsider is especially prominent in the Gospel of Luke. Luke's gospel is especially attentive to "the unqualified." The Abrahamic references suggest that Jesus, after the model of Abraham, is the way in which "unqualified outsiders" are blessed:

a. The Magnificat of Mary (Luke 1:46–55) is a song about the reversal of destinies wrought by God, especially on behalf of the "unqualified," the "handmaiden of low estate" (v. 48), those of "low degree" (v. 52), the "hungry" (v. 53). It cannot be unimportant that the revolutionary statement of blessings beyond the normal provision ends, "as he promised to our fathers, to Abraham and his seed forever."

b. In Luke 13:10–17, the Abraham tradition is involved in the account of a crippled woman. By her infirmity, she yields a picture of rejection. For eighteen years she has lived under a curse. Remarkably, Jesus properly identifies this nameless woman as a "daughter of Abraham" (v. 16).

c. In the parable of Luke 16:19–31, there is a clear contrast drawn between the "rich man," the one obviously blessed, and the poor man, Lazarus, who lacks every mark of blessing. The narrative is about the reassignment of blessing toward the one who has lived under curse. Therefore, it is the poor man who is called to Father Abraham (v. 22). Father Abraham, even in this quite derivative teaching, is one who blesses the outsider.

d. In the well-known narrative of Zacchaeus (Luke 19: 1–10), the tax collector is obviously a despised outsider. Jesus announces salvation for him and asserts that this utterly rejected man is indeed "a son of Abraham" (v. 9).

These four texts together suggest that Luke has grasped the radical character of the Abrahamic blessing.

6. This promise of 12:1–3 dominates our pericope. It stands between the immobilized family of 11:30 and the responsive family of 12:4ff. Things are changed from the one to the other by this promise. Yet, though the text is fully focused on the promise in God's speech of verses 1–3, it is verse 4 which announces the motif which characterizes all of chapters 12:1— 25:18. God's call to Abraham is accepted and embraced. Abraham went (v.4)! He believed the promise. He obeyed. He asked no questions. Believing the promise without any visible evidence is what is meant by faith (even though that term is not yet used). The Bible is shaped to show that God here forms a family to embrace the call and believe the promise. And he went! Abraham stands as the prototype for all disciples who forsake everything and follow (Mark 10:28). The remainder of the drama of Abraham and Sarah is to probe that embrace, to find out if it can be honored, and to assess the cost of such a decision.

The Family in Pilgrimage

In the remainder of this unit (12:4–9), we may identify three dimensions of the narrative which can be pursued usefully.

1. This text introduces the metaphor of journey as a way of characterizing the life of faith. If the geographical notes (vv. 5–9) are to be trusted (and there seems no reason for doubt), the journey of Abraham encompasses the land with special reference to Shechem and Bethel, the great northern shrines. He moves toward the south, the Negev and especially Hebron, where the Abraham tradition has its locus. (The reference to "oak of Moreh" is obscure.) Though the broad outline of geography is to be accepted, the reference to sojourning should not be understood simply as physical movement. It is not clear that Abraham is to be regarded as a nomad whose business carried him hither and yon. And it is even less likely, as has been

121

suggested, that he be reckoned as a merchant who moved in regular caravan. More likely, this particular reference is to be understood not only as a historical or geographical note, but as a theological program. The life of faith is one which keeps Israel in pursuit of the promise of land. But Abraham is not one who finally arrives at his destination. He trusts the promise. But his life falls short of grasping the fulfillment. He is in the land. But he does not yet possess it.

a. The metaphor of journey or sojourn is a radical one. It is a challenge to the dominant ideologies of our time which yearn for settlement, security, and placement. The life of this family is matched by the way of Yahweh himself. Thus Yahweh is understood not as a God who settles and dwells, but as a God who sojourns and moves about (II Sam. 7:4–6). In the David tradition which protests against royal absolutism, Yahweh is presented as a God who is known especially in his lordly freedom. This family is called to the same kind of freedom marked by precariousness and danger, the same risk Yahweh himself takes by sojourning with Israel.

b. The metaphor of journey as a way of speaking about faith is utilized by the New Testament in important ways.

1) Christian discipleship is understood as a following of "the way" (Matt. 8:22; 9:9; 10:38). The "way" as a metaphor is not precisely characterized, but it is variously the way of Jesus, the way of the cross, the way of suffering, the way to Jerusalem. The term marks Christians as those who live in a way contrasted to every fixed and settled form of life. They pursue a God who finally will be at peace with no human arrangement that falls short of the Kingdom in its practice of justice and freedom. "The way" clearly brought the early church into conflict with all the false ways of self-securing.

2) In the great recital of pilgrimage in Heb. 11, Abraham and Sarah are presented as people who claimed no home. They only pursued a risky promise (11:8–12). The recital in Hebrews may be noted in relation to our passage for several reasons. First, such a pursuit of promise can never be one-generational. Each generation trusts that if the promise is not now fulfilled, it will be given to a next generation. Thus, the text stands in opposition to the one-generational ideology of our culture, which demands everything now. Second, this chapter is not simply a celebration of great names from the past. It is an appeal for fidelity in the face of present persecution. It affirms

122

that the anti-promise mode of human community must be countered and resisted by this more powerful way of living.

3) In a passionate appeal to the church at Corinth (I Cor. 4:7–13), Paul makes use of the sojourn theme:

> To the present hour we hunger and thirst, we are ill-clad and buffeted and homeless.

That is the present state. But of the present, Paul further observes *(a)* everything we have is a gift (v. 7), *(b)* redemptive behavior can be practiced (v. 12), and *(c)* to do so makes one despised by the world (v. 13).

Clearly, the metaphor is no way to be well-thought-of in the world. To be on this journey is to live in a way which makes the community despised, at odds with the world, and certainly not understood. The "Abrahamic minority" lives always as a threat against a world which has embraced barrenness and called it vitality.

2. The text of Gen. 12:5–9 appears to be quite self-conscious theology. Abraham's initial entry into the land is faced with the reality of Canaanites. Of course. The promise is not given in a void. The reality of Canaanites (which means those who do not believe the promise) poses difficult questions. What right can one have to the promised land when it is already occupied by others? An answer depends on the sociology which one assumes. If Israel is understood (as perhaps in Judges and Joshua) as a desperate, displaced community, then to ask about the legitimacy of the Canaanites is a luxury that cannot be afforded, any more than any oppressed people can ask first about the well-being of the oppressors.

But that is not the situation assumed in Genesis. Here it is better to recognize that the presence of Canaanites points to two religious realities. First, the promise of God is never easy to believe and practice. It must always be believed and practiced in the midst of those who practice more effective and attractive ways. Abraham is called always to be a minority report among those who live and manage society against the promise. Second, Abraham is called to a relation with the Canaanites. Whereas some older commentators see the Canaanites simply as embodiments of paganism to be resisted, Von Rad rightly sees that Abraham is brought by God "into a completely unexplained relationship" with the Canaanites. On the one hand, there is no evidence in the Abraham tradition of conflict

123

with the Canaanites. (See the same issue in Gen. 34.) The Canaanites are, perhaps, a temptation to Abraham, for their ways were surely attractive in contrast to the slow-paced way of Yahweh's promise. On the other hand, there is also no evidence that Abraham seeks to convert them. Abraham's work is not to convert and build a church. Rather, he is to live among them, to practice and believe the promise. His task is not to impress or even to bear witness to God, but simply to permit the reality of blessing to be at work. The statement of verse 6 suggests a delicate living of a promissory presence which is neither to destroy nor convert but to mobilize the power of life in behalf of the others.

3. We may note the phrase, Abraham "called on the name of the Lord" (v. 8). Initially, the text suggests that Abraham is the builder of altars, and the phrase undoubtedly refers to cultic practice. But more may be seen in it.

a. "To call on the name" means to turn to the one named as the single referent of life. Thus, the cultic practice of Abraham expresses a life-identifying decision he had made in verse 4. It is appropriate to link this decision of Abraham to the primal commandment, to have "no other gods." Luther's well-known interpretative comment on the commandment is that "whatever your heart clings to and relies upon is properly your God." Abraham's calling on Yahweh's name means that he had resolved to cling to none other than to the promise-maker. Even among the Canaanites, the building of an altar is an assertion that the promise-maker is being trusted. It is a polemic against every other god and every other loyalty. Abraham's act in making this visible decision stands in the tradition of 4:26.

b. Calling on God's name encompasses the whole of life. On the one hand, to call on the name is the fullness of *praise:*

O give thanks to the LORD, *call on his name,*
    make known his deeds among the peoples!
Sing to him, sing praises to him,
    tell of all his wonderful works (Ps. 105:1–2)!

On the other hand, it is passionate *petition* by those in need:

The snares of death encompassed me;
    the pangs of Sheol laid hold on me;
    I suffered distress and anguish.
Then *I called on the name of the Lord:*
    "O LORD, I beseech thee, save my life" (Ps. 116:3–4)!

These two examples reflect the parameters of the life of faith: praise and petition, well-being and distress. And in each, there is a turning to Yahweh and to no other.

c. If this formula in 12:8 is to be understood simply as a step in the history of religion, too much should not be made of it. But if we discern here the faith of the community, then this text may be linked even to the sweeping claim of Acts 4:12:

> "And there is salvation in no one else, for there is *no other name* under heaven given among men by which we must be saved."

The use of the formula in Acts 4:12 presents an interesting suggestion for our exposition. In Gen. 12, we have now seen the juxtaposition of *(a)* the promise of blessing to the nations and *(b)* the act of calling on the name of Yahweh. The former (12:3 *b*) affirms an *inclusiveness for all peoples;* the latter (12:8) asserts an *exclusive loyalty to Yahweh.* That same combination of "horizontal inclusiveness" and "vertical exclusiveness" appears in Acts. In Acts 3:25, the inclusive promise is given for all persons. In Acts 4:12, the exclusive claim is made for the one name. Together, they are used to appeal to "the men of Israel" and to make testimony to the "rulers of the people and elders." The combination warns against both a sociological exclusiveness and against a religious accommodation.

Genesis 12:10—13:18

In 12:1–9, Abraham is presented as the perfectly faithful man. He is called and he goes. He relies only on the name (12:8) and word (12:1–4*a*) of this God who has suddenly inverted his life. The call of God has been fully embraced. That is where the history of Israel begins. Undoubtedly, Abraham is offered as a model for the faith of Israel (as Heb. 11 attests). But taken alone, the model is unconvincing. In that presentation, Abraham seems to be almost plastic. Faith is not that easy. Faith is always a battle. Even father Abraham must struggle for faithfulness. The two episodes we now consider, 12:10–20 and 13: 1–18, give fleshly reality to the problem of faith. In these two episodes, the question of faith arises in two forms. Will this God keep his "outlandish" promises? Will the sojourning man and

125

woman be able to trust the promise? The two questions are not the same. But they always come together. The texts now considered are counterpoints to 12:1–9. The themes announced in 12:1–9 must be explored and tested in the demands of reality.

The two narratives that we have grouped together, 12:10–20 and 13:1–18, originally had nothing to do with each other. But they have been brought together in the construction of the tradition. Our exposition will suggest that they form a perfect pair, negatively and positively probing the issue of faith.

The two narratives require skill in story-telling. In broad movement, they follow the same structure. Both begin with a problem, the famine (12:10) and an over-crowding of flocks (13:2–7). Both end happily—Abraham departs rich (12:16, 20), Abraham journeys with a fresh promise of land (13:14–17). In both, the structure places a decisive reference to Yahweh between the beginning problem and the ending resolution. In 12:17, the Lord afflicts Pharaoh. In 13:14, the Lord makes a promise. Each narrative is constructed so that the reference to Yahweh appears somewhat extraneous. Without Yahweh's intervention, each narrative might make a good story. But it would not be the story of faith and faithlessness it now is. The text claims that life is shaped like the narrative itself. The decisive intrusion of Yahweh is at the point where the promises are greatest and the risks the highest. We will consider the two episodes separately and then reflect on their juxtaposition.

Abraham in Egypt

12:10–20, quite in contrast to 12:1–9 presents Abraham as an anxious man, a man of unfaith. He is ready to secure his own survival because at this point he does not trust exclusively in the promise. Luther shrewdly observes that Abraham, "let the Word get out of his sight." The text indicates that the temptation of unfaith comes immediately after his best resolve to faithfulness. (Thus the juxtaposition is not unlike that of Mark 8:27–33. In vv. 27–30, Peter is celebrated for his great faith. In vv. 31–34, he is immediately rebuked for his lack of faith.)

1. Several critical issues need to be considered.

a. The text is an independent unit and appears to be an interruption in the narrative which moves easily from 12:9 to 13:2. Moreover, the narrative is likely not originally an Israelite story, for it reflects a common theme of the "danger to the ancestress." Israel has appropriated a common tale for its own

126

purposes. That this is a common theme is evident in the parallel episodes of 20:1–18 and 26:7–11. Evidently, the theme was popular in and important to Israel. The relation of these parallel accounts is obscure. Following Gunkel and Van Seters (*Abraham in History and Tradition*, pp. 167–183), 12:10–20 appears to be the earliest form of the three. This presentation in 12:10–20 contains dimensions of inscrutable mystery which the other versions attempt to resolve. As there seems no particular advantage in sorting out the obscure relations of the three versions, it will be best to leave them aside and deal with the form of the text as we have it.

b. It has been argued, especially by Speiser (*Genesis*, AB 1969, pp. 89–94) that the tale reflects an older Hurrian practice that a wife could be "adopted" as a sister, elevating her to a higher social position. This would argue for a historical basis for Abraham's ploy and show that he was not in fact lying to the Egyptians. But whatever may be the antecedents (which are doubtful), the present form of the story cannot be understood in that way. The story clearly depends upon the admission that Abraham was lying.

c. Following Peter Weimar, the passage is presented in a chiasmus which may be used in retelling the story (*Untersuchungen zur Redaktionsgeschichte des Pentateuch*, BZAW 146: 16):

v. 10 introduction; action of Abraham

    vv. 11–13 first scene: speech of Abraham

        vv. 14–16*a* second scene: action in Egyptian court

    vv. 17–19 third scene: speech of Pharaoh

v. 20 conclusion: action of Pharaoh.

The introduction and conclusion concern the action of the two principals, Abraham and Pharaoh. The first and third scenes concern speeches of the two principals. In the center stands the main transaction, between the two. But in that center stands the intrusion of Yahweh, which surprises the principal characters, and perhaps the narrator as well. Yahweh is now the principal actor.

2. The narrative is clear enough. For the sake of the promise, Abraham leaves the well-being of Mesopotamia. Immediately, he discovers that the promised land is famine land. The

127

threat of famine requires him to deal with the imperial reality of Egypt. There follows the interaction between the ruthless empire (which needs to explain nothing to anyone) and this resourceless man, whose only resource is a promise which the empire will not acknowledge. The narrative presumes the ludicrous interface of force and helplessness. (The contrast is characteristic of biblical faith, e.g., in Exod. 1:15–20, where the contrast is between Egyptian women and Hebrew midwives, or in John 18:33—19:16, where the unequal encounter is between Jesus and Pilate.) As so often in the Old Testament, in this text we are dealing with minority literature of survival. It is a narrative told by a powerless community to maintain its courage, identity, and dignity in the face of overwhelming odds and unresponsive power. The story itself redresses the imbalance between imperial reality and helpless faith by introducing Yahweh, the new reality which neither the hungry father nor the king had reckoned with.

a. The story permits Israel to mock and laugh at the empire, the Egyptian empire, or any other form of oppressive power. The story might still serve that function for the faithful community when it is a minority needing to maintain its courage and identity in the face of overwhelming odds and hostile values. The story offers humor which should be fully exploited: the shrewdness of father Abraham, the irresistible beauty of mother Sarah (in the present form, an aged beauty), and the crippling lust of Egypt and its Pharaoh. Of all the women available in the empire, they want mother Sarah! So the story has a sociological function. It moves in the arena of liberation, of dramatic and linguistic delegitimization of imperial authority.

b. Our exposition must face the morality of the narrative. Abraham is a desperate man who will act in prudential and unprincipled ways, even endangering Sarah to save himself. Luther goes to great lengths to salvage the morality of Abraham. Calvin says simply that he did not rely on the grace of God as he was called to do.

c. But our interpretation has to do neither with humor nor with morality. It concerns the strange way in which Abraham is caught up in the history of God's blessings and curses. There is much here that is not and must not be explained. The real action transcends both the scheme of Abraham and the prudence of Pharoah. It is not explained why God would smite Pharaoh (v. 17) when it is unambiguously Abraham who has

128

created the problem. Nor is there any hint of how Pharaoh knew that his smiting was in any way linked to the destiny of Abraham and Sarah (vv. 18–19). There are some extraordinary gaps which have not been covered over. They do not concern the narrator. It is enough that they are hidden in the inscrutable workings of God.

Perhaps the narrative is a testing of both Abraham and Yahweh. Abraham has been told, "By you all families will be blessed." The narrative makes clear that Abraham may indeed have the power to cause a blessing for an outsider. But Abraham also has the power to curse others (also in 12:3). The strange calculus of the narrative is that Abraham's shabby action does bring curse. However, the curse is not on himself (as we might expect in a good moral lesson), but on the innocent others. Both Abraham and Pharaoh are on notice: It is dangerous business to deal with Abraham. Something powerful is at work here, more powerful than the father or the empire. When Abraham acts faithlessly, as he has obviously done, curse is released in the world. The faith and/or faithlessness of Israel matters not only to Israel. It is decisive for the nations. In this strange way, Israel has the capacity to impact the affairs of nations. That is anticipated in the programmatic promise of 12:3*b* and now demonstrated in this narrative.

d. The other inscrutable element in the story is that, for all his cowardice, Abraham continues to be protected by Yahweh. The God who first promised will still rescue Abraham from Pharaoh and cause a blessing (vv. 16, 20; 13:1, 2). Thus, the narrative considers two kinds of testing. First, would Abraham believe the promise? Clearly *no.* And that disbelief brings death (v. 17). Second, would Yahweh keep his promise? Unambiguously *yes,* far beyond any reasonable expectation (cf. II Cor. 1:19–20). The graciousness of God is fully confirmed. The faithfulness of Israel, in its very first testing, is found wanting. As Von Rad observes, "The bearer of the promise is the greatest enemy of the promise." But even if Abraham cannot risk the promise, it is not voided. God will keep the promise in spite of Abraham. Abraham had refused to "cast all your anxieties on him." But it is nonetheless true that "he cares about you" (I Pet. 5:7). After the morality and the political humor, the major themes of the narrative endure: the overriding faithfulness of God and the cowardly faithlessness of Israel. The text brings the listening community face to face with "the deep mystery of God's

129

power" which works its own way in history. Neither Pharaoh nor Abraham can finally control the power of blessing. God presides over that in his own free ways.

Abraham and Lot

13:1–18 provides a telling counterpart to 12:10–20. The question of Abraham's well-being now takes the form of land. Is there enough land? How shall the land be managed? How may it be kept and how will it be lost? In contrast to 12:10–20, in this narrative Abraham is presented as a marvelous model of faithfulness. As the older uncle, he might have preempted the good land. But because he believes the promise, he does not doubt that he will finally receive the land God wants him to have. He risks everything by permitting Lot to choose. Whereas the intervention of Yahweh in 12:17 brought curse, in 13:14, the parallel intervention brings blessing.

1. The narrative may originally have served tribal purposes.

a. This narrative is commonly related to Gen. 18—19 as part of a cluster of stories about Lot. Verse 13 seems to provide such a connection. The story probably has an older ethnological function, to explain why certain tribes who are non-Israelite received and are entitled to certain portions of the land. But as we shall see, the present narrative is no longer interested in that question.

b. David Daube (*Studies in Biblical Law,* 1947, pp. 28–36) has suggested that the action first of Lot (v. 10) and then of Abraham (v. 14) reflects the legal practice of coming into possession of the land by the capacity to own whatever can be seen. Thus the invitation of Yahweh to Abraham (vv. 14–17) is a concrete way of bringing Israel into legal possession of the land (cf. Deut. 3:27; Luke 4:5 and perhaps Isa. 39:1–4; Mark 11:11).

c. As in the previous episode, this narrative is clear in its movement. Both Abraham and Lot have prospered, blessed by Yahweh (cf. 30:27–30). Now there is need for more land because of their prosperity. At some stage of the narrative, this may have reflected conflict between Abraham and other, perhaps older, groups in the land. But that historical basis is now lost to us. While the need for more land, water, and grass holds the potential for conflict, the story surprises us. There is no conflict on the part of Abraham. In contrast to the calculating self-serving of 12:10–20, here Abraham is magnanimous in the ex-

130

treme. Whereas his inability to trust the promise had made him fearful in the preceding tale, here his trust of the promise makes him gracious and generous. His practice of the promise enables him to be a source of life for Lot (one of the nations, cf. 12:3*b*) and permits blessing to come upon both of them.

2. The text invites reflection upon the way in which trust in the promise of God permits a different perception, even of economic reality. The common economic view in which modern persons are schooled, capitalists and Marxists alike, is *scarcity*. Social policy, personal conduct, and international politics are conducted on a presupposition of scarcity. From such a presupposition, it follows that conflict, competition, and aggression are appropriate ways with economic matters. That was obviously the mind-set of the hirelings of both men (13:7–8). The matter of dividing up the wealth is a place at which the *power of the promise* and the *ideology of scarcity* come into urgent conflict.

a. In Luke 12:13–21, Jesus is confronted with the same issue. The request for judication is premised on the lack of abundance. The response of Jesus is well-known. He transforms the issue of inheritance and division into the issue of covetousness. He characterizes covetousness as a way of death. The rich man in Luke 12:13–21 (perhaps the same rich man as in Luke 16:19–31 who yearned for father Abraham, perhaps the rich man who presides over Egypt) had more and more and more until he squandered himself to death. The concluding statement of Jesus is a telling one in which he contrasts "treasures for self" and "rich toward God" (Luke 12:21). In verses 22–31, Jesus asserts that the alternative to covetousness is reliance on the good gifts of the father. It is pertinent to the contrast of our two stories that in Luke 12:15–31, Jesus associates with each other the three elements of covetousness (v. 15), anxiety (vv. 22, 25), and little faith (v. 28). That triad of elements in the narrative of Luke 12 is not remote from our story of Gen. 13. Here also is a need to divide the inheritance. Among the shepherds of the two men there are hints of covetousness (v. 7). But there is not a shred of coveting on the part of Abraham. (Lot does not figure in these calculations. He is passive in the narrative.) In contrast to 12:10–20, here Abraham is not now anxious about his life (cf. Luke 12:22). He is presented as the man of faith, content to rely on the promise of God. Therefore, he acts as a man "rich towards God" (Luke 12:21).

131

b. The theme of inheritance is explicit in Luke 12:13–21

and implicit in Gen. 13. It receives special attention in Galatians 3—4, a text closely related to the Abraham tradition. Paul's consideration of the issue is commonly viewed as quite "spiritualized." We must take care that the concrete historicality of the theme of "inheritance" is not lost. Paul faithfully understood the intent of the Abraham narrative. Paul's argument is that the good gifts of God, however they are characterized, finally depend on their quality as *gift*. They cannot be seized, grasped, or possessed, for to do so is to pervert what is promised. Thus in Gal. 3:18 he concludes:

> For if the inheritance is by the law, it is no longer by promise; but God gave it to Abraham by a promise.

The problem for Abraham is to trust only the promise. This he does in 13:1–18, in contrast to 12:10–20. Our text, joined with the commentary of Gal. 3 and Luke 12, brings together the claims of the promise and the realities of economic life. The vocation of Abraham is to live in an economy of promise, which appears to every adherent of the "law" as foolishness. But the family of Abraham is called to be heirs, not predators, purchasers, or thieves.

The Juxtaposition of 12:1–20 and 13:1–18

Both texts, 12:10–20 and 13:10–18, are illuminated by placing them in tension. It is the relation between the two which poses the hard issue of faith.

1. We are concerned not with a romantic religious idea, but with a changed perception of social and economic reality. In the first narrative, Abraham is concerned for survival in the face of imperial power. In the second, the crisis is about real flocks and water. In the first, Abraham is intimidated, but he does not finally capitulate to the power of Pharaoh. In the second, Abraham rejects the ideology of scarcity and acts on a different perception because he does not doubt God's promise.

If the current foreboding about energy and ecology has any validity, in time to come adherents to these texts will have to decide about the reality of God, about the validity of the promise, and about our "little faith" in the goodness of God which can change our perception of reality. Our natural wont is to confine grand statements about trust and promise to private matters and religious questions. But just as it pressed Abraham himself, the text presses the family of Abraham to decide about

132

the relation between the reality of the promise and other more compelling realities.

2. When the reality of God and other realities meet, various responses are possible. These narratives do not flinch from that. They have no interest in a whitewash of father Abraham. Indeed, the two narratives explore the alternatives. In the first, Abraham is self-seeking and self-serving. He trusts in no resource beyond his own shrewdness. He is willing to sacrifice others for his survival.

In chapter 13, Abraham is very different. He takes no thought for himself or for tomorrow (cf. Matt. 6:15–34). In 13:1–13, one might guess that the virtue of Abraham is its own reward. But it is only in verses 14–17 that the story-teller comes to the point. In these verses, the promise of land is stated in a full fashion, well beyond the hopes of 12:1–3, 7. These verses consist only in the speech of Yahweh. The speech consists of two imperatives:

"Lift up your eyes and look (v. 14). . . .
Arise, walk through . . . the land" (v. 17).

And these are matched by two motivational clauses:

". . . for all the land which you see I will give to you (vv. 15–16).
. . . for I will give it to you" (v. 17*b*).

The speech of Yahweh is not an addendum, though it may be a "later tradition." Now the entire narrative exists for the sake of this speech. The speech is unexpected. Abraham did not know this ending when he risked in verse 9. The promise always lies outside the purview of the person of faith. It is not too much to suggest that here Abraham anticipates the teaching of Matt. 6:15–33. He does seek only the righteousness of God. And verses 14–17, perhaps added, are like "all these things shall be yours as well."

3. The contrast between the two narratives could not be sharper. In the one Abraham is "anxious about his life, what he will eat and drink" (Matt. 6:25). In the other, Abraham risks everything for the sake of the promise. But the text does not permit us to choose between the two. The first story sounds a note of realism. The second portrays a daring faith. But the narrator never suggests that one is preferred to the other nor that one may be valued at the expense of the other. Both are there. Both are remembered and treasured by the community.

133

The two together (and neither alone) present faith the way it really is. Like Abraham, we are strange mixtures of prudence and trust. But in both, the gospel is at work. In both narratives, the promise-making, blessing-giving God is at work. The trust of Abraham matters in these narratives. But it does not matter finally. What matters finally is the faithfulness of Yahweh to this family.

Focused on father Abraham, 12:10–20 shows his weak faith which doubts the promise and so brings *trouble.* Conversely, 13:1–18 shows Abraham believing and bringing *well-being.* Yahweh intervenes each time. In the first, he intervenes in deathly ways but stands by Abraham. In the second, he intervenes only late, but at the right time for Abraham. The texts leave the community of faith with decisions to make. But the narratives also affirm that however those decisions are made, Yahweh keeps watch over his promise.

Genesis 14:1–24

The most enigmatic chapter in Genesis, chapter 14, seems to stand utterly alone and without connection to any of the sources or strands of tradition found elsewhere in the book. Apparently, it is placed here because of the reference to Lot in verses 12–16, thus having it follow the Lot narrative and chapter 13.

The text consists of three segments. The relationship between them is not clear. They include *(a)* a report on an international war (vv. 1–11); *(b)* an intervention of Abraham for the sake of Lot (vv. 12–16), and *(c)* a subsequent encounter with Melchizedek, king of Salem (vv. 17–24). The final section seems to hold the most possibility for theological treatment and will be our primary concern in exposition after we have briefly summarized some critical matters for the entire chapter.

Critical Issues

The analysis and assessment of this chapter are exceedingly difficult.

1. The historical data (especially related to vv. 1–11) is quite obscure. Scholars have assigned it everywhere from the Middle

134

Bronze to the Maccabean period. No certain judgments can be made on the identification of the kings of verses 1–11, though the dispute among them may have been over mineral rights. The various historical identifications which have been suggested are far from secure.

2. The intervention of Abraham into the battle on behalf of Lot (vv. 12–16) is a curious statement and ill-suited for the kind of narrative the first part of the chapter appears to be. It may be placed here as a fiction to enhance the reputation of Abraham for his prowess and generosity on behalf of his kinsmen. In any case, the association suggested between Abraham (vv. 12–16) and general public history (vv. 1–11) is unique in this text.

3. While the encounter with Melchizedek (vv. 17–24) is of peculiar interest, it is also enormously difficult. Melchizedek may be linked with Zadok, the later priest of David (II Sam. 8:17; I Kings 1:8ff.) if "Salem" (v. 18) is an early reference to Jerusalem. On that basis, it is argued that the text refers to the sacred place of Jerusalem and is placed here to serve the interests of the Davidic establishment. The effect would be to relate Israel to earlier Canaanite cultic practices and also to the memories of Abraham, thus giving historical legitimacy to an upstart regime. However, the evidence is less than compelling for such a theory. Our knowledge of associations between Israelite tradition and Canaanite religion is as thin as our knowledge of the political history reflected in verses 1–11.

4. The reference to the tithe (v. 20) suggests not a pious act but a formal obligation. Thus, tithe is not a "free-will offering," but acknowledgement of a relation to a superior by a subordinate.

Four Expository Observations (vv. 17–24)

1. Special attention should be given to the doxological formula of verses 18–20. This is a very old formula, likely pre-Israelite and perhaps placed here in David's time. The God mentioned is not the God of Israel, but "God Most High" *(El Elyon),* the high God of the Canaanite pantheon. The poem would seem to be a hymn addressed to a Canaanite deity whose functions and glories are only later assigned to Yahweh, the God of Israel. The formula "Most High God" is a very ancient one and is assigned to Yahweh late. It is striking that the title is used especially in Daniel (3:26; 4:17, 24, 25, 32, 34; 5:18, 21; 7:18, 22,

135

25, 27) in a later tradition that presents an especially high doctrine of God. It is used in contexts in which the sweep of faith
goes beyond the history of Israel to make universal claims for
this God.

a. This text can be valuable in helping persons to understand the strange and powerful ways of syncretism. While syncretism is indeed problematic, it is also a way in which alien
functions are taken from other gods and reassigned to the God
of Israel as an enhancement of his glory. In this text, "Yahweh,"
rendered "Lord," is mentioned in verse 22 only and not in the
poem (vv. 19–20). But even that reference is commonly regarded as late on the basis of the textual versions. The different
versions reflect not simply manuscript uncertainty but the history of a struggle by which the God of Israel usurped the functions of other gods and came to be confessed as the High God
of Canaan and all else. The text in its present form certainly
means to identify the God who watches over Israel as the God
of the universe. But the process must have been one of intense
theological conflict. The outcome is not unlike the effort of the
early church in identifying and confessing *(a)* "the maker of
heaven and earth" as also *(b)* the "father of our Lord Jesus
Christ."

The doxology (vv. 19–20) reflects this dual agenda. It consists of two parallel lines naming God and ascribing blessing.
But following that double naming of "God Most High," the
ascriptions go in opposite directions. The first (v. 19) refers to
the creator God, the second (v. 20) to the historical deliverance
of Israel. In the hands of Israel, this dual construction dares to
claim that the God who calls Abraham and gives Isaac is indeed
the God worshiped in Canaan as the God of fertility even
though the Canaanites did not know his true name. The Canaanites worshiped him as "Most High God," but it was the liberated Israelites who knew his name.

b. This peculiar adjustment in divine claims reflects political upheavals and power struggles. The struggle is illuminated
by the sophisticated theological assertion in the mouth of Paul
(Acts 17:22–31). There Paul's argument is that the "unknown
God" is now known. He is not an idol to be manipulated but is
a Lord who compels repentance. In a way parallel to that of
Paul, our text covers a complex religious history by asserting
that Israel knows the name of this God. In the present form of
the text, Melchizedek the Canaanite (vv. 19–20) calls God only

"God Most High," whereas it is Abraham in response (v. 22) who discloses the true name. It is only Abraham and not the priest of Salem who knows the name of God. This text provides opportunity to reflect on the name and character of God and the way he is fully known in concrete historical disclosure.

In the New Testament, the same title is used (Mark 5:7; Luke 8:28; Acts 7:48; 16:17) in contexts linked to Jesus and acts of saving power. (Cf. also Heb. 7:1 to which reference will be made.)

2. The Canaanite formula (now claimed for Israel's God) makes the claim that this God, the one who stands by Israel, is "maker of heaven and earth." Appeal to God as creator is not simply a way of speaking about the origin of "the cosmos." It is a way of grounding faith in a time of crisis in the deepest reality about which we can speak. This doxological formula becomes an assertion that we are not and need not be self-made. The power of life stands outside us and is given to us.

Norman Habel ("Yahweh, Maker of Heaven and Earth," JBL 91:321–37 [1972]) has shown that this formula has become a standard liturgical one in Israel. He has isolated five closely paralleled uses (Pss. 115:15; 121:2; 124:8; 134:4 and 146:6). In none of these is there a concern about how the world came to be. Rather, each of them speaks about the present reality of the same God who makes a difference now. In three of them (Pss. 121:2, the best known to us; 124:8; 146:6) the formula carries with it the notion of "help" *('āzar)*. Thus, creation faith yields a remarkable confidence about the helper:

> When other helpers fail, and comforts flee,
> Help of the helpless, O abide with me.
> (Henry F. Lyte, "Abide with Me," 1820.)

The other two uses (Pss. 115:15; 134:4) do not mention *help*. But they speak of *blessing,* the power for life. This doxological formula invites Israel to think in the largest scope about the power of life that has been made available to us. More than any other in Genesis, these verses in chapter 14 (cf. 24:3, 7) invite us to take creation faith out of the arena of "origins" and see it as source for life, buoyancy, and joy in the trials of the day. The use of the same formula in the psalms gives this great cosmic claim a personal casting as a resource for the most intimate dimensions of personal faith.

3. The encounter of Abraham with the King of Salem (vv.

137

21–24) concerns taking booty from war and giving credit for victory. Abraham is victorious and apparently has captured an abundance of goods as well as people (v. 16). The following exchange between the two parties is instructive. Abraham refuses the invitation of the king to act in an acquisitive way (v. 23). Instead, he makes a faith affirmation. He will not rely on the king nor give the appearance of relying on him (cf. Judg. 7:2). He will rely only on the God whose name he knows and to whom he has sworn an oath (v. 22). The well-being and prosperity which Abraham already has and which he is yet to receive is not to be credited either to military or political machinations, but only to the free gift of God.

In that regard, we may return to Psalm 146 just mentioned. The psalm offers a double use of the theme "help," once with our term *'āzar*" (v. 5) and once with *"t*ešû'āh*" (v. 3), which means "saving help."

> Put not your trust in princes,
> in a son of man, in whom there is no *help[t*ešû'āh]*
> When his breath departs he returns to his earth;
> on that very day his plans perish.
> Happy is he whose *help['ezrô]* is the God of Jacob,
> whose hope is in the LORD his God,
> who made heaven and earth (Ps. 146:3–6*a*).

The contrast concerns *(a)* the help of princes (in our text, the king of Sodom) and *(b)* help from the creator of earth and heaven. The statement of Abraham in Gen. 14:22–24 is a militant statement of faith and also a polemic against the pretensions of the king. Psalm 146 contrasts human (princely) power and the maker of heaven and earth. And in Dan. 11:34–36, human power is declared "little help" *('āzer)* and is contrasted with the God of gods. This gospel, common in all three texts, asserts a singular trust in the true God to the disregard of all other pretensions of support. Abraham's utter reliance upon God's gift is powerfully affirmed by Paul against every notion of self-reliance:

> For who sees anything different in you? What have you that you did not receive? If then you received it, why do you boast as if it were not a gift? (I Cor. 4:7).

Here Abraham is already presented as one justified only by his faith in God. He refuses to boast or to confide in his own strength (cf. 15:6).

4. Curiously, the major interest of this chapter for many will be the reference to Melchizedek in Heb. 5:6–10; 6:20; 7:

1–28. However, in chapter 14 it is apparent that Melchizedek is marginal. The references in Hebrews have only the most tenuous connection to our chapter. Undoubtedly, Ps. 110:6, given a christological reading early in the history of the church, is the middle ground which establishes a connection between our text and Heb. 5—7. The psalm is quoted generously in Hebrews, whereas our text is not so extensively used.

The relation of our text to Hebrews is established by an intensely typological reading of the text. That relationship appears to rest on two points: First, Melchizedek blessed Abraham. Since a superior always blesses an inferior, Melchizedek must be the prototype of the only real high priest, Jesus Christ, who can claim superiority even to Abraham. Second, Melchizedek can be such a type for Jesus Christ because he is "without father or mother or genealogy, and has neither beginning of days nor end of life . . ." (Heb. 7:3). From this typology, three interpretive observations may be made:

a. It is futile to seek a connection between Melchizedek and Jesus in any historical way (cf. Heb. 7:16). The connection is based on other kinds of parallels which are theological and not historical.

b. The text does not claim that Jesus is derived or descended from Melchizedek but rather is "like" him (7:15) or belongs "to the order of . . ." (Heb. 6:20; 7:11). The linkage concerns a similarity of *function* rather than any identity of person. Any attempt to penetrate behind the typology into history is illegitimate. But the claim made for the function should not be overlooked. The writer of Hebrews seeks to ground the authority of the gospel in something beyond history. The inscrutable appearance of Melchizedek provides a way for such a trans-historical claim.

c. The text of Hebrews is not interested in Melchizedek except as a metaphor and a way of speaking. The real issue is the superiority of Jesus to other mediators. That superiority is finally not based on associations with Melchizedek but on the resurrection, a very different grounding:

> . . . who has become a priest, not according to a legal requirement concerning bodily descent but by the power of an indestructible life" (Heb. 7:16).

139

Our text in Genesis contributes nothing substantive to Hebrews. At the most, it provides a figure of speech for a christological concern which lies well beyond our text. The type of

Melchizedek is not concerned with *continuity or derivation* but with *a free gift from God.* This is a decisive claim against religious silliness often associated with such a shadowy figure.

Genesis 15:1–21

This chapter is pivotal for the Abraham tradition. Theologically, it is probably the most important chapter of this entire collection. It has been judged by many scholars to be the oldest statement of Abrahamic faith, from which the others are derivative. It has been utilized by Paul in a distinctive way for his great teaching on justification by faith. There is no doubt that this chapter offers crucial resources for the themes of *faith* and *covenant.*

Abraham and Sarah were called out of their barrenness (11:30) by God's powerful word (12:1). Their pilgrimage of hope had begun on no other basis than the promise of Yahweh (12:1–4a). The *promise* of Yahweh stood over against the *barrenness.* But when we arrive at chapter 15, the barrenness persists. That barrenness (which the promise has not overcome) poses the issue for this chapter. The large question is that the promise does delay, even to the point of doubt. It is part of the destiny of our common faith that those who believe the promise and hope against barrenness nevertheless must live with the barrenness. Why and how does one continue to trust solely in the promise when the evidence against the promise is all around? It is this scandal that is faced here. It is Abraham's embrace of this scandal that makes him the father of faith.

The Crisis of Faith (vv. 1–6)

The movement of verses 1–6 is worth noting in detail:

(v. 1)	Yahweh's fundamental promise
(vv. 2–3)	Abraham's *protest*
(vv. 4–5)	Yahweh's response
(v. 6)	Abraham's *acceptance.*

Following the fundamental statement of promise, Abraham protests, doubting that such a promise can be accomplished in the circumstances. Yahweh responds to the doubt with a double statement of assurance. In the conclusion of verse

6, Abraham accepts the promise. The two assurances of Yahweh (v. 1 and vv. 4–5) are parallel. The believing response of Abraham (v. 6) is contrasted with the resistance (vv. 2–3).

The entire passage is one of sharp exchange in which Abraham stands face to face with God and seeks to refute the promise and resist the assurance. Clearly, the faith to which Abraham is called is not a peaceful, pious acceptance. It is a hard-fought and deeply argued conviction. Abraham will not be a passive recipient of the promise. He is prepared to hold his own. His freedom in the face of God is not unlike the freedom of the creation in Gen. 1:1—2:4a. This Lord invites and permits but will not coerce. Abraham is forced to faith no more than the creation is forced to obedience.

1. The narrative report makes a new beginning with an abrupt "fear not" from God (v. 1). It is a word of greeting, but it is also a word which shatters. It disorients Abraham who was fearful for his future. He had concluded by now that there would be no change. The call from barrenness was a false alarm. If barrenness prevails, then the promise is null. But this God will not leave it there. He speaks (as in 12:1) with a word that reestablishes the promise. The promise is now presented with a somewhat different image: "Your reward will be great." The "reward" is not specified, but it refers to the land (cf. vv. 18–21).

The use of the term "reward" calls for comment. While the Hebrew term *śkr* sometimes suggests economic settlement and may be rendered "wage," this usage implies gift and not *quid pro quo* (cf. the different usage in the Jacob narrative 29:15; 30:28; 31:7). Here the reward is not a prize that is earned but a special recognition given to a faithful servant of the king who has performed a bold or risky service. Abraham and Sarah are called to live their lives against barrenness. The "reward" calls them to live as creatures of hope (cf. Heb. 11:10) in a situation of hopelessness. The theme of "reward" poses one of our most difficult issues in interpretation. Clearly, trusting is not the cause of fulfillment, for that would reduce things to *quid pro quo*. On the other hand, it is clear that only those who hope will be given the gift. This does not make a very logical argument. But it is a key insight of biblical faith. It has been learned not as a theoretical matter but as an experience of God's grace. The gift of God is given especially to those who trust and who will risk according to what is promised. The same difficult affirmation is made in the Beatitudes of Jesus. They conclude in Matt.

141

5:12 with a promise of "reward in heaven." In Matt. 5:46, the reward for the hopers is contrasted with the "reward" of those who live in resistance and mistrust. And in Matt. 6:1, 2, 5, 16, a contrast is made between the rewards given by human persons and the rewards of God which cannot be forced but only received in trust. Three times the contrast is stated:

"They have received their reward" (vv. 2, 5, 16).

". . . your father who sees in secret will reward you" (vv. 4, 6, 17).

It will not do to spiritualize the rewards given. Clearly, the reward for Abraham is the land. And even in such a teaching as Mark 10:29–30, the rewards are eternal life, but also "houses and brothers and sisters and mothers and children and lands, with persecutions. . . . " In the same way, in Mark 9:41 "reward" is linked to concrete caring after the manner of Jesus. Because of the prominent role of Abraham in Hebrews 11, the mention of reward in that chapter is worthy of special attention, albeit with reference to Moses:

He considered abuse suffered for the Christ greater wealth than the treasures of Egypt, for he looked to the reward (v. 26; cf. 10:35).

It is hazardous to speak of rewards as these texts do, for they may be heard as bargains or bribes. And yet it is attested that faithful trust makes a difference and that God does respond in generosity to those who trust. It will not do either to be silent on the question or to leave the subject to religious hucksters who promise all kinds of benefits in their religious retailing. Rather, the rewards must be articulated as the generous response of God to those who heed his call and share his life. That is what is offered Abraham in the face of barrenness.

2. But the reward of land requires having heirs. Land is never for one generation. The capacity to transmit land for long generations to come is required. So the large promise depends upon the quite concrete matter of an heir. We have returned (in vv. 2–3) to the problem of being without child. God has not yet done the one thing needful for the sake of the future. Can the closed womb of the present be broken open to give birth to a new future? It will take an heir to break it. An *heir* stands in contrast to a *slave* who only continues the hopeless present. Abraham and Sarah could possess many slaves. But a slave is no sign of the future, for slaves bespeak necessity, fate, compulsion.

What is needed is an heir to break the power of necessity (cf. Jer. 2:14).

Abraham issues a double protest: "I continue childless/no offspring" (vv. 2–3). The Hebrew text of verse 2 is notoriously difficult. But its meaning is clear enough. Because Abraham has no son he is chagrined at the prospect that an adopted slave-boy will be his only heir. The practice of making a slave an adopted heir may reflect an older Hurrian practice. In any case, the anguish of Abraham is that he has no son. And no "reasonable substitute" will do. Juxtaposed are the powerful promise (v. 1) and the equally powerful refutation (vv. 2–3). The utter impossibility of the promise to this family becomes evident. Abraham knows what is possible. He lives in restless torment, finds God's promise without persuasive power.

3. After the double protest (vv. 2–3), Yahweh reasserts the promise one more time (vv. 4–5). The text is unambiguous. Nothing more is offered except the word. The strategems of adoption or of human biology are not doors to the future. Abraham and Sarah are left as they were in chapter 12, with only the reality of this strange language. Yahweh speaks his lordly majestic word which governs all of biblical faith: "Your own son will be your heir" (v. 4).

The response of God to Abraham is not a fool-proof argument like the brief of a lawyer. It comes in two parts: *(a)* in verse 4, the word again; and *(b)* in verse 5, a sign, a glance at the heavens. But the sign proves nothing. How could it be that the multitude of stars is a promise of a son? We must not misunderstand the universe of discourse at work here. It is not an argument, but a revelation. This is a vision, a disclosure that surprises old reality. We are struggling, as was Abraham, with the emergence of a certitude that is based not on human reasons but on a primal awareness that God is God. And that certitude is given in this dark moment to Abraham. He knows, and the knowing can only be credited to the work of God's brooding care. The same God who gives the promise is the one who makes it believable. Only the new awareness that God really is God provides ground for Abraham's safe future. Perhaps Ps. 8 can be heard as a commentary on this strange disclosure by seeing the stars and the heavens:

143

> When I look at the heavens . . . the
> moon and the stars (cf. Gen. 15:5),

what is man [heir?]
        or the son of man [Isaac?].

The psalm makes a connection between the awe of creation and the greater awe of this royal creature to whom God especially attends. If the stars and the heavens are awe-filled, how much more concern for the future of this family? (See the same reasoning in Jer. 33:19–26.) It is the caring majesty of God that makes the connection. The same God who makes stars beyond number can also make a son for this barren family. And we understand no more about the one than about the other.

4. The result: *he believed* (v. 6)! The verse which ends the unit is the focus of our text. As is well known, this has been a key text from Paul to Luther. The text poses the issue of what faith is and how it comes. There is nothing in verses 1–5 which amounts to persuasion. The new promise (vv. 4–5) offered no new data not already known to Abraham when he refused (vv. 2–3). The most suggestive interpretive point in this text is its structure. The two parts (vv. 1–3 and vv. 4–6) are structured the same. In each there is a promise and a response. The promises are the same in substance. But the two responses are very different. The first (vv. 2–3) is a disbelieving protest or lament. The second (v. 6) is an act of faith. The interpretive question is, why the difference? What moved Abraham to a new response? Surely it is not because he feels new generative powers in his loins. Nor because he has new expectations for Sarah. The new promise for his life is not any expectation of flesh and blood. Rather, he has come to rely on the promise speaker. He has now permitted God to be not a hypothesis about the future, but the voice around which his life is organized.

a. Abraham has repented. He has abandoned a reading of reality which is measured by what he can see and touch and manage. That new orientation is not a generalized religious notion that "everything will work out all right." He is not guilty of pious abdication. Rather, it is a quite specific response to a concrete promise from a known promise-maker. The faith of Abraham is certain of one point. There is a future to be given which will be new and not derived from the present barrenness. He believes that God can cause a break point between the exhausted present and the buoyant future. He believes in a genuine Genesis.

b. While alike in substance, there is one difference between the approach of God in verse 1 and verses 4–5. The second

144

approach includes a *sign*, a clue to the movement of God is discerned in ordinary realities. The multitude of stars is received by Abraham as a sign of the power of God in his life. The sign is not proof or demonstration, but it is a sacrament to those who can discern the connection between the concrete visible and the promised. Abraham engages in sacramental discernment (cf. I Cor. 11:29). Exposition of this element in movement of Abraham from the *protest* (vv. 2–3) to *belief* (v. 6) may make reference to the signs of Jesus, especially in the Fourth Gospel (e.g., John 2:11, 23).

c. But finally the new reality of faith for Abraham must be accounted as a miracle from God. The faith of Abraham should not be understood in romantic fashion as an achievement or as a moral decision. Rather, the newly ready Abraham is a creature of the word of promise. The situation of Abraham is paralleled to the confession of Peter (Matt. 16:15–17). Abruptly and without explanation of cause, Peter makes this same leap in his confession: "You are the Christ, the Son of the living God." The gospel narrative also wants to ponder the question: How does such a man come to such a confession? How is faith possible in the life of unfaith? The response of Jesus indicates the miracle which faith is:

"Blessed are you, Simon Bar-Jona! For flesh and blood has not revealed this to you, but my Father who is in heaven."

That is how this faith of Abraham is. He did not move from protest (vv. 2–3) to confession (v. 6) by knowledge or by persuasion but by the power of God who reveals and causes his revelation to be accepted. The new pilgrimage of Abraham is not grounded in the old flesh of Sarah nor the tired bones of Abraham, but in the disclosing word of God.

5. This statement is a revolutionary moment in the history of faith. "It was reckoned to him as righteousness" (v. 6). Von Rad has seen (but it was clearly anticipated by Calvin and Luther) that Abraham is now abruptly *designated* as one well pleasing in God's sight. The text announces afresh what it means to be the human creatures we are created to be, that is, to be righteous. It means to trust God's future and to live assured of that future even in the deathly present. This discernment of righteousness means the end of every "*-ism*" (not only moralism, dogmatism, pietism, but also existentialism, positivism, Marxism, capitalism, humanism), for every -ism is a way of

keeping control of the present. This new righteousness means to relinquish control of the present for the sake of a Genesis. Abraham is a "new creation; the old has passed away, behold, the new has come. All this is from God . . . we might become the righteousness of God" (II Cor. 5:17–18, 21). No other Old Testament text has exercised such a compelling influence on the New Testament.

a. This text is especially important to the Pauline argument of Rom. 4 and Gal. 2—4. Paul has well understood the claim of this text. The future of God's goodness is open to those who trust themselves to that future, seeking neither to hold on to the present nor to conjure an alternative future of their own. But, Paul has also understood that finally it is not faith which makes the difference. Faith responds to an already given grace. This faith is not simply an embrace of the goodness which meets us in the world, but a reception of the *goodness of God promised* in spite of the way the world is. The faith of Abraham is not in anything he sees in the world, but in a word which will overcome the barrenness of the world. Faith is reliance on God's promise of overcoming the present for a new life (cf. John 16:33).

b. It is important in the letter to the Galatians that Paul sees that the *freedom* of the new righteousness has important ethical implications. Thus, in Gal. 5:21, he uses the symbol of the inheritance. Those who manifest the fruit of the spirit (vv. 22–23) are those who live in the land of promise. The fruit of the spirit is the active practice of promise in the life of the human community.

c. It is remarkable that this same text is used in James 2:23f. It is conventionally argued that James either misunderstands or distorts Paul or that he holds to a kind of Jewish Christianity which fails to discern the power of the gospel. But this text suggests that James develops a full dialectic of faith and works which Paul in his passion did not assert. James is often read as though he urges works as the only real way of faith. But it can also be argued here that works keep faith possible, that acting out of the conviction of the promise is in fact a bodily, incarnated way of enacting the promise. "Works," then, is not an extrinsic demonstration, proof or price, but an essential ingredient in sustaining the promise. The promise must be practiced by God's alternative community. James understood the reality of the gospel in the same realistic way Alcoholics Anonymous

146

understands the importance of *doing* the promise. And so the church can sing:

> In work that keeps faith sweet and strong,
>   in trust that triumphs over wrong.
>   (Washington Gladden,
>   "O Master, Let Me Walk with Thee" 1879).

d. The Synoptic Gospels, especially Matthew, are aware of the battle for faith in the church. The disciples are presented as those who have great difficulty in receiving, trusting, and affirming the power of the future as it is evident in the person, teaching, and action of Jesus. On the one hand, the gospel narrative reports the amazing gift of faith that wells up at odd moments. Thus, there is appreciation of the powerful faith of the centurion (Matt. 8:10–13), of the friends of the paralytic (9:2), of the woman with the hemorrhage (9:22; Luke 8:48), of the woman whose daughter had a demon (Matt. 15:28), of the woman of the city (Luke 7:50), of the blind man (Luke 18:42) and of the lepers (Luke 17:19).

In each of these cases, faith was the ready reception of newness given by the presence of Jesus. Each of them had a closed future of sickness or misery. But each of them willingly abandoned that closed situation, not reluctant to receive the "reward" given them in the gospel. Jesus affirms that it is their faith which lets the gift be given:

> Your faith has made you well (Matt. 9:22; Luke 8:48; 17:19).
>
> Your faith has saved you (Luke 7:50).

The ones who are barren and hopeless become the practitioners of faith. They are the ones who do not doubt the promise and so allow the new age to surge upon them.

As H. J. Held has shown, faith is a problem to the church when it clings to the problematic present and so shuts out the kingdom (*Tradition and Interpretation in Matthew*, 1963, pp. 206f. and *passim*). Thus in Matt. 6:30; Luke 12:28, the disciples are "men of little faith" because they are anxious about eating and drinking. Caught in the storm (Matt. 8:26), they are "men of little faith" because they believe the storm is stronger than Jesus. In Matt. 14:31, Peter is a "man of little faith" because he doubts his ability and/or the power of Jesus. The disciples are "men of little faith" (16:8) because they understand nothing of Jesus' capacity to feed and are preoccupied with the present

147

bread supply. And in their inability to cast out demons, they have "little faith" (17:20; cf. 21:21; 28:17).

As in Genesis, the problem of faith is not presented in the gospels as a problem for those who have never been marked as believers. What Matthew knows and what Genesis shows about Abraham is that faith is an issue precisely for those who have heard God's call to new life and intend to embrace that call.

The Binding in Covenant (vv. 7–21)

The issue of faith has been clearly posed in the Abraham tradition. We may consider the ways in which 15:7–21 report on the confirmation of that act of faith. In their present form verses 1–6 and 7–21 may be considered as the relation between an *act of commitment* and *dramatic affirmation* of that commitment. (Concerning the history of the text, it may well be that the two portions had no early relation to each other and that 7–21 is the old text.) This text may be considered in three parts:

1. Verses 7–11, 17 (especially vv. 9–11, 17) present a curious ritual act that is probably very old. While the specific details of the action are obscure, the act suggests a solemn and weighty binding of the two parties to each other. Perhaps this is some kind of blood oath to visibly reinforce the promise (cf. Jer. 34:18). In restrained fashion, verse 17 suggests that somehow the mysterious and unseen presence of Yahweh is engaged in this action.

2. Verses 12–16 contain a historical reflection on the course of the promise in the history of Israel. Perhaps these verses deal with the question of why the promise is so long in being kept. The verses survey in prospect the history of Israel with special reference to the oppression in Egypt and the Exodus from Egypt. (It is precarious to draw any specific conclusions from the chronology of v. 13.) This theological reflection in the form of a dream message contains three assertions of importance: *(a)* The promise will be kept. The word is sure and need not be doubted. *(b)* The promise will be delayed, for historical reasons given. *(c)* Abraham, to whom the promise is first given, need not be anxious over the delay. It is enough for him to be assured that it endures to the next generation. He may confidently embrace his old age and his death.

This text is offered as a theological explanation for the delay. As such it is a useful theological piece. For in the life of

148

faith, those who have trusted most passionately sometimes find that the promise is not given (as 15:2–3). One response to unkept promises from God is to engage in theoretical discussions of theodicy and to explain the justice of God. But this text is not prepared for such a discussion. It prefers to keep the question well within the bounds of historical explanation. In that regard it is not unlike the reasoning of Judg. 2:1—3:6. Such reflections are to be taken neither as specific historical reports nor as very compelling theological reasons. They do reflect, however, on the awareness that there is a deep problem for a faith that believes in historical enactment of promises, for history is profoundly recalcitrant and does not yield easily to promise. But this text at least does not flinch from very long waiting, even from generation to generation.

To wait a very long time emerges as an overriding theme in this chapter, and indeed as a theme throughout the Abrahamic tradition. Abraham has no heir and he must wait yet longer (vv. 1–6). The waiting extends over the generations (vv. 13–16). Perhaps interest in the wait as well as the mention of faith caused this passage to be taken up in Hab. 2:2–4. That passage, which provides a link to Paul, not only affirms that "the righteous will live by faith," that interpretation is well known, but the passage also affirms,

> If it seem slow, wait for it;
> it will surely come, it will not delay (Hab. 2: 3).

The problem of faith is waiting, even when the delay seems unending. That may be a useful interpretive contact with persons of our time. In the Promethean way we have of immediately making our own future, we are not accustomed to waiting. In our impatience we are prone to conclude that if it is not given now, it will not be given. Abraham's impatience (vv. 2–3) reflects the same judgment. But gifts may not be forced. Futures stay in the hand of the God who gives them. As we have already seen in 12:10–20, even this model figure of faith was tempted to form an immediate alternative future of his own making.

3. Verses 18–21 conclude the theological statement with a *covenant* issued as a promise of *land*. This is the only Abrahamic text which might possibly reflect covenant as a part of the old Abrahamic tradition. (The other uses in Gen. 17 are certainly later.) The covenant has been given liturgical expression in verses 9–11, 17. Here the covenant is simply a promise.

149

It is one-sided as a commitment on the part of God to Abraham and exacts no comparable allegiance from Abraham to God. It is a commitment of free grace.

The unqualified commitment of God in verses 18–21 has its counterpart in verse 6. In both passages it is affirmed that God's movement toward Abraham is free and unconditional. Abraham need only trust. The land promised seems to anticipate the holdings of the united monarchy. It can be claimed that verses 18–21 describe the actual borders of the monarchy at its high point under Solomon (cf. I Kings 4:24). Thus the promise is articulated from the perspective of one dramatic fulfillment.

4. It is the *covenant promise of land* which unifies verses 7–21. The initial promise of God is about the land (v. 7). And the initial question of Abraham (v. 8, not unlike the protest of vv. 2–3) is about the land. The promise and question of verses 7–8 at the beginning and the promise of verses 18–21 at the end provide an envelope for this unit. Between the initial promise and the concluding promise there is a liturgical act (vv. 9–11, 17) and a historical reflection (vv. 13–16), both of which are rather obscure. But the overriding agenda of the passage is that *(a)* God is a promise-maker, *(b)* Abraham is a promise-bearer, and *(c)* the substance of the promise is land. Until the promise is kept, covenant is the way the promise is practiced.

The text of Gen. 15, taken as a unit, asks whether Abraham can, in fact, *trust.* And it asks if Yahweh can, in fact, *be trusted.* It is faith which permits Abraham to trust and God to be trusted. It is unsure faith that wonders about the delay. The issues are set here. The remainder of the Abrahamic narrative explores the answers.

Genesis 16:1—18:15

The tension and incongruity could not be sharper than in chapter 15. The assurance of 15:4 could not be clearer: "Your own son will be your heir." Yet it has not happened. Quickly, 16:1 restates the new issue for the tradition, that the promise has not been kept. Will there be an heir? Is there still a future? Can God be trusted?

In this section, we consider three distinct pieces, 16:1–16; 17:1–27 and 18:1–15. In different ways, all three texts revolve around this issue of faith in a God whose promise tarries too long. In this discussion, there will be brief comments on the first two elements and then focus on 18:1–15 as the richest possibility for exposition. At the end of 18:15, there is still no resolution. The promise is still in limbo. Sarah is still without child. The whole narrative presses to the birth in chapter 21. The task of exposition is to portray the anguish of these texts. That anguish turns out to be labor pain, but that is not known here. These texts present the creation "groaning in labor ... groan inwardly as we wait for adoption as children, the redemption of our bodies. For in this hope we were saved" (Rom. 8:22–24—author's translation). These first parents of faith might well have made that same statement. The story of their lives is the story of hopeful but impatient groaning as they wait for the redemption of their bodies and of their history.

While the three units focus on the same theme, they have no natural connection with each other. They are of different sources and reflect the varied ways in which Israel responded to this troublesome delayed promise.

The Promise to Ishmael

Chapter 16 is an early and non-reflective narrative which requires quite open-ended story-telling, for there is much here that is not clear. To maintain the power of the story, it is important that it be left unclear. The story is premised on the twin realities of continued barrenness and on the prominent presence of Ishmael who could not be ignored. It is possible that some version of the story stopped with verse 6, which marks an ending with the expulsion of Hagar. But as it now stands, the entire chapter is incomplete and looks to chapter 21 for its fruition. The folklore character of verses 1–6 has similarities with 12:10–20 and reports on a family triangle of trouble with which Abraham can hardly cope. No moral judgment need be rendered against the alternative device for securing a son, as this may be attested as a proper legal practice elsewhere in the biblical period. But theologically, the narrative asserts that Abraham and Sarah did not believe the promise. As in 12:10–20, Abraham takes the promise into his own hands again, unwilling to wait for God to work his inscrutable purpose. Calvin calls their faith "defective." That is the main issue to be pursued.

151

Faith is not easy. It calls for a persistence which is against common sense. It calls for believing in a gift from God which none of the present data can substantiate.

1. From the perspective of the faith of Abraham and Sarah, the story is oddly presented. It is structured as a Hagar story. The beginning in trouble (vv. 1–6) is matched by the resolution of the birth (vv. 15–16). Between the beginning in trouble and the ending in birth, the middle section (vv. 7–14) marks the intervention of God through the speech of an angel. Only by inference is this story concerned with Abraham and Sarah.

As in 12:17 and 14:14, verse 7 marks the intervention. This is a curious break in the story. It shows that all parties—Abraham, Sarah, Hagar, Ishmael—would have left well enough alone. All parties except God! It is God who reopens the issue. The positive implication is that God is turned toward the outsider. But in terms of the vitality of the promise, the negative implication of the narrative is that Ishmael is a temptation for Abraham to trust in the fruit of his own work rather than in the promise (cf. 17:18). Thus, Ishmael is a testing which complicates the narrative. Paul has transformed Hagar-Ishmael into a sign of the law that is excessively imaginative (Gal. 4). Yet Paul has seen correctly that even in the Ishmael story itself, Hagar and Ishmael function as an alternative to the promise. They are visible evidence that in the short run, initiative can be taken from God and things will be better.

2. The middle section (vv. 7–14) is dominated by the speech of the messenger, again showing that divine speech is decisive. Thus, the angel speaks four times: *And he said* . . . (v. 8); *The angel of the* Lord *said to her* . . . (v. 9); *The angel of the* Lord *also said to her* . . . (v. 10); *And the angel of the* Lord *said to her* . . . (v. 11). The four speeches build until the final one in verse 11, which is a birth announcement.

a. The birth announcement presents a history alternative to Abraham-Sarah which is also blessed by God. It concludes (v. 13) with a blessing for the banished one. It is vigorous blessing, but it is not the Abrahamic blessing of the land. It is a blessing to be in another place, out of the promised land, living by his own resources, that is, not by the primal promise.

b. The middle portion concludes with an obscure etiology (vv. 13–14). Theologically, we may best follow Frank Cross (*Canaanite Myth and Hebrew Epic,* 1973, p. 46) in seeing here one presentation of the High God El, whose claims are reassigned to Yahweh (cf. 14:19–20). Historically and linguistically, we cannot determine the meaning of the phrasing. Apparently, the name is something like "the God who sees me lives." While that holds some interpretive possibility for the character of this God who cares for the banished, it should not be pursued away from the main issue. The disclosure was not greatly valued in the tradition and is best left in its obscurity.

3. The Ishmael presence suggests two things. Seen vertically, with reference to God, it asserts that God has not exclusively committed himself to Abraham-Sarah. God's concern is not confined to the elect line. There is passion and concern for the troubled ones who stand outside that line. Seen horizontally, from the agenda of Abraham-Sarah, Ishmael is a temptation not to trust the promise. The very child who discloses the *passion* of God for the outsider is no small *threat* to the insider.

The first narrative portion ends with nothing resolved. Sarah's initiative (v. 2) in circumventing the promise has brought conflict (cf. Prov. 30:21–23). Now the promise is jeopardized by this alternative.

The Promise of Everlasting Covenant

Chapter 17 introduces a completely different world of language and presupposition. Whereas chapter 16 preserves the playfulness of anecdote, chapter 17 is ponderous, disciplined, and symmetrical. It is agreed that the text belongs to the P tradition and is more self-conscious in its statement than 16 (J). But the issue is still the same: the powerful claim of the promise and the equally powerful reality of being without an heir. We may suggest four elements which will be useful in exposition.

1. The *promise* to Abraham is here most fully and solemnly asserted. The promise is given in the stylized pattern of P. Throughout P, the promise does not simply crop up at incidental times. It is thematic and is carefully placed to guide the narrative (cf. 1:22, 28; 9:1, 7; 28:3; 35:11; 47:27*b;* 48:4; Exod. 1:7). As presented by P, the whole narrative is now subsumed under the promise. The promise *(a)* is linked to creation, for the language is the same (vv. 6, 20; Gen. 1:28). Thus, Abraham is the first fruit of the new creation. He is the bearer of what is intended in creation. He is indeed "the new creation" (Rom. 8:23; II Cor. 5:17; James 1:18); *(b)* is a *royal promise* (v. 6, 16, 20), undoubtedly connecting Abraham to the Davidic hopes of II Sam. 7; *(c)* is an *"eternal" promise* (vv. 7, 8, 13, 19) assuring

153

permanent well-being in the land; *(d)* concerns the *fundamental relation* of Yahweh and Abraham as belonging to each other. Thus, the promise concludes, "I will be their God" (v. 8). This is a promise more fundamental than even the land. While the action is singularly unilateral and talks only of God's commitment to Abraham, the formula clearly presumes the unspoken counter-theme, "You shall be my people." (Cf. Exod. 6:2–7 for the full formula of P. Cf. also Jer. 7:23; 11:4; 24:7; 31:1, 33; Ezek. 11:20; 14:11; 34:24; 36:28; 37:23, 27.) It is evident that this formula became crucial for Israel (in P as well as in Jer. and Ezek.) precisely in the sixth century exile when normal external supports were collapsing. Undoubtedly Heb. 11:16 is a commentary on this promise: "Therefore God is not ashamed to be called their God." He is not scandalized to be the God of exiles. The promise is a grand and comprehensive one. The point is not lost on Abraham. All of it depends on an heir. The large visions of God require concrete historical reality. And that is not yet given.

2. Closely related to *promise,* perhaps even an alternative version of it, is *covenant* (vv. 2–7). In the entire Abraham narrative, only 15:18 elsewhere refers to covenant. It is likely that the strange ritual of 15:9–11, 17 is an old ritual of covenant-making. But only now is the claim and reality of covenant clearly presented. It is probable that the specific patterning of covenant presented here is relatively late. Nevertheless, as the tradition now stands the covenant is the primary metaphor for understanding Israel's life with God. It is the covenant which offers to Israel the gift of hope, the reality of identity, the possibility of belonging, the certitude of vocation.

3. The central portion of the text (vv. 10–14) is concerned with *circumcision,* the sign and seal of trust in the promise and entrance into the covenant. This text permits reflection on the importance of concrete, institutionalized religious symbolism.

Interpretation must take care not to be distracted with questions about the religious history of the institution. We do not know about the origins of circumcision though they may relate either to quasi-magical practice or to a concern for hygiene. In Exod. 4:24–26 and Josh. 5:2–9, there are older accounts of the practice in Israel. While the practice is older than our text and not confined to Israel, it does have peculiar theological importance for Israel after 587 B.C., when the usual institutional supports for the community disappear. In exile,

154

circumcision helped give identity to the "insiders" of faith who had been declared "outsiders" by Babylon.

Most of the theological issues, as distinct from phenomeno-logical ones, may be comprehended in four affirmations:

a. Circumcision as a liturgic act gives important concrete signification to a theological affirmation. What is said and thought must also be *done*, not only for its dramatic and edu-cational effect, but because "belonging" is in fact accom-plished in this act. The signifier has a role in the things sig-nified. Biblical faith is never cerebral. It is always lived and acted. Belonging to this strange community and trusting in a scandalous promise requires a mark of distinctiveness. Cir-cumcision announces that Israelites belong only to this com-munity and only to this God.

b. Circumcision as a positive theological symbol functioned in Israel as a metaphor for serious, committed faith. Thus, the tradition speaks of the circumcision of the heart (Lev. 26:41; Deut. 10:16; Jer. 4:4; 9:26; Ezek. 44:7). The image suggests yielding affections and will to the covenant partner (cf. Rom. 2:29).

c. Such religious symbols/acts hold enormous potential for empowerment of faith. But there is also risk, for the symbol may lose its theological intent and vitality. It then takes on a life of its own. And in its autonomy, it may become an empty form, nurturing self-deception. Or it may become an instrument of oppression and conformity. As an empty form or as a lever of conformity, it immobilizes rather than empowers. This is appar-ently what happened to the symbol of circumcision. No doubt that is what caused controversy in the early church (Acts 15: 1–5) and evoked the strictures of Paul (Rom. 2:25; 4:12; Gal. 5:2–12; 6:12–16; Col. 3:11). In Christian exposition, it will be important not to limit this critical awareness to the sign of circumcision in which the church has no investment. It is equally important to ask about the temptation to autonomy in our own signs, symbols, and sacraments. Thus, for example, is it possible that baptism has also taken on a life of its own which has no intrinsic relation to the claims of faith?

d. The tradition of circumcision is of importance to Chris-tians, for it illuminates the practice of baptism as an entrance into a new life, a new loyalty to a new community. It is ironic that for all the polemics in the New Testament against circum-cision which is regarded as an empty form or even a barrier to

155

the gospel, nonetheless circumcision is utilized as a type for understanding the meaning of baptism:

> In him also you were circumcised with a circumcision made without hands, by putting off the body of flesh in the circumcision of Christ; and you were buried with him in baptism, in which you were also raised with him through faith in the working of God, who raised him from the dead. And you who were dead in trespasses and the uncircumcision of your flesh, God made alive together with him, having forgiven us . . . (Col. 2:11–13).

The intent in circumcision is also intended in baptism. And like circumcision, baptism has potential either as an energizing symbol for faith or a negative alternative to faith. Thus, Christians have a dialectical attitude toward the institution of circumcision. On the one hand, they are aware of its temptation to become an empty practice. On the other hand, they know no better model for understanding their own sacraments of life and faith. In handling this text, it will be important to keep this dialectic alive and visible.

4. The entire text of Gen. 17 concerns binding Abraham to God in *radical faith.* Yet by verses 17–18, Abraham completely doubts the promise, laughs a mocking laugh, and appeals to the son already in hand. Abraham, the father of faith, is here again presented as the unfaithful one, unable to trust, and willing to rely on an alternative to the promise.

a. We are now able to see the function of Ishmael as a threat to the promise. Abraham is no longer pressed to believe in an heir to be given, for he already has one, albeit in a devious way. Abraham is willing to stake his future on Ishmael. He does not fully understand the promise and its strange character. The laugh and the reference to Ishmael (vv. 17–18) are attempts to avoid the deep and unsettling claim God now makes on him.

b. The failure of Abraham at this point is comparable to the obduracy of the disciples who either do not understand or cannot believe the promise of the gospel. In Mark 8:14–21, the disciples witness the miraculous feeding of 5,000 (Mark 6:30–44) and the 4,000 (Mark 8:1–10). But as soon as the question of bread comes up, they understand nothing. They are unable to believe in the life-giving, future-creating resources present in the person of Jesus. Almost in resignation, Jesus acknowledges their lack of understanding (v. 21). The failure to understand is not a matter of intelligence but of will. They do not understand because of hard hearts (6:52).

156

More acutely, the disciples understand nothing of the vocation of crucifixion or the future of the resurrection. In the passion sayings of Jesus (Mark 8:31; 9:31; 10:33–34) they either resist (8:32), do not understand (9:32), or quarrel about the future (10:35ff.). In every case, they miss the point that in Jesus the power of God is at work to create a newness underived from what is old.

The parallel of the disciples' misunderstandings to the unfaithfulness of Abraham in our text is more than *formal.* There is a second *substantive* connection. The same crisis of faith is present to both. Like the disciples who fail to discern the life-giving power of the bread (I Cor. 11:29), so Abraham fails to discern in God's promise the capacity for new life. As the disciples' inability to understand the passion sayings, so Abraham is unable to accept the discontinuity between barrenness and heir upon which the covenant is premised. The power of God will give a child of promise. But Abraham clings to a son of the flesh. Unlike Peter in his great confession, Abraham understands nothing.

c. The issue in this exchange about Ishmael is exploited in Gal. 4:24–31 by Paul. Paul has seen that the children of necessity cannot inherit. Only the children of free gifts and open promises can enter the Kingdom. The text reflects on transformation from the world of *compulsion* to that of *gifts.* Ishmael is not without his value. Indeed, in 17:20 there is a great promise to him (princes, not kings; contrast v. 6). However, the issue turns on verse 21 and the adversative "But." The primal promise is never to Ishmael. It is solely to this other son, the son given only by grace (cf. a comparable adversative in II Sam. 7:15, perhaps not unrelated in terms of theological tradition).

The Laughter of Sarah

18:1–15, in contrast to the disciplined statement of chapter 17, has more freedom and imagination. It belongs to an earlier stream of tradition with some affinities to chapter 16. It admits of suspense and excitement in the telling, so that the disclosure at its center requires narrative form and expects skillful dramatic presentation.

The primary critical question concerns the identity of the visitor. In the opening scene (vv. 2–8) as well as the departure (v. 16), it is "three men." But in verse 1 as well as the main confrontation of verses 9–15, it is "the LORD." There is no need

157

either to harmonize the two versions or to divide into sources or to seek a Christian statement of the Trinity here. The story is an unreflective account of a revelatory disclosure. That is enough. The vacillation of identity heightens the hidden source from which the disclosure comes. The interpreter will do well to present the story as it is and allow for a playfulness in this regard.

The narrative divides into two parts:

1. In the preliminary section, Abraham is the key actor (vv. 1–8). He dominates the scene in a series of active verbs. An atmosphere of hurry is created (vv. 6–7). Abraham is exceedingly deferential. The narrative wants us to understand that something unexpected and peculiarly important is about to happen.

2. In the second part of the narrative (vv. 9–15) everything is changed. The pace is slowed to allow for the weightiness and drama of the transaction. The initiative has passed to the "stranger(s)." Abraham is a quiet recipient of the news. The point of the narrative (for which vv. 1–8 is the only stage setting) is a birth announcement (v.10). (This announcement has important parallels to the announcements of Judg. 6:12–18 and 13:6. Luke 1 is surely conscious of this narrative.) The form of the announcement with its dramatic sense of amazement matches its substance. The surprise is yet another speech-event in which the world of Abraham and Sarah is decisively changed. Their world of barrenness is shattered by a new possibility that lies outside the reasonable expectation of their perceptual field.

The story is constructed to present the tension between this inscrutable speech of God (that comes as promise) and the resistance and mockery of Abraham and Sarah who doubt the word and cannot believe the promise. Israel stands before God's word of promise but characteristically finds that word beyond reason and belief. Abraham, and especially Sarah, are not offered here as models of faith but as models of disbelief. For them, the powerful promise of God outdistances their ability to receive it.

Once again, this story shows what a scandal and difficulty faith is. Faith is not a reasonable act which fits into the normal scheme of life and perception. The promise of the gospel is not a conventional piece of wisdom that is easily accommodated to everything else. Embrace of this radical gospel requires shatter-

158

ing and discontinuity. Abraham and Sarah have by this time become accustomed to their barrenness. They are resigned to their closed future. They have accepted that hopelessness as "normal." The gospel promise does not meet them in receptive hopefulness but in resistant hopelessness. This story embodies a statement of irony, for the total Abraham/Sarah story is about a call embraced. But in this central narrative, the call is not embraced. It is rejected as nonsensical. And indeed, if no new thing can intrude, if newness must be conjured from present resources, the promise announced here truly is nonsensical.

3. But our interpretation must focus on the overwhelming question of the Lord (v. 14): "Is anything impossible for the LORD?" This question means to refute and dismiss the protests of the hopeless couple. The refutation is not stated as a proposition, assertion, or proclamation but as a question. It comes as a question because the gospel requires a decision. And that decision cannot be given from above. It must come from Abraham and Sarah.

a. "Is anything too hard for the LORD?" That is the question around which this confrontation revolves. It is an open question, one that waits for an answer. It is the question which surfaces everywhere in the Bible. We must say it is the fundamental question every human person must answer. And how it is answered determines everything else.

If the question of the Lord is answered, "Yes, some things are too hard, impossible for God," then God is not yet confessed as God. We have not conceded radical freedom to God. We have determined to live in a closed universe where things are stable, reliable, and hopeless. If, on the other hand, the question is answered, "No, nothing is impossible for God," that is an answer which so accepts God's freedom that the self and the world are fully entrusted to God and to no other. The question must not be given this answer lightly or easily. The way the story hopes we will answer is to yield utterly to this gracious one, to let the initiative for our lives flow from our hands.

b. To do the impossible! The gospel in this text reaches beyond our frames of reference. It breaks out of the parameters of reason, wisdom, morality, and common sense. It questions normal epistemology. It shatters accepted value systems. It is the heaviest criticism available about our definitions of reality.

4. Very much depends on the answer of Sarah and

159

Abraham. Their answer is a negative one (vv. 12–15). There is a curious dialogue at the end, humorous but filled with pathos: "Sarah: denied saying, 'I did not laugh. . . .' He said: 'No, but you did laugh.' " And here it is left, quite unresolved. The laughter of disbelief seems to refute the invitation implicit in the question. Abraham's and Sarah's world of possibility has been assaulted. But they have beaten off the attack. The story leaves them thinking their presumed world is still intact.

But not everything depends on their answer. The resolve of God to open a future by a new heir does not depend on the readiness of Abraham and Sarah to accept it. God keeps his own counsel and will work his own will. It will happen, if not in a context of ready faith (which is here denied), then in a context of fearful, resistant laughter. The narrative ends. Sarah and Abraham still doubt.

But the word has been uttered. Sarah and Abraham and the listening community can never again live pre-promise. All their lives are now impacted by this promissory word which will find its own fulfillment. The Bible is a testimony finally "fully convinced that God was able to do what he had promised" (Rom. 4:21; cf. Josh. 21:43–45), whether we are ready or not.

5. While the final biblical testimony is convinced of God's ability to do the impossible, the question of this text continues to circle throughout the history of Abraham's family. Is anything too hard for God? Is God's sovereign power finally limited to our expectations? It is a question that is easily translatable: Is God God? Or is their some other norm or power which limits this? Can the world finally say "no" to the creator? Can Sarah and Abraham finally keep their future closed in spite of God?

a. The question comes to the oppressed Israelites in the face of the Philistines (Judg. 13:18–25). They ask concerning the gift of a young deliverer who will invert history. The question is also posed in the exile. First, would God really abandon his people (Jer. 32:27); and then, is God able to raise his people from death to newness, from barrenness to hope (Jer. 32:17)?

b. In the New Testament, this is the same question asked concerning Elizabeth (Luke 1:37). And Mary is presented, in contrast to Sarah and Zechariah, as the one who did not doubt (v. 38). Indeed, she is a model for the faith of the community, "for she believed there would be a fulfillment of what was spoken to her from the Lord" (v. 45).

160

But the question does not linger with babies and birth narratives. It moves to the impossibility of discipleship, the impossibility of faith, and the impossibility of new community. Every believer and every believing community knows about the futility of our best faith, of our deep resistance to the gospel just when we intend faithfulness. In that recognition, this lordly word to Peter and the disciples is the very same lordly word given first to Abraham and Sarah and then to the whole church: "With humans it is impossible, but not with God for all things are possible with God" (Mark 10:27—author's translation). Finally, in the mouth of Jesus the question to Abraham and Sarah is uncompromisingly answered. It is answered by this one who faced fully that God is free to be God. Jesus calls his followers to embrace that radical faith with him. "Nothing will be impossible to you" (Matt. 17:20).

c. The exposition we have urged leaves itself open to misunderstanding, as though faith makes every desirable thing possible. But not everything is promised. What is "possible" is characterized only as everything promised by God. That is, only what corresponds to God's good purposes is possible. He has promised a future in a new community, but not everything we would seek.

To the disciples seeking salvation in Mark 10:27, Jesus gives his uncompromising answer. Poignantly, the issue surfaces for Jesus himself in the scene at Gethsemane. There he, too, seeks and raises the question of Gen. 18:14, praying: "Father, all things are possible to thee" (he affirms what he affirmed in 10:27 to the disciples). "Remove this cup from me; yet not what I will, but what thou wilt" (Mark 14:36). Everything is possible to God —except one thing. The one thing not possible is the removal of the cup. What God will not (cannot?) do is to circumvent the reality of suffering, hurt, the cross. Thus, our text does not permit a casual triumphalism that simply believes everything is possible. Because of the character of God, everything is possible for those who stay through the dark night of barrenness with God. For Abraham and Sarah, there is no simple, painless route to an heir. And when we come to the shattering of Genesis 22, we shall see that the *"impossibility* of God" freely given is not a painless, tension-free possibility.

161

Thus the strangers departed (Gen. 18:16) with the question still unanswered. The answer is given only provisionally in

Genesis, always waiting to see if God can do what he says. Faith is a scandal. The promise is beyond our expectation and beyond all evidence. The "impossibility possibility" of God deals frighteningly with our future. No wonder Sarah was frightened (cf. v. 15). These three episodes (16:1–16; 17:1–27; 18:1–15) together serve to extend the uncertainty of the promise in 15:4. The promise is given. But the community is called to a long wait (cf. Mark 14:37–42).

Genesis 18:16—19:38

This unit contains three distinct elements. At the center is the story of Sodom and Gomorrah (19:1–29). Anticipating that narrative is a remarkable theological reflection (18:16–32). Appended to the Sodom story is an old narrative about the children of Lot (19:30–38). The three pieces are varied in their texture and presupposition and come from different hands. They are held together by the figure of Lot. The whole unit is loosely linked to 18:1–15 by the device of "the men" in 18:16, 22, who in 19:1, 15 have become the "angels/messengers," though here as well it might be read "men." Though the stories had no original connection, the "men/messengers" device is employed for placing them back to back with the theological reflection of 18:16–32 set between them. As it stands, then, there is a parallel presentation of *(a)* the visitation of the messengers to Sarah and Abraham (18:1–15) and *(b)* the disaster of Sodom and Gomorrah (19:1–25). Both are presented as strange intrusions by God.

The "strange men" in Gen. 18:1—19:29 have two tasks. One is *to promise a beginning.* This is done in 18:1–15 with Sarah and Abraham. The other task is *to effect an ending.* This will be done in 19:1–28. The awesome task of God (and his messengers) is to cause both *beginnings and endings.* Displacement is caused for Abraham and Sarah and for Lot. It is God's singular power to cause both beginnings and endings (cf. Deut. 32:39; I Sam. 2:6; Isa. 45:7; Ps. 75:7). Times of beginning and ending are times when the mystery of life becomes most urgent and when the hardest theological questions must be asked. Peter Berger has termed such intrusions of God *Rumors of*

162

Angels (1969). There are two kinds of "rumors of angels" in this text, a rumor that an heir is to be given (18:1–15) and a rumor that a city is to be destroyed (19:1–28). One is as inscrutable as the other.

This text must be interpreted with extreme care. It easily lends itself to conclusions which are wooden, mechanical, and concrete-operational about the reality of God. Unless interpreted carefully, this passage will be taken as support for mistaken theological notions that are uncritical and destructive. The most obvious dangers of perverse interpretation relate to *(a)* the stylized and stereotyped description of judgment and destruction (19:24–28); *(b)* the appeal to numbers in 18:26–32 which will too easily reduce God's righteous purposes to arithmetical calculation; and *(c)* the offense of Sodom which in popular usage and perhaps in 19:5 is homosexuality. If these three factors—stylized judgment, numerical calculation, and a simplistic moralizing on homosexuality—are brought together according to popular understandings, the text will yield a teaching remote from the gospel. The following discussion suggests that such conclusions are far removed from the intent of the text.

The text admits of rich expository possibility because it juxtaposes an early unreflective tale (19:1–28) and a self-conscious theological teaching (18:16–32). As we shall see, 19:29 is the hinge by which the two texts may be brought together. Because 18:16–32 seems to be a later reflection on the early narrative of 19:1–28, we will begin with the earlier material so that we may understand the subsequent reflection. (Chapter 19, verses 30–38 will be treated as an independent unit.)

The Destruction of Sodom and Gomorrah (19:1–28)

This narrative about the visitation of God with its generalized view of wickedness and its stylized notion of destruction (19:1–28) does not seem to belong to the historical narratives of Israel. It is more akin to the comprehensive statements about human history found in Gen. 3—11. It is only the connection to Lot which has dictated its placement in the Abrahamic materials. Without that linkage, this story has no more historical rootage than the stories of Cain or Noah. The story (together with 18:16–32 and especially 19:29) is structured to show the tension between the *faith of Abraham* and the *waywardness of humanity.*

163

INTERPRETATION

1. The initial visitation (vv. 1–11) parallels the visitation of Abraham in 18:1–8. In both cases, the host practices hospitality. Here, of course, the practice of hospitality is much more demanding and perilous. (The episode of vv. 4–9 is parallel to the sordid account of Judg. 19.)

Of late, special attention has been given to the nature of the sin of the men of Sodom. Aside from the popular name of "sodomy" from Sodom, the text does not give much help in determining the offense. The act is identified only by a desire to "know" *(yd')* (v. 5). That term, in this narrative, is now popularly taken as a desire for homosexual relations. This is supported by the parallel of Judg. 19:22–25. Judges 19 also uses the term *nebālāh* ("folly") to characterize an unacceptable sexual act. (Cf. 34:7 for the only other use of the term "folly" in Genesis.)

It is likely that interpretation can go in a more general or a more specific direction. It is possible that the offense of Sodom is understood with specific reference to sexuality. But if such a reading is accepted, the turbulent mood of the narrative suggests gang-rape rather than a private act of either "sodomy" or any specific homosexual act.

However, the Bible gives considerable evidence that the sin of Sodom was not specifically sexual, but a general disorder of a society organized against God. Thus in Isa. 1:10; 3:9, the reference is to injustice; in Jer. 23:14, to a variety of irresponsible acts which are named; and in Ezek. 16:49 the sin is pride, excessive food, and indifference to the needy.

It is likely that interpreters will disagree about the "sin of Sodom," but the evidence in any case shows that the Bible itself did not agree that the sin was homosexuality. The use of the term "outcry" in 18:20–21; 19:13 argues in the direction of a general abuse of justice. (Cf. Isa. 5:7 without any explicit indictment. Cf. also Luke 10:8–12.) It may be that sexual disorder is one aspect of a general disorder. But that issue is presented in a way scarcely pertinent to contemporary discussions of homosexuality.

2. Gen. 19:15–23 offers a digression in which the one being saved is reluctant and resistant. This unit may originally have been an independent tale concerned with the name of the village Zoar. In its present place, this particular conversation with Lot suggests two important motifs. First, the imperative to flee (v. 17, cf. v. 20) is a standard form used to warn someone

164

to escape from a general destruction of war (cf. Josh. 6:17, 22; Jer. 6:1). Like Rahab, who is given special attention, Lot and his family are made an exception to the general destruction. Second, the special attention to Lot as an exception to the general rule is cited as the special "loyalty" of the Lord (v. 19) by which God "spares" (v. 16) through a special recognition of him (v. 21). This is peculiarly meaningful language. But as the narrative now stands, we are given no reason for the special rescue. Only at the end (in v. 29) does the narrator give us the reason. The reason finally given turns out to be quite unrelated to the event or to Lot. It is grounded only in Abraham, who appears to be remote from the entire story.

3. The imagery of destruction (vv. 24–28), "a rain of brimstone" is surely a stylized image (cf. Deut. 29:23; Isa. 34:9; Ezek. 38:22; Ps. 11:6; Job 18:15; Luke 17:29; Rev. 9:17–19; 14:10; 19:20; 20:10; 21:8). It has become a conventional usage without intending literal detail. It is used for its general dramatic effect. It has been popularly taken as a historically descriptive term. While such descriptive language undoubtedly has its base in an actual experience of volcano or earthquake, it surely has become poetic imagery especially utilized by apocalyptic traditions which break out of historical descriptive language. It is a characteristic way of speaking about the most horrible judgment on human history that is thinkable. Tamer images are inadequate for such judgment. Used in this way, the imagery need not be taken literally. Thus in Isa. 30:33, it is clearly figurative. The imagery attempts to speak seriously about God's judgment of the world. But there is no warrant for a one-dimensional literalism to which some may be tempted by this passage. The powerful imagery should not cause us to miss the structural development of the narrative. These verses are in fact a *sentence* of death which respond to the general *indictment* of verse 13.

4. The reference to Lot's wife (19:26) is commonly explained as a comment upon a notable salt deposit, perhaps by the Dead Sea. Notice the use made of the tradition in Luke 17:32 where it is related to more intense discipleship. Here, also, Sodom's destruction is used in the context of apocalyptic teaching.

165

5. Having examined the Sodom passage in episodes, we may now consider the structure of the entire passage. It is the structure which discloses the intent of the whole. The unit

consists of two dissonant elements; the large public narrative and concern for the special destiny of Lot.

a. The large public narrative, having to do with the wicked city, is a simple presentation of a lawsuit in which disobedient people are punished.

(1) There is an *indictment* in 19:13 for sin of a generalized kind:

> . . . because the outcry against its people has become great before the Lord . . . (cf. 18:20).

(2) There is a *judgment of death* in 19:24–29 on the basis of the indictment:

> Then the LORD rained on Sodom and Gomorrah brimstone and fire from the LORD out of heaven; and he overthrew all the cities
> . . .

The structure is essentially theological and conventional, reflective of the prophetic faith of Israel. It closely parallels the lawsuit form we have seen at the beginning of the flood narrative. The theological claim is that humanity (the two cities) has been *disobedient* to Yahweh and must be *destroyed*.

Insofar as Genesis 19 revolves around indictment and judgment, it presents a view of moral reality that is widely shared in popular religion. It does not need any special advocacy because it is commonly held by all sorts of people who have never reflected on the matter but who are inclined to link the rule of God with moralistic matters. That is, God is the one who punishes "sinners." The primary structure of chapter 19 reflects a simple teaching of retribution in which "good people prosper and evil people suffer" and die. The narrative has a quite uncomplicated assumption which lives in both secular and religious circles. This retributive theology is the simplistic premise of much wisdom teaching in the ancient world. It is the ground for blood-thirsty revenge in contemporary society. There are enough texts and enough practical experiences to make such a view credible. Interpretation faithful to the gospel need use no energy on behalf of such a world-view. That is why the text is misunderstood if chapter 19 is taken alone. It permits a "scare theology" of moralism which, by itself, is remote from the gospel. As we will see in our next section, this rather obvious theology is criticized and modified by a fuller statement of the gospel in the text now linked to 19:1–29.

b. A *counter-theme* in the narrative is the *special destiny* of Lot. This counter-theme appears in the practice of hospitality (vv. 1–11) and then in the rescue (vv. 15–23). Thus, we may contrast the two statements about *Sodom* and *Lot:*

	of Sodom:	of Lot:	
the assessment:	guilty (v. 13)	hospitable (vv. 1–11)	
lawsuit			*deliverance*
the judgment:	destruction (vv. 24–28)	rescue (vv. 15–23).	

The two patterns are nicely woven together.

The rescue of the "remnant" presents an alternative to the general destiny. But it is apparent that the rescue of Lot and his family has no general significance. It does not alter the essential pattern of retribution. The religion offered here is still closed and fated.

c. Only in verse 29 does the juxtaposition of the *judgment speech* (against Sodom) and the *special rescue* (of Lot) receive comment. The narrator has shrewdly held the main point until now. The difference is not in Lot nor even in Yahweh, but in Abraham. The remembering of Abraham is as crucial here as is the remembering of Noah in 8:1. This narrator does not permit even remembering Abraham to make a difference in the total narrative. Abraham's impact is limited to Lot. In that respect, the impact of Abraham is much less than that of Noah in the parallel narrative. This narrative still waits for a "better" gospel.

A Theological Critique

The argument of 18:16–32 seeks to break open the closed, fated view of the world given in 19:1–28.

1. Gen. 18:16–32 embodies a kerygmatic critique of the popular religious conviction which is dominant in 19:1–28 and perhaps written in direct response to it. If the two chapters are taken on the same plane, then chapter 19 prevails, at least in terms of dramatic impact. But if 18:16–32 is understood as a bold and tentative theological probing, then it raises a hard theological issue that will never again be silenced by the simplicity of 19. That issue is still not silenced: Is there in the gospel an alternative way of being in the world? Or are we consigned to the brimstone that inevitably follows our failed, faithless action (19:24–28)? In his study of wisdom literature, Hartmut

167

Gese has observed that Israel has largely taken over a retribution scheme that is taught all over the ancient Near East (*Lehre und Wirklichkeit in der Alten Weisheit,* 1958, pp. 45–50). But it is the peculiar problem and persistent possibility of Israel that its fresh discernment of God provides for the intrusion of grace between the indictment (19:13) and the punishment (19:24–28). Our exposition concerns how that graceful wedge (18:22–33) is asserted as criticism of the *quid pro quo* of retribution (19:1–28). Much is at stake theologically in this issue, for we must decide if there is good news, even for Sodom. Much is at stake pastorally, for countless persons are trapped in this closed structuring of reality and yearn for the intrusion of grace.

2. As 18:22–33 is offered as a critique of 19:1–28, so Abraham dramatically offers a critique of Yahweh. It is as though Yahweh rather simplistically accepts popular practice reflected in 19:1–28 until Abraham raises the question of 18:22–33. It is as though Abraham is Yahweh's theological teacher and raises a question that is quite new for him. The question concerns Yahweh's willingness to set aside the closed system and approach the world in another way. Abraham is the bearer of a new theological possibility. He dares to raise risky questions with Yahweh.

The relation of Abraham and Yahweh in this passage is worth noting in detail. We may observe a remarkable textual problem which illuminates the matter. As it stands, the text in 18:22 now says, "Abraham stood before the Lord," suggesting the subordination of Abraham to Yahweh. This is what we should expect. But a very early text note (not to be doubted in its authority and authenticity) shows that the text before any translation originally said, "Yahweh stood before Abraham." The picture is one which agrees with our comment about Abraham as Yahweh's theological instructor. It is as though Abraham were presiding over the meeting. But that bold image of Yahweh being accountable to Abraham for this theological idea was judged by the early scribes as irreverent and unacceptable. Therefore, the text was changed to read as we have it. But the earlier version suggests with remarkable candor what a bold posture Abraham assumes and how presumptuous is the issue he raises. Whether the textual change is accepted or not, this text reports that Yahweh must think a quite new theological thought. God is pressed by Abraham to consider an alternative.

3. In 18:17–19, Abraham is legitimated by God most re-

markably. These three verses are especially rich in expository possibility. They leave no doubt that Abraham stands, in all his humanity, as the historical bearer of Yahweh's purposes. He is the one chosen, blessed, and charged by Yahweh. He is the one to receive all of God's promises. The text offers not only a remarkable statement about God but also about Abraham. (These powerful credentials enable Abraham to issue his challenge to Yahweh in vv. 22–33.) Three points should be noted:

a. The promise of 12:1–3 is reiterated (v. 18), including the reference to other peoples (here perhaps Moab and Ammon via Lot; cf. 19:30–38). In that regard, 19:29 is a crucial text linking Abraham to the well-being of the others. As we shall see, that verse shows Abraham is effective in his vocation for the others.

b. The "chosenness" of Abraham is expressed, the only time it is stated so explicitly (v. 19). With high irony, the term used is *yada*, "to know," precisely the word used in 19:5 for the defense of Sodom. This point should not be lost in interpretation. The identical verb is used for Yahweh's choice of Abraham and Sodom's aggression against the strangers.

c. The chosenness of Abraham is not an end in itself. Its purpose is to do Yahweh's purpose of righteousness and justice (v. 19). This is the only occurrence of this word pair (righteousness and justice) in Genesis. The word pair elsewhere is used to summarize the teaching of the prophets (Isa. 5:7; Amos 5:7, 24; 6:12; Jer. 23:5; 33:15). In Isa. 5:7, the two words occur together in juxtaposition with "outcry," the same word that is used in Gen. 18:20–21 against the cities (cf. 19:13). Gen. 18:19 is widely regarded by commentators as an intrusion into the text, as a teaching alien to the Abrahamic tradition which is excessively demanding and conditional. But as it now stands, the verse offers a sharp contrast between Abraham's vocation and the popular view of retributive justice in 19:1–28. The vocation of Abraham (1) contrasts with the viciousness of Sodom, and (2) provides occasion to ask about Yahweh's righteousness. The righteousness and justice of Abraham are not simply moral obedience. They are also a passion for the well-being of the very ones who have violated God. Calvin says of Abraham that in this passage he has a "sense of humanity." As a result, Abraham calls into question the sense of humanity operative in the sinful city and on the part of Yahweh. Yahweh's sense of humanity is no more acceptable to Abraham than is the practice of Sodom.

169

The narrative takes pains to establish Abraham's uncommon qualifications and authority so that he may daringly raise with Yahweh a question that must be raised. Like its counterpart in the flood story (cf. 6:6), this text offers a remarkable theological innovation. In the flood narrative, the innovation was about the pain in the heart of God. Here the innovation concerns God's valuing the righteous more than craving the destruction of the unrighteous.

4. Verses 17–19 present Abraham as Yahweh's unexpected associate in matters theological. This prepares us for verses 23–33. In these verses, Abraham raises the question which explodes not only the presuppositions of the old story of chapter 19 and popular presuppositions about morality but also (if we may put it so), the presuppositions Yahweh holds about indictment and punishment. In the words of Schmidt (*De Deo,* BZAW 143: 150–156[1976]), the question is this: "Can God, if he is really God and not a capricious tyrant, destroy an entire city?" That is, can God who is genuinely God be content with the unflinching indictment-punishment scheme of chapter 19? Or must the true God intervene in his gracious freedom and free graciousness to break apart the bond of indictment and punishment?

a. The subject of these central verses (18:23–33) is righteousness. They ask about the nature of God's righteousness and its power and authority in the face of wickedness. The relation of the innocent to the guilty (note the shift to juridical language) does not concern the rescue of the innocent remnant from the great company of the wicked.

To be sure, such a preoccupation with the special individual in the face of collective guilt seems to surface in chapter 19 in relation to Lot and his family. And it is an important agenda in Ezek. 14:12–20; 18:5ff. There it is affirmed that the righteous can save themselves from the punishment of the whole. But Ezekiel is clear that they can save only themselves. For Ezekiel, there is no "acquittal by association," no vicarious righteousness that one may have in behalf of another. In this text, however, Abraham dares to press beyond Ezekiel and to raise that very question.

b. The conventional calculus, reflected in Gen. 19, is that innocent people have power only to save themselves. Guilty people can take down with them others who may be innocent. But the guilty may not be saved by those same innocent ones. That is, the future-creating power of guilt is stronger than that

170

of innocence. With all proper deference to such conventional theology, Abraham asks two pressing questions:

Will you indeed destroy the innocent with the guilty (18:23)?

Shall not the judge of all the earth do justice (18:25)? In these questions, Abraham urges God that he should act like God and not like a childish, score-keeping litigant.

Between the two questions in verses 23 and 25c is sandwiched the double refrain (v. 25):

Far be it from thee . . .
Far be that from thee!

That standard translation of the assertion is weak and misleading. It is really a cry, "That is profane!": contaminated, impure, polluted. That is, Abraham urges that such a practice is unworthy of the holiness of God, for the holiness of God must preclude what is profane. The argument is not based on what is morally attractive but on the character of God's holiness. If God should act in such a calculating way, he diminishes and jeopardizes his own holiness. Thus Abraham (or the innovative theologian speaking in this role) forges a link between the *compassionate justice of God* (in his dealing with human history) and *God's holiness* (in his own claim to be God). What is at issue is not simply *equity in human history* but *the character of God.* While Abraham is never irreverent or insulting, the boldness and force of his argument is reminiscent of Job in his most passionate argument (cf. Job 31:35). And the reasoning of Abraham parallels that of Ezekiel, who finally concludes that God is gracious, not because of the claims of the guilty, but for the sake of his own name, his own reputation (Ezek. 20:9, 39). Note that in Ezek. 20:9, "that it should not be profaned," the Hebrew term "profaned" is the same as that twice used by Abraham ("far be it . . ." RSV) in verse 25. Thus, hope for humanity comes to be rooted in God's defense of his own character and reputation. That is precisely the ground of Abraham's challenge to God here.

c. On the basis of such an argument, Abraham gets down to concrete cases concerning the relative vicarious power of righteousness and wickedness. Conventionally, a few guilty people can cause the destruction of the whole community and the power of innocence is limited to the innocent persons themselves. The questions of Abraham carry another possibility

171

which God must now consider. It is the possibility that innocent people have the capacity to save others and the power to override the destructiveness of guilt. That is the theological principle urged. The remainder of these verses is an exploration about the quantity of innocent people it will take. The process, like barter in a Near Eastern bazaar, moves from fifty to ten.

We need not focus on the numbers, for that is a literary device and not to be taken literally. Schmidt has suggested that the numbers refer to military or administrative units. It is like asking how many military companies are needed for the security of the division (cf. Exod. 18:25; Amos 5:3). The numbers are incidental. The principle is established. The result of the argument is that it will take only a very small number of righteous ones to save a community, even though it is largely populated with guilty people. According to the dramatic movement of the account, that represents a major move on God's part. God is now more attentive to and more moved by those who obey than those who do not. Such an argument questions every caricature of God as the score-keeper and guardian of morality who is ready to pounce and judge and punish. No, God is more ready to celebrate, acknowledge, and credit for all the right-relatedness of a few.

d. The discussion ends with a dismaying abruptness. First, its abruptness is striking because it ends at a figure of ten (v. 33). One might insist, if we were calculating mathematicians, that that ending shows there must be ten and that nine will not do. But, one would fail to see the point. Rather, the conversation breaks off because the point is established that the power of righteousness overrides evil. The dramatic exploration need not be carried further. Second, the narrative is abrupt because after the deep struggle of chapter 18 the story of chapter 19 goes ahead as though nothing is changed. That is likely so because (1) chapter 19 is old traditional material that could not be altered in the telling and (2) because the dialogue of chapter 18 is a new theological probing that only raises a fresh question still to be pursued rather than reaching a firm conclusion as a basis for chapter 19. The possibility raised by Abraham is perhaps too radical. It is suggested and then left to germinate in the heart of God. The issue remains between *new affirmation* (18:23–33) and *old tradition* (19:1–28). The principle of a new righteousness is affirmed in 18:22–33. These verses (19:1–28) sound as though the concern is only to rescue the innocent (Lot and his

172

family) without a care for the guilty. The popular theology of
19:1–28 moves in the direction of individualism and will be
easily accepted by conventional believers. Previously, 18:22–33
carries with it a more difficult theology that will be intellectu-
ally more demanding. It stands against the usual moralism of
each receiving his or her due. It is the good news of 18:22–33
and not the convention of 19:1–28 that moves toward Jesus of
Nazareth. And like a subtle reprise, even in the conventional-
ism of chapter 19, 19:29 adds one whisper from chapter 18. Lot
is saved not by his righteousness but vicariously by the power
of Abraham:

> So it was that, when God destroyed the cities of the valley, *God
> remembered Abraham,* and sent Lot out of the midst of the over-
> throw, when he overthrew the cities in which Lot dwelt.

By the new mathematics of 18:22–33 (and 19:29), *one* is enough
to save (Rom. 5:15–17).

5. This teaching of a new righteousness which has power to
save may be pursued in several directions.

a. As a minority report, this teaching is reflected in other
Old Testament texts. In his remarkable exegesis, Von Rad has
pointed to two crucial texts.

1) First, Hos. 11:8–9 (which we have considered in relation
to the flood narrative) presents the move made by God in his
own embrace of righteousness. In an explicit reference to
Sodom and Gomorrah (in v. 8, Admah/Zeboiim—Sodom/
Gomorrah), God breaks out of the convention to say that he will
not destroy. He resolves not to act like "man," that is, so that
the guilty are punished, but to act like God (which is all
Abraham asked). That is very different. The contrast of God and
"man" is the contrast of saving mercy and retributive vengeance. Worth noting is the verb *haphak,* rendered "recoil" in
the RSV of Hos. 11:8: affecting God's innards in shattering ways.
This verb is the same used in Gen. 19:21, 25, 29 and is rendered
"overthrow" to describe the earthquake. Hos. 11:8–9 asserts a
new dimension of God which is closely related to our narrative.
This text argues that God has taken the earthquake into his own
person rather than against the city and that God will not be
defined by human conventions. This does not mean that God is   173
indifferent or careless or no longer concerned about guilt, but
that he turns those passions upon himself for the sake of the
world.

2) The other text worth noting (as Von Rad has done) is Isa. 53:5, 10. Perhaps this is the quintessence of biblical teaching about vicarious suffering in redemptive ways. This poem seems to have made a premise of the question raised in Gen. 18. It is now assumed that the innocent one has saving power in the lives of others, not by easily preempting the guilt of others, but by the capacity to receive it into one's own body and there to rob it of its deathly power and passion.

b. This story has characteristics reminiscent of the flood narrative of Gen. 6:5—9:17. There we have seen that in the crucial turn of 8:1 everything hangs on the miracle that "God remembers." In our present text, 19:29 partakes of both the older teaching of 19:1–28 and the new proposal of 18:16–33. In that pivotal verse, the turn again happens because "God remembers." In the flood narrative, creation is saved because God remembers Noah, the one who is righteous (6:9). In our text, Lot and his family are saved because God remembers Abraham, the righteous one. The "turn" ending the flood (8:1) is paralleled by the "turn" which limits the brimstone (19:29).

c. The capacity of one to save others is the ground of Paul's argument about the righteousness of God in Rom. 3:21–26. The righteousness of God known in Jesus Christ is a righteousness apart from the law:

> This was to show God's righteousness, because in his divine forbearance he had passed over former sins; it was to prove at the present time that he himself is righteous and that he justifies him who has faith in Jesus (vv. 25–26).

For Paul, righteousness apart from the law means that God has given up calculations, exactly the proposal of Abraham in 18:22–33. Thus, our text stands as the source of a powerful theological claim. It announces that the freedom of God has broken the death-grip of the indictment-judgment scheme. The capacity to break that scheme (which condemns us all and every city) is the substance of God's holiness. So far as the Abraham-Sarah tradition is concerned, the categories have shifted from *barrenness/heir* (Gen. 15:1–6), where Abraham's faith battle was fought, to *wickedness/rescue.* The categories have changed, but the issue is the same, namely, God's readiness to break the death categories of necessity that imprison our lives. It is the faithful man Abraham (Gen. 15:6; Rom. 4:3) who discerns that God breaks the hopelessness of barrenness and the fearfulness of wickedness by his overriding holiness.

d. The reality of God's *new righteousness* is asserted in 18:22–33. The new righteousness is not calculating, is not for selected individuals, and is not a passive administration of deserved consequences. Rather, the new righteousness is an active power to overcome evil in the world.

6. While our text concerns the new righteousness in the life of God, we may note that the new righteousness concerns human faith and conduct as well. Thus in Matt. 5:20 and Rom. 10:1–5, the disciples of Jesus are enjoined to a new righteousness reflective of God's new righteousness. The quintessence of that new righteousness is summarized in Matt. 5:43–48 as love of enemies. That indeed is God's new righteousness: He loves his enemies and overcomes the hostility aimed at him (cf. Eph. 2:14–16).

a. There are resources here for a staggering new announcement of the person, power, and holiness of God. Many people live in a terror of God which is rooted in moralism, assuming that God has no other agenda than to keep the indictment-punishment scheme operative. Indeed, that seems to be the premise of the appeal for faithfulness in II Pet. 2:6–10. In that situation of persecution, the apostle appeals to a rather undeveloped notion of retribution. But our text will break the stereotype. God is not an indifferent or tyrannical distributor of rewards and punishments. Rather, God actively seeks a way out of death for us all.

b. On the other hand, there is a bold pastoral resource here for a new valuing of human vocation. It is easy enough to grow cynical and imagine that nothing matters anyway, for evil is too overwhelming. It is equally easy to grow selfish as if there is some private well-being available to us. This text refutes both. First, there is no private escape, for there is solidarity among us and we are in it together. (This is the argument of 18:22–33, though in 19:29, the older theology reappears.) Second, the virtue and obedience of faithful persons are valued by God and have redemptive potential.

7. The text ends in 19:27–28. Abraham goes to see. And what he sees is the smoldering, utter quiet after the devastation. All life has been silenced. There is only death—and hopelessness. It is a dramatic scene which we have no difficulty conjuring. It is a scenario available in a quick way by nuclear warfare,

or in a slow way by the squandering of our resources, or simply by the slow cancer of inhumaneness. It is a scene well within our imagination and within our grasp. That is what father Abraham had to see. The story urges that we must see it as well. There we stand! We are thrust into our vocation of caring obedience. It is the resource that can turn wrath and keep death at a distance. With Abraham, we must study the scene of destruction and know something urgent about God's call to us.

In considering that call, we may return to the choosing of Abraham in our text. In 18:19, Abraham is celebrated as God's precious choice. In this quite self-conscious teaching, Abraham is offered as a way to think about ourselves as faithful. He is, of course, a model of rectitude in his own person. By him many are blessed. But most remarkably in this text, the faithfulness of Abraham consists in boldly pressing God to be more compassionate. He does not flinch from urging God and even offering himself as a theological teacher to God so that God may think more clearly and responsibly about his own vocation. There is something unembarrassed about Abraham which helps us to see intercession as nearly strident in the face of God. We must not miss the point. This revolution in the heart of God (cf. Hos. 11:8–9) is because Abraham intervened. Intercession does matter (cf. James 5:16). This is not *pro forma* prayer. The prayer of Abraham goes beyond that of Job (Job 31). Job prayed only *for himself* in his presumed righteousness. Abraham prays *for the others* who are recognized by all as unrighteous. Abraham disputes with God about the meaning of his Godness. It is clear to both Abraham and to Yahweh (in that order) that God is not a tyrant but really God. And from that flows good news.

The Family of Lot

We need only mention 19:30–38 as a saga not related to our main consideration. It appears to be a primitive story to explain the origin of two tribes who are designated as bastards. Doubtless it is a story which would have been more popular in Israel than in Moab or Ammon. We should observe, however, that no stigma is attached to the action of the mothers in the narrative. In fact, they appear to be celebrated for their bold and heroic action, which surely stands beyond convention. In any case, the new children at least come of pure stock. Lot and his daughters are clearly treated as members of the family of promise. In an odd way, this is one more evidence of the inclusive attitude of

176

Genesis toward other peoples. If Lot is saved because of Abraham (cf. 19:29), then it is also true that Moab and Ammon are blessed because of Abraham (cf. 12:3; 18:18).

Genesis 20:1—21:34

In these two chapters we shall take up themes already encountered. In 20:1–18, we are concerned with a motif already found in 12:10–20, Abraham's use of Sarah for his own safety. In 21:8–20, we again have to do with the contention caused by Ishmael, a theme related to chapter 16. In between the two (21:1–7), the birth of Isaac, the child of promise, is finally reported in an understated account.

The narrative of barrenness draws closer to the promised birth. But it is an unsure and circuitous route to the fulfillment of the promise. As part of that circuitous route, the present narrative is a strange assortment of materials, the order of which appears to be unintentional. We have grouped these two chapters together partly for convenience and partly because the Abimelech materials of 20:1–17 and 21:22–34 form an envelope. Enclosed within the Abimelech-Abraham account is the narrative of the two sons of Abraham in 21:1–21 (Isaac in vv. 1–8 and Ishmael in vv. 9–21). The material on the two sons will primarily concern us. We will begin our comment with the Abimelech narratives.

Abraham and Abimelech

1. The material in 20:1–18 is recognized widely as an alternative version of the same themes in 12:10–20. Here, however, the theme has much less of the folklore flavor and much more self-conscious theological tone. (Reference should be made to the comments on the earlier passage of 12:10–20.) It appears that the shaper of 20:1–18 had before him the older material which strangely presented Abraham caught in a bald lie. That material has now been reworked along other lines, making them less damaging to the reputation of Abraham. The text will be especially useful in teaching situations to explore the internal interrelations of Scripture and to study the dynamic and intentionality of the traditioning process.

177

INTERPRETATION

a. This text has been carefully shaped. As Weimar has seen (*Untersuchungen zur Redaktionsgeschichte des Pentateuch* BZAW 146: 69–72), the text is set in a neat series of three groups of speeches. First, the scene is set (vv. 1–2) with a framework of sojourn. Then follow (1) the speeches between Yahweh and Abimelech (vv. 3–8), (2) the speeches between Abimelech and Abraham (vv. 9–13), which are presented as *controversies,* and (3) the speeches and actions of Abimelech and Abraham which appear as *conciliatory* (vv. 14–18). In the first scene, we may be amazed that Abimelech the foreigner has his own intense interaction with Yahweh, the God of Israel, without the mediation of the Israelites. The discussion between Abimelech and God is like a lawsuit. Abimelech is accused, gives his defense, and is found innocent. The vindication of Abimelech uses the word "integrity" (vv. 5, 6), a word used to describe great piety. It has been applied to Abraham (Gen. 17:1) and to Job (Job 1:1, 7; 2:3), the utterly pious man. Here it is the non-Israelite who is pious.

The second scene (vv. 9–13) is a dispute between the Israelite and the non-Israelite. Abraham's excuses for himself are feeble and unconvincing. While he reports that he acted because Abimelech did not fear God, it is evident that (1) Abimelech did fear God, and (2) Abraham feared many things more than he feared God. Thus the contrast is made that the one most directly called to faith and fear is the one who models faithlessness and fearfulness. And so Calvin can say, "Abraham attributed less than he ought to God's providence." The contrast between Abimelech and Abraham is not unlike the contrast Jesus makes between the trusting outsiders and the resistant insiders: "I have not found such faith in all of Israel" (Matt. 8:10). Here Abimelech models faith lacking in Abraham, the father of faith.

Nonetheless, the concluding reconciliation (vv. 14–18) presents Abimelech completely dependent upon and subservient to Abraham. Abraham emerges from the narrative with his power and authority not only intact but enhanced. That is, the one who lied (even though the narrative tries to put a positive reading on it in contrast to 12:10–20) is still the one preferred. The morally upright one is still dependent on Israel. The preeminence of Abraham here rests not on Abraham's virtue, but on God's promise.

b. The story has a strangeness about it, perhaps because

178

the theological narrator wanted to make a point that ill-fitted the traditional material with which he had to work. As it stands, the text makes the claim that Abraham is the chosen of God, not by words (which are lacking), nor even by faith (which is feeble here), but only by God's incredible grace. Thus, we can hardly advance on Calvin's thematic summary, "The infirmity of man and the grace of God." The infirmity of both men is evident. But God's grace overrules. It overrules with Abimelech in keeping him from a deathly sin (v. 6). It overrules even more completely with Abraham. Morally devious though he is, it is his prayer which is heard (vv. 7, 17). It is not only, as Paul has argued, that Isaac is a son only by the promise (Gal. 3—4). It is even the case that Abraham is the father only by the promise. This man who nearly brought death to Abimelech by his scheming (v. 3) is still the means by which God gives life and blessing (vv. 17–18). Unworthy as he is, he is God's chosen way of life to the nations.

2. The material in 21: 22–34 contains a number of fragmentary pieces which revolve around Abimelech and provide etiological material about Beersheba related to "seven," "oath," and "well." These verses appear to continue the Abimelech theme from 20:18 without interruption. The unit begins with a programmatic theological statement, "God is with you." That formula is a summary theme of divine leadership which becomes even more central in the promise to Jacob (28:15). The narrative has the non-Israelite affirm the primal position of the Israelite. As we have seen, God is with Abraham in his unqualified graciousness.

But that does not make Abraham easier to trust. Therefore, this narrative pursues a covenant to bind Abraham to Abimelech in mutual loyalty *(ḥesed)* (v. 23). The remainder of the narrative reports *(a)* the making of the covenant, *(b)* the taking of solemn oaths and *(c)* the handling of a dispute over water rights. It may be useful to reflect here on the slippage that is apparent both to Abimelech and Abraham concerning the difference between the *vertical affirmation* ("God is with you") (v. 22) and the *horizontal reality* ("deal with me loyally") (v. 23). A just way in power relations in the human community does not naturally flow from right faith. Provision must be made for institutional guarantees of the social dimension. While Abraham is celebrated as a designated man of God, in the arena of human commerce he must fully pay his due as must all the

179

others. No one interprets his designation by God as a proper means of securing economic advantage.

The Birth

In the context of the two Abimelech passages of 20:1–18 and 21:22–34, we arrive finally at the birth of the awaited child. In 21:1–18, we have the central fulfillment within the Abraham tradition. The birth of the child is the fulfillment of all of the promises, the resolution of all of the anguish. And yet this narrative is peculiarly understated. One could almost miss the point. Except for the mention of "old age" (vv. 2, 7), this account does not even acknowledge there has been a problem. The fulfillment seems strangely anticlimactic after the troubled anticipation. This report seems oddly detached from what has gone before.

1. But this in no way diminishes the crucial character of the text. Everything hangs on it. This is evident in the opening verse, which contains the double refrain: "As he said" *('āmar)*, "as he promised" *(dābar)*. This is no birth brought about by natural processes. Natural processes had all been found wanting. This is an unwarranted birth in every usual sense. It now comes only by the promise of God. The text holds together the *word of God* and the *birth of the child.* Indeed, the whole story depends on that coupling. It insists that one cannot separate the *eternal purpose of God* and the *concrete biological reality.* Twin temptations always face the church in the practice of its faith. On the one hand, there is the temptation to cling to the word of God in an excessively spiritual way and to minimize the fleshly concreteness of the birth. On the other hand, there is the inclination to cling singularly to the reality of the birth in an excessively secular way and regard the word of promise as of no importance.

Concerning the former, under the influence of Von Rad, patriarchal interpretation by biblical scholars has fully appreciated the power and overriding importance of promise in these narratives. Nonetheless, it seems evident that in most modern settings it is a difficult task to bear effective witness to the promissory character of faith. To do so requires a break with our prosaic world-view which does not believe in active, world-changing words from God. Our propensity is somehow to accommodate this strange mystery to our reason so that our conventional world is unshattered by this inexplicable event.

180

But the announcement of birth by promise is not the primal claim of the text. Rather, it is that the promise is kept to this *old-age pair.* Alongside the difficulty of promissory proclamation in a world of technical reason, there is also among us the alternative temptation to romanticize the promise and remove it from the arena of historical reality. Care must be taken that the promise is seen as fulfilled to none other and through none other than these the world regarded "as good as dead" (Heb. 11:11–12).

2. These two dangers (classically identified as ebionism and docetism) of course appear in our understandings of the birth of Jesus. In that regard, those who take a high view of the virgin birth tend to deny not only the human father but also the mother. Conversely, those unaccustomed to scandal regard the entire assertion of a peculiar birth as meaningless religious rhetoric. The problem of expressing this finely balanced gospel faithfully is the key problem of an incarnational faith: life comes only through *promise;* the promise comes only in *the body of the hopeless ones.* Like the birth of Jesus, Isaac's birth is announced by the *angels* (18:1–15). But the birth is not apart from the *tired, aged reality* of Abraham and Sarah. The promise has fleshly fulfillment.

3. The birth is as promised. Everything depends on the power and loyalty of the promise-maker. Surely it is in direct reference to this that Paul can say, "It is not as though the word of God had failed" (Rom. 9:6). That is the faith issue which exposition of this text must face. The word of God is scandalous. It never comes to fruition as we expect it. Some conclude it fails and they are driven back to their own seemingly adequate resources. Others conclude it fails but have no resources and so are driven to despair. Even father Abraham cannot release the child of the slave-woman (cf. 17:18). Even this father of faith flinches from the radicalness.

The son comes from the couple who is "as good as dead." There was in them no reason for hope. Kerygmatic faith rests on the candid affirmation that human reality does have within it ground for hope. That is why Paul (Rom. 4:17) must link the birth of Isaac to *(a)* the creation of the world *ex nihilo* and *(b)* the resurrection of the dead. Thus Ernst Käsemann has argued that *resurrection* (from the dead), *justification* (only by grace), and *creation (ex nihilo)* are all affirmations about the same reality (cf. H. H. Schmid, "Rechtfertigung als Schöpfungsge-

181

schechen," in J. Friedrich, W. Pohlmann, and P. Stuhlmacher, eds., *Rechtfertigung*, 1976, p. 403). They bear witness to the peculiar power of God to evoke new life by his graciousness, not out of a "life-potential," but in a situation where there is nothing on which to base hope. Like the Pauline presentation of justification, the birth of Isaac drives us away from ourselves to total and singular reliance upon the God who is found faithful.

"Miracle" (and this is a miraculous birth) is not the violation of a natural order. It is the concrete assertion that God is faithful to his promises. Miracle is having disclosed again that we are not bounded by necessity but by the freedom of God's love, offered in faithfulness.

4. For that reason, Sarah laughs (v. 6). Beyond the etymological explanations which link Isaac to "laugh," and beyond doubtful embarrassment, Sarah laughs because "God has made laughter for me." By his powerful word, God has broken the grip of death, hopelessness, and barrenness. The joyous laughter is the end of sorrow and weeping (Matt. 5:4; Luke 6:21; John 16:20–24). Laughter is a biblical way of receiving a newness which cannot be explained. The newness is sheer gift—underived, unwarranted. Barrenness has now become ludicrous. It can now be laughed at because there is "full joy" (John 16:24). No wonder birth, and especially the birth of Isaac, stands as a principal model in the Bible for God's faithfulness. It is precisely by the surprise and impossibility (cf. 18:14) of Isaac that the fortunes of Israel are inverted. Gunkel, therefore, rightly connects this passage to Ps. 126:

> When the LORD *restored the fortunes* of Zion,
> we were like those who dream.
> Then our mouth was filled with laughter,
> and our tongue with shouts of joy;
> then they said among the nations,
> "The Lord has done great things for them."
> The LORD has done great things for us;
> we are glad (Ps. 126:1–2).

"Restoring fortunes" is the way Israel speaks about the end of exile (Jer. 29:14; 30:3; 33:7, 11, 26). Isaac is the end of every exile in the kingdom of necessity.

182

The Other Son

Upon the weaning of Isaac (v. 8) our narrative abruptly changes moods. Verses 9–21 are about the conflict between the

son of promise and the son of the slave woman. This narrative
has important points of contact with chapter 16.

The conflict between the two sons, between the two
mothers and within the reluctant, ambiguous father, is complex (cf. 16:1–6). The story knows what it wants to tell. Isaac is
the child of the future. But the story has no easy time imposing its will on the characters. Ishmael will not be so easily reduced. He has some claims. He has a claim because he is the
oldest son of father Abraham. He is not adopted, not an intruder, but born to the man of promise. And Abraham is not
ready to discard him (cf. 17:18). The father is not yet ready to
relinquish the realities of primogeniture. (See the same anguish for Isaac with his oldest son, 27:37.) But most compelling, God has this special commitment to Ishmael (cf. 16:7–12).
For some inscrutable reason, God is not quite prepared to
yield easily to his own essential plot. And so like two men coping with a cantankerous woman, God says to Abraham, "Let
Sarah do what she wants. Do not worry because I will make it
right" (vv. 12–13). In the midst of this narrative about Isaac,
there is extended attention to a promise of being a great nation (v. 18) and an assertion of God's abiding presence with
Ishmael (v. 20) even as with father Abraham (v. 22). Most
movingly and most delicately, Ishmael is given water in the
wilderness (v. 10). God cares for this outsider whom the tradition wants to abandon. There is no stigma attached to this
"other" son. All are agreed on the preciousness of Ishmael—
Yahweh, angel, Hagar, Abraham—all but Sarah. She has a
vested interest which closes that reality to her.

So the *celebrated* birth of Isaac and the *anguished* settlement of Ishmael are set in juxtaposition. The one has rights
which are honored. The other evokes laughter and is celebrated. This text does not force us to choose. And that should
give us pause. The text is unambiguous: Isaac is the child of
promise. That much is not in doubt. The narrative knows the
"canonical" story must be presented. That story is an Isaac
story. But the text is equally clear that God is well inclined
toward Ishmael. The "other son" is not to be dismissed from the
family. The narrative holds us to the tension found so often in
this narrative, the tension between the one *elected* and the
not-elected one who is *treasured*. It is, of course, evident that
Ishmael's promise is short of the full promise given to Isaac. And
yet it is a considerable promise not to be denied. God is atten-

183

tive to the outsider (cf. 30:17). God will remember all the children like a mother remembers all her children (cf. Isa. 49:15).

The History of the Two Sons (Gen. 21:1–21)

1. The predominant exegesis of this narrative is again that of Paul in Galatians 4. It is clear that both pairs, Hagar-Ishmael and Sarah-Isaac have now become theological types. Powerful theological meanings are assigned to them that run well beyond the claims of this text. Hagar and Ishmael, children of Mt. Sinai, are located in the kingdom of necessity, coercion, and fate. Sarah and Isaac, heirs of Mt. Zion, are located in the kingdom of gift, freedom, and destiny. Christian interpretation of our Genesis text (when juxtaposed with that of Gal. 4) has two tasks: *(a)* to be clear that the Genesis narrative does not contain all of this typology but *(b)* that our Christian tradition has now chosen a certain lens through which to view the narrative. The test for the expositor is not to insist on the "original" meanings of the narrative, but to find the ways in which interpretation illuminates our human lot in the context of the gospel. Without being reductionist in a Pauline-Lutheran sense, it is clear that the fate of "natural man" and the "pilgrimage of the children of promise" are two distinct ways in which life can be discerned. Isaac is a *gift* to be explained in no other way than as a wonder. And Ishmael is a child gotten by skillful *determination and planning.* As oldest son, Ishmael is the child of "entitlement" in possessing all natural rights. Thus, the allegory of Paul is not remote from what is claimed in the Genesis account. It is clear that living in the world of skillful determining, planning and competence is problematic. Such a way easily crushes the spirit and consigns one to the world of compulsion, control, and alienation. Such a way tries to live "by bread alone" (cf. Deut. 8:3). Against that, Paul understood that to live in the arena of "wonder" is the way to freedom and joy.

2. The juxtaposition of the two sons in this chapter also permits us to reflect on Jesus' parable of the two sons (Luke 15:11–32). While there is no explicit link between the texts, the flow of argument is quite parallel. In the parable, the older son with all the rights pleases the father, obeys the rules and deserves much. He is Mt. Sinai embodied (perhaps not unlike Ishmael). But the younger son receives life as a gift. As we have seen with reference to Luke 13:16; 16:19–31 and 19:1, the Lukan gospel understands the intent of the Genesis narrative here. The exegesis of Paul and the parable of Jesus, like the

narrative of Genesis, understand that God's freedom is not limited by barrenness, old age, or primogeniture. God alone has power to make new.

Genesis 22:1–24

This chapter is among the best known and theologically most demanding in the Abraham tradition. It poses acute questions about the nature of faith and the way of God with his faithful creature. In many ways, this narrative brings the Abrahamic tradition to its dramatic resolution. The chapter forms a counterpart to the call to faith at the beginning of the cycle (12:1–4a). In 22:18, the promise of 12:3 is reaffirmed. To be sure, there are other chapters yet to follow. But after this one, the dramatic intensity of the whole is noticeably relaxed. Thus, our present text serves as a way to bring together the main affirmations of the Abrahamic tradition.

We have considered Abraham under the general heading, "God's Call Embraced." With some vacillation, Abraham has been a man of faith, trusting in God's promise. This is most directly evident in his ready departure in 12:1–4, his response to the promise in 15:6, and his embrace of circumcision in 17:22–27. All of that has come to fruition in 21:1–8 in the birth of Isaac. After that birth, what could come next to extend the dramatic development of the tradition is not readily apparent. If the story of Abraham had ended with the birth of Isaac (21: 1–7), we would have a tale of origins.

But in our present text, unexpected things happen. Only now do we see how serious faith is. This narrative shows that we do not have a tale of origins, but a story of anguished faith. The narrative holds rich promise for exposition. But it is notoriously difficult to interpret. Its difficulty begins in the aversion immediately felt for a God who will command the murder of a son. Erich Auerbach (*Nemesis,* 1953, 12) has discerned that this text, like others in Israel, is "fraught with background" and is presented to permit free play of interpretation. The intent is not clear. It requires some decisions by the interpreter.

185

The narrative is principally confined to verses 1–13. Verse 14 is a place name etiology which has been attached. Where some have urged cultic emphases here, our exposition must try to stay with the theological claim of the text. It is of no value to find in this story an exchange of animal sacrifice for human sacrifice, as it addresses much more difficult issues.

Verses 15–18 are commonly regarded as a secondary addition. However, our exposition will indicate these verses are not inappropriate in the setting of the narrative. No comment will be made here on the genealogical data (vv. 20–24).

The Structure of the Passage

1. We may begin our study by observing the intricate and symmetrical construction of the passage. The text is organized around three series of summons/response statement interchanges (with other variable elements):

Series 1	Series 2	Series 3
Summons by God (v. 1)	Summons by Isaac (v. 7)	Summons by Angel (v. 11)
Abraham's response (v. 1)	Abraham's response (v. 7)	Abraham's response (v. 11)
God's command (v. 2)	Isaac's question (v. 7)	Angel gives release (v. 12)
	Abraham's statement (v. 8)	

We may observe the distinctive way in which the second series is presented. The first and third series have only a/b/á, that is, summons, response, address. But peculiarly in the second series, we have a/b/á/b́, summons, response, the question by Isaac, and *a fourth element* (in v. 8). This fourth element falls outside the normal structure and is therefore noteworthy: "God will provide himself the lamb for a burnt offering, my son." There can be little doubt of the cruciality of this statement on structural grounds. It is without parallel in the first and third series. It stands utterly alone as the point of stress, violating the normal pattern of the three parts.

2. The second structural feature we may observe is the parallel between the command (v. 2) and the resolution (v. 12):

186

Take your son, your only son Isaac, whom you love . . . (v. 2)

You have not withheld your son, your only son . . . (v. 12).

These two verses provide the limits of the drama. The first creates the crisis. The second resolves the crisis. The actual crisis takes place between verses 2 and 12 and is articulated in verse 8, which we have already observed as decisive. Thus verse 8 stands between and plays against verses 2 and 12. Verses 2, 12 express the inscrutable intention of God. We know no more about the resolution of verse 12 than we do of the command in verse 2. We do not know why God claims the son in the first place nor finally why he will remove the demand at the end. Between the two statements of *divine inscrutability* stands verse 8, offering the deepest mystery of *human faith and pathos.*

3. We should observe that substantively (though not necessarily in terms of structure) there is a close linkage between verses 1 and 12 in another way. Verse 1 sets the test, suggesting God wants to know something. (Notice the intent of God to "know" in 18:21, which also leads to a crisis.) It is not a game with God. God genuinely does not know. And that is settled in verse 12, "Now I know." There is real development in the plot. The flow of the narrative accomplishes something in the awareness of God. He did not know. Now he knows. The narrative will not be understood if it is taken as a flat event of "testing." It can only be understood if it is seen to be a genuine movement in the history between Yahweh and Abraham. The movement is from "take" (v. 2) to "you have not withheld" (v. 12), and from "test" (v. 2) to "now I know" (v. 12). The move in both forms is accomplished by the affirmation in verse 8, an enigmatic statement of unqualified trust. It is only verse 8 that permits the story to move from its problem to its solution. The verse contains the primary disclosure about God: "God will provide." In the same verse, we also have the main disclosure about Abraham: "he trusts."

The Interplay of Abraham and God

In turn, we shall consider the situation of Abraham and of Yahweh in this narrative.

1. The narrative locates Abraham before a word.

a. As we have seen, three times Abraham is addressed and three times he answers, "Behold, here I am." That is the most we know about the location of Abraham. He stands before a word. He is addressed. He answers immediately and faithfully. His response to Isaac in the second speech is the same as his

187

response to God in the first and third speeches. Addressed by the purposes of heaven or the pathos of earth, he is a man ready to be addressed. He does not flinch from answering. To be addressed is to know that he is grounded in another and that he does not retain initiative for his own existence. Abraham knows that. That is the radical obedience of Abraham. He understands fully that he is a creature of the word. There are no reasons (in this narrative, in contrast to some others) within his own person to *dispute, delay, or resist the address.* As in 12:4, his response is full and immediate.

b. Verse 8, which we have seen to be structurally central, merits special attention. "God will provide." It is a statement of utter trust and confidence, but one that is quite open-ended. Abraham does not tell Isaac all he wants to know because Abraham himself does not know. He does not know at this moment if Isaac is God's act of provision. He does not know that God will provide a rescue for Isaac. It could be either way: Isaac or an alternative to Isaac. Abraham does not know, but he trusts unreservedly. He is the man ready to commit his way:

> Commit your way to the Lord;
> trust in him, and he will act (Ps. 37:5).

Abraham finds his only refuge in the divine provider whom he finds inscrutable but reliable. Abraham has turned from his own way to the way of God which lies beyond his understanding (cf. Isa. 55:8–9) but upon which he is prepared to act in concrete ways.

2. The narrative leads to a new disclosure of God. At the beginning, God is the *tester* (v. 1). At the end, God is the *provider* (v. 14). These two statements about God form the ultimate frame for the story. Calvin and Luther are candid and unflinching before this contradiction in God. Calvin says, "The command and the promise of God are in conflict." Luther says this is a "contradiction with which God contradicts himself." The *promise* of God is that through Isaac your descendants will be named (21:12; cf. Rom. 9:7). The *command* of God is that Isaac must be killed. It follows that there will be no descendants, no future. We are back to barrenness. The entire pilgrimage from 11:30 has been for nought. Abraham has trusted the promise fully. Now the promise is to be abrogated. Can the same God who promises life also command death?

The expositor must take care not to explain, for it will not

188

be explained. But without explanation, the text leads us to face
the reality that God is God. The narrative concerns Abraham's
anguished acknowledgment that God is God. The narrative
may be connected to Exod. 20:1ff.: The God who *delivers* is
the one who *prohibits* any alternative God, any alternative
trust. He insists on being trusted only and totally.

I am Yahweh your God, who brought you out . . .   [deliver]
You shall have no other gods before me.   [prohibit]

God is shown to be freely sovereign just as he is graciously
faithful. That God provides shows his gracious faithfulness. That
God tests is a disclosure of his free sovereignty. Abraham comes
to an awareness that the two marks of God are always encountered together. The problem of this narrative is to hold together
and embrace both the *dark command* of God and his *high
promise.* This strange contradiction in the heart of God is another glimpse of the same reality we have seen in the flood
narrative (6:6–7; 8:20–22). Luther is correct to say that no
human reason or philosophy comprehends these two marks of
God. Faith is the readiness to answer to this strange contradiction in God. Faith says "yes" to the promise, which is no small
matter. It also says "yes" to the command which makes the
promise only a promise.

3. There are important parallels to this episode in the narrative of Job 1—2. Like Job, Abraham is a blameless man (17:1)
who fears God exceedingly (cf. Job 1:1, 8; 2:3). Like Job,
Abraham is prepared to trust fully the God who gives and who
takes away (cf. Job 1:21). It may be that in probing this text,
appeal to the Job narrative will be useful.

The poem of Job may very well reveal to us the innards of
Abraham which chapter 22 keeps discreetly hidden. The dialogue of Job with his friends (Job 3—27) and with God (Job 29
—31; 38—42:6), expresses the wonderment and dismay of this
utterly faithful man who finds the costs of God in deep tension
with the joys of God. Neither the Joban poetry nor this
Abraham story are about evil or the justice of God. Rather, they
ask about faith which, as Kierkegaard has shown, drives us to
dread before the self is yielded to God.

The text moves past the clear and prominent theme of
Abraham's perfect obedience to the issue of God. Perhaps the
expositor may lead the listening community to be inquisitive
about this word "God." What do we mean when we say that

189

precious word? What different meaning does the word have in serious faith from that in the innocuous single-dimensional piety of civil religion? In what ways are we prepared for the God of Job and Abraham who gives and takes away, who promises but also commands and tests? In the same way, to what extent are we prepared for the radical God who meets us in the Crucified One who is risen? With these two God-fearing men, we are urged to move beyond Job's friends as well as beyond contemporary simple civil piety which knows no dread and which goes from strength to strength.

4. This narrative yields this question about God: Does God really test in this way? The premise of the story is that he does.

a. It is evident in Exod. 20:20; Deut. 8:16; 13:3; 33:8 that testing is a common theme for a time of syncretism, like the Ahab-Jezebel period (cf. I Kings 17—19; 21). The term "testing" *(nāsāh)* is prominent in Deuteronomy, which faced syncretism most directly. The testing of Israel by God is to determine if Israel would trust only Yahweh or if it would at the same time look to other gods. But to understand "testing" (or "proving"), it is necessary to consider not only *nāsāh,* the word used in our text. Alongside it reference should be made to *bahan,* also "testing." (Cf. Pss. 7:9; 17:3; 26:2; 66:10; 81:7; Prov. 17:3; I Chron. 29:17 and the numerous uses in Jeremiah, 6:27; 9:7; 11:20; 12:3; 17:10; 20:12.) The imagery of this term (different from *nāsāh*) is a more directly juridical concept. In addition, reference may be made to testing by *Satan,* particularly to the personification in Job 1—2. These terms together with *nāsāh* make clear that testing is no marginal notion in the faith of Israel. It occurs only in a faith in which a single God insists upon undivided loyalty, a situation not applicable to most civil religions. Testing is unnecessary in religions of tolerance. The testing times for Israel and for all of us who are heirs of Abraham are those times when it is seductively attractive to find an easier, less demanding alternative to God. The testings which come in history (and which are from God) drive us to find out whether we mean what we say about our faith being grounded solely in the gospel.

b. In our sophistication, we may find the notion of "testing" primitive. But Christians may take no comfort that this is in the Old Testament. The same issue is clear in the New Testament. Nowhere is it more visible than in the Lord's prayer. How odd that settled, complacent believers pray regularly, "lead us not into temptation" (Matt. 6:13; Luke 11:4). The prayer com-

190

mended by Jesus is that God should not put us in a testing situation where we are driven to choose, decide, and risk for our confession of faith. The prayer is the petition that our situation of faith may not be so urgent that we will be found out. The prayer bespeaks fear that we will be found wanting if such testing comes.

The early church in the New Testament knew there were times of testing (cf. Mark 13:9–13; I Pet. 1:7; II Pet. 2:9). One dimension of testing is the temptation to accommodate the world, to yield to the pressures which lead to a compromised confession. The testings make clear the deep conflict between the purposes of God and the purposes of "this age." For the most part, faithful people cringe from having to decide. Few respond as readily as Abraham. This narrative asserts that we must decide about relying only on the promise. The testing is finally inescapable.

5. But there is a second issue here concerning God. While it is not ordinarily raised, it is equally difficult. The narrative begins with the testing by God. But the narrative ends with God providing. That statement may be taken for granted. But it is no less problematic. It is no less an act of radical faith on the part of Abraham to concede the last statement than to accept the first statement. To assert that God *provides* requires a faith as intense as does the conviction that God *tests*. It affirms that God, only God and none other, is the source of life. Abraham's enigmatic statement (v. 8) and the conclusion (v. 14) confess that the alternate ram did not appear by accident, by nature, or by good fortune (v. 13). They mean, rather, that the same God who set the test in *sovereignty* is the one who resolved the test in *graciousness*. In a world beset by humanism, scientism, and naturalism, the claim that God alone provides is as scandalous as the claim that he tests.

The term "provide" (vv. 8, 14) is difficult. It is an unusual translation of the term *rā'āh*, otherwise rendered "see." Karl Barth (*Church Dogmatics* III, 3, pp. 3, 35) helpfully links the term to *pro-video*, "to see before," "to see to," "to see about." Thus, the Latin rendering nicely makes the connection between "see" and "provide." Barth appeals to our text as the ground for his entire understanding of providence, the doctrine of God's full provision of what is needed for his creatures. Theologically, the difficulty with God as provider may be understood in two ways. First, the notion is problematic for our modern

191

reasonableness with reference to specific gifts. Quite concretely, the visible emergence of the ram is credited to the "seeing for" which God did. Second, to link our word "see" generally to the affirmation of providence makes the broadest claim possible that life is held in the purview of God and that we are destined to live according to his good will. Barth links this to a general concern for care and preservation. While the word itself appears to be awkward in the narrative, the generally accepted rendering of it in terms of *pro-video, pro-vide, providence* opens up important theological resources. This confession of Abraham (v. 8) and the conclusion drawn (v. 14) make clear that the entire episode of testing is set in the context of God's good care and sustaining concern.

The Old Testament elsewhere acknowledges God's providential and benevolent action in the narrative of manna (Exod. 16:15), in the resolution of leadership (I Sam. 16:1, 17), and in the extravagant recognition of the goodness of life (Pss. 104: 27–30; 145:15–19). God is the one attentive to the needs and hungers of his creatures.

The same radical affirmation about God the provider is evident in the New Testament. The same church which prays about the *testing* prays for the *providing*. The Lord's prayer acknowledges that there is no other source of provision. And so the church prays daily for bread (Matt. 6:11; Luke 11:3). The New Testament church confessed that it is only the sustenance of God that makes life possible (Matt. 6:25–33; 7:11; Mark 6: 30–44; 8:1–10; Eph. 3:20–21).

The Mystery of Testing and Providing

The life of Abraham, then, is set by this text in the midst of the contradiction between the *testing* of God and the *providing* of God; between the sovereign freedom which requires complete obedience and the gracious faithfulness which gives good gifts; between the command and the promise; and between the word of death which takes away and the word of life which gives. The call to Abraham is a call to live in the presence of this God who moves both toward us and apart from us (cf. Jer. 23:23). Faithful people will be tempted to want only half of it. Most complacent religion will want a God who provides, not a God who tests. Some in bitterness will want a God who tests but refuse the generous providing. Some in cynical modernity will regard both affirmations as silly, presuming we must answer to

192

none and rely upon none, for we are both free and competent. But father Abraham confessed himself not free of the testing and not competent for his own provision.

1. The text asserts that God is this way with his people. There are deep problems with affirming that God both tests and provides. The problems are especially acute for those who seek a "reasonableness" in their God. But this text does not flinch before nor pause at the unreasonableness of this story. God is not a logical premise who must perform in rational consistency. God is a free lord who comes as he will. As the "high and holy One," God tests to identify his people, to discern who is serious about faith and to know in whose lives he will be fully God. And as the one among the "humble and contrite," God provides, giving good gifts which cannot be explained or even expected. We are not permitted by this narrative to choose between these characteristics of God (cf. Isa. 57:15).

Luther finally had to say that this contradiction of testing and providing (of the promise of Isaac, the taking of Isaac, and the late rescue of Isaac) will only be reconciled in the word of God. Short of the word of God, our reason and our faith are baffled. That word which reconciles is that he who is dead lives. It is the word of resurrection which leads us through this text to the God who surprises us with life. That is not to say simply that Isaac would be raised had he been killed. For that is speculation and is not the claim of the text. Heb. 11:17–19 links Isaac to the power of the resurrection, but not in terms of raising a dead man. Resurrection concerns the keeping of a promise when there is no ground for it. Faith is nothing other than trust in the power of the resurrection against every deathly circumstance. Abraham knows beyond understanding that God will find a way to bring life even in this scenario of death. That is the faith of Abraham. That is the faith of the listening community. And that is the meaning of the ram at the last moment. A substitute is not brought by Abraham but given by God in his inscrutable graciousness.

2. The dialectic of testing and providing, of taking and giving, may be linked appropriately to the reality of Jesus of Nazareth. In the three Marcan passion sayings to his disciples (Mark 8:31; 9:31; 10:33–34), Jesus each time speaks of crucifixion and resurrection. These two events belong together and cannot be separated. The two together, the giving of Jesus' life and his receiving of new life, summarize his claim. They assert all the

193

news available to the church. The crucifixion of Jesus is the
✓ ultimate expression of the testing of God. Like Abraham, Jesus
in Gethsemane (Mark 14:32–42) is in a situation where he must
choose. In that situation, Jesus and the Father find that Jesus,
like Abraham, trusts only the promise. And just as the passion
sayings speak of the testing of the crucifixion, they also speak of
the resurrection as God's ultimate providing. The resurrection
is the miracle by which God provides new life in a situation
where only death is anticipated. The dialectic of *testing/provid-
ing* in our narrative becomes the dialectic of *crucifixion/resur-
rection* in the faith of the church.

3. Our narrative illuminates the life of Jesus, with special
reference to crucifixion and resurrection. In a parallel way, the
story expresses the character of faithful discipleship. The structure of the text corresponds to a central teaching on discipleship: "For whoever would save his life will lose it; and whoever
loses his life for my sake and the gospel's will save it" (Mark
8:35).

4. Paul understands this. In his letter to Corinth, he brings
the themes to a marvelous junction. In writing about worship
of idols, he concludes: "God is faithful, and he will not let you
be tempted beyond your strength, but with the *temptation* will
also *provide* the way of escape, that you may be able to endure
it" (I Cor. 10:13). It is the same God who tempts and provides.
The connection is that God is faithful. In the end, our narrative
is perhaps not about Abraham being found faithful. It is about
God being found faithful.

Genesis 23:1—25:18

The Abraham narrative has now run its course and reached
its goal. Its sweep from 12:1 to 22:19 stretches from an initial
trust in the promise (12:1–4) to a final radical risk of the heir
(22:1–14). The Abraham tradition in its main part is enveloped
by the promise of 12:1–3 and its reiteration in 22:15–18. Now
194   the promise can be transferred to the next generation. In the
chapters now before us, we deal with three elements in the
transition of the promise to the generation of Isaac: *(a)* the

death of the *mother* (23:1–20), *(b)* a *wife* for the son and heir (24:1–67) and *(c)* the death of the *father* (25:1–18). These transitional elements are presented after relaxation of the main tension of the narrative in 22:1–13. These present chapters function in the Abrahamic narrative much like 34—36 in the Jacob narrative and 47:28—50:26 function in the Joseph account. They treat necessary concerns. But in each case, they lie outside the main dramatic development.

The Burial of the Mother (23:1–20)

This self-contained unit (23:1–20) concerns the burial of Sarah, the one who had lied for Abraham (12:10–20), mocked at the promise (19:8–15), and finally laughed the Easter laugh (21:6). The structure of the passage is straightforward. It begins with the need for a grave (vv. 1–4) and concludes with the resolution of the problem (vv. 17–20). Between the problem and the resolution stands a long, detailed narrative of negotiation (vv. 5–16) which enables the movement to resolution.

It may be that the narrative reflects genuine practice of negotiations which are inordinately polite and carefully conducted to secure the best price. It is commonly thought that the narrative reflects careful legal procedure as the way of securing a clear title properly attested by witnesses. While specific parallels to Hittite practice in the second millennium has been suggested, the practice more likely reflects a still more common Near Eastern procedure.

Perhaps the narrative reflects no more than a specific commercial transaction. Nowhere is there any mention of God. The narrative gives no hint of any theological intention. It may best be left at that. In any case, beyond the actual securing of the grave, one may note the almost humorous style of negotiations, governed by the verb "give" (vv. 4, 9, 11, 12) which is only a euphemism for buying and selling. If there is one thing neither party intends to do, it is to "give" anything away. This tone is culminated by the speech of Ephron (v. 15). He finally, reluctantly, names an amount, probably a high amount and in effect says, "What is 400 shekels among friends?" The answer is, "A lot." But that is the basis of the settlement. (The maneuvering for a suitable settlement is reminiscent of intense bargaining between Abraham and God in 18:23–33.)

Perhaps the narrative should be left in this restrained way,

195

as an actual report of a transaction without more meaning intended. If, however, we are to press beyond this, three expository comments are in order:

1. There is a suggested incongruity between Abraham's self-effacing identity (v. 4) "a stranger and sojourner," and the title the Hittite commander uses for Abraham (v. 6), "a prince of God." The RSV offers an alternative rendering of the address as "a mighty prince." Such a rendering is, of course, possible; but it cannot be unimportant that the Hebrew adjective is *"elohim"*— "God." If this translation be accepted, it suggests that, for the narrative, it is the *landless sojourner* who is *God's prince.* It is the landless one who bears all the promises and lives in hope. It is this very incongruity which intensifies the main concern of Genesis. Luther correctly draws attention to a suggestive New Testament link in Eph. 2:19. The landless Abraham, by the power of the gospel, is made a fellow citizen. By the end of our narrative (vv. 17–20), Abraham has fully acquired land and "belongs" in a new way.

2. It is possible that securing the grave with a clear legal title is a symbolic but concrete guarantee of possession of the whole land. Since the text is assigned to the Priestly tradition and dated to the sixth-century exile, the memory of this transaction reassures exiles, those again made "strangers and sojourners." They do, in fact, have a secure place. This little piece of land signifies the whole land, certainly promised and undoubtedly to be possessed.

3. Special reference may be made to Jer. 32:1–15, probably a contemporaneous text. This is the only other passage in the Old Testament in which such elaborate care is taken with a land title. Perhaps the intent of Jer. 32 is to interpret Gen. 23. In that text, the action is as careful about legal procedure as in our text. But Jer. 32:15 explicitly gives a theological reading to the legal action: For thus says the LORD of hosts, the God of Israel: Houses and fields and vineyards shall again be bought in this land.

The legal action of purchase is a full investment in a promise against the present circumstance. To be sure, such a reading of Gen. 23 goes beyond the explicit statement of the text. It presumes that this text, like others in Genesis, has promise just beneath its surface. Thus Abraham and Sarah "acknowledged that they were strangers and exiles on the earth," and "make it clear they are seeking a homeland" (Heb. 11:13–14). Thus even the death of the mother is shaped to be an occasion for deep trust in the promise.

A Wife for the Son and Heir (24:1–67)

The second piece in these transitional materials (24:1–67) concerns the son and heir. This material has no special relation to chapter 23. It has a quite different style and tone. However, in the finished shape of the text they are linked (24:67) so that Sarah's death and Isaac's marriage are nicely joined together.

As Von Rad has seen, the narrative easily divides into four scenes, each featuring a different combination of characters: (1) vv. 1–9, *Abraham and the unnamed servant;* (2) vv. 11–27, *the servant and Rebekah;* (3) vv. 28–61, *the servant and the kinsmen of Rebekah;* (4) vv. 62–67, *Isaac and Rebekah.*

The narrative has novelistic features not unlike the Joseph narrative. It is quite extensive and moves in a leisurely but clearly disciplined way through its plot. Each scene is designed to serve a particular function, so that the whole is carefully shaped. At the same time, however, there are leisurely points of humor along the way; and these should be relished in the telling.

The problem of the narrative is to find the proper wife for Isaac so that the promise may have a future. This goal is not overstated and perhaps only provides a context for the story. If this goal is taken seriously, it could be seen as reflecting, on the one hand, aversion to *Canaanites* (cf. 26:34; 27:46—28:9). On the other hand, it attends in a positive sense to the *Aramean* connection, not otherwise stressed in the Abraham story (cf. Deut. 26:5). But those concerns lie outside the dramatic coherence of the story which is restricted simply to the drama of finding a wife with proper credentials.

1. In the telling of the story, the first (vv. 1–9) and fourth (vv. 62–67) scenes are essential for announcing the *problem* and stating the *resolution.* But the dramatic power is in the two middle scenes.

a. The first scene (vv. 1–9) presents Abraham as an intensely determined and utterly believing man. Of special note is the double use of the formula "Yahweh, God of Heaven," (vv. 3, 7), unusual here and perhaps suggesting a distinctive origin for the story.

197

b. The second scene (vv. 11–27) is nicely enveloped by the prayer of vv. 12–14 and the doxology of vv. 26–27, indicating the prayer has been answered. The key word in the scene is "steadfast loyalty" *(ḥesed)* found twice in the prayer (vv. 12, 14) and again in the responding doxology (vv. 26–27). Abraham has entrusted the whole matter to Yahweh. The servant, too, has found God to be fully trustworthy. Between the two prayers of verses 12–14 and 27 is a playful narrative (vv. 15–28) in which the servant enjoys looking at the lovely woman and assessing the wealth of her family (v. 21). The motif of "prosper" is introduced. The humor of this scene is that Yahweh's prosperity is quite an earthy matter: *(a)* proper genealogy, *(b)* good looks, *(c)* many camels, *(d)* a virgin (how could he know?). The blessings of heaven come packaged for earth!

c. The third scene (vv. 28–61) is a long one. It is especially extended by the eloquent speech of the servant (vv. 34–49) which repeats the whole matter in detail. This rhetorical device is a useful one for developing suspense and holding the attention of the listener. Note that the long speech is bounded by blessing:

Yahweh has blessed my master . . . (v. 35);

I . . . blessed the LORD (v. 48).

The speech in turn is bracketed by two statements of Laban with formidable theological content (vv. 31, 50). The structure is this:

v. 31 Laban: Come in, O *blessed* of the LORD . . .

v. 35 servant: The LORD has greatly *blessed* my master . . .

v. 48 servant: I bow my head and *bless* the LORD

v. 50 Laban: This thing comes from the LORD. . . .

Laban's response (v. 50) is complete adherence to Abraham's plan. It is later echoed in Laban's complete surrender to Jacob (31:29). It is, of course, important for the story that Laban speaks here as a Yahwistic believer, not only knowing the name, but conceding everything to him. The narrative pursues its foremost theological claim somewhat facetiously. On the one hand, it is surely important that Laban speaks the name of Abraham's God. But on the other hand, the narrative is tongue-in-cheek. Laban has just seen the rings, bracelets, and camels (v. 30). He may not be a true believer, but he is no fool, either!

d. The resolution of the plot occurs at the end of scene three (vv. 52–60), in which the necessary arrangements for the dowry are handled in ceremonious and decorous fashion. In this scene, we may note the recurrence of two motifs. First, the servant asked for loyalty from Yahweh (vv. 12–14), and for steadfast love and faithfulness (v. 27, *ḥesed* and *'emet*). He asks in the same words for loyalty and fidelity from Laban (v. 49). Second, the issue of prosperity posed in verse 21 has now been answered (v. 56). The scene ends (vv. 60–61) again with the blessing theme, this one corresponding to that of Abraham (v. 1). As Abraham of the old generation ended richly blessed, so Rebekah, mother of the future generation, begins in blessing and with a rather imperial mandate for the land already promised (cf. commentary of 22:17 on the formula). The reception in scene four (vv. 62–67) is a happy one. The note of "comfort" (v. 67) brings an end to the matters of transition.

2. The following motifs should be noted:

a. The entire family, the whole world of Abraham, is richly *blessed.* There is no need for conflict. Everything is right and good. The motif of blessing begins with Abraham (v. 1, restated in the identity of the servant in v. 31) and is sustained to the departure of Rebekah (v. 60). The blessing of Yahweh is matched by the servant's blessing of Yahweh (v. 27, restated in v. 48).

b. Closely related, the motif of *prosperity* runs throughout the story (vv. 21, 40, 42, 56). That theme will later surface in the Joseph narrative (39:2–3, 23). But already here we have a literary genre (novel) adequate to express the resilient power of God's providential care.

c. We have already observed that the use of *"loyalty"* with *"fidelity"* is important. The pairing occurs twice here. It is asked of God (vv. 12, 14) and received from him (v. 27). It is asked of Laban (v. 49) and received, though not explicitly expressed. That formula, *ḥesed* and *'emet,* is a favorite way of speaking about a full, trustworthy relation.

d. A fourth theme is the hidden, inscrutable guidance of God. Already the servant knows he has been led (v. 27) and he repeats that conviction (v. 48). Yahweh has done nothing directly. There has been no sign or signal. There has been no seeking after or requesting guidance, but only the willing acknowledgment after the fact. The mention of the angel (v. 40) is most peculiar and nothing is made of it in the narrative. Perhaps the angel is a device whereby this "leading" is con-

199

nected to the wilderness sojourn. More likely it puts the reader on notice that this seemingly "natural" sequence of affairs consists in more than meets the eye. God is at work here. Only the discerning believer discerns the angel. Others will regard these remarkable events as "good luck."

Use of the guidance motif is worth special attention. The term *nāḥāh* (RSV, "led") occurs nowhere else in Genesis. Its two characteristic uses refer *(a)* to guidance in the wilderness sojourn (Exod. 13:17; Ps. 60:9; 78:14; 53; 108:10), and *(b)* to personal well-being as a request in time of stress (see especially the Psalms of lament, 5:8; 27:11; 31:3; 43:3; 73:24). Surely the best known usage is Ps. 23:2–3 which is a statement of utter confidence in God's benevolent care:

> He *leads* me beside still waters;
>   he restores my soul.
> He *leads* me in paths of righteousness
>   for his name's sake. (author's italics)

The leadership theme is most aggressively stated in our narrative (v. 14) and is repeated in verse 44. It is asserted that the girl is the one Yahweh "appointed" for Isaac's wife. The word "appoint" is unusual for this usage, but it indicates the high theology of the narrative. The story has no doubt that it is the precise, concrete purpose of Yahweh which has governed these events.

In summary, then, these four themes together provide ways to think theologically about this narrative: (1) *blessing from God and to God,* (2) *prosperity,* (3) *steadfast loyalty and fidelity (ḥesed and 'ᵉmet),* and (4) *God's leadership.*

3. In many ways, the story appears to be "secular." It takes human experience seriously and God is nowhere active in the story. This is a prime example of Von Rad's "Enlightenment literature" (cf. *Old Testament Theology I,* 1962, pp. 48–56). Wolfgang Roth ("The Wooing of Rebekah," CBQ 34: 177–87 [1972]) suggests the narrative bears the marks of sapiential influence. At the same time, the story is a profound statement of faithfulness to God, not only as we expect it from Abraham, but also in the words and actions of Abraham's servant and Laban.

a. The narrative reflects the conviction that all events are under Yahweh's providential care. He will bring events to a good end. Admittedly, Yahweh does nothing visible. There is an oath in Yahweh's name (vv. 3, 7). There is a petition to Yahweh (vv. 12, 14). There is a thanksgiving to him (v. 26–67). This is not

200

foremost a statement about Yahweh's deeds (as some other parts of the Abraham tradition are) but a presentation of how it is to live in an ethos in which life is accepted and perceived as a gift from Yahweh's hand. The narrative does not have Yahweh intervene or intrude. But it offers a world-view in which there are no parts of experience which lie beyond the purpose of God. In this, as in so many ways, the narrative has kinship with the Joseph narrative (cf. 50:20). How things emerge are attributed to Yahweh's watchful presence.

b. It may well be asked of such a narrative: Does God in fact lead and guide in such a way? The answer will not emerge directly from the text. This text does not stress the leadership of Yahweh as much as it emphasizes the faithful following of the actors. The principal characters accept a reading of reality related to Yahweh. They interpret events accordingly. For its seeming naïveté, this narrative is a mature reflection on faith. It asks people not first of all to anticipate the faithfulness of God, but to read it in retrospect. We do not always know the gifts of God in advance. But given a perspective of faith, we can in subsequent reflection discern the amazing movement of God in events we had not noticed or which we had assigned to other causes. Thus we are like the servant of this narrative (v. 21) who must study the matter to draw a conclusion. Only after such reflection can one draw such a conclusion and assign a meaning (as in vv. 26–27, 48, 56).

The text provides an important opportunity to help persons think about faith, what it is and how it comes. In a culture which grasps for visible signs of faith, which is driven toward scientism, and which falls for too many religious quackeries, this story stands as a foil against easy and mistaken faith. The workings of God are not spectacular, not magical, not oddities. Disclosure of God comes by steady discernment and by readiness to trust the resilience that is present in the course of daily affairs. There is an understatedness about the action of the narrative. But it is not reticent about faith. It is an understatement that is ready to be sustained and profoundly grateful when gifts are given.

c. The expected response to this story may be a new awareness of the buoyant serenity in which faith lives. Of course it is possible that such a reading of reality is a deception. But that is the risk of such a perception. The servant and Laban may be mistaken in their acknowledgments, but the narrative pre-

201

cludes such a thought. The narrative defines our life-world in affirmation and not in suspicion. Such a reading must not be done lightly. And it is not for everyone. Luther has wise words about the way this narrative claims things for God: "According to the law, one may not prescribe anything to God; But according to the gospel, the godly who are without the law may do so." Luther is clear that the faith modeled by the servant in this story may not presume too much or claim too much. And so he commends the prayer of the servant: "Make it occur. Grant that all things will come about of themselves" (vv. 12–14). The faith of this narrative is one in which things occur seemingly as they will and yet are credited to God. The text nurtures a mature faith that resists both easy romanticism and hard cynicism. Thus the listening community can sing about the One who leads, even when we seem to be walking of our own accord:

> Lead us, Heavenly Father, lead us
> O'er the world's tempestuous sea;
> Guide us, guide us, keep us, feed us,
> For we have no help but Thee,
> Yet possessing every blessing,
> If our God our Father be.
> ("Lead Us, Heavenly Father, Lead Us," James Edmeston, 1821)

The faith offered here is for those who are willing to be led. The mandate of Abraham (v. 7) looks back to 12:1 and sets such faith precisely where it must be lived, between the old place abandoned and the new place not yet received. In retrospect, such persons are able to confess God's incredible and prompt attentiveness (v. 15; cf. Isa. 65:24).

The Death of the Father (25:1–18)

The third element in these chapters (25:1–18) reports the death of Abraham and the final settlement of the promise on Isaac. We need not linger on the marriage of Abraham to Keturah (vv. 1–4) and the keeping of concubines. While Calvin extensively criticizes Abraham in this regard, Luther concludes that he had these other relations only because of his pious concern to produce an heir for the promise. In any case, these verses probably reflect a genuine historical report and indicate the fruitfulness of Abraham.

These notes may be useful on this text:

1. Verses 5–6 attend to the relation between Isaac and Ishmael. Here there is no negativity toward the other sons.

202

They are not dismissed out of hand but are properly cared for by the father. Nonetheless, the text quickly establishes the qualitative difference. The others receive "gifts" (v. 6). To Isaac, he gave "all" (v. 5). Isaac receives the blessing almost as a tangible, identifiable substance (v. 11). The text provides a striking presentation of the tension between *election* to promise and a *generosity* which embraces all peoples.

2. Verses 7–10 may be utilized to reflect on what it means to die a good death. Abraham had lived a long, blessed life. He had a good burial plot. The death of Abraham is peaceable because he dies midst the generations, confident that all things valuable have been transmitted to his son(s). It is never stated but everywhere assumed that dying is an event in the company of hope (Heb. 11:17–19). But even Abraham cannot die hopefully in the midst of the generations unless he has lived there. Such a minor note in the text may offer a useful contrast with our excessive individualism. We die in isolation because we tend to live the same way (Rom. 14:7–9).

3. Verse 9 notes that the burial is supervised by both sons, the son of right and the son of promise (cf. 35:29). This note also expresses a solidarity among the brothers (cf. Ps. 133). There is no doubt that the story is tilted toward Isaac. And yet it does not deny Ishmael or his claims. (This is also clear in the genealogy of vv. 12–18.) In verse 19, the text moves to Isaac as we would expect. But it does not ignore the other brother. Even in this Isaac tradition, Ishmael is not a man without a story and a future. These are not pursued here. But they are not denied either. He also has received gifts (v. 6) and bears a blessing (cf. 16:11–12; 21:17–21). The tension within the family of Abraham is reflected and left unresolved, at least until the promise is fully kept (cf. Isa. 19:23–25).

Perhaps this notation is useful for those who will ask about election to promise. Why does the choice happen in what seems to be arbitrary ways? What about the others? The answer is not equitable and may not satisfy. But it permits the surmise that the house of this father has more than one room (cf. John 14: 1–2). Ishmael is an unexpected way to conclude the Abraham story!

PART THREE

The Jacob Narrative: The Conflicted Call of God

GENESIS 25:19—36:43

> God chose what is foolish in the world to shame the wise, God
> chose what is weak in the world to shame the strong, God chose
> what is low and despised in the world, even things that are not,
> to bring to nothing the things that are, so that no human being
> might boast in the presence of God (I Cor. 1:27–29).

The narrative about Jacob portrays Israel in its earth-
iest and most scandalous appearance in Genesis. The narrative is not edifying in any conventional religious or moral
sense. Indeed, if one comes to the narrative with such an
agenda, the narrative is offensive. But for that very reason,
the Jacob narrative is most lifelike. It presents Jacob in
his crude mixture of motives. This grandson of the promise
is a rascal compared to his faithful grandfather Abraham
or his successful father Isaac. The affirmations of faith in this
narrative are especially robust. The narrator knows that the
purposes of God are tangled in a web of self-interest and self-
seeking.

The narrative offers two general affirmations which provide the tension that holds our interest. First, God has *chosen
and destined* this man Jacob in a special way. The initial designation of Jacob is inscrutable (25:23). We are not told why God
wills this inversion of "natural right." But as the narrative is
given to us, it is this designation by God which brings Jacob to
well-being and prosperity. In an earthy way, this is a statement
about justification by grace. God has taken one who is "low and

204

despised" and has overturned conventional power arrangements.

But it is also this designation by God that begins the *trouble* (25:29–34; 27:1–45) that is to mark Jacob's entire life. This is the second reality which holds the narrative in tension. Even as the designated of God, Jacob lives a troubled life. He has conflicts with all those around him. It is the juxtaposition of *special designation* and a *life of conflict* that is the mainspring of the narrative. Apparently, it is the commitment of God to this troubled man which causes the conflict. In the end, it is this same commitment from God which resolves the conflicts in his favor. The narrator knows that the election is a blessing and a burden. The narrator, however, is not completely captivated by the special position of Jacob in the will of God. There is a curious fascination with and inclination toward Esau, the son who has "natural rights." It is almost as if the narrator could not resist the inclination. The claim of Jacob seems to advance even against the wish of the narrator. The claim is so powerful that eventually it will shape the stories in its own way.

Critical Issues

The critical issues in the Jacob materials are complex and largely unresolved.

1. While the narrative of Jacob now has some coherence, it is comprised of a variety of materials which probably had independent development. Gunkel concluded that the narrative contained four kinds of independent material: *(a)* Materials of *Jacob with Esau* (25:19–34; 27:1–45; 27:46—28:9; 32:3–21; 33:1–17), *(b)* materials of *Jacob with Laban* (29:1–30; 30:25—31:55), *(c)* materials concerning the *sons of Jacob* (29:31—30:24), and *(d)* materials related to *theophanic and cultic encounters* (28:10–22; 32:1–2, 22–32). This ordering of materials reveals the main elements of the Jacob narrative. In addition, our exposition includes the single narrative about Isaac (26) and a collection of miscellaneous materials in 33:18—36:43. As we shall see, these latter materials appear to be appendices which come after the basic resolution of the narrative.

2. It is probable that these materials reflect a long traditioning process of the northern tribes. That process apparently was related to the great shrines, with special connections to the shrine at Bethel (cf. 28:10–22; 31:13; 35:1–15). The materials developed around several themes and without reference to

205

each other. Only later was this formed into a coherent narrative. As it now stands, the arrangement has considerable artistry. But that is no doubt a late development in the traditioning process.

3. This narrative was developed and transmitted in the north of Israel, without relation to the southern tribes, and without reference to the southern figure of Abraham or the claims of the royal establishment of Jerusalem. This means that the texture of the narrative is much less restrained and disciplined than the Abrahamic tradition. Even in its completed form, the narrative does not need to serve any goals external to itself (see p. 138, e.g., for royal aspects of Abraham). As a result, it can express puckish humor and doubtful morality. At the same time, it can make a more unembarrassed claim for the purpose of God in overturning conventions on behalf of Jacob. This tradition permits candor about the offensiveness of Israel and the resilience of God in relation to that scandal.

Westermann has suggested two ways in which the Jacob narrative may be contrasted with the Abraham narrative ("Types of Narrative in Genesis," *The Promise to the Fathers,* 1980, pp. 74–78).

a. The Abraham narrative is concerned with a "vertical" problem, the movement of the promise from father to son. It is preoccupied with the relation of the generations and the securing of an heir. By contrast, Jacob struggles within his own generation. There is conflict with wives and uncle, but especially with his brother. Much more than the Abraham story, this narrative is realistic about power and position in the family, about the practices of promise and deception, about wages and departures and reconciliation. The narrative is attentive to all those interactions which betray or enhance humanness and the well-being of the family.

b. The Abraham narrative is preoccupied with the issue of *promise.* It revolves around two questions: (1) Will God keep his promise of an heir? (2) Will Abraham and Sarah trust in and rely only on the promise? While the motif of promise is obviously present in the Jacob narrative, it is noticeably subdued (cf. 28:13–15; 31:13; 35:11–12). The story, rather, is dominated by the motif of *blessing.* Westermann has shown that *promise* and *blessing* are quite distinct issues. Whereas promise might per-

206

mit staying with more "religious" issues, the theme of blessing presses the narrative toward earthly and earthy realities.

Jacob cares continually about matters of prosperity, fertility, and well-being which are received or lost in normal life processes. The narrative appropriately begins in the womb (25:22–24) where the mystery of life is granted. The blessing later given to Jacob and denied Esau (27:27–29) contains an important focus on fertility. That same agenda is evident in the narrative about the sons (29:31—30:24). The names of some of the sons are explained with reference to fertility (cf. 30:11–12). The same theme is used in Jacob's mysterious capacity to manipulate the breeding processes of the sheep (30:37–43). And even in the enigmatic narrative of 33:18—34:31, the pragmatic judgment of Jacob (34:30) recognizes the need to come to terms with the Canaanite realities of land, prosperity, and property.

4. The historical questions related to the text are obscure. It is evident that there are old materials here which contain unreflective elements of folklore. Further historical placement of materials is obscure. There have been attempts to relate social practices to the Middle Bronze period, especially to Hurrian parallels. Those attempts are now in question. The Laban materials, and especially the covenant of 31:44–54, suggest a time of Israelite interaction with the Arameans but more cannot be said. Chapter 34 likely reflects some early interaction with the population of Shechem and evidence from the Amarna period may be pertinent. But for purposes of our exposition, we need not assume more than that we have old materials which contain some authentic memories from the past of Israel.

Theological Affirmations and Possibilities

The final form of the narrative is undoubtedly shaped with theological intent. These motifs stand out as possibilities for exposition.

1. We may begin with attention to the structure of the tradition. The whole is roughly arranged in concentric circles. The framework or the outer circle is provided by the Esau materials which stand at the beginning (25:19–34; 27:1–45) and at the end of the main story (32:3–21; 33:1–17). Inside of these were placed the two theophanic narratives of Bethel (29:10–22) and Penu'el (32:22–32). And inside that is the narrative of the conflict with Laban (29:1–30; 30:25—31:55). Then at the very

207

center is the story of the birth of the children (29:31—30:24). Thus, the entire narrative is developed to move from the overriding conflict with Esau to the most treasured blessing of the sons and on to the resolution of the conflict. Clearly, the oracle of designation (25:23) governs the narrative. The overall structure moves from the estrangement (25:19–34) to the reconciliation (33:1–17). This framework poses the question about blessing: Will God give the blessing he asserts? Will Jacob trust only in the blessing? Can the purpose of God in fact invert the normal rights of primogeniture? That is the issue which shapes the narrative. It concerns the capacity of God to transform power relations and bring to well-being those who are "low and despised" and without claims of priority. The resolution of that issue is given in 33:1–17. It is a characteristic resolution for Jacob. It is not clear and unambiguous as things are for Abraham. When Esau leaves for Seir and Jacob comes to Succoth (33:16–17), it is not evident that the "older shall serve the younger." Yet the narrator would not have us miss the fact that Jacob does have the land. Esau must go far away to settle. Without a very explicit statement, the narrative affirms that the initial oracle of 25:23 has come to fruition. Again God's gift of blessing has no visible or necessary connection to the conventional ordering of life.

The blessing taken from the brother is the overriding theme, presented in the outer framework. Moving for the moment past the second and third structural circles to the central narrative, we find the second major question of blessing: Will this younger one be blessed with sons? That is the issue of the internal narrative of 29:1—31:55, and more precisely of 29:31 —30:24. That most internal account begins in barrenness (29:31) and ends in the birth of Joseph (30:24). God has added! The blessing is given. Barrenness is overcome. The power of life is at work for this younger one.

2. The call of God places Jacob in a series of unrelieved conflicts. The entire narrative is marked by strife: (*a*) There is the overriding dispute with Esau which shapes the tradition. (*b*) There is the dispute with Laban which is like a chess game between two very clever players. (*c*) There is hint of a dispute with Rachel concerning whose fault it is that they have no child (30:1–2). (*d*) There is a sharp dispute with his sons over how to live in Canaan (34:30; by inference see also the dispute of 35:22). (*e*) There is the awesome dispute even with God, in which Jacob will concede nothing easily (32:22–29). Jacob is a

208

man who will contest every step of the way with every party.

But the dispute is not of Jacob's making. It is evoked by God's initial oracle (25:23). The narrative affirms that the call of God is not only a call to well-being. It may be a call to strife and dispute.

3. The challenge to primogeniture is a primary area of conflict. It is announced in the opening oracle and is faced with reference to Esau and the daughters of Laban. The conflict of Jacob is a conflict not with "spiritual" realities, but with the ways in which human life has been institutionalized. Primogeniture is not simply one rule among many. It is the linchpin of an entire social and legal system which defines rights and privileges and provides a way around internecine disputes. But that same practice which protects the order of society is also a way of destining some to advantage and others to disadvantage. That world of privilege and denial is here disrupted by the God of blessing who will sojourn with the "low and despised" (cf. Luke 7:34). This narrative, then, is a radically revolutionary announcement. It dares to call into question a conventional settlement of power. The governing oracle and the narrative which flows from it are not disinterested. They are an attempt to arrange the blessings in an alternative way. And with that attempt, painful possibilities are reopened. Many things are placed in jeopardy.

4. Theological exposition will not focus on the person of Jacob. He holds our attention and warrants it. But finally the text concerns the God of Jacob. By quoting from Paul (I Cor. 1:27–29), we have pointed to a God who violates the world's notions of wisdom and strength. Jacob is a scandalous challenge to his world because the God who calls him is also scandalous.

We are not told why God challenged the legitimated convention of the community by designating this "heel" of a man (25:26). But he does! It is this same God who will later struggle with Jacob and leave him crippled (32:22–32). At many points the narrative presents the inscrutable, dark side of God. It offers a radical theological affirmation which has been appreciated by Paul. The God of Israel comes to and sojourns with the unworthy and unvalued until they are brought safely home (cf. 28:15). It is that scandalous God who finally settled on a Crucified One as the way to make all things new. Thus, this oracle of inversion is not simply a political program of preference for Israel over Edom or Aram, though it may be that as well. It is also a disclosure about this God. To be faithful to the call of such a God brings conflict because this God himself evokes and enters into conflict with the way the world is organized.

5. This narrative presents a strange juxtaposition of themes. It is a collection of conflict tales, especially concerning Esau and Laban. But in the midst of them are the accounts of divine encounter (28:10–22; 32:22–32; cf. 32:2–3; 35:1–15). That juxtaposition is important for our exposition.

The two kinds of narratives, of *human conflict* and of *divine confrontation,* cannot be separated from each other. On the one hand, we cannot simply focus on the "religious" encounters, as much interpretation tends to do. On the other hand, Jacob does not live in a history that is flat and one-dimensional. The two dimensions of reality are of a piece. Thus, the Bethel vision of the "ramp" (28:10–22) comes in Jacob's flight from his brother who wants to kill him. The crippling encounter at Penu'el (32:22–32) comes in the midst of great anxiety about reconciliation with that same brother. There are no troubled dimensions of human interaction which are removed from the coming of the Holy God. And there are no meetings with the Holy God apart from the realities of troubled human life. That juxtaposition is a statement about the God who comes and the human life into which he comes. *Human extremity* and *divine intrusion* are correlated with each other. It may be that the juxtaposition of texts is late in the traditioning process. But they are now shaped that way for a reason. From that shape we learn how it is that the Holy God impinges upon human power struggles and how it is that human realities are transformed by these assaults from God.

6. In the midst of its concern for Jacob, the narrative has an unusual and positive fascination with Esau. The narrator is like Isaac who cannot quite let go of his oldest son (27:37–38). This attention to Esau may be because he was remembered as the more attractive person. The narrative never argues that Jacob is more attractive. It claims only that he is designated by God, in spite of his own merit or lack of it.

The positive presence of Esau warns against claiming too much for the elect one, as though the whole economy of God has been committed to him. The narrative asserts that the mystery of God has more to it than this amazing choice of one man. Both brothers have claims, and the narrative does not deny them. In subsequent tradition (cf. Obad.; Mal. 1:2–5; Heb. 12:12–17) Esau is used as a negative type. But in this narrative,

210

the handling of Esau reminds us to hold every claim for Jacob loosely and provisionally.

7. Exposition of this text will make ready contact with persons in our time who belong to the *"third generation."* Jacob is not like the first generation of Abraham with its serene and confident faith. Nor is he like the second generation of Isaac with his effective and prosperous living. In contrast to these two, this child of the third generation lives in conflict and trouble all his days. Jacob has an attraction and a gift for those who find their lives in conflict, who yearn and even connive for the security of a blessing, who await upheavals but greatly fear them, who seem always to face combat on earth and with heaven. Some of these members of the "third generation" have been harshly crippled in their struggles, but prevail, like Jacob at Penu'el. Others still wait for such a transforming meeting.

A Schema for Exposition

The chart suggests the movement of exposition in what follows. The large framework consists of the *conflict with Esau* (25:19–34; 27:1–45, and derivatively 27:46—28:9, informed by the oracle of 25:23) and the *reconciliation with Esau* (32:1–21; 33:1–17). Within that is the *conflict with Laban* (29:1–30; 30:25 —31:42) which ends in a *covenant with Laban* (31:43–55) even if something short of a reconciliation. And within that, at the center, is the narrative of the *births* (29:31—30:24) which moves from *barrenness* (29:31) to the *birth of Joseph* (30:24). It is the birth of Joseph which marks a turn in the entire narrative (30:34). After that event, Jacob looks toward the land and toward his brother Esau. In the midst of the conflicts are placed the two major encounters with God (28:10–22; 32:22–32). The encounters occur at crucial places in the sequence of conflicts. Thus, the sweep of the narrative is from the oracle of 25:23 to the reconciliation with Esau and the settlement in Succoth (33:15–17). The basic tension announced in the oracle is resolved by the meeting of the brothers. In this narrative the "horizontal" stories of conflict with Esau, Laban, and Rachel are matched by the "vertical" narratives of meetings with God. Together they show both how sure and how disputed is the gift of an unmerited blessing.

211

The materials in 33:18—36:43 occur outside the main dramatic structure of the narrative. They serve to form a transition and to give closure to the narrative. In these materials three things are evident: *(a)* The family now settled in the land (cf. 33:17) faces new problems of security and fidelity in a different context. *(b)* Jacob's family is in some disarray. The details are given now which the earlier taut narrative did not include. *(c)* The reconciled brother Esau is still very much in view and is valued positively.

Genesis 25:19–34

This unit begins the story of Jacob which extends through chapter 36. It announces the main themes of that narrative. The unit is divided into two parts. Verses 19–28 present the birth of Jacob and Esau and the pre-natal mystery that marks the birth. It is already apparent here that this child of the family of promise is marked in special and problematic ways. The second element (vv. 29–34) presents the well-known interaction of the brothers, who strike a bargain of food and birthright. The two parts juxtapose the inscrutable power of God with the self-serving cleverness of human desire. We will see that even in the latter, God's purposes are at work.

The Pre-birth Destiny (25:19–28)

Everything is ready for this birth to be announced (vv. 19–28). The genealogy is secure (25:1–18). Great pains have been taken to secure a proper mother for these heirs of the promise (24:1–62). There should be an easy transition to the next generation.

1. But the birth must happen in barrenness (v. 21). This new generation begins as it did for Abraham and Sarah (11:30). There is an incongruity here. The father is the special child of promise (21:1–7). And the mother is of good stock (25:20). But in this best possible arrangement, there is barrenness. There are no natural guarantees for the future and no way to secure the inheritance of the family. It must trust only to the power of God.

As with Abraham, the problem of the heir is not a riddle in biology (cf. 18:1–15; 21:1–7). It is, rather, a statement about the power of God and the needfulness of this family of promise. Other families might have been free to invent and govern their own future. But this family is marked by promise. It receives life

212

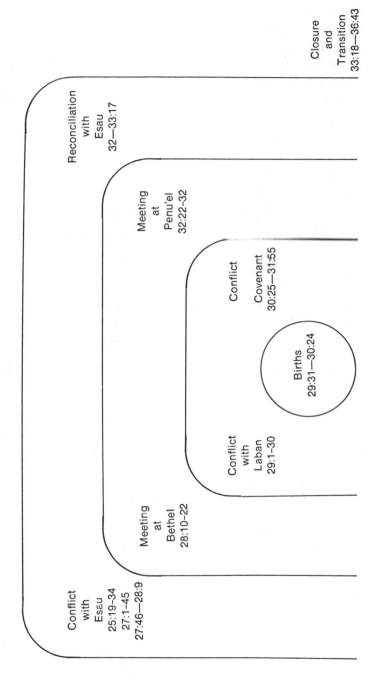

GENESIS 25:19—36:43: THE JACOB NARRATIVE

Reconciliation
with
Esau
32—33:17

Closure
and
Transition
33:18—36:43

Meeting
at
Penu'el
32:22-32

Conflict
Covenant
30:25—31:55

Births
29:31—30:24

Conflict
with
Laban
29:1-30

Meeting
at
Bethel
28:10-22

Conflict
with
Esau
25:19-34
27:1-45
27:46—28:9

Isaac
[26]

as an unexpected gift. Promise requires an end to grasping and certitude and an embrace of precariousness. It is only God who gives life. Any pretense that the future is secured by rights or claims of the family is a deception (cf. Matt. 3:9).

The role of the mother and the father in this birth narrative is that of prayer. It is their task to cast themselves solely on God (cf. Ps. 55:22). To pray as they must is to know that life is given as a gift. Sarah and Isaac and all who come after them in this family of promise are children of gift: ". . . He gave power to become children of God; who were born, not of blood, nor of the will of the flesh nor of the will of man, but of God" (John 1:12–13). Those who would enter this text may discover that they are children of promise, wrought only by the will of God (James 1:18). Paul's self-affirmation echoes the claim made here for the heirs of Isaac: ". . . he who had set me apart before I was born, and had called me through his grace . . ." (Gal. 1:15). That is how it is with these twins. They are not only born. They are called. They live because prayers are answered and words are spoken. They are not given life naturally. Their destiny is shaped by the One who first spoke them into life. When Jacob and Esau are born, their life is already decisively shaped by this Other One to whom their parents pray. Their life is encompassed in a mystery of graciousness before they see the light of day. Barrenness cannot be overcome by the shrewdness of the parents. It can be dealt with only by the Lord of life.

2. The birth is a gift and a marvel. But it comes in conflict (vv. 22–28). From the beginning, Jacob is destined to be a man of combat. The paradoxical marks of *gift and conflict* dominate the Jacob narrative. We are frequently surprised by his well-being and his good fortune. But it is the conflict which concerns us at this point. There is a realism about this text which challenges romantic piety. One might have expected that a birth given in such graciousness would be for a creature who is removed and protected from conflict. But this child of *gift* is called for the sake of *conflict.* His life cannot be otherwise. It is not a conflict he has chosen. He is "scripted" before he is born. And we are not given any reason.

a. The conflict is evident to Rebekah even before the birth is a burden to her (v. 22). The narrator wants us to know there is a dark power at work in the life of Jacob. He is born to a kind of restlessness so that he must always insist, grasp and exploit. His life is a trouble not only for himself but for those around

214

him. Thus the statement about the church in the Fourth Gospel might be used to characterize this enigmatic son:

> "If the world hates you, know that it has hated me before it hated you. If you were of the world, the world would love its own; but because you are not of the world, but I chose you out of the world, the world hates you" (John 15:18–19).

b. The narrator wants us to know we are not faced with a physiological problem of pregnancy. Rather, we are confronted with a theological reality (v. 23). It is stated baldly and without explanation:

> And the Lord said to her, . . .
> "the one shall be stronger than the other,
>   the elder shall serve the younger."

The text credits the shattering career of Jacob to the speech of God. God does not explain or justify. God simply announces. God not only gives an unexpected birth (v. 21). But he locates this new child in contentious relation to the other son.

The oracle of 25:23 casts its power over the entire Jacob narrative. The Israelites must have wondered about this patriarch who was always in trouble. They concluded that it was part of the purpose of God which would not be explained but only accepted and confirmed.

The oracle is against all conventional wisdom. It makes a profound theological claim. It affirms that we do not live in a world where all possibilities are kept open and we may choose our posture as we please. It does not deny freedom. But it requires us to speak also about *destiny,* about the working of this Other One who will have a voice in the future. There are some options that are closed and some choices denied this people of God. Jacob had some freedom. He could stay or go. He could fear or care. But all his freedom is bounded by the choices God has already made on his behalf.

God has the power to make promises and keep them in spite of any human expectations. This is the premise of the Exodus narrative: God makes a distinction for Israel against Egypt (Exod. 11:7). That is the premise of the ministry of Jesus: the poor, the mourning, the meek, the hungry and the merciful are the heirs to the kingdom (Matt. 5:3–7). This God does not align himself only with the obviously valued ones, the first-born.

c. This oracle speaks about an *inversion.* It affirms that we are *not fated* to the way the world is presently organized. It is

215

conventional wisdom in the world of Isaac and Sarah that the older son should have preeminence (cf. 29:26). As we have seen (cf. pp. 182–184, 207–209), the law of primogeniture is very old. It asserts that the oldest should be first and favored (cf. Deut. 21:15–17). It claims that some have "natural rights" which cannot be questioned. From that assumption of "natural rights," a whole theory of societal relationships is derived. In most societies, that network of rights and privileges is taken as normative and ordained of God. It is the way order is maintained. It determines the criteria for justice and equity. It is a way by which social privilege is established and authorized beyond question.

This oracle expresses a scandalous decision on the part of God. To call into question the "non-law of primogeniture" is to tamper with a fundamental conviction of society (cf. Robert Alter, "A Literary Approach to the Bible," *Commentary* 60: 74 [1975]). In this oracle, Esau is not judged or condemned. It is simply asserted that his accident of birth is not a title to privilege. Thus God works a basic inversion of social right. The oracle discloses something crucial about God. It affirms that by the power of his promise, God is free to work his will in the face of every human convention and every definition of propriety. Jacob is ordained as a man of conflict because the God who wrought him is a God in conflict as well. By the inverting promise of this God, Jacob embodies a challenge to every societally sanctioned arrangement.

d. To understand the affront of this text, we may reflect on the meaning of the "younger one" in the Bible, the one without right on his side. These include the widow, the orphan, the sojourner (Deut. 10:18; 14:29; 26:12; Ps. 146:9). In the New Testament, the "younger one" may be identified with "publicans and sinners" (Matt. 9:10–13; 11:16–19; 21:32).

The oracle concerns and anticipates the gospel affirmation that the "first shall be last, and the last first" (Matt. 19:30; 20:16; Mark 9:35; 10:31; Luke 13:30). For this reason, we have taken the Pauline affirmation of I Cor. 1:28 as an interpretive clue to Jacob: "God chose what is low and despised in the world to bring to nothing the things that are." In that ancient world, the younger son is "low and despised." But by the power of the oracle (and by trickery), this younger son "supplants" (cf. Gen. 27:36) his brother. The last becomes first.

e. Yet at birth, Jacob was not first. He had battled in the

216

womb (v. 22). He had been promised preeminence (v. 23). But he came second (v. 24–26). The two boys are described and explanations are given for their names (vv. 25–26). The name of Jacob is unclear, but the usual rendering is either "heel," that is, the one who kicks his way out, or "supplanter," the one who would displace his twin. Either reading of his name adds to the foreshadowing of a life of conflict, beginning even at birth.

And if that were not enough, verses 27–28 show further that the matter of conflict will dominate the life of the two sons. The narrative is explicit. The two parents who prayed so passionately for a son have now chosen sides. At birth, in name selection, in vocation, and even in parental preference this narrative has prepared us in every way for Jacob's life of conflict.

f. The narrative does not accommodate our discreet sensibilities. It is without guile or apology. It does not waver from the exasperation of Rebekah (v. 22). It does not apologize for the partisan character of the oracle (v. 23). It is not even embarrassed by (nor does it bother to explain) the blatant preference by the parents (v. 28). Like its main character, this narrative is indiscreet and at times scandalous. It shows God and his chosen younger one aligned against the older brother, against the father, and against the cultural presumptions of natural privilege. Jacob is announced as a visible expression of God's remarkable graciousness in the face of conventional definitions of reality and prosperity. Jacob is a scandal from the beginning. The powerful grace of God is a scandal. It upsets the way we would organize life.

The Bargain Between the Brothers (25:29–34)

The negotiation of the brothers (vv. 29–34) forms a counterpart to the inscrutable way of God (vv. 19–26). Things moved darkly (vv. 19–26), by the hidden will of God (v. 23). Here things are governed by human need (Esau) and human cleverness (Jacob). There is nothing hidden or mysterious about the need or about the cleverness. But the brothers do more than they know. They proceed as though they themselves could resolve the issue of priority and right. They discuss as though none were involved except the two of them. What they do not know (and what is evident only by the juxtaposition of vv. 19–28 and vv. 29–34) is that their bargaining works to implement the pur-

217

poses of God. Those purposes were already at work in the womb of mother Rebekah. "The elder shall serve the younger." The exchange of birthright is the first step in that mysterious inversion. In the juxtaposition of texts, there is no conflict between divine promise and human ingenuity. The one is an instrument for the other. Through both, the power of God is at work and will have its way. This juxtaposition of texts anticipates the verdict of 50:20: "You meant evil against me; but God meant it for good." The action of verses 29–34 in relation to the oracle of verse 23 affirms that, "He who began a good work . . . will bring it to completion (Phil. 1:6).

1. The text begins and ends with these statements about Esau:

> Esau was famished (v. 29).
>
> Esau despised his birthright (v. 34).

These are the two circumstances of Esau, before the dialogue and after the dialogue.

The dialogue is the means whereby Esau moves from *hunger* at the beginning to *despising* at the end (vv. 30–33). In the dialogue each brother speaks twice. In his first speech, Esau speaks of hunger and pottage (v. 30). But Jacob deftly changes the subject (v. 31). There is no more speech about eating. The other three speeches (two by Jacob, one by Esau) are about the right of the firstborn and the ceding of that right. Jacob is shown to be a hard bargainer. He must have a solemn oath. Almost as an afterthought does the narrator note that Esau gets his food (v. 34).

2. The narrative depends upon the contrast of *pottage* and *birthright*. "Pottage" here is an unusual word. Its only biblical use is in this story. It is part of a dexterous play on words. "Pottage" translates the Hebrew *'ādôm*. It is modified by the adjective "red," also *'ādôm*. The latter is the same word used to describe the redness of Esau at birth (v. 27). Both words, "pottage" and "red," consist in the Hebrew letters *'dm*, the same letters in "Edom," the people embodied in Esau (cf. Gen. 36: 16–43). Thus the word play of *"Edom/red/pottage"* cleverly asserts that Esau is a man (and the Edomites a people) peculiarly destined for pottage and not more. The implicit contrast is the claim that Jacob/Israel, though younger, is destined for birthright. The remainder of the Jacob narrative is the suspenseful account of the way in which this claim becomes reality.

The contrast of birthright and pottage should not be inter-

218

preted as a contrast of spiritual and material, as is often done. The birthright is fully as historical and material as is the pottage. It concerns security, prosperity, fertility, and land. Rather, the contrast is to be sought in two factors:

a. The contrast is between *deferred* and *immediate* material blessing. Esau is hungry and cannot wait. We are not told if Jacob is hungry. Perhaps he also is hungry. But he can wait (cf. 29:30). In its posture of faithfulness, Israel is prepared to wait because it does not doubt that God can be trusted (cf. Heb. 2:2–4; Isa. 40:28–31). Waiting can be done if one does not doubt the outcome (cf. Rom. 5:3–5). Jacob is here the figure of trusting Israel, able to wait.

b. The contrast is between material blessings that can be *taken, managed, and controlled* and well-being that must be received only as a *gift*. Esau is presented as one who must take initiative in his own life. Jacob (here but not always elsewhere) is the man who will depend not on grasping and seizing but upon the sureness of God's promise. None of this is to enhance the person of Jacob nor to deny that he is shrewd and knowing. It is not argued here that he is good or honest or respectable. As the narrative stands, such moral distinctions are disregarded. What is clear is that Jacob, in contrast to Esau, believes in futures to which Esau is indifferent.

Perhaps the narrative understands about older and younger. Perhaps the older son, the one born to rank and right, must have things under control. By contrast, the younger, from a position of weakness, has learned early to seize gifts and take risks for them. See the insight of Jesus (Luke 15:11–32) on the way of the older and the younger. Finally, the older rests upon his rights and virtues which are nothing more than pottage (Luke 15:29–30), whereas the younger trusts himself fully to the good gifts of the father (Luke 15:21–24).

3. This narrative has received important treatment in two New Testament expositions of it.

a. In Heb. 11:20–21, Jacob is named among those who believed in the promise. (Note that Esau is also mentioned as having a blessing.) In Heb. 12:12–17, Esau is used as an illustration of those who do not believe the promise. The primary call of the letter to the Hebrews is for disciplined obedience in the face of persecution. The urging throughout is that waiting for and believing in the sure promises of God will lead to blessings of "rest" (Heb. 4:11) and inheritance (6:11–12). Those who do not believe promises and want more immediate satisfactions

219

will no doubt compromise the faith for the sake of easier gains: pottage. Esau becomes a type for those who do not trust the promise and accommodate themselves. The issue for the listening community is how to believe the promises seriously enough to withstand alternative forms of food which are immediately available and within control. (Cf. Mark 8:15. Perhaps the "leaven of the Pharisees" is another form of pottage.)

b. Paul appeals to this text (Rom. 9:6–13) in his tortuous argument about the relation of Jews and Christians. Paul's argument is that God in his freedom need not honor the right of the firstborn but is free to assign the birthright as he chooses. The calling of the Christian community is not a sign of the rejection of the Jews but is an assurance that "the word of God has not failed" (Rom. 9:6; cf. Josh. 21:43–45). Paul's bold interpretation curiously casts the Jews no longer in the role of Jacob(/Israel), the younger brother of promise. They are now in the role of Esau, the older brother of legitimated right. Paul appeals to the mystery and offense of the younger brother with the birthright in order to assert that God's grace is free and scandalous. The unlegitimated one may be the bearer of God's purpose.

In 9:15, Paul offers an ingenious image. As if inviting Isaac, Rebekah, and Esau to listen to Moses, Paul brings together the issue of Gen. 25:19–34 and the claim of Exod. 33:19. The oracle of Gen. 25:23 is a concrete embodiment of the more reflective statement of Moses: "I will have mercy on whom I will have mercy; I will have compassion on whom I will have compassion." There is no way to seek behind this for explanation. The justification is hidden in the purposes of God. That is what the Jacob narrative is about. The world is filled with "practitioners of primogeniture." They are any who insist on their culturally bestowed rights and privileges. These will not welcome the new community of the younger. If such guardians of the present order have a means, they will eliminate the younger to preserve their particular privilege (cf. Mark 3:6; Luke 19:47). (The argument offered here is not a Christian polemic against Jews. It is rather a comment on every social situation in which the younger deals with the older.) God has inscrutable mercy on "younger ones." And the promise does not fail!

220

Neither in our text of 25:29–34 nor in the Pauline argument are things resolved. The bold emergence of the younger one to prominence is only anticipated. This text does not do more than invite the listening community to wait with Jacob.

Genesis 26:1–34

This chapter contains the only primary material we have concerning Isaac. (In chapter 24, Isaac is not a principal actor. That narrative serves to conclude the Abraham story. In chapters 25 and 27, Isaac also is not a principal but serves to introduce the Jacob materials.) All the tradition tells us about him is essentially confined to this one narrative. In an earlier stage of the process of tradition, he was probably an important figure in the area of Beersheba and Gerar in the south. It may be that he competed with Abraham of Hebron as a southern figure of stature. But all of that is disregarded in our tradition, which presents him only as a transition from Abraham to Jacob.

This chapter is made up of an odd assortment of materials. Whatever unity it has appears to be secondary. The chapter includes (*a*) a primary statement of the patriarchal promise (vv. 1–5), (*b*) a third presentation of the wife-sister motif (vv. 6–11; cf. 12:10–20; 20:1–18), (*c*) a series of narratives about the pursuit of water in conflict with the Philistines (vv. 12–25) which leads to Gerar (vv. 17–22) and finally to Beersheba (vv. 23–25), (*d*) a conclusion (vv. 26–33) which reiterates the blessing (looking back to vv. 1–5) and a treaty with Abimelech (returning to the themes of vv. 6–11), and (*e*) verses 34 and 35 containing an isolated report anticipating 27:46—28:9.

The chapter presents only brief episodes of Isaac's story. He is primarily remembered as the precious son of a great father and the beguiled father of a scheming son. But as we shall see, the figure of Isaac is made the bearer of an important and distinctive theological perspective.

Out of this array of materials, the expositor may identify two facets of the blessing theme: *the theological claim* of blessing from Yahweh and blessing as *prosperity judged by worldly standards.* It is the pairing of the facets in this text which is important for exposition.

1. The entire chapter is preoccupied with the theme of blessing. In the Abraham story, the blessing is cast in the lan-

221

guage of the promise (vv. 3–4; cf. 12:1–3; 18:18; 22:15–18). In the total sweep of patriarchal narrative, the promise seems to belong primarily to the Abraham stories. But now it is extended to each of the lead characters. It is spoken over Jacob (28:13–14) and indirectly over Joseph (46:2). But for Isaac as for Joseph, the promise theme appears to be extraneous to a narrative oriented to blessing. Blessings are acknowledged as *gifts from God.* A firm theological claim is being asserted. The blessing is evident in (*a*) the traditional blessing of vv. 2–5 and 24 (with the pious response of an altar, v. 25), (*b*) the affirmation of Abimelech, "the LORD is with you" (v. 28; cf. vv. 3, 24 and concerning Abraham (21:22) and Jacob (28:20), (*c*) the Philistine recognition of v. 29. (The mention of the Philistines throughout this chapter may pose a historical problem depending on when it is dated. However, such a problem is not at issue for our interpretation. The Philistines appear as another device for articulation of the blessing. In any case, the text appears not to be a historical narrative but a theological statement.)

2. The blessing theme is this-worldly. In its main import, chapter 26 is not concerned with long-range hopes for what will be given in some distant future. Rather, it is celebrative of the present working out of prosperity and well-being in quite visible form. Isaac enjoys *great prosperity, judged by worldly standards,* apart from any theological notion. Thus, Isaac has a good harvest (v. 12) and is "very wealthy" (v. 13). He is blessed "a hundred-fold" (v. 12). (In the New Testament, blessing received "a hundred-fold" is a result of faithfulness [Matt. 19:29; Mark 10:30] and of responsiveness to the word of the kingdom [Luke 8:8].) Isaac's good fortune is evidenced in the finding of water (vv. 17–22, 32), in reference to fertility (v. 22) and in the ready capitulation of Abimelech and the Philistines (vv. 26–31).

The worldly blessings of Isaac are given formal summary expression in the judgment of verse 13: "And the man became rich, and gained more and more until he became very wealthy." It is important that the term "great" *(gdl)* is used three times, the same term used for Abraham ("great nation, great name" in 12:2) and for Solomon ("greater throne," "great throne," "excelled" [I Kings 1:37, 47; 10:23]), the prototype of Israelite blessedness.

3. The narrative in its present form finds no conflict or tension between the *theological claim of blessing from Yahweh* and *prosperity judged by worldly standards.* In a very general

way, the theological claim of verses 3, 24 forms a framework for the narrative of prosperity, though the climactic statement of Abimelech the non-believer (v. 28) falls beyond verse 24. The *eyes of faith* discern the reality of blessing in the language of *promise*. So the whole chapter is made into a statement about promise. But the *eyes of the world* discern the same reality as *prosperity*. Promise and prosperity are not different, however. The promise of God is the source of prosperity. Later of course (as in Job), that equation is questioned. But this narrative does not face such an anguished possibility.

But the narrative does not insist on such an articulation. It is sufficient that the blessings are received and recognized. Truncated as it is, the Isaac narrative is contrasted with the Abraham narrative in which the promise is always put as something of a question. And it is contrasted with the Jacob narrative so beset with conflict. Here there is only a minimum of conflict and that is nicely resolved. Here the promise is asserted and presumed but not at all in question. Here the tradition of promise is used as a vehicle for a theology of blessing.

A Theology of Blessing

In an intellectual climate in which we are pressed to choose between Jerusalem and Athens, between religion and secularity, this narrative offers an important resource for holding together *profound faith claims* and *worldly experience*. The graciousness of Yahweh (which is at work everywhere in this chapter) wells up as natural benefit for the world of this man.

The picture of Isaac offered here is parallel to the blessed man of Psalm 37:

Trust in the LORD, and do good;
     so you will dwell in the land, and enjoy security.
Take delight in the LORD,
     and he will give you the desires of your heart.
Commit your way to the LORD;
     trust in him, and he will act.
He will bring your vindication as the light,
     and your right as the noonday. . . .
But the meek shall possess the land,
     and delight themselves in abundant prosperity. . . .
The LORD knows the days of the blameless,
     and their heritage will abide for ever;

223

they are not put to shame in evil times,
>> in the days of famine [cf. Gen. 26:1–2] they
>>> have abundance. . . .
Wait for the LORD, and keep to his way,
>> and he will exalt you to possess the land; . . .
Mark the blameless man, and behold the upright,
>> for there is prosperity for the man of peace
>>> (Ps. 37:3–6, 11, 18–19, 34, 37).

This psalm has close connections with wisdom traditions. The picture of Isaac may also have derived from such a perspective. In any case, Isaac is "a man of peace" (vv. 29, 31; cf. Ps. 37:37) for whom all God's blessings operate. The narrative testifies to the benevolent ordering of life which has gifts to give. Not much is made in the Isaac narrative of obedience as a condition for blessing. The gifts are simply given. And yet two dimensions of obedience are worth noting. First, verse 5 has a remarkable reference to the obedience of Abraham, looking back to 18:19 (cf. 19:29). This text seems to affirm that Isaac prospers because of the obedience of his father. Second, Isaac is characterized as one who trusts Yahweh (v. 25), like his father before him (cf. 12:8; 13:4).

We may observe three dimensions of blessing as the narrative moves from the theological premise of verse 3 to the worldly recognition of verse 28.

1. Verses 6–11 utilize an old tradition of which we have already seen parallels. (Probably the closing formula of v. 11 is an ancient and stylized one to which the narrative has been attached [cf. Judg. 21:5; Exod. 21:12–17; I Sam. 14:39]. The formula itself existed independently of the narrative but is used here to strengthen the narrative.) But this version of the wife-sister episode is even more positive than 20:1–18, which ends in God's intercession. This account has an unexpected conclusion (vv. 26–31), ending in covenant (v. 28), blessing (v. 29), and oath (v. 31). Isaac, a man of blessing, enters into a solidarity with those less blessed. He is a model citizen, like Job (cf. Job 31:1—34), who also causes a blessing for others (cf. Gen. 12:3). Isaac is a man of peace. He not only lives peaceably, but he causes peace for those around him. He not only receives blessing but bears and causes blessing. Thus the wife-sister narrative is used for a very different message.

224

2. The disputes over water rights may reflect actual historical reality (cf. 13:7). (It is impossible to determine the economic

base of Isaac, though there is evidence of agrarianism [v. 12] and shepherding [v. 20]. He appears to be a person who controlled considerable land in a mixed economy.) Those episodes are now ordered according to etiologies for the names of wells, thus "Ezek" (v. 20), "Sitnah" (v. 21), "Rehoboth" (v. 22) and "Beersheba" (v. 33). In the final form, Beersheba is the most important though it does not seem intrinsic to the narrative. Special attention should be given to the name, "Rehoboth," "The LORD has made room for us" (v. 22). This term expresses a major motif of the blessing theme. Israel is frequently concerned for "room" or "space." (Cf. Pss. 4:1; 31:8 "broad place"; 66:12; 80:9.) That agenda reflects the awareness of people who have had no safe place. It is an abiding agenda for Israel, so often facing exile. The metaphor in the name Rehoboth may be turned psychologically toward "breathing space" or sociologically toward *Lebensraum*. This is a God who gives space (cf. John 14:2). As elsewhere in this chapter, the large promise of land is nicely made concrete in the specific blessing of a well (and derivatively, space).

3. The chapter concludes with the climactic affirmation, "We have found water" (v. 32). (V. 33 is an appended etiology and v. 34 is an isolated note. Neither relates to the main narrative.) This statement (v. 32) is the decisive verdict on Isaac as a man genuinely blessed.

The specific figure of water, while quite concrete here, is used elsewhere in a more impressionistic way. Thus we may refer to the lack of water in Amos 4:7–8, to the distinction of living water and self-made water in Jer. 2:13–14 (cf. Deut. 11:10–12), and to the metaphor of water applied to Jesus (John 4:1–15). Related to the water reference of John 4, note the theological claim of John 1:45 in a statement paralleled to that of our verse 32.

It is not suggested that water in chapter 26 is anything but concrete. But such a reference stands at the beginning of a tradition in which the image is developed in quite theological ways. The "water of life" is both the news of *the giving God* and *the gift* he gives. With the figure of water, as in other ways throughout the chapter, theological claim and worldly reality converge.

225

4. The movement of chapter 26 compresses the sojourn of Isaac into a brief account. But even in brevity, it spans a movement from *famine* (v. 1) to *water* in Beersheba (vv. 32–33). At

the beginning, the life of this son of promise is precarious. At its end, Isaac is safely settled and richly blessed. And Isaac knows, as the narrative announces, that "every good endowment and every perfect gift is from above..." (James 1:17). Like his father, Isaac calls on the name of and relies only on Yahweh (v. 28). Yahweh is one who is known in the blessing of sowing (v. 12), in the prosperity of flocks and herds (v. 16), in water and in peace (v. 27). In a quite understated way, this narrative uses the formula of promise (vv. 3–4, 24) to announce the goodness of a blessed world. The narrative provides a theological nuance different from that of the father before or the son after. The Isaac narrative invites reflection on a world teeming with generously given life. That abundant life is recognized as blessing to those who will receive and share it. The chapter presents a world-view in which *affirmation of the world* and *gratitude to God* are held integrally together.

Genesis 27:1–45

This chapter forms a counterpart to 25:19–34. Together, the units of 25:19–34 and 27:1–45 deal with the two related themes. On the one hand, they concern the transmission of the promise and the inheritance from one generation to the next. There is in Genesis no one-generational faith. There is always the problem of the promise being safely entrusted to the next generation. Here, as elsewhere, that vertical move from *generation to generation* causes a crisis. Indeed, that crisis evokes much of the action in the patriarchal narrative.

On the other hand, and more intensely, these two narratives concern the tension and rivalry in the next generation between the two brothers. That is, the horizontal problem *within the generation* is more acute than the vertical problem between the generations. The narrative does not report simply that the promise is given to the next generation, but that it is given to Jacob the younger at the expense of Esau the elder. In the finished form of the tradition, it is clear that the oracle of 25:23 governs even here. It has been inscrutably decreed that the younger shall receive what might have been automatically entrusted to the older.

226

Our text unfolds in four dramatic movements. It traces a tense interaction between four members of the family, each of whom has a distinct role to play. In the midst of these actions, the inscrutable power of the blessing works its will. At the beginning, the old father must give his blessing before he dies (vv. 1–4). At the end (vv. 42–45), the younger son has the blessing. But the blessing makes him a fugitive. As it tells of the strange turn of events, the narrative is not without irony. It knows that the blessing, surely intended for good, has become a source of heavy anxiety. The blessing so passionately sought is a burden. The cunning younger son never anticipated that. The blessing has its own way, notwithstanding the intent of any of the four players in this family drama.

The Juxtaposition of Blessing and Duplicity

(Note: Our exposition has repeatedly found a remarkably insightful device of composition in the traditions. Theological statements are made by means of the often surprising juxtaposition of two themes in one narrative. As a result, each theme may make its own statement and then be a part of yet another significant affirmation by means of the pairing and the consequent tension. See also pp. 210, 221–222).

As we shall see, this narrative is a carefully crafted drama. But before considering the dramatic development of the whole, we may observe that behind the characters, the narrator has presented an unexpected interplay between the power of blessing and the practice of deceit.

1. A proper interpretation of this narrative requires attention to the meaning of blessing. The assumptions made in the text may seem foreign to us. This narrative requires the expositor to step outside the rationality of our world into a different world where another kind of transaction is possible. This family in Genesis is preoccupied with blessing, as though it matters more than things visible. As it is here sought and given, the blessing combines all of the *primitive power* of a spoken word (which has a life of its own) with the *high theological claim* of special vocation for its addressee. No more than the story itself are we permitted to choose between the primitive power discerned in the blessing and the theological claim derived from it. There is no blessing without that life-changing claim. And there is no new vocation without that mysterious designating act. Blessing is understood as a world-transforming act which

227

cannot be denied by modern rationality. For the son as for the father, indeed for the entire family, the matter of the blessing is as dangerous as it is compelling.

a. The pursuit of blessing characterizes existence as *inter-generational.* Parents and children have a deep stake in each others' destinies. The narrative refutes every notion of individualism which assumes that every individual life and, indeed, every generation is discreet and on its own. The generations are inalienably and terrifyingly bound together (cf. Heb. 11:39–40).

b. The narrative presumes that *symbolic actions have genuine and abiding power.* Symbolic actions (like laying on hands) are not empty gestures signifying nothing. This ritual act is a decisive event in which something has been done irrevocably (cf. 48:18–19). More happens than meets the eye.

c. This narrative assumes and affirms that *spoken words shape human life.* Language is not simply an exercise in propaganda and manipulation (as it tends to be in our modern world). Words here are not a matter of indifference which may be attended to or not, as is convenient. Here, when words are spoken by authoritative persons in proper contexts, they have a substance. They mean what they say. They must be handled with respect, for they are means toward life or death (cf. James 3:10).

d. This narrative offers a *fresh discernment of the nature of power.* It eschews mechanistic views which equate power with force. It understands that power, the capacity to shape the future, lies not in weapons and arms, but in the use of language, gesture, and symbol.

Like so many others in Genesis, this narrative invites the listening community into the "strange new world of the Bible." Our exposition must suggest a critique of our presumed life-world which tends to be flat and one-dimensional. That is, language only describes what is. Newness is not expected or thought possible. Life is defined by the present, what can be handled, explained, and managed. This narrative insists that all who claim the memory of Israel are sacramental creatures. Words and gestures, promises and claims, matter for humanness and humaneness. These have a power that technical capacities cannot void or even diminish. To hear this text requires the suspension of our usual perceptual world so that we may discern an alternative which holds better promises.

There is pathos in this text, for the sons as well as for the father. It lies in the awareness that nobody wants to live a life that is unblessed. Nobody wants a life without the special words and gestures that bind that life to a precious past and a promised future. The narrative becomes aware that somebody is destined to lesser blessing. One son cannot have the full blessing, for there is only one such blessing. The intrigue in this narrative is as keen as the stakes are high. This whole family knows that without the power of the blessing, life has no fresh possibility and no new beginning. The unblessed are those left empty-handed with only pragmatic forms of power, mechanistic ways of speech, and futures only they can shape. For all these reasons we can appreciate the "holy zeal" of Rebekah (Calvin), the detached stridency of Jacob, and the pathos of the father and his first-born.

2. Even though the blessing has such power, it is given in fragile ways. In this narrative, the blessing is at the behest of intrigue and deception. Though we might be interested in the blessing, the drama depends on the duplicity initiated by Rebekah and implemented by Jacob. Without it there would be no narrative and conventional inheritance by the first-born would prevail. But this is no conventional story. The practice of primogeniture is broken, and it is that break that concerns us. But we cannot overlook this fact: The break for the blessing comes by trickery.

As with the narrative about the pottage (25:29–34), so here the narrator does not explain or justify. Indeed, the narrator seems unaware of the incongruity that may appear to us: a *blessing* gotten by *deception!* While that may be a problem for us, we do better to stay inside the story itself, to perceive that the narrative is simply that way (as is life itself). Settlement of property and inheritance is seldom achieved without coveting and calculation. That is how it is in this family. The story is powerful enough to speak for itself. The narrative exemplifies what is generally true of Genesis. This is not a spiritual treatise on morality. It is, rather, a memory of how faith moves in the rawness of experience. We must leave it at that.

3. The narrative functions as a parallel to 25:27–34. The statement of Esau in 27:36 recognizes that the stories are parallel. J. P. Fokkelman observes a possible play on words in "blessing" *(bᵉrākāh)* and "birthright" *(bᵉqorāh)* (*Narrative Art in Genesis*, 1975, pp. 99). Both narratives serve the same function,

to make concrete the inversion anticipated in 25:23. Perhaps the two narratives were transmitted in separate circles of tradition and only late brought together. Thus, 27:36 may be an effort to harmonize materials that go over the same ground. But even if they serve the same purpose, there are two important differences.

a. In 25:27–34, there is nothing mysterious or deceitful. The negotiation between the brothers is open and honest, even if exploitative. Jacob does nothing treacherous. By contrast, in our narrative of 27:1–45, we are in another milieu. The entire plot is focused on a carefully planned deceit. Unlike the matter of the birthright, the blessing is secured here not by hard bargaining but by shrewd misrepresentation.

b. We have found very little narrative development in 25:27–34. There we saw only one moment and no movement of scenes or plot. Our exposition is theological because the text itself is intentionally proclamatory. By contrast, 27:1–45 is artistically shaped with skillful development and tantalizing rhetoric and pace. The theological claim is discreet and understated. And when it is done, we are left with mixed responses and unresolved issues. Thus, our exposition of this text must be more attentive to the structure and movement of the narrative. Compared with 25:27–34, this text calls for patience to permit the narrative to take the lead and make its own case.

The narrative carries listeners to emotional extremities. Yet it also practices severe restraint in setting limits on the characters and the actions. Therefore, it does not lend itself to reduction or summary. It requires the listening community to participate in the turns and pauses of the action. The best exposition is to lead the listening community through the action and to share in the struggle.

Given such delicate expression, this struggle is at two levels. Up front, there are the four family members locked in a fated dispute. But behind that family quarrel is the interface between blessing and deception. The blessing seems to have its own power toward the younger son. Yet the mother and her son manage it by their cleverness. One may wonder if the blessing would have turned out differently without the deception or if the deception was the deciding factor. Yet, one senses that while the deception appears to turn the blessing, in fact the deception is only a tool for the blessing to go a way already decided upon. But one is not sure. For that reason,

230

conclusions must be restrained. It is best to follow the contours of the narrative.

The Drama in Four Scenes

Gunkel has already seen that the extended narrative of chapter 27 is easily cast into four scenes with a transitional conclusion in verses 41–45:

Scene I.	(vv. 1–4)	The father prepares to bless his older son
Scene II.	(vv. 5–17)	The mother schemes for her younger son
Scene III.	(vv. 18–29)	The younger son deceives the father
Scene IV.	(vv. 30–40)	The father grieves with his older son.

1. There is a symmetry to Scene I (vv. 1–4) and Scene IV (vv. 30–40). Both concern Isaac and Esau. These two scenes might have been the whole story had there not been an intrusion. But Jacob is always and everywhere an intruder. The first scene begins with the resolve of the father to give his blessing, transmit the promise, and settle the inheritance. Both the father and the son, "heir apparent," assume that it is their proper business to engage in a regular transmission to the elder son. It would seem a fitting closure to the life of the father. Thus far, we are given no hint of anything exceptional.

2. Scene II (vv. 5–17) features the shrewd mother and her precious son. The scene requires little comment. It is clearly an act of deception. One would not expect it in the Bible from the son whose future has been guaranteed by the oracle. This family for whom so much is at stake cannot permit the transmission of the blessing to pass routinely. The fascination of the tradition with Jacob is based on his refusal of routine subordination. Rebekah is willing to risk curse for the well-being of her precious son (cf. 13).

3. But it is in Scene III (vv. 18–29) that the issue is joined.

a. All the power that can be mustered to seize the future comes into play. The father is eager to settle the future on his elder. Driven by his mother (and the oracle of 25:23?) to have his own way, Jacob is zealous to overcome his mistaken status not corrected in the womb. Jacob sets himself against the clear intent of his father and every social convention.

231

Characteristically, Jacob will not be denied. He will have his way. He becomes accustomed to having his way. The father gives the blessing he wants to give. But he gives it to the son whom he does not want to have it. Surely, there is more working against Isaac than the cunning of Rebekah. There is also the power of God at work for Jacob. From the beginning, Isaac cannot resist it.

b. Given and received in duplicity, the blessing is massive and unqualified.

1) The blessing concerns the things of the earth, fertility, well-being, prosperity—shalom (v. 28). Westermann (*Blessing in the Bible,* Chap. 2) has shown how blessings concern especially the things of the earth. Even that most familiar blessing of Num. 6:24–26 ends with such a wish for shalom: "The LORD give you shalom."

2) The blessing speaks of the things of history, of political power and preeminence (v. 29a). In this conflict between brothers, Esau is locked into a place of subordination. The blessing is that the elder shall "bow down" to Jacob. The entire Jacob narrative has a strange irony. For in 33:3, 11, there is "bowing down." But it is not as anticipated in this text. One is left to wonder who in fact has triumphed. The outcome is characteristic for this man of conflict, for this narrator of shrewdness. On the larger canvass of politics, Israel (=David?) is given preeminence in the family of nations (cf. II Sam. 8:1–14, especially vv. 13–14 on Edom/Esau).

3) The most formidable hedge of protection is given (v. 29 b), one which looks back to the word to Abraham (Gen. 12:3) and forward to Balaam (Num. 24:9). Now the die is cast. The blessing has worked its way, albeit by treachery. The transition to the next generation is achieved. The younger son has worked his will in spite of his father. The blessing has reached its locus through a world-changing duplicity.

4. In Scene IV (vv. 30–40), neither the father nor the older son expect anything other than a routine settlement. Neither knows about the diabolical action in the intervening scenes.

a. The language in Scenes I and IV (the only ones involving Esau) concerns the blessing. The father and the older son are determined to live in a world where the symbolic power of language is at work. They know nothing of treachery or deceit. Perhaps they do not need to, for they are not the younger son. They are able to rely on and benefit from a very different social reality. The expectation of Scene I has been, "that I may bless you" (v. 4). Scene IV resumes this, "that you may bless me" (v. 31).

b. Then abruptly, there is the terror-filled turn: "Isaac trembled an exceedingly great trembling" (v. 33). In an instant, everything is clear to him. His whole beautiful dream for a peaceful and proper closure to his life has been irreversibly shattered. Even his presupposition that he is master in his own house is destroyed. The son makes a claim that both are prepared to accept: "I am your son, your first-born" (v. 32). But something is at work which neither of them can control. Their claims on each other are irrelevant. It is ironic that the very blessing which was to bind the generations into a peaceful whole has now become the instrument of a deathly divisiveness.

There is here deep communion between the father and the son. Both of them are helpless. Both have been dealt a mortal blow. They do not need to say very much to each other. The story-teller is delicate and does not intrude into this private and precious moment of the characters. The expositor must practice the same restraint. The narrative provides a moment of self-recognition for any hearer simply because life is like that.

c. The older son, the son of entitlement (cf. Deut. 21:15–17) still cannot believe what has happened, even after he sees clearly. He urges bitterly and passionately: "Bless me, even me also" (v. 34). But the father knows more than the son. He knows that things are beyond his power to recall. Every father would want to make it all right for his son (cf. Matt. 7:9–11). But Isaac knows that the power of the blessing is larger than both of them. It will have its own way in spite of them both. Esau pauses long enough to articulate the hatred which will drive his life for the next twenty years (v. 36). Then he returns to the issue at hand, the blessing. No one wants to live an unblessed life. The father does not wish such a life for his son. What pathos passes between the son who must have the blessing and the father who cannot give it! The narrative makes ready contact with every parent whose dream for the child is fractured. Every parent wants to "fix it" and make it right for his/her precious child. But it is beyond the parent, always, because other things are at work that do not yield to us. And so the parent is a mixture of hurt and failure and sorrow. Precisely at the moment of deepest kinship comes this strange impotence. The pathos is shared by the two, by the father who is honored but duped, and by the son whose birthright is spent.

d. Blessings are to be spoken in solemn assurance. But not

233

this one. All that is left now is a desperate whimper which the son can hardly hear and the father cannot bear to speak. Now empty-handed (vv. 39–40), he gives a blessing which is scarcely a blessing to his precious son. It must have been spoken in tears of weakness and hopelessness. The last words are a faint hope (v. 40*b*). There will be an end to the yoke. The conclusion is not what either had wished. But there is a vision of freedom even for the "other" son.

Isaac could not let his son Esau go without a blessing. He lingers with him and fashions something of a blessing. Surely Isaac, as the tradition presents him, can still remember the anguish of Gen. 22 when father Abraham had to take his son, his only son, the one whom he loved (v. 2). And now Isaac in yet another context must turn loose his son whom he loves into a threatening world where the blessing has been turned against him. Esau, his beloved child, is not the child of promise. And yet, cautiously, understatedly, he also bears a promise. This lesser promise (vv. 39–40) keeps the story from being narrowly and ideologically Jacobite. There is a broadness here that requires a vision even beyond Israel. There is a promise to the nations. In the midst of Jacob's coup, liberation for other peoples is also envisioned. No wonder others not of the lineage of Abraham also find in Genesis a root promise for human liberation: for "you shall break his yoke from your neck" (v. 40).

It is so pale a hope. We are left with all kinds of questions: Why only one blessing? Why not recall and reissue the blessing like a car manufacturer? But both the father and the son know better. We are not dealing with a "previously owned" blessing, like a used car. That first blessing has been spoken. There are tears and pathos, bitterness and hatred. But it is over and gone. And all parties know it.

Inscrutable Blessing and Dangerous Future

Jacob is the son before whom the future now lies—with the help of Rebekah. In the narrative, neither Jacob nor Rebekah evokes any positive feeling from the listener. They are nearly cardboard figures in a larger game. If we feel toward them at all, the feeling is probably contempt. By contrast, our sympathies run to Isaac and Esau. That is how the story has been told. But for all our attraction to them, Isaac and Esau are beside the point.

1. The text confronts us with an incongruity. The story is fashioned deliberately to bring our sympathies to those who are

beside the point. Because it is done with such consummate skill, we may be confident that it is not an accident. It is a subtle but deliberate way of saying that the blessing will work in spite of human character and quality and in spite of our inclinations in another direction. The blessing of God has its way whether we are attracted to or repelled by the object of the blessing. The narrative shows God strangely at work for Jacob without regard for our emotions about Jacob.

Given the oracle of 25:23 and its undoubted continuing importance for the Jacob tradition, we may dare to conclude that the real issue here is not primarily about Isaac and Esau, nor about Rebekah and Jacob. It is, rather, about the power of the blessing in the service of God's purpose of inversion. It is dynamic of the blessing that makes moral censure of Rebekah irrelevant. For this narrator, Rebekah plays a role she does not know about and did not choose. There are no hints in the entire narrative that she knows what she is doing (cf. Luke 23:34). We know only from 25:19–34 about the larger mystery at work here. The assertion at the beginning, at the birth, was inexplicable. We do not know why, "The elder shall serve the younger." That issue continues into this episode. The bargaining for the birthright (25:29–34) and the scheme for the blessing (27:1–45) implement the oracle in ways unrecognized by every participant. God has evoked the conflict. The conflict causes pain or shame to every player. But God does not shrink from the conflict, for a holy purpose is underway.

2. The way of God will not be explained. The narrative invites the listening community to marvel rather than to explain. The reality of blessing is not simply the result of human ingenuity. Nor is it a matter of good luck. The narrator hints here at what becomes explicit to Balaam (Num. 23:7–12). Balaam was hired to curse, but try as he would, he could not curse those whom Yahweh would bless. Balaam discovered he was not free in the face of such divine decision: "Must I not take heed to speak what the Lord puts in my mouth?"

The difficult part for us is that this is not an incidental religious curiosity in the Bible. It is, rather, a persistent theme which runs toward that strange company gathered around Jesus. The scandal there is the same. The ones whom all partisans of "primogeniture" would reject as unqualified and unworthy are the very ones invited to the festival of blessing (Luke 5:30; 14:12–14, 21; 15:1–2; 19:7).

235

3. The blessing has its course to run, one way or another. The narrative must now turn its attention to the realistic recognition that such an unfair act evokes new ways of resentment and dispute (vv. 41–45).

It is ironic that the bearer of the blessing becomes a fugitive. He is a fugitive from all the usual claims of family and propriety. He is a fugitive from the well-ordered world of law. The world can little tolerate persons who seize blessings and find ways to have birthrights by intrigue. By every conventional standard, such a one is unqualified. He constitutes a threat to the known and habitable life-world (cf. Mark 5:19; Luke 19:47). Though Jacob is thrust into an inimical existence, he has been offered alternatives beyond the world's usual assumptions. That is the perilous, hopeful way of God.

Genesis 27:46—28:9

These verses are an intrusion in the primary narrative. They are unrelated to what precedes and to what follows. The main narrative advances naturally from 27:45 to 28:10 without them. At the same time, these verses look back to 26:34–35 which, as we have seen, are also inappropriate in their context.

It is usual to assign these verses to the Priestly tradition. They are dated, then, to the exile when the traditionists faced a particular theological crisis. Believing people were set in a cultural context where they were tempted by various religious and cultural alternatives. The theological agenda of these verses, therefore, and the agenda of exile, is the identity and distinctiveness of the Israelite community in the face of assimilation. The acute threat of assimilation came to be symbolized by the problem of mixed marriages.

By placing this text at this point in the tradition, the traditionists accomplished two things for the Jacob narrative. First, they included a mild criticism of Esau, also reflected in 236 26:34–35. This is the only criticism of Esau in the Genesis narrative. It is what we might expect in the exilic period when Edom/ Esau is a threat to Israel (cf. Mal. 1:2–5). Second, this unit gives an alternative reason for Jacob's flight from his family to his uncle Laban in Haran. In the primary narrative of 27:41–45, his flight is unambiguously to save his own life from the anger of Esau. But this Priestly narrative minimizes that family conflict and gives a positive, theological reason for the journey, that is, so that Jacob can find a suitable wife within the family circle. Thus, the Priestly tradition would prefer to transform the narrative into a parallel with Gen. 24. That attempt is without success because the claim of the main narrative is more compelling. That narrative asserts that Jacob went in fear for his life, not for the sake of family purity. At best, this later narrative offers a minority report which would make things more positive and more intentional theologically.

The Movement of the Passage

The three segments of the text (27:46; 28:1–5; 6–9) do not flow easily from one to the other. They lack the coherence of sustained narrative. Rather, the text is didactic in style and form. This is not story but teaching, and we must focus on its didactic intent.

1. In 27:46, the account begins in a complaint by Rebekah. (It has the same mood and tone as her earlier lament in 25:22.) In the total narrative, such a remark is unexpected and out of character. But as an introduction to a teaching, it is clear enough. To a passionate, faithful member of the family, assimilation through mixed marriage is a horrendous prospect.

2. The main portion of the text is 28:1–5.

a. After 27:1–45, we would not expect Isaac to dismiss his scheming son with such a blessing. But this text posits a family in harmony, quite unlike the main tradition. The speech of Isaac contains two elements: (1) Verses 3–4 provide the conventional promise to the fathers expressed in the distinctive language of the Priestly tradition (cf. 17:1–8; 35:11–12; 48:3–4; Exod. 6:2–8). (2) More importantly, verse 1 contains the central teaching of the entire text: "You shall not marry one of the Canaanite women." The unit is built around this warning about mixed marriage which will jeopardize the faith of Israel and the promise of land. The prohibition is in the same form as the prohibitions of the ten commandments and is offered with the same gravity and urgency. The issue of assimilation is perceived as life-and-death for Israel. The traditionists know that trust in seductive alternatives in exile will lead to the destruction of this family.

237

b. An important incongruity will be noticed. On the one hand, the syncretism feared in the prohibition concerns the *Canaanites*. That is the substance of this stereotyped formula. On the other hand, the narrative about Rebekah's fear concerns the *Hittites*. It is probable that the text is concerned with neither Canaanites nor with Hittites but with the principle of purity. Neither Canaanites nor Hittites are real historical factors in the sixth century. Van Seters ("The Terms 'Amorite' and 'Hittite' in the Old Testament," VT 22:64–84 [1972]) is correct in urging that these terms have lost all concrete historical meaning in this text. They now have a theological "ideological" intention, referring to those outside the identifiable "orthodox" religious community of Israel. Thus, the terms "Canaanite" and "Hittite" in our text refer to any people not under the discipline of covenant, the demands of Torah, and ritual obedience. (Cf. Ezek. 16:3, likely a text contemporary to our text, for a theological use of "Hittite.") What is urged is not ethnic or racial purity but disciplined intentional identity in the face of pagan or disbelieving cultures. The issue was an important one in exile and after exile as reflected in the reforms of Ezra and Nehemiah (Ezra 10:9–17; Neh. 13:23–27). It is predictably an important issue wherever a zealous minority community of faith must maintain itself against an attractive dominant cultural alternative.

3. In the concluding part of the text (vv. 6–9) the central teaching on syncretism is repeated (v. 6), this time with reference to Esau. Not only Jacob, but Esau as well, must be attentive to the need for purity in the community of Israel. There can be no compromise in the family of Israel.

The Issue of Purity and Syncretism

This text poses the issue of faith and culture, an issue given classical expression by H. Richard Niebuhr in *Christ and Culture*. That is not a primary issue for the dominant tradition of Genesis, which tended either to be at ease with culture (as in the Solomonic period) or had the energy to transform culture (as in the period of Joshua and Judges). It is when the community of faith is itself endangered by syncretism and domestication that this text may speak an important word. Faith becomes endangered either by persecution or by accommodation. In the exile of Israel, both dangers were operative. Psalm 137 suggests a sense of being persecuted. But more likely, it was the seduc-

238

tive power of an alternative religion which was the greater threat to Israel. Either persecution or accommodation requires the community of faith to draw lines of discipline to maintain itself and sustain its energy.

1. This text will seem odd to tolerant "melting pot" America, which has worked hard to overcome destructive religious sectarianism and has learned to practice ecumenism and even "mixed marriage" with some degree of humaneness. The text will not be compatible with the inclinations of those who believe that being "in the world" is not necessarily to be "of the world." It will run counter to those who believe sectarianism is a danger far more threatening than syncretism or assimilation to cultural values.

But in principle, the text requires the faithful community to recognize that "Canaanite/Hittite" alternatives can be a danger to the community. There are times when concrete steps of discipline must be taken for the purpose of identity and survival. This text invites the listening community to ask what time it is and to decide which posture of faith *vis-à-vis* culture is now required. The text was shaped at a time when cultural embrace and accommodation had gone on long enough to be a threat. In such times, an assertion of distinctiveness and discipline is important. In the contemporary church, careless syncretism may mean an embrace of consumerism in an acquisitive society or an uncritical positivism in ethical matters.

2. There will be a temptation for some to regard this text as "Old Testament legalism" as contrasted with the graciousness of the New Testament. But in the New Testament as well, there are a variety of postures on this issue. New Testament texts reflective of the same crisis do appear, especially in those addressed to the church at Corinth. Presumably, the Corinthian congregation lived at the brink of syncretism. In I Cor. 7:14–15, Paul urges staying and living with unbelievers because the issue of harmony is more urgent than that of purity. But in II Cor. 6:14–18, written to the same congregation but in another situation, Paul takes a quite different position and rejects any partnership with non-believers. Clearly Paul does not offer an unambiguous model. But the various responses of Paul as well as our text suggest that the community of faith must be self-conscious and intentional about its relation to cultural values. Only then can it assess the dangers of syncretism.

3. What the expositor makes of this text depends on

239

whether one's assessment of the community of faith in culture tilts toward Paul's judgment of *harmony over purity* (as in I Cor. 7) or toward *disengagement for the sake of faithfulness* (as in II Cor. 6). In any case, it is clear from this text that there are times when the community of faith cannot be preoccupied only with cultural engagement, outreach, and ministry. There are times when it first asks about its own life, its discipline and the practice which makes for identity, faithfulness, and power. At such times, the possibility of a necessary disengagement from culture for the sake of the promise is clearly supported by this text.

However, it is important in such contexts to recall that "mixed marriage" is not to be treated from this text as a concrete issue in itself. It is a symbolic expression of the problem of syncretism on a broad front. Given the church in modern Western culture, "mixed marriage" is no longer a primary dimension of the church's manifest enculturation. Taken concretely, the prohibition would not get at the real issues of syncretism and domestication in our time. Those issues in our time more likely concern political and economic dimensions of public morality.

Expository Possibilities

1. Linked to the command to disengage (28:8) is the articulation of the most profound blessing, the blessing of Abraham (28:3–4). Could it be that only in singular reliance on the promise (i.e., with cultural alternatives rejected) is the gift of God present with power? (That realization is also evident in Gen. 22:1–13 in which the *promise* requires even the *risk* of the son.)

2. The summons to disengagement and the accompanying promise send Jacob to exile. (Remember that the Priestly text is addressed to exiles.) Disengagement from culture for the sake of faith results in being displaced persons. This is a sophisticated theological motivation for sojourning, in contrast to the quite concrete fear of 27:41–45.

3. Even Esau (not the son of the promise, but still a son) responds to the prohibition to marry with the family of purity. The tradition is not at all parochial or sectarian at this point. In the issue of enculturation versus disengagement for faithfulness, Esau clearly is reckoned among the faithful. The Esau reference hints that the community of faith may act in disciplined ways without becoming exclusivistic. At this place where

Esau could easily be disowned for his violation (cf. 26:34–35), he is included among those who honor the prohibition.

Genesis 28:10–22

For the first time in the Jacob narrative, this unit moves away from the strenuous conflicts of human interaction. Now we have a direct confrontation between Jacob and the God who has been at work in the battle for the birthright. As Gunkel has seen, this episode, together with the parallel encounter at Penu'el (32:22–32), form the skeletal structure for the entire Jacob story.

This narrative is structured to include, (*a*) a context of journey (vv. 10–11) which gives the text continuity with 27:45. The journey motif is resumed in 29:1. But the journey motif is not important to this episode and only provides a framework for (*b*) a theophanic encounter (vv. 12–15) which includes both a visual experience (v. 12) and a speech of promise (vv. 13–15), and (*c*) the response of Jacob to the encounter which includes a vow of faithfulness (vv. 20–21) and cultic responses to the event (vv. 17–19, 22).

The encounter occurs in a place where Jacob would not expect a religious experience. It is not even a place whose name is known until the encounter. Jacob is a fugitive now outside all the protections of conventional meanings and social guarantees.

Shakespeare has offered empassioned, eloquent testimony to the dread of such banishment:

> Ha, banishment! Be merciful, say "death;"
> For exile hath more terror in his look,
> much more than death. Do not say "banishment." . . .
> There is no world without Verona walls,
> But purgatory, torture, hell itself.
> Hence banished is banish'd from the world,
> And world's exile is death. Then "banished"
> Is death mis-term'd; calling death "banished,"
> Thou cut'st my head off with a golden axe,
> And smilest upon the stroke that murders me
> (*Romeo and Juliet*, Act III, Scene III).

241

Moreover, the encounter takes place not in wakeful control but in a time of vulnerable yielding, while he is asleep. The encounter is completely at the behest of God, who through it all retains the initiative. Jacob is helpless to conjure the meeting. In any case, such an event is scarcely a priority for him. He seeks only his own safety from his brother, not likely to be found through such an encounter. He has no religious agenda.

This narrative raises difficult questions about the nature of an encounter with God. On the one hand, we may be tempted to imagine that this is a "primitive" religious report that has no pertinence to modern reality, for we have "outgrown" such matters. Or on the other hand, we may wish to explain it psychologically and deny its objective reality. But neither of these will do. The narrative shatters our presuppositions. It insists the world is a place of such meetings. The expositor must take care not to explain or explain away. The startling element in the narrative is not the *appearance* of God, for religious phenomena are still with us in all sorts of ways. But here, the amazement is not in the appearance. Rather, *it is God!* The element in the narrative that surprises Jacob and seems incredible to us is not the religious phenomenon of appearance. It is the wonder, mystery, and shock that this God should be present in such a decisive way to this exiled one. The miracle is the way this sovereign God binds himself to this treacherous fugitive. The event is told as an inexplicable experience. It cannot be assessed by any comparisons or norms outside itself.

The Journey

The framework of the journey (vv. 10–11) is not very important except that the event happens "between places" where nothing is expected. It happens between safe, identifiable places. Here everything is risky. It is enough in this memory that a *"non-place"* is transformed by the coming of God into a *crucial place.* The transformation takes place during sleep, when Jacob has lost control of his destiny. He will not resist this Other One in the night. And in the process, this "non-person" (i.e., *exiled, threatened*) is transformed by the coming of God to a person crucial for the promise.

The Coming of God

242   In such encounters as this one (vv. 12–15), there are often two elements, the visual and the auditory. While the former may fascinate us, the point of exposition must be the speech. It

is the speech of God which changes things. Other gods may appear. This one makes self-binding promises.

1. Our interpretation must not linger too long on the visual elements (v. 12). Three phenomena are noted, each of which can be pursued for its "religious" dimension.

a. The meeting happens in *a dream*. The wakeful world of Jacob was a world of fear, terror, loneliness (and, we may imagine, unresolved guilt). Those were parameters of his existence. The dream permits the entry of an alternative into his life. The dream is not a morbid review of a shameful past. It is rather the presentation of an alternative future with God. The gospel moves to Jacob in a time when his guard is down. The dream permits news. It is here, as elsewhere in Genesis (cf. 31:10–11, 24; 37:5–10), a means by which the purpose of God has its say in the life of this family.

b. The news is that there is traffic between heaven and earth. The object described is probably a *ramp* rather than the conventional "ladder." It refers to something like the Mesopotamian ziggurat, a land mass formed as a temple through which earth touches heaven. Such a ramp as a religious figure reflects the imperial religion of the culture. But now it has become a visual vehicle for a gospel assertion. Earth is not left to its own resources and heaven is not a remote self-contained realm for the gods. Heaven has to do with earth. And earth finally may count on the resources of heaven. Paul Minear (*To Heal and to Reveal,* 1976, Chap. 2) has explored "heaven" as a metaphor by which the Bible refers to the reality of *promise* related to the purposes of God. That is the substance of the vision. It shatters the presumed world of Jacob. He had assumed he traveled alone with his only purpose being survival. It was not hard then to conclude that divine reality was irrelevant. Now it is asserted that earth is a place of possibility because it has not been and will not be cut off from the sustaining role of God. In this image are the seeds of incarnational faith, of the power of God being embodied in a historical man. Thus our text points to the statement of Jesus (John 1:51).

c. The figure of the ramp is enlivened with the presence of *angels.* These are not, of course, winged creatures, but royal messengers of God who act to do his bidding. As indicated in the promise (vv. 13–15), the message they bear is that the promissory Kingdom of God is now at work. The old kingdom of fear

243

and terror is being overcome. God comes where he is not anticipated. That, after all, is the real issue of this text: Is there a coming of God who transforms human reality? These together —dream, ramp, angels—answer "yes." These visible features introduce a new reality into the life of Jacob. While interpreters have often paid excessive attention to these elements in verse 12, they are preparatory. The center of the text is the speech of God. The visual elements are the vessels in which the treasure of promise is given.

2. The narrative moves to the real agenda of the speech of the Lord (vv. 13–15). It is not an angel who speaks (v. 13), or even "God." It is *the LORD*. The Lord's speech is a promise.

The phenomena of divine *appearance* are vehicles for a *promise*. The story expresses God's intrusion into human reality which redefines everything. Jacob came to this deserted place, fleeing for his life, undoubtedly without promise. He departs from this encounter changed by the only thing that can change, a word which makes available an alternative future.

a. The promise at the heart of this text and of all the patriarchal stories is the now "standard" promise (vv. 13–14) set in stylized language. It affirms the promise of land for Israel and the promise of well-being for others by Israel. The promise of land is the same which had concerned Abraham and Isaac (12:1, 7; 13:15; 26:3–4). It is the promise which had been surreptitiously given Jacob in the oracle of 25:23, only now it is clear and unambiguous. The promise for the well-being of others (cf. 12:3; 18:18; 22:18; 26:4) again protects the narrative from self-interest. It expresses the counter-theme, urging the promise-receiver (Jacob) out beyond his own narrow interests.

b. But the promise speech extends beyond the standard promise to the fathers. Verses 13–14 appear to be predictable and conventional in the patriarchal narrative. But verse 15 is a promise addressed peculiarly to Jacob. It is a promise not needed by those like Isaac who live their lives without conflict. But Jacob faces special dangers. This promise is God's attentive response to his circumstance of danger. The "behold" of verse 15 breaks new ground—pay attention! The promise to this younger son is three-fold:

244

1) "I am with you." That, of course, is the intent of the ramp-ladder. Heaven has come to be on earth. This promise presents a central thrust of biblical faith. It refutes all the despairing judgments about human existence. A fresh under-

standing of God is required if we are to be delivered from the hopeless analyses of human possibility made by pessimistic scientists and by the poets of existence. God commits himself to the empty-handed fugitive. The fugitive has not been abandoned. This God will accompany him. It is a promise of royal dimension. In fact, such promise later is addressed to another man in jeopardy for God's sake (Jer. 1:19). Then it is reasserted to this whole community called Jacob when the community is in a desperate place of exile (Isa. 43:1–2). It is the name finally assigned to Jesus of Nazareth ("Emmanuel, God with us," Matt. 1:23), who was indeed God with his exiled people:

> O come, o come Emmanuel
> and ransom captive Israel.

And this same promise was his last word to the Matthean church (Matt. 28:20), "I am with you always."

The introduction of this formula dare not be treated like a cliché. It is the amazing new disclosure of Jacob's God, one who is willing to cast his lot with this man, to stand with him in places of threat.

2) The first promise is about a *presence.* The second promise is about an *action:* "I will keep you." The word presents the image of the shepherd who will *protect* Jacob. Israel deals with the good shepherd who cares for and protects the helpless sheep in every circumstance. Again, the promise refutes the notion that Israel is left to its own resources. That promise to this man in conflict is perhaps the basis for much other reflection in Israel. Reference is easily made to Ps. 121, which includes the word "keep" six times. The conventional benediction of Num. 6:24–26 may be usefully linked to Jacob in distress, for it begins, "The LORD bless you and keep you." The angels have not been mentioned since verse 12. But it is worth noting that our word "keep" is used with the angels in Ps. 91:11–15:

> For he will give his angels charge of you
> to *guard* you in all your ways. . . .
> Because he cleaves to me in love, I will deliver him;
> I will protect him, because he knows my name.
> When he calls to me, I will answer him;
> I will be with him in trouble,
> I will rescue him and honor him.

245

The keeper of Israel guarantees the lives of those who are exposed and defenseless. In the Cain narrative (Gen. 4:9), the murderer refused to be "keeper" for his brother. Now this fugitive from his brother has a better "keeper," the Lord himself (cf. p. 60).

3) The third element of the blessing (v. 15) becomes even more specific, the promise of *homecoming*. This promise is recalled (31:13) when Jacob at long last ends his exile. The theme of exile/homecoming can touch the experiences of many persons in a world of displacement. The experience of Jacob makes contact with others in the community of this tradition who are also fugitives from some violation of a brother. For that community of fugitives, the good news is the promise of homecoming.

Thus, *accompaniment, protection, homecoming:* a full complement of good news. All of them are staked on the trustworthy word of promise (v. 15). No wonder the narrative seeks to set the word in a dramatic context of solemn authority by means of dream, ramp, and angels. But finally Jacob, like all of this family, is left with only a word. As the narrative moves toward its fulfillment in chapters 31—33, it is clear that God does watch over his word and bring it to fulfillment.

The Trusting, Responding Man

The promise comes in a dream. But the response of Jacob is in his wakefulness (vv. 16–22). Jacob is the trusting man. He finds the world of the dream more convincing than his old world of fear and guilt. In his wakefulness, he resolves to embrace the new reality of the dream. He accepts the fact that the kingdom is at hand. He is prepared to repent and believe. He repents, deciding here and now to abandon his old presuppositions of fear for the new reality of assurance. Jacob comes to understand that his undefended sleep in a lonely place has been the entry way for God's awesome power (v. 17). This was the time and place when the sovereign goodness of God preempted initiative for his life. His certitude in that moment, believing the old promise (vv. 13–14) and trusting in the new promise (v. 15), is echoed by Paul in his lyrical conclusion:

For I am sure that neither death, nor life, nor angels, nor principalities, nor things present, nor things to come, nor powers, nor height, nor depth, nor anything else in all creation, will be able to separate us from the love of God in Christ Jesus our Lord (Rom. 8:38–39).

The dream has made this clear. God has to do with Israel. Heaven has to do with earth.

1. Jacob's response (vv. 16–22) is a clear unity. But we may consider it in two parts. First (vv. 16–19, 22), there is attention to the *place* of the encounter. A nameless place "between places" has become a decisive place. And the cruciality of that place is marked by the founding of a shrine.

a. We have seen that theophanic narratives are often remembered to establish the legitimacy of cultic places (16:14; 22:13–14). In some stage of this tradition, the narrative no doubt functioned to legitimize the shrine city of Bethel. The mention of "Luz" in verse 19 suggests this was an older shrine of another religious tradition which is here being claimed for the Israelite tradition. The reference to Bethel here is an exceedingly important one for the Jacob tradition. The Jacob narrative has special links to Bethel (cf. 35:1–15). Moreover, there are hints to suggest that after Jerusalem, Bethel may be reckoned as the most important city in the Israelite tradition (cf. Amos 7:10–17; II Kings 23:15–20).

b. Also to be noted are the cultic acts of erection of a sacred pillar (cf. 35:14) which may reflect an older non-Israelite tradition and the payment of a tithe which may suggest endowment to ensure the continuation of the shrine. Attention to cultic matters ensured the permanence of the place and the durability of this tradition of founding.

2. But in addition to the place, there is attention to the *promise.* Jacob recapitulates the promises (vv. 20–21) in a way that corresponds to God's statement of verse 15.

a. The promises here given and received are echoed in Psalm 23:

1) He is with me:	I will not fear, for thou art with me (v. 4).
2) He will keep me:	He makes me lie down, he leads me, he restores my life, he leads me (vv. 2–3).
3) He will give me bread to eat:	He prepares a table before me in the presence of my enemies (v. 5).

247

4) I come again to my father's house in peace:	I will dwell in the house of the Lord forever (v. 6)

The psalm is not a cliché, but a studied summary of the best promises of God and the deepest yearning of Israel.

b. The appearance of God leads Jacob to make deep commitments and overriding decisions. The appearance does not leave Jacob free to be an interested spectator of some religious phenomenon. The appearance presents a word of promise which demands a decision. Jacob now decides in ways that reshape his existence, for promises are covenantal acts. God makes promises to Israel. And in response, Israel makes vows to God. Vows are not contracts or limited agreements, but yieldings that reorient life.

In the church tradition of German pietism (from which this commentator comes), the most solemn vow was at the end of the catechism for confirmation:

> Lord Jesus, for thee I live,
>   for thee I suffer,
>   for thee I die.
> Thine I will be in life and death.
> Grant me, O Lord, eternal salvation.

The vow of Jacob may have special pertinence for the church on occasions of church membership and confirmation decisions. It models life-orienting decisions.

c. Jacob's vow matches the promise (v. 15). First, Jacob decides the God question. He trusts the promise-making God: "The LORD shall be my God" (v. 21). Second, the vow takes concrete cultic form. It leads to sustained, disciplined worship (v. 22a). Third, the vow leads to the concrete act of tithe (v. 22b). Tithe here is not a religious offering, but a recognition that the land belongs to its real owner.

Jacob the trickster is now bound to this God who presides over all the trickery yet to come in the narrative. God has been committed to Jacob since the oracle of 25:23. But only now is Jacob also bound. Jacob's response strikes one as a genuine act of faith. But Jacob will be Jacob. Even in this solemn moment, he still sounds like a bargain-hunter. He still adds an "if" (v. 20).

248

Genesis 29:1—31:55

The extended narrative of Jacob's sojourn with Laban is a continuous, relatively self-contained account. It is continuous in the development of its main plot, even though there is ground for discerning different layers of tradition. It is self-contained in that it begins with Jacob's entry into Laban's sphere (29:1) and it ends with a departure (31:55). Nowhere else is the Laban connection so fully developed in the tradition. For that reason, it probably is a narrative that had its own independent development. It is nicely placed between the theophanies of 28:10–22 and 32:1–2, 22–32. The narrative is broadly structured with the first (29:1–4) and last units (31:43–55) being friendly. Within those, there is a deception of Jacob by Laban (29:21–30), answered by Jacob's deception of Laban (30:25–43). At the center is a narrative about the offspring of Jacob which seems to be independent even within this larger unit (29:31—30:24). Thus, the narrative may be seen in this outline:

29:1–4 preliminary meeting—a kiss of meeting

    29:15–20 meeting with Laban and contract

        29:21–30 deception of Jacob by Laban

            29:31—30:24 the offspring

        30:25–43 trick of Laban by Jacob
        (31:1–16 is a theological reflection)

    31:17–42 meeting with Laban and dispute

31:43–55 covenant and departure—a kiss of departure.

To be sure, this schematization is not completely symmetrical, and it should not be forced. It is offered simply as a way of ordering the materials to show (*a*) that it is neatly placed in an envelope of entry and departure, and (*b*) that at its center stands the relatively independent unit of the birth of the children. The materials beginning in 30:25 are somewhat more diverse and do not permit close schematization.

We observe in this structure a deliberate theological state-

249

ment. The narrative is presented so that at its center is the birth of the children in 29:31—30:24. Everything before that is preparation, especially securing the wives who mother the children. Without being explicit, the narrative addresses the overriding issue of transmission of the inheritance (promise) to the next generation. Immediately after this unit, upon the birth of Joseph (30:22—24), preparation begins for return to the land (30:25). Thus, the sojourn in Haran is now understood as a way of securing heirs. The old agenda of flight from Esau is in abeyance until chapter 32.

Recurring Motifs

Before considering the text in its various units, we may give attention to several recurring motifs. Their presence in the narrative suggests a delicate and artistic narrator who tells a story of some subtlety.

1. The story should be heard as a *humorous* narrative designed for entertainment. Its inherent playfulness is heightened by the fact that it is partisan lore. It permits the Israelites not only to laugh with the success of their hero, but to laugh at Laban. And through Laban, they laugh at their perennial antagonists, the Arameans. The humor is not disinterested. It is partisan and polemical. Among the points of humor are (*a*) the initial meeting with Jacob and the shepherds (29:1-8) in which he chides their laziness; (*b*) his meeting with Rachel, in which he moves the large stone, clearly an exhibition of virility for the maiden (29:9-12); (*c*) the careful and shrewd bargaining of Laban and Jacob, in which both have met their match and each refuses to make the first offer (30:25-36); (*d*) the ludicrous scene of Laban "feeling around" in the tent for the household gods while Rachel sits on them hidden in the camel's saddle (31:33-35). The apparently helpless daughter foils the accusatory father. The unlikely event is intensified by her menstrual condition. (The ritual impurity of menstruation would—or should—have made any association with the gods a still greater offense.)

Too much should not be made of any of these points. It is enough to know that the teller and the listener understand that some things are going on in this drama that do not need to be brought to full verbalization.

250

2. The humor is lightened by several allusions to *magic and superstitious manipulation.* It is not clear how seriously these

ought to be taken. Possibly, they are old folklore elements which are perpetuated without being particularly valued by our narrator. But they are there and should be appreciated as ways in which the story is paced and suspense sustained.

a. This includes the fascination with and use of aphrodisiac fruit, mandrake (30:14–18). Little is known about mandrake. It is a plant believed to increase sexual effectiveness. Does the mandrake give assistance toward pregnancy?

b. In a more extended incident, Jacob manipulates the breeding of sheep by the use of sticks, as though the sight of different colors of sticks caused different breeding (30:37–43). The story-teller apparently relishes this story, embellishing it with exaggerated (though not decipherable) vocabulary with reference to "striped, speckled, and spotted."

c. Finally, we may note the curious, deferential comment of Laban (30:27), "I have learned by divination. . . ." Perhaps he learned by divination, but all he needed to do was look (v. 29)! The narrator intends the Israelite listener to enjoy and celebrate this odd man, Jacob, for whom there are strange, positive powers at work.

3. The theme of Jacob as *a man of conflict* continues to be advanced in this narrative. We already have seen Jacob in conflict with his father and with his brother. In this narrative, there is conflict with Rachel over the lack of a child. She seems to blame Jacob, and he protests strongly (30:1–2). The later use of the mandrake suggests that the barrenness is the burden of Jacob, in spite of his denial. Hence the conflict. Of course the primary conflict is between father-in-law and son-in-law. The entire narrative of Jacob and Laban, from the marriage ploy (29:21–30) through the division of property (30:-32–43) to the departure (31:17–42), is one long recital of conflict. Even the benediction of 31:49 is an acknowledgment of the unresolved conflict. Even at the end, there is only a truce, not a resolution.

4. In interpreting the narrative, attention should be given to the ambiguous and ambivalent *character of Jacob*. He is at times an unseemingly deceptive man. At other times, he seems to be a believer, or at least he is able to sound that way. As Terence Fretheim proposes, it is possible to dissect these matters and assign the more scandalous Jacob to the realism of the J tradition and the pious Jacob to the E tradition which offers him as an exemplar of faith ("The Jacob Tradition," *In-*

251

terpretation 26:419–36 [1972]). That may be an effective way of handling the material. But such literary division is not to be pressed too far. It is possible and necessary to see that in the faith of Israel, these matters come together. It is this earthy man through whom the resilient purposes of God are being worked out. The purpose of God is somehow operative in the places of scandal and deception. Even Luther tries too hard to explain away the sordidness of the narrative. One would expect Luther, especially, to affirm that God's promises have no interest in moral rectitude. But the text is clear enough. Precisely in this doubtful character the promise of God is being fulfilled.

The promise of 28:15 is that Jacob should return to his land. But the narrative affirms that he can and will return only when he has heirs. Thus, the narrative moves toward that fulfillment in 31:13. The prosperous, blessed man is now ready to reenter his patrimony. This now blessed man is none other than the deceptive, embattled Jacob of the other episodes. In the midst of the ambiguities, the promise is having its way.

The Drama from Exile to Return

The flow and movement of the narrative may be portrayed in three distinct scenes, centering in the narrative of the births.

1. The opening section (29:1–30) sets the stage, introduces the characters, and hints at the conflict to come. The characters are quickly sketched: Laban the devious (vv. 21–27); Leah the older (vv. 17, 26); and Rachel the beautiful (v. 17). Skillful storytelling then leads the listener from idyllic harmony through deception and conflict and finally to love and preference as harbingers of things to come.

a. The introduction of Jacob to the family of Laban (v. 1–14) is a scene of idyllic harmony, with parallels to the travels of the servant of Abraham (24:10–21; cf. the less idyllic parallel of Exod. 2:15–21). The refugee has things break for him in good fortune. The happy meeting climaxes in the formula of friendship and/or kinship in the mouth of Laban (v. 14; cf. Gen. 2:23; II Sam. 5:1). This scene of solidarity and bonding ill prepares us for the discord which follows. Nothing is claimed here of a theological character. Things happen fortuitously. Only those who know of the hidden voice of 28:15 can discern God's leadership of Jacob.

b. The idyllic picture of solidarity is quickly shattered by

252

the aggression of verses 15–29. Laban abruptly introduces the topic of payment (v. 15). Perhaps there is an intended irony. Laban dares to speak of "wages," *śkr* (cf. 30:28; 31:7), when for father Abraham (15:1) it is clear that only Yahweh can give the "reward" *(śkr)* that is needed? See the discussion, pp. 140–141. In any case, Laban appeared to be friendly at first (vv. 15–20) Then more deceptive than friendly (vv. 21–27). Since 25:27–34 and 27:1–45, we have known that Jacob was an effective trickster. But now he has met his match in Laban. Here Jacob is on the receiving end. He is done in. The one led and accompanied by God (28:15) is duped by his uncle. The reasoning of Laban has its own logic. And the irony of it is striking and perhaps a fair retaliation to Jacob. Since the early kick in the womb (25:-22), Jacob has struggled with the "natural" rights of the older. Only by subterfuge had he settled that with his own brother. And now it meets him again. The resistant reality of primogeniture blocks his love even as it blocks his inheritance. Leah is older, Rachel must wait. And so also Jacob must wait. But this time, Jacob has no trick to reverse the matter. He must wait. And he does. God is at work keeping promises again, but the keeping of promises can be delayed.

c. This introductory scene is brought to its conclusion with the cryptic statement of verse 30. The terseness of the statement is like that of 25:28, where parental preference caused trouble. And as we shall immediately see, trouble comes again to this man unable to take things as they are. Perhaps only Jacob's unbending determination is at work here. Or we may conclude that God is at work with his promises against the "natural" order of Laban. But God has not yet made an appearance in this story. In any case, two competitive sisters, a husband caught between them, and an exploitative father-in-law are not the most likely data for narratives of faith. But that is what this narrator has to offer. And by now, that should not surprise us in Genesis. Of such stuff are "beginnings" made.

2. The "supplanter" who cannot accept the usual order of things still must struggle for his future, as we find in the middle section of our narrative (29:31—30:24). This is the focus of the narrative. It portrays the way to the next generation as a way of conflict. The sons are born in rivalry, envy, and dispute. Undoubtedly, this presentation of sons is a mapping of the tribes of Israel. But in the narrative itself, they are simply children, yearned for, given, yet given in the midst of anguish.

253

a. The narrative begins with barrenness (v. 31). After Sarah (11:30) and Rebekah (25:21), we are not surprised. There is no easy, natural way toward the future. The future of Israel will not be worked by human mechanizations, not even by mandrake. There is irony here. Rachel, the one who is beautiful (v. 17) and loved (v. 30) is also the barren one. It is this barrenness that becomes the premise of all that follows. It is the occasion for the rivalry of the sisters (30:14–15). It is the motivation for the device of the maids (30:3–13). It is the cause of the names of the children, given to celebrate and to gloat. But all of that is to come. Now we know only that the one who is to mother the next generation of Israel is barren.

b. The narrative focuses on Rachel. But there is an interlude for Leah (vv. 32–35). Of four sons given to her here, three are named with reference to Yahweh:

The Lord has looked upon my affliction (Reuben) (v. 32)

The Lord has heard that I am hated (Simeon) (v. 33)

I will praise *the Lord* (Judah) (v. 35).

The names have no philological grounding. But they are crucial for the story. When birth is given it is not a human achievement, but a gift from God. So Leah, the one not beautiful and not loved, is blessed by God. But then, she also ceases to bear (v. 35). She now joins in the anguish Rachel has known all along.

c. Now the narrator must return to Rachel (30:16–21). Her situation is only more acute because of the "success" of Leah. The narrative portrays this odd triangle of Jacob and his wives in struggle and pathos. Something is surely amiss in this family. There is acrimony as the players seek to decide the fault. Rachel transfers the guilt to Jacob (vv. 1–2). But he will have none of it. He answers sharply. His rhetorical question (like that of his son in 50:19) is a statement of abdication. But implicitly, it is also a theological conclusion. For all the playfulness of this story and for all the inventiveness of the family, the future belongs to God. Both birth and barrenness, fertility and denial of fertility, are in the hands of God.

The family uses two devices to overcome the disaster of barrenness (vv. 3–21). First, there is recourse to handmaidens as surrogate mothers, a device first used by father Abraham (Gen. 16:2). First Rachel (vv. 3–8) and then Leah (vv. 9–12) use this alternative solution. And it works! Except that it only works as it did for Sarah and Abraham. There are children, but not the one still awaited. The second device is the use of mandrake (vv. 14–16). This incident seems to be more of a folklore motif and not much is made of it.

But the narrative is subtle. Rachel manipulates the mandrakes. But it is Leah (vv. 17–21) who has the children. And finally when Rachel conceives, it is not because of mandrakes but because God remembers (vv. 22–23). The narrative is a delicate balance. On the one hand, there are mandrakes and handmaidens and names of children which suggest the powers of fertility. There is a suggestion that births can be wrought by careful planning. But at the same time, there is the overriding theological affirmation: God is the only cause of new life. The ambivalence in the narrative reflects the situation in which faithfulness is always at issue.

d. But the narrative waits for verses 22–24. Since 29:31, it has been waiting for this moment. All the rest—sons from Leah, children by handmaidens, intrigue by mandrakes, fault-finding between the man and the woman—all of that has been a means of delay, or perhaps avoidance. Only now (in 30:22) does the narrative resolve the issue of barrenness from 29:31: God remembered—God heard—God opened! The shame of 29:31 is overcome. The child is named (30:24). And the God of Israel is named for the first time since 29:35.

The stress of the entire narrative of 29:31—30:24 is the movement from barrenness (29:31) to conception and birth (30:23). That movement is accomplished by no human action. It comes by the faithful, inexplicable *remembering* and *hearing* of Yahweh. For bereft Israel, God's remembering is the only source of hope. It is the ground later on for the hope of exiles (Isa. 49:15). Other than the faithful memory of God, there is no reason to expect an heir or a future. But he remembers. It is the same remembering that turned the flood for Noah (8:1). It is the same remembering that salvaged Lot from the destruction (19:29). That remembering is the heart of the gospel. It will not be explained. It can only be affirmed, celebrated, and relied upon. That is how it is with Rachel. That is how it also is with Leah (29:33; 30:17). The two mothers of Israel, the loved and not loved, the beautiful and not beautiful, discover together 255 that barrenness is not a problem for human solution. New life is God's gift. The seemingly incidental assertion of Leah in 29:32 is the claim of the entire narrative. God looks upon the affliction of his children (cf. 31:42). The action of God in this narrative prompts Luther to ask, "Does God have no other occupation left than to have regard for the lowliness of the household?" Luther's question receives an answer not only here but in the good news of Luke. In both narratives, it is indeed the occupation of God to care for the lowly, unloved, second-born, and barren ones. (Cf. Luke 1:48, 52 which become the premise of that entire Gospel.) It is only because of the remembering and hearing of God that finally there is Joseph. Because of God's faithfulness, the story of this family has yet another chapter. When Joseph, the awaited one, is born, this narrative of birth ends abruptly. "God has added." The Lord has added more than might be asked or manipulated or coerced. Perhaps the assertion of verse 24 anticipates little Benjamin, who is yet to come (cf. 35:16–18). The narrative leaves the way open for the future.

3. After the birth narrative, the final element (30:25—31:55) is a counterpart to 29:1–30. It resumes the conflict with Laban. It also anticipates the return to the land of promise from which Jacob had fled. This narrative moves in a rather rambling way. Its burden is to show that Jacob bears a promise that will not fail. In each of its parts, this final section of the narrative contains both elements of entertainment and a straightforward theological assertion.

a. Immediately upon the birth of Joseph, Jacob initiates plans for a return (30:25–43). The interaction between Jacob and Laban is shrewd and careful bargaining. Jacob asks for his wives and children (v. 26). Laban responds by talking of wages (v. 28; cf. 29:15; 30:28). Laban is accustomed to buying what he wants. Here he apparently wants to persuade Jacob to stay in his service. The repartee between them is designed for enjoyment (vv. 27–30). Laban makes the opening gambit: "If you will allow me to say so, I have learned by divination that the LORD has blessed me because of you." And Jacob, with unconvincing modesty, concedes the point: "For you had little before I came, and it has increased abundantly; and the LORD has blessed you wherever I turned." But a theological point is also made. Yahweh is the giver of prosperity. And it is given through the person of Jacob. Laban is dependent on Jacob for the gift of God's blessing. The worth of Jacob is established. He will come at a high price, as Laban admits (v. 28). The story takes a surprising turn. Jacob's statement (v. 31) confounds and rejects Laban.

256

Jacob will not be beholden to Laban in any way (cf. 44:21–24). He will take his chances with his inscrutable good fortune. He is boldly self-confident. Verses 31–41 describe a series of actions which are beyond explication. They need not be understood, but only narrated. They are intended to evoke amazement. The narrative makes no explicit theological claim. The surprising turn in Jacob's favor is given in verses 42–43. Things happen in the course of events without comment or explanation. But the attentive listener knows. Jacob's success comes not from his magic or his manipulation of sheep, but from the watchfulness of God over his decree (25:23). The formula of inversion (vv. 42–43), which affirms the increase of God's chosen one, is used elsewhere in various forms: *(a)* to characterize the rise of David (II Sam. 3:1), *(b)* to mark a beginning for Jesus (Luke 2:52), and *(c)* to trace the flourishing of the early church (Acts 6:7; 9:31; 12:24; 19:20). All these uses testify to the power of God at work in ways that reorder the future and make newness possible.

b. A much more self-conscious theological assertion than we have found elsewhere in our narrative is contained in 31: 1–16. The assertion is framed by references to the family of Laban. The opening challenge of the *sons of Laban* (vv. 1–2) is contrasted in the conclusion, with the compliance of the *daughters of Laban* (vv. 14–16). Jacob's pilgrimage under the leadership of Yahweh is set in the context of Laban's family, sons and daughters.

The call of God (v. 3) governs the entire narrative. It is like that given to Abraham in 12:1, calling for an abrupt departure. And the promise of accompaniment is reasserted from 28:15. The only explicit mention of Yahweh in the passage is here as the one who calls. Jacob recites the recent history of the promise, alluding three times to the leadership of God, but without invoking the name of Yahweh:

> "But the God of my father has been with me" (v. 5). . . .
>
> "but God did not permit him to harm me" (v. 7). . . .
>
> "Thus God has taken away the cattle of your father, and given them to me" (v. 9).

This recital is followed by still another recapitulation of the promise from 28:13–15 as the sanction for his departure from Laban (vv. 11–13). The daughters of Laban find the argument compelling.

257

This unit forms a theological summary to the whole of

chapters 29—31. Until now, things have proceeded as if naturally or even by accident. Jacob has been led to his kin. He has found wives and prospered. He has received sons. Now are things made explicit. It is as though the narrative did not want us to miss the intent of the whole. It wants to affirm that all of Jacob's life is kept (cf. 28:20) and valued by this God who works inversions for the sake of the promise. Finally, all the action with the father-in-law, wives, and children is subordinated to the mandate to go back to the land.

c. The final section is the account of departure (31:17–55). The departure is not unlike negotiations of Moses with Pharaoh (Exod. 5). In both cases, there is anger, exploitation, and pursuit. And in both, there is inevitable escape because God calls.

This part of the narrative contains a most peculiar series of interactions, no doubt intended to heighten the suspense and the humor. But throughout these, there is a clear affirmation, conceded now even by Laban, that God has been at work to prosper and protect Jacob. It is not a concession we would expect from Laban, but even he cannot resist the dream of God (31:24, 29). Like Israel from Egypt (Exod. 10:26; 11:2), Jacob did not go empty-handed but richly blessed. And all the blessings, prosperity, and wealth are credited to Yahweh:

> "If the God of my father, the God of Abraham and the Fear of Isaac, had not been on my side, surely now you would have sent me away empty-handed. God saw my affliction and the labor of my hands, and rebuked you last night" (31:42).

Everything is credited to God. Laban receives thanks for nothing. With this one assertion, Jacob refutes Laban and any help he might claim to give (cf. 30:31), thus making an affirmation of the free gift of his God. As Gunkel has observed, the grateful faith of Jacob is an echo of Psalm 124:

> If it had not been the LORD who was on our side . . .
> then they would have swallowed us up alive,
>   when their anger was kindled against us; . . .
> Blessed be the LORD,
>   who has not given us
>   as prey to their teeth! . . .
> Our help is in the name of the LORD,
>   who made heaven and earth (vv. 1, 3, 6, 8).

The God of Israel emerges as the one who orders all events. It is this God who has taken sides and turned events toward the overriding promise. All else is pressed into the service of this plan to get Jacob back to the right place with well-being and prosperity. The one who left as an empty-headed fugitive has become a man of means because of this God.

This championing by the God of Israel permits a playful yet important contrast between Yahweh and the household gods of Laban. The God of Jacob orders and transforms the affairs of history. By contrast, the household gods of Laban do nothing. They must be protected—even by a menstruating woman (31:15). Those gods may be tokens of inheritance, but they cannot impact real events. They are gods who "cannot do good or ill" (cf. Zeph. 1:12). In contrast to Yahweh, they are objects to be carried about (cf. Isa. 46:1–4). The fortunes of this family depend upon the contrasting character of God and the gods.

A Pattern of Inversion

The narrative of 29:1—31:55 is shaped to suggest a large inversion and within it a smaller but nonetheless crucial inversion. The larger one shows the transformation of Jacob, the empty-handed fugitive, into a man of means and well-being. The more intense one shows the barren Rachel made the mother of the precious, awaited son. The pattern may be seen in this outline:

29:1–30 the empty-handed fugitive

      29:31 the barren mother

          30:22 *God remembers and hears*

      31:23–24 God adds the son and Rachel rejoices

30:25—31:55 Jacob bargains as a man of power and authority.

In the course of the story, the transformations and inversions seem to happen almost by themselves. But throughout the narrative, the narrator places in the mouths of the players affirmations of the actual situation with Yahweh (cf. 30:27, 30, 42–43; 31:3–13, 42–43). The narrator and the family of the narrator trust fully in the work of this hidden but effective inverter.

With their complicated interrelations, this family is a microcosmic presentation of our "common lot." All of them—Jacob, Rachel, Leah, Laban—pursue the same issue. All of them know a future is coming which frightens them. They are not ready for it. At the same time, they crave it and they dread it.

259

None of them can bring that future. None of them can keep it from coming. None of them can prepare for it adequately. The struggle is the same for husbands, wives, fathers. It is the same struggle whether this story is read as a conflict over descendants or over property. It is a quarrel about the future. It is a battle for the future which the combatants want to take into their own hands. It is a battle against the closedness of history, against the threats—no heirs, wrong-colored sheep, and misplaced gods. But none can have their future as they wish it—not Laban, who is finally tricked; not the barren wives; not even Jacob. That same battle against a closed history is still present to us. History may appear to be closed with the collapse of public institutions, with the shortage of energy, with the ways of technology which outstrip our humaneness. What is to come leaves us filled with a mixture of hope and dread. This narrative for the family of Jacob and for the listening community is subtle but sure. On the one hand, history is not closed because God has surprises yet to give. But on the other hand, the future will be shaped in God's promised way. And no human scheme or device can do more than delay that sure future. In the meantime, truces and alliances are made (31:32–54). But they are at best provisional in the face of this persistent One.

Genesis 32:1—33:17*

In these chapters, the narrative resumes the story of the Esau conflict, left unresolved in 27:45. In that verse, Jacob fled for his life, empty-handed. Now by the command of God (31:13) he returns to Esau and the land as a prosperous man (32:5). The Laban narrative of chapters 29—31 is independent and intrudes into the primary narrative, having little effect on the problem of Esau. The continuity of this text is with 27:1–45. In the intervening materials, nothing has changed in relation to his wronged brother. On the one hand, Jacob is still estranged from his brother. On the other hand, he is blessed by God, who from the beginning has disrupted relationships with the brother.

260

*In chapter 32, the numbering of verses used here follows that of English translations. In each verse, the corresponding Hebrew is one number higher.

The narrative concerning Esau is sustained and well crafted: It begins with the initial exchange which heightens anxiety (32:3–6). It continues with a careful stratagem for the meeting (32:7–21). It culminates in a guarded but friendly meeting and reconciliation (33:1–17). The entire movement is from aggressive conflict (27:41f.) to a reconciliation in which both brothers prosper. At the last, they are able to put the quarrel safely behind them. The narrative is thoroughly secular, leaving the brothers alone to work thingsout. (The references to God in 33:5, 11 are conventional and stylized.) The account is acutely sensitive to the emotional extremities of fear, calculation, and distrust.

In the midst of this narrative built on human calculation, there are statements which are noteworthy for their theological acumen. These include a brief theophany (32:1–2), a fearful prayer (32:9–12) and an extended encounter (32:22–32). There is little doubt that the two theophanic episodes (32:1–2, 22–32) have had an independent life and been incorporated into the narrative. The prayer of 32:9–12 represents a nearly pure form of prayer and is highly stylized. But finally, our interpretation is not permitted to treat these pieces separately. We must discern the intent of the whole picture. We are offered the remarkable juxtaposition of an account of anxious, human reconciliation together with one of the Bible's most imposing religious encounters. As the narrative attests, this trickster is truly a man of many parts!

Preparation for Meeting

Although the whole of this text has remarkable unity, we may divide our exposition into two parts: preparation and meeting. Because of the way in which the theophany (32:1–2) and the prayer (32:9–12) are placed in the text, it will be apparent that preparation for the meeting has a *theological* as well as *pragmatic* dimension.

1. The preparation is introduced with an abrupt appearance of the angels of God (32:1–2). The report has a clear parallel in Josh. 5:13–15, also placed at the awesome moment of entry into the land of promise. Now, however, the report is related to the narrative that follows. Although terse, it alerts the listener. There is more going on here than meets the eye. For all his straining to manage his affairs, Jacob is no stranger to the powerful reality of angels (cf. 28:12; 31:11). While the text is

261

restrained, probably the angels are protective agents gathered as a bodyguard to usher this man back to safety to the promised place. This is, after all, no casual journey. It has been commanded by God's messenger (31:11–13).

Calvin has drawn attention to the convergence of our themes in Ps. 34, a psalm which illuminates this episode:

> I sought the LORD and he answered me,
>   and delivered me from all my fears. . . .
> This poor man cried and the LORD heard him,
>   and saved him out of all his troubles.
> *The angel of the Lord encamps*
>   *around those who fear him, and delivers them.*
> O taste and see that the LORD is good!
>   Happy is the man who takes refuge in him! (vv. 4–8).

The "angel encamps and delivers" (v. 7), parallels the language of our narrative. And as in Jacob's prayer, the Psalm has the parallel of the poor man, the prayer for deliverance, the promise of good, and finally, the assertion that no good is lacking (v. 10).

The angels belong to the fabric of the story. They are a way of the strange power of God. God is here at work. Military metaphors are needed to express the protection given Jacob. The narrative begins with a "safe conduct" for Jacob, assured by God.

2. With such an assurance, Jacob makes the first contact with his brother (vv. 3–8). In verses 1–2, Jacob had received messengers from God (angels). Now, he sends messengers to Esau (v. 3) and, in turn, receives his messengers back (v. 6). By this double use of messengers, the narrator refuses to let the two dimensions of this account—toward God and toward Esau—be separated from each other. The preparation is for two kinds of meetings, as we shall see. These verses need little comment. But the story must be told carefully. We may observe three dimensions to these verses which will aid in the proper presentation of the narrative.

a. Jacob enters the negotiations with great fear and anxiety (v. 7). Perhaps his fear is something of a match to the anguish he earlier caused his father and brother (27:33–34). There is no hint of remorse on his part. But he is not unaware of the wrath of Esau or that he himself is the wrong-doer. One senses in his actions that he does not regard the wrath of Esau as unwarranted.

b. Jacob approaches the meeting with extreme deference, the kind of deference appropriate to a wrong-doer in the face of the offended. The careful preparation of Jacob is no doubt a measure of his fear. He is not normally a deferential man. After 25:27–34 and 27:1–45, we expect Jacob to assert himself and prevail, but not to defer. But something is at work here beyond Jacob. The power of primogeniture against which he had struggled, with his brother (27:19, 32) and with his wives (29:26), seems to endure. He cannot have his way by force. The formula of deference here is, "If I find favor in your eyes" (v. 5), used subsequently three times (33:8, 10, 15).

c. Because of his fear and because of his strategy of deference, here and in the development of verses 13–21 and 33:1–11, the story is shrewdly and slowly paced. This is a dangerous and ominous meeting. It must not be rushed. Every step must be measured, for any miscalculated move could be fatal. The narrator has found a style to carry the listening community along the tortured and risky way to reconciliation. The listener is not invited to know the outcome until the last moment. The brothers have to wait to see how it all would turn out. The listener must wait with the brothers.

3. The preparation involves more than a stratagem. Because of his shrewdness, Jacob can *plan.* Because of his vulnerability, Jacob must *pray.* In verses 9–12, we are offered the only extended prayer in the book of Genesis. Because it is well stylized, the prayer is easily seen in four parts:

a. Jacob addresses God, placing God and himself in the flow of the generations (v. 9). He asserts that he is a recipient of promise and has acted because of that. Affirming that God has made promises, he now means to hold God to them. Thus, even the address contains an insistence.

To be sure that God is attentive to it, the promise is restated in the address. The imperative here is "return to your country and to your kindred." While it is not a complete parallel (cf. 28:15; 31:13), the promise surely refers to the call to Abraham: "Go from your land, from your kindred, from your father's house" (12:1). Here only the first two elements are parallel. But the third, "your father's house" is contained in the reference of the address to "God of my father" (cf. 28:21). Thus the return to which Jacob refers is not only his own homecoming after the flight of chapters 27—28. It is also the homecoming of Abraham, who had left long ago. Jacob is presented as completing the

263

sojourn which has been underway for three generations. Something more is at stake here than simply reconciliation with Esau. The family of Abraham now finally comes to its own country and that concerns Yahweh as much as Jacob.

The presence of the heavenly escort (32:1–2) suggests that the homecoming of Israel here is as decisive and momentous as that of Israel in Isa. 40:1–11, where there is also an accompanying guard (v. 10) and an end to exile. The fugitive character of Jacob is understood as the exile of the whole people of Israel. This prayer looks to homecoming. Jacob asserts that the entire matter of homecoming has been God's idea, not his. (In 27:43, clearly the idea of flight was that of neither Jacob nor Yahweh, but Rebekah. But the larger sojourn of Abraham was indeed in response to the call of Yahweh. The same device of reminder is used by Moses in Num. 11:11–15 to motivate Yahweh to act.)

b. As a motivation for God's protection, Jacob next affirms God's past goodness to this unqualified man (v. 10). He does so in a mood of proper deference (cf. II Sam. 7:18–20; I Kings 3:7). Jacob is deferential to God, as he is to Esau. In the prayer, Jacob marvels at the inversion of his fortune. He was a desperate, poor man. Now he is rich and powerful (cf. Deut. 10:22; I Pet. 2:10). His new state can only be explained by the power of God. Jacob concedes that there is nothing in himself which could have caused this change.

1) The word "least" (v. 10) is not an incidental adjective, as we might conclude from the customary translations. It is the governing verb, "I am smaller." The self-identification of Jacob thus alludes to the miracle against primogeniture. It is a primal theme of biblical faith that God has cast his lot with the little ones (cf. Matt. 10:42; 18:6–14) against the strong of the world (I Cor. 1:18–25). It is so with Gideon (Judg. 6:15–18) and with David (I Sam. 16:11) and is recognized in the pathos-filled intercession of Amos (7:2, 5). In this "littleness," Jacob has always "stood" only because of God.

2) The formula of "steadfast love and faithfulness" (*ḥesed* and *'emet*) is Israel's most frequent characterization of God (cf. Exod. 34:6). It comes to full light in Jesus of Nazareth, who is "full of grace and truth" (John 1:14). In his prayer, Jacob knows the heart of God is steadfast and faithful. He knows that he himself is a miracle wrought by this God. Jacob is empty-handed before God. He becomes a paradigm for all who are children of

the gospel who live only by God's gracious faithfulness (cf. Luke 7:22).

c. On the basis of the address (v. 9) and the affirmation as motivation (v. 10), Jacob now makes his petition (v. 11). There is an appeal for a present show of mercy. Jacob knows he is in a dangerous situation. Jacob puts himself in the best possible light, praying with both deference and boldness. But in fact, his entire prayer can be heard in one imperative word: *deliver* (v. 11). It is perhaps ironic that the verb deliver (*nṣl*, v. 11) is the same verb used in Gen. 31:9, 16 to describe God's action in taking from Laban to give to Jacob. As God has "snatched" property for Jacob from Laban, so Jacob prays to be "snatched" from the power of Esau. In this petition, Jacob prays the most characteristic prayer of the biblical community (cf. Pss. 7:1–2; 31:15–16; 59:2–4; 142:6–7; 143:9; 144:11).

d. Looking at the prayer as a whole, we see a carefully crafted statement. It is given closure by a phrase which looks back to the beginning:

"... I will *do* you *good*" (v. 9)

"... But thou didst say, I will *surely do* you *good*" (v. 12, author's translation).

The second formulation has an infinitive absolute ("surely") which makes the verb "do good" much stronger. This is an important nuance usually lost in translation. The prayer has a strong conclusion, appealing to the initial statement of promise. The prayer is the voice of a man accustomed to stating his best case. In this brief prayer, Jacob is deferential. But at the same time, he intends to hold God firmly to his promise of "good." The blessing he hopes for is that his life shall be kept from the anger of his offended brother.

The prayer is not immediately answered. It is enough to have prayed it. Jacob returns to his own devices. But in the midst of them, he is a man who looks outside himself for well-being. Yet while Jacob may be in need of help, he does not beg. He will hold his own with his brother, even as he does here with Yahweh.

4. The final preparations for the meeting are made (32:13–21). The paced and dramatic presentation of gifts is designed to impress Esau with Jacob's generosity and with his considerable power and wealth. It is clearly an act of appease-

265

ment. The reflection of Jacob (v. 20) and the strategy speak for themselves. We may particularly note the play on the word *face* (vv. 20–21; cf. Heb. 11:21–22):

> I may appease his *face* with the present that goes *before* me, and afterward I will see his *face;* perhaps he will lift my *face*. So the present passed *before* him (author's translation).

The intensity of the statement is evident when it is recognized that the Hebrew for "face" and for "before" is the same word, *pen*. The term is used five times here. As we shall see (in 32:22–32 and 33:1–17), the theme of "seeing the face" is an important one. Here the term is used as a posture of servility by one unworthy to look upon the face of the other. Yet Jacob hopes that the stronger party will pardon and accept, that is, "lift his face" to recognition and well-being (cf. 40:20–21). Jacob engages in an act of self-abasement. That posture is further heightened by the use of "appease," (v. 20). The term is *kpr*, seldom used in secular contexts and usually rendered "atone." The word suggests the gravity of the meeting. Jacob has now done everything he can. He has made careful and calculated preparations to play upon the sympathies of his brother. He has made petition to Yahweh and entrusted himself to his care. Now there is the waiting. As we shall see, the "meeting" to come entails more than Jacob anticipates.

The Two Meetings

The text holds a curious development for Jacob. He anticipates one meeting, with Esau. But he has two meetings, first with the dreaded stranger in the night (32:22–32), and only then with Esau (33:1–17). It will become evident that the two meetings are related to each other. The night encounter (32:22–32) is not placed accidentally or casually. It takes on a special function in this precise location.

1. The encounter of 32:22–32 is perhaps the most extensively interpreted text in the patriarchal materials. Its rich expository possibility is based in part on its lack of clarity, which permits various readings. In any case, it is an ominous encounter with an unnamed opponent possessing divine qualities.

a. The identity of the "man" (v. 24) is obscure. In much interpretation, it has been understood as a demon or a Canaanite numen. While that may have been the intention in some earlier form of the narrative, that does not help us to interpret the present form. Others have proposed that the shadowy antagonist was Esau in some earlier version. In that case, the night meeting is an anticipated scenario of the next day.

Perhaps it is important that the narrative is not explicit. In its opaque portrayal of the figure, the narrative does not want us to know too much. It is part of the power of the wrestling that we do not know the name or see the face of the antagonist. To be too certain would reduce the dread intended in the telling. It is most plausible that in the present form, the hidden one is Yahweh. On the way to *his brother* whom he wants to appease, Jacob must deal with *his God* to whom he has made intercession (32:9–12). (The careful juxtaposition of brother and God in the destiny of Jacob is closely paralleled in the Cain narrative of 4:1–16.) But if it be Yahweh, we are shown something other than the promise-filled aspect of Yahweh known in the daylight. Now Jacob must deal with the terrifying face of the deity, hidden in sovereignty and not to be appeased or even found out. The adversary is identified only as "a man," which leaves all the options open. The power of the stranger is as much in his inscrutability as in his strength. Jacob anticipates the wrath of his brother. But first he must face an assault from the deity. In the middle of the night, the forms merge and overlap. Perhaps in pondering this scene, the narrator, too, could not make out the forms very well. He could not discern whether the adversary is God or Esau. Surely there is more than Esau at work here. But it is not without reference to Esau. In the night, the divine antagonist tends to take on the features of others with whom we struggle in the day.

b. The wrestling (vv. 24–25) is hardly described. We know only that it lasted all night (cf. Ps. 6:6). It must have been nearly an even match. What a man this Jacob is! He may be frightened of both God and his brother. But in the fray, he will hold his own with either one. The hidden One has the power to injure Jacob even though he does not finally defeat him. At daybreak, the stranger wants to leave. Is it because he loses his power when seen or because he must preserve his hiddenness? Perhaps. In any case, Jacob and his nemesis come nearly to a draw. Neither can quite have his way. But if this other one is God, what does it mean to say that Jacob has come to a draw with him? What kind of God is it who will be pressed to a draw by this man? And what kind of man is our father Jacob that he can force a draw, even against heaven? This is no ordinary man. And certainly no ordinary God! Clearly, this is no ordinary story.

267

c. In verses 26–29, we are offered a remarkable dialogue. After the wrestlers are exhausted in conflict, they are reduced to speech. Breathlessly, they engage each other. There are three exchanges. Jacob takes the initiative in only one of these:

(1) The man: "Let me go, for the day is breaking."
Jacob: "I will not let you go unless you *bless* me" (v. 26).

(2) The man: "What is your *name?*"
Jacob: "Jacob."
The man: "Your name shall no more be called Jacob, but Israel, for you have striven with God and with men and have prevailed" (vv. 28–29).

(3) Jacob: "Tell me, I pray, your *name.*"
The man: "Why is it that you ask my name?"
And there he *blessed* him.

The three exchanges fit together only curiously.

1) In the first (v. 26), Jacob is the stronger party. He has an advantage and he knows it. He exploits the situation to seek a blessing. Since chapter 27, we have known he would do anything to get a blessing. Now he seeks a more weighty blessing (v. 26). But for the moment, that request is ignored. It is not denied but held in abeyance. It is as though the stranger changes the subject, seeking more likely ground on which to gain advantage. The stranger finds Jacob as quick with words as with wrestling.

2) In the second exchange (vv. 27–28), the stranger has the stronger part. The upshot is a new name and, by implication, a new being. Jacob had asked for a blessing. Perhaps he dreamed of security, land, more sons. But what he got was a new identity through an assault from God. He had been named Jacob—"heel/trickster/over-reacher/supplanter." Each of these is true, but not flattering. Now he is "Israel." The etymology of "Israel" is disputed. Perhaps it means "God rules," "God preserves," "God protects." But whatever the etymology, a new being has been called forth. He is now a man (and a community) linked not only to a nemesis of the night but to a promise-keeper of the day. Something happens in this transaction that is irreversible. Israel is something new in the world. Power has shifted between God and humankind (cf. Luke 8: 45–46). Israel is the one who has faced God, been touched by God, prevailed, gained a blessing, and been re-

named. There is something new underway here about the weakness of God and the strength of Israel. The encounter will not permit a neat summary of roles, as though God is strong and Jacob is weak, or as though things are reversed with Jacob strong and God weak. All of that remains unsettled. But new possibilities are open to Israel that have not been available before. In the giving of the blessing, something of the power of God has been entrusted to Israel. Unlike every other such relation in which God rules and humankind obeys, Israel is a newness which has prevailed with God. And so he comes to his brother changed. He has new power. Perhaps, therefore, he does not need to press his power so fully with his brother (cf. I Cor. 1:25; 15:43; II Cor. 12:9; Heb. 11:34).

3) The third exchange (v. 29) is an act of incredible boldness. In the other two, the stranger has spoken first. Now Jacob is buoyed by the new disclosure (v. 28). Now he assumes a priority. He reverses roles and dares to ask the name of the stranger, even as he has been asked his name (v. 27). He wants to know God's name, the mystery of heaven and earth. Like the couple in the garden (Gen. 2—3), Jacob/Israel wants to overcome all the distance. The stranger did not win (v. 25). But he did not lose either. And so he will not grant as much as Jacob asks (cf. Exod. 33:18–23). Jacob has gained a great deal, but the name of God has not yet been given. (That must wait for Moses —Exod. 3:14). The stranger stops short of that ultimate gift. He returns to the first request (v. 26), on which he had been silent. That much will be given. He blesses. And then he departs. Or perhaps then Jacob permits him to leave. The issue is unresolved. We cannot tell at the end how it all comes out. We cannot tell if the stranger leaves in his freedom, or whether Jacob permits the departure. In any case, the stranger has maintained his inscrutable role. He is not forced to tell his name. But on the other hand, Jacob receives the blessing he so craved. God remains God, his hiddenness intact. But Jacob is no longer Jacob. Now he is Israel.

That is how Israel comes on the horizon. Israel is not formed by success or shrewdness or land, but by an assault from God. Perhaps it is grace, but not the kind usually imagined. Jacob is not consulted about his new identity. It is given, even imposed. When daylight comes, the stranger is gone. And so is Jacob. There remains only Israel, who had not had a good sleep that night. Now there is Israel, blessed and named. Israel is born

269

in the combat where he asked about God's name. That is who Israel must now be on the way to the brother.

d. Verses 30–32 offer Jacob's immediate reflection on the event. (Likely v. 31, with reference to Penu'el ["face of God"] presents a justification for a place name. Verse 32 contains a derivative explanation of a ritual practice. But neither etiology need detain us.) What remains on the next morning is the same man, but now decisively changed. He has changed in two ways. First, he has *a new name—Israel.* This narrative is not about religious encounters in general. It is a quite concrete assertion about the forming of Israel, no more nor less. Israel's identity is not only that he has to do with God, but that he has been peculiarly "victimized" by the assault of God. That is what marks Israel in its obedience and its disobedience.

Second, the same man is decisively changed by a *new limp.* It is not impossible that the damage to the "thigh" means Jacob was assaulted in his vital organs. Thus, the "limp" refers to the mark left on his very manhood and future. This is no minor injury. He was wounded by his wrestling with God (v. 25). Meeting this God did not lead, as we are wont to imagine, to reconciliation, forgiveness, healing. It resulted in a crippling. Those are the marks of Israel. The *new name* cannot be separated from the *new crippling,* for the crippling is the substance of the name. So Jacob's rendezvous in the night is ambivalent. He has penetrated the mystery of God like none before him. Jacob has dared to do what the Israel of Moses will not dare (Exod. 19:21–25; 20:18–20). And he has prevailed. But his prevailing is a defeat as well as a victory. There is a dangerous, costly mystery in drawing too near and claiming too much.

Frederick Buechner has called this event *The Magnificent Defeat,* and it can be read that way. It is a defeat because he limped. It is magnificent, nearly Promethean, in the prevailing. There is a different nuance if one should say, "The Crippling Victory." Jacob did gain a victory. And he limped every day thereafter to show others (and himself) that there are no untroubled victories with this holy One. Only now can Jacob understand that his exclamation of 28:16 (cf. 32:2) should not be made lightly: "God is in this place." That is cause for dread as well as exultation.

270

e. This narrative reflects some of Israel's most sophisticated theology. On the one hand, Jacob/Israel soars to bold heights of a Promethean kind. But then, he is corrected by a limp, affirming that only God is God. On the other hand, Jacob is a cripple with a blessing. Israel must ponder how it is that blessings are given and at what cost. This same theology of weakness in power and power in weakness turns this text toward the New Testament and the gospel of the cross. This same dialectic stands behind Jesus' encounter with his disciples (Mark 10:35–45). They want thrones, an equivalent to asking the name. Jesus counters by asking them about cups, baptisms, and crosses. Like Jacob, they are invited to be persons of faith who prevail, but to do so with a limp. Karl Elliger ("Das Jakobskampf am Jabbok," ZTK 48:31 [1951]) suggests that Jacob's struggle with a holy vocation may hint an anticipation of the Crucified One.

The exclamation of Jacob is a telling one (v. 30). It characterizes Israel as having access to the life of God in most peculiar ways. The statement contravenes conventional religious judgments (cf. Exod. 33:20; Judg. 6:22–23; 13:22). Israel does see and live. But it is not suggested that the seeing leaves one the same, unscathed. He lived, but he lived a new way, with new power and with new weakness. And then he faced his brother.

2. The second meeting is with Esau (33:1–17). This is the one for which Jacob was better prepared. We have the initial negotiation (32:3–8) and the careful strategy (32:13–21). The observed meeting itself is presented in a carefully stylized, almost ritual manner. The telling must be as careful and paced as is the well-orchestrated narrative.

a. The approach (vv. 1–11) is dominated by two phrases.

1) Three times (vv. 8, 10, 15) the phrase is used, "If I find favor in your eyes" (cf. 32:5). The interplay of the brothers proceeds as if all the claims of primogeniture were operative. Esau is the one feared.

2) The verb *bow down* is used to good effect with an ironic reverse allusion to the blessing of 27:29:

> He himself went on before them, *bowing himself* to the ground seven times, until he came near his brother (v. 3). The maids drew near, they and their children, and *bowed down* (v. 6). Leah likewise and her children drew near and *bowed down* (v. 7). And last Joseph and Rachel drew near, and they *bowed down* (v. 7).

271

The scene is solemn and tense. The arrangement indicates that Rachel and Joseph are the most cherished ones and the ones to be protected.

b. By verse 12 the reconciliation has been accomplished. Esau has accepted the generous gift. There is the departure (vv. 12–17), which ends with an etiology for Succoth (v. 17). This section contains only one noteworthy element. Esau apparently departs in trust and invites Jacob to come with him. He acts in good faith. But Jacob begs off with a not very convincing excuse (vv. 13–15) and finally does not go with Esau at all. Even in this last ostentatious reconciliation, Jacob still deceives. He acts in contradiction to what he has said.

As a result, one cannot be sure. Has the whole notion of a transformed Jacob been a ploy without substance? Or is it serious? Probably, we are not meant to know. We do not know whether Jacob is genuinely changed or if this is more of his posturing. Perhaps he even exaggerated the limp to impress his brother. Perhaps Esau does not know, nor does the story-teller. It may be that Esau leaves the scene not knowing if he has won or if he has been duped. In any case, on the public face of it the brothers have been reconciled. The main issues set in motion in 25:19–26 have been resolved. The main tension of the Jacob narrative has reached its culmination.

The Two Meetings and Reconciliation

The ostensible subject of this narrative is the meeting with Esau (33:1–17). But that meeting is now set alongside the meeting with the night stranger (32:22–32), whom we judge to be Yahweh, with shadows of Esau present. The juxtaposition of the two offers a warning. God will not be taken lightly or easily. There will be no cheap reconciliations. On the way to the affronted brother, Jacob must deal with the crippling (and blessing) God. The Israel that goes on to the reconciliation with the brother is not only buoyant and successful, he also limps.

1. The story of brotherly reconciliation must be held together with the statement of dreaded holiness. The meeting with God and the meeting with the brother run together in the experience of Jacob.

The narrator knows this interrelatedness by the way he has arranged the statements on the motif of *face: (a)* "Afterwards I shall see his *face* . . ." (32:20). *(b)* "For I have seen God *face to face,* and yet my life is preserved" (32:30). *(c)* "For truly to see *your face* is like seeing the *face of God*" (33:10). It is hard to identify the players. In the *holy God,* there is something of the *estranged brother.* And in the *forgiving brother,* there is something of the *blessing God.* Jacob has seen the face of God.

272

Now he knows that seeing the face of Esau is like that. We are not told in what ways it is like the face of God. Perhaps in both it is the experience of relief that one does not die. The forgiving face of Esau and the blessing face of God have an affinity. Perhaps it is to meet the dread that can be measured. In both cases, there is a prevailing, but also a crippling. The crippling is not to death. The forgiving is not unqualified.

Not for a minute does the narrator confuse God and brother, heaven and earth. But it is seen that the most secular and the most holy overlap. Permission to be Israel (and not Jacob) depends on wrestling and prevailing. But it also requires meeting the brother. Perhaps it takes meeting the brother to regard the limp as a blessing. The religious encounter and the renewal of the relation are not the same. But they come together and must not be separated.

2. The theme of reconciliation touches the narrative about God and the narrative about brother. The text is realistic. Reconciliations are seldom as unambiguous as we anticipate. Jacob's encounter with God left him an empowered, renamed cripple. His reconciliation with his brother included deception. The two meetings belong together in promise and in caution.

a. The theme of reconciliation may point us to the distinctive Pauline statement (II Cor. 5:16–21). In that text, we are invited to discern a new creation. The old has passed away. While the texts of Gen. 32—33 and II Cor. 5:16–21 are very different, there are parallels. In both, the beginning is in the reconciling work of God. In both, there follows the mandate to horizontal reconciliation. The Pauline insight may help us understand the odd juxtaposition of Penu'el and Esau. The limping of Penu'el may keep us from speaking flippantly about the "New Being," for the New Creature may be marked by limping as the sign of newness (cf. II Cor. 4:7–12).

b. In another arena, we read these other words:

No man has ever seen God [not even Jacob?]; if we love one another, God abides in us and his love is perfected in us. . . . If anyone says, "I love God," and hates his brother, he is a liar; for he who does not love his brother whom he has seen, cannot love God whom he has not seen. And this commandment we have from him, that he who loves God should love his brother also (I John 4:12, 20–21).

273

Love of God and love of brother belong together. It remains to ask about seeing and loving. What does it mean to be children and heirs of that man—crippled and blessed, bowed down and forgiven? More than one answer will be given. But all the answers must pass through the prism of the Crucified One. He is the one who knows fully about limping and blessing, about bowing down and forgiving.

Genesis 33:18—34:31

This unit is one continuous story. It seems to have no relationship with anything before or after. In the present arrangement of narratives, it poses a new agenda for Jacob and his family. In 25:19—33:17, the main theme is the flight of Jacob from Esau and the *return* to Esau and the land. The primary account is the story of a fugitive surviving away from the land and returning to it with a blessing. But in this narrative, Jacob has come to the land and is settled in it. The new problem in this narrative is survival and faithfulness *in the land.* Israel has a quite new theological agenda for which the old postures are less than adequate.

Historically, we can say little about the narrative. We know that Israel had old and significant ties with the city and region of Shechem (cf. Josh. 24; Judg. 9). Indeed, Shechem became a major point of reference for pre-monarchial Israel. It is probable that Israel never faced major conflict with the other inhabitants of Shechem (the Canaanites), but was able to achieve a peaceful accommodation. The Amarna Letters from the fourteenth century indicate a social movement in Shechem which had affinities with the Israelites, thus predisposing the inhabitants to friendship with them. Perhaps this narrative reflects the anguished and ambiguous way in which marginal peoples coped with a new situation of land and prosperity. The theme of the narrative is Israelite accommodation to non-Israelites in the land. The polemical casting of the text suggests this was a much disputed issue in Israel. Some favored more accommodation. Some resisted accommodation.

The story consists of two major movements, with an introduction and conclusion:

274

33:18–20	introduction: settlement in Shechem
34:1–12	seduction and negotiation by Shechem
34:13–29	retaliation by the sons of Jacob
34:30–31	conclusion: dispute between Jacob and his sons

The Settlement and Accommodation

The problem of settlement and accommodation has been marginally reflected in 26:34–35; 27:46—28:9. But here the issue is put more sharply. The contrast between the approach of the two texts is telling. Gen. 27:46—28:9 is a late text and has the ideological coloring of the Priestly tradition. Our present text is much earlier and much more visceral in its response to the question.

1. The narrative is introduced by a report of Jacob coming to the city, purchasing land (cf. Gen. 23), and building an altar (33:18–20). The story is made more complicated by the fact that Shechem is treated as a person, but the reference is also to the city and to the culture it represents. We cannot be sure whether we are dealing with personal interactions or with disguised tribal history. This is the case not only with Shechem but with Simeon and Levi later in the story (34:25–31).

Archaeological remains indicate Shechem was a major shrine before the appearance of Israel. The building of the altar (33:20) may point to the act of claiming an older cult place for Israelite use.

2. The crisis of the narrative is introduced in 34:1–7. Dinah has been mentioned previously in 30:21. But neither here nor in that text does she appear in other than a passive role. Most plausibly, the liaison of Dinah and Shechem refers to the interaction (and intermarriage?) of Canaanites and Israelites. The narrative is a bit artificial for an actual event. The report on Shechem is obviously given from a polemical Israelite perspective (v. 2). While there is indication that his intentions were not entirely dishonorable (v. 3), the story is tilted against any good intention he may have had.

Major interest in these verses may be focused on two words.

a. The action of Shechem is interpreted as "defilement" *(ṭāmē')* (v. 5; cf. vv. 13, 27). This term is found nowhere else in Genesis, though later it is a normal term in the Priestly tradition with reference to ritual purity (cf. Lev. 5:2; 11:25, 28; 12:2, 5; 15:18; 22:8—RSV renders "unclean"). This text uses the word in a distinctive way. Here, Israel intensifies its notions of right and wrong by presenting the issue as one of ritual purity. That is, a linkage is made between sexuality and ritual correctness. Ricoeur (*The Symbolism of Evil,* 1969) has shown that an elemental notion of ritual uncleanness is more powerful, more

275

compelling, and (as here) more dangerous than a judgment of moral guilt. That is, the woman is not simply taken. She is made ritually unacceptable. It is this elemental passion regarding "defilement" which lies behind the outraged retribution that follows. The shift of images from *guilt* to *defilement* makes the issue much more outrageous in the perception of Israel. (The use of "defilement" here may be understood as parallel to the kind of emotional power the word "communist" has had in recent American politics. Both are terms capable of evoking powerful responses without reference to political reality.)

Clearly, this articulation is not the disciplined, detached reflection of professionals on the problem of uncleanness, as in he later Priestly tradition. Rather, this narrative evidences the unsophisticated and irrational response of a passion unencumbered by reflection.

b. A second term of note is "folly" *(nᵉbālāh)* (v. 7), also used nowhere else in Genesis. It is not only folly but "folly *in Israel.*" The action is linked to the special identity and vocation of Israel among the Canaanites. Here, as often elsewhere, the term is connected to sexual violation. In confronting "folly," we have to do with the deepest realities and passions of the community (cf. Deut. 22:21; Judg. 19:23f.; 20:6; II Sam. 13:12; Jer. 29:23). All of these passages use the same word, *nᵉbālāh.*

3. The proposal of Hamor (vv. 8–12) builds upon the positive statement of verse 3. He is genuinely conciliatory and wishes to make settlement on whatever terms Israel wishes. Thus, there is an incongruity between the harsh judgment made by Israel (vv. 1–7, 26f.) and the positive attitude of Hamor (vv. 8–12). Their differences in perception are at the root of the trouble. For Israel, Shechem's act is seen as perversion. To Hamor, it is an opportunity for cooperation.

Deception and Retaliation

Resolution of the action begins in verse 13.

1. The response of the sons of Jacob (vv. 13–17) is one of religious zeal, but not an unreasonable zeal. The proposed condition of settlement seems a proper one, even to Shechem. The solution offers benefit to both parties. On the one hand, it permits *cooperation* and intermarriage. On the other hand, it insists on the *religious peculiarity* of Israel which must be honored.

a. The term "defile" is again used (v. 13). Thus the Israelite reading of the situation is not mitigated by the open-ended

276

conciliatory proposal (vv. 8–12). Israel sees the situation as one between the violated and the violator. That can only be rectified by concession on religious requirements.

b. The term "defile" is further intensified in relation to the term "disgrace" *(ḥerpāh)* (v. 14). This term is again an unusual one, used elsewhere in Genesis only in 30:23. With the use of "disgrace," "defilement," and "folly," the rhetoric of the narrative makes clear how deeply the action of Hamor had touched the sensitivities of Israel.

There is no hint in the son's proposal of anything but good faith, even if it is good faith that is tinged with rancor and a reluctance to compromise. The offer even concludes with a hint of a larger unified community, "one people" (v. 16).

2. Hamor persuades his people to accept the condition (vv. 18–24). The conditions do not seem unreasonable to him or to his people. His speech persuading the community provides three motivations which carry the day (vv. 21–23).

a. There is no reason not to be friendly and to meet unimportant conditions which will make cooperation possible (v. 21). Shechem need not take the symbolic action of circumcision seriously, no matter what Israel means by it.

b. There is a hint of largeness of vision (v. 22) with the phrase "one people" echoing the invitation of verse 16. One should not make too much of it, but in secular and pragmatic terms, the two allusions offer an ecumenical vision.

c. But we should not be overly impressed with the first two arguments. The third argument is no doubt the compelling one (v. 23, also 21*ab*). Acceptance of the religious condition will advance economic interest. The secular vision of Hamor is informed by economic interest. For the Shechemites, there is no problem in using religious ritual for the sake of economic gain.

d. For their own mixed, highly pragmatic reasons, the men of the city accede to the conditions (v. 24). There is no debate or contention. Accommodation seems obviously the most profitable and secure recourse to the people of Shechem.

3. Finally the story reaches its real action (vv. 25–29). The proposed condition had been accepted by the Shechemites. Only now it becomes clear that the sons of Jacob were not acting in good faith. In fact, they had no serious interest in the religious scruple. They valued their religious act no more than Shechem did.

277

a. Again, the governing word is "defile," now the third and key usage of the term (v. 27). The Israelite reading of the situation has not changed. They are not interested in accommodation, cooperation, or even ratification. They have no vision of social cooperation, of ecumenical community, or even of economic advantage. Their perceptual field is informed only by vengeance.

b. Insistence upon circumcision was posed not for purposes of faithfulness, but for purposes of social control and exploitation. It is not considered an act of faithfulness nor an end in itself, but only a means to another end, and an ignoble one at that. This most precious symbol of faith has now become a tool of inhumanity. (Cf. Rom. 4:1–2 on the religious symbol in the service of social control.)

c. The exacting description of plunder indicates that the retaliation is completely disproportionate to the offense (vv. 25–29). The impassioned partisan vision of reality reflected in the words "defilement," "folly," and "disgrace" now comes to a violent expression. Because the single act of Hamor is read through these emotional lenses, there is no possibility of humaneness or cooperation. The Israelite passion for the community has now worked its destructive end.

d. But the passionate vengeance is transparently self-serving. What they seized, they did not destroy as an act of faithfulness (cf. I Sam. 15:3, 14–19). Rather, they kept it for themselves so that their taking was not an act of righteous indignation, but an act of confiscation for self gain.

4. The concluding exchange between Jacob and his sons (vv. 30–31) makes an odd and unexpected ending to the narrative. Until now, Jacob has had no part to play in the narrative. He has deferred to the judgment of his sons (v. 5). Now he has regrets.

In this narrative, Jacob is the seasoned voice of maturity. He has lived a long time. He has not flinched from conflicts as they have come to him. But now he rebukes such a childish religion which will endanger its own life rather than face realities. There is, of course, a place for passion and zeal. But Jacob recognizes his marginal, minority position in Shechem. He counsels, therefore, a low profile and an effort to get along with more powerful neighbors. His response is not one of great faith, but of clear-headed pragmatism. Luther finds Jacob's words much too pragmatic: "They are not words of faith but simply words of the murmuring flesh and struggling faith." Jacob does not appeal to promises. Here he reacts as a sensible, fear-

278

ful man. In his chastening of his sons, he uses two telling words.

a. He accuses his sons of bringing "trouble" *('ākar)*. This same word is used in the narrative of Joshua and is coupled with the same term we have rendered "folly" (Josh. 6:18; 7:15, 24–25 —RSV: "shameful thing"). In the Joshua narrative, the Israelites have done *folly* (7:15) and caused *trouble* (6:18; 7:24–25). In our text, Shechem has done *folly,* but Israel has caused *trouble.* Like Achan in Joshua 7, the sons of Jacob have coveted. They have coveted their religious peculiarity. They have coveted their moral rectitude. And finally, they have been corrupted by their passion to covet the lives and the property of their neighbors.

b. Jacob knows that as a result, he is made a *stench* (RSV: "odious") to Shechem. The actions of his sons have made him abhorrent to his context. That is a painful blow to this one who has been a homeless refugee all his life. Now he has come into the land and has become a rejected presence as a result of this foolish action.

c. Sadly, at the end of the narrative Jacob's sons have learned nothing and conceded nothing (v. 31). They are fixed on the narrow sexual issue. The sons remain blind to the larger economic issues, blind to the dangers they have created, blind to the possibilities of cooperation, and blind even to the ways they have compromised their own religion in their thirst for vengeance and gain. The narrative ends with a question (v. 31). Things are unresolved. The father does not speak again. We do not know if he has been persuaded. It may be that he despairs of teaching his sons anything.

5. This narrative will surely not be widely used in theological exposition. But it poses hard questions to the community of faith. It speaks about the convergence of *elemental passion, economic advantage, religious scruple,* and *ecumenical vision.* It asks the community of faith to decide for faith in the midst of such convergences. All these factors are present in the story in conflict and ambiguity. The controversy of Jacob and his sons indicates that more than one conclusion is possible. If Jacob had had his way, the settlement with Shechem would have been honored. But the unresolved ending hints that a more sectarian and destructive settlement prevailed. The issue is a continuing one for Israel. This story portrays a resolution of passion. Implicitly it urges a more pragmatic settlement. But above all, the episode will not permit escape from the burden of facing the

279

issue. Passion is often a strange mixture of religious fervor and animal craving. And passion is always in tension with cool pragmatism, seeking survival through planned action. Faith must live and move and decide within that tension. It is an issue which the community of Jacob must face whenever it comes to the prosperity and stability of the land. The land always comes with people who have another vision (cf. 12:6). They must be dealt with, whether passionately or pragmatically or, perhaps, faithfully.

Genesis 35:1—36:43

These chapters contain miscellaneous materials not centrally important to the tradition. They include:

35:1–4   a cultic pilgrimage from Shechem to Bethel
35:5–15   a theophany at Bethel
35:16–21 the death of Rachel/the birth of Benjamin
35:22–26 the sons of Jacob
35:27–29 the death of Isaac
36:1–43 the genealogy of Esau.

These materials do not seem to have a particular relation to each other, though they function to give closure to the narrative of Jacob. We will consider several elements as independent units. Because some elements may be regarded as only of secondary interest, they will be passed over without mention (cf. 35:22b–26).

Events at Bethel

We have already seen in 28:10–22 (cf. 31:13) that Bethel is a most important city and shrine and that it is crucial for the Jacob tradition. Here two important events are linked to that shrine.

1. The narrative of 35:1–4 with its ritual of purification is an appropriate counterpoint to chapter 34.

a. Though it may have had no original connection to that narrative, it now stands as its foil. The *purification rite* of Shechem-Bethel in these verses serves as a response to the *defilement* of Gen. 34. We have seen the dominance of the word "defile" in 34:5, 13, 27. It is here answered by the term "purify" *(ṭāhar)* (v. 2). The terms "defile/purify," *(ṭāmē'/ṭāhar)* are paired in ritual prescriptions (cf. Lev. 11:47; 16:19). This may be the reason for the present arrangement of the text. The term "purify" is used only here in the ancestral narratives (and elsewhere in Genesis only in 7:2, 8; 8:20 in the flood narrative —RSV "clean"). Its use is as noteworthy as "defile" *(ṭāmē')* in the preceding narrative.

b. As much as Genesis 34, this text knows that faithfulness in the land among the Canaanites is a risky business. But this text knows, as chapter 34 does not, that Israel cannot either *leave* the land or *kill* all the Canaanites. Israel must find a way to stay in the land with the Canaanites and yet practice faithfulness. The way chosen to do this without either destructiveness or accommodation is by way of *radical symbolization.* Israel engages in dramatic ritual activity as a mode of faithfulness. It is apparent that this ritual (later used at Shechem, cf. Josh. 24:23) permits Israel to be Israel in the land. The tradition affirms there can be dramatic disengagement from the powers and practices which endanger faith and deny humanness.

c. Philip Carrington has suggested that in the Christian tradition, this same disengagement from alternative values is enacted in the sacrament of baptism (*The Primitive Catechism,* 1940, Chap. 4). In his study of New Testament formulae of baptism, Carrington has identified a four-fold scheme: (1) putting off evil; (2) the code of subordination; (3) watch and pray; (4) resist the devil/stand firm. Carrington has identified a number of New Testament texts which reflect this pattern that he judges to be from catechetical instruction for baptism. While we do not have the entire pattern in our text, the first element is clearly reflected. Thus, we may suggest a parallel between the ancient rite of purification and the Christian practice of baptism, both of which seek disengagement from the values and powers of the world around the faithful community. It is an act of *purification and renunciation,* as we may observe in these texts:

> In these you once walked, when you lived in them. But now *put them all away:* anger, wrath, malice, slander, and foul talk from your mouth (Col. 3:7–8).

> *Put off* your old nature which belongs to your former manner of life and is corrupt through deceitful lusts, and be renewed in the spirit of your minds, and *put on* the new nature, created after the

281

likeness of God in true righteousness and holiness. Therefore *putting away* falsehood . . . (Eph. 4:22–25).

So *put away* all malice and guile and insincerity and envy and all slander (I Pet. 2:1).

Therefore *put away* all filthiness and rank growth of wickedness and receive with meekness the implanted word, which is able to save your souls (James 1:21).

. . . let us also *lay aside* every weight, and sin which clings so closely, and let us run with perseverance . . . (Heb. 12:1).

These texts urge renunciation of sinful ways. Until our own time, traditional formulae for baptism have called for "renouncing the vainglories of the world." Thus in the Christian tradition, the renunciation of foreign gods has been translated as renunciation of sinfulness. Israel believed that the symbolic removal of foreign gods, purification, and change of garments were effective in disengagement from their real power. In parallel fashion, Christian baptism is understood as disengagement from the powers of evil.

Exposition of this passage in our time may need to ask about the false powers and loyalties which must be rejected. And it will want to ask about the symbolic actions which might accomplish disengagement. Marie Augusta Neal suggests that the faithful are now called to disengagement from "economic aggression" which has both economic and spiritual dimensions (*A Socio-Theology of Letting Go*, 1977). Thus, we may discern continuity from the Israelite purification practice concerning foreign gods, to the baptismal renunciations in the early church, to the mandates for disengagement in our time. This community of faith is continually engaged in dramatic and genuine *relinquishments* of Canaanite alternatives.

d. The ritual action in this passage involved a change of garments (v. 2). This is a specific liturgical act of "putting off" and "putting on." The writer of Ephesians, in what may be a baptismal tract, calls the church to "put off your old nature," and "put on the new nature, created after the likeness of God, in true righteousness and holiness" (Eph. 4:22–24). In our text, this was an actual physical change of clothes. Perhaps the same is true in some early forms of Christian baptism. In any case, there is no doubt that the metaphor of being reclothed is utilized in the early church (II Cor. 5:4; Eph. 6:13–17; I Pet. 5:5; Rev. 3:4; 16:15).

2. The second part of this Bethel tradition reiterates mate-

rial which has been encountered elsewhere. There is again the establishment of the shrine by means of altar (v. 7) and pillar (v. 14, cf. 28:18, 22). But, as is usual in such theophanic appearances, it is the speech which matters most.

a. The name change (v. 10) is a second version of the change of name already announced in the Penu'el episode of 32:27–28. Though the connection of this text to 35:1–4 is secondary, the connection serves well an exposition attentive to the parallel of baptism. In 35:1–4, the baptismal parallel had to do with *renunciation,* purification, and change of garments. Here, the parallel concerns the *name change* (cf. Isa. 43:1). A new person is formed. A new community is convened. It is called forth in the land as an alternative to the Canaanite culture in which it is placed.

b. Bethel is the place of the promise (cf. 28:13–15). The fundamental promise of the land to the fathers is again repeated (vv. 11–12). We have seen in Gen. 17:1–8 that this version of the promise is probably from the Priestly tradition. The Priestly agenda might have influenced the placement of this appearance after the older narratives of *defilement* (v. 34) and *purification* (35:1–4). It is to *defiled* Israel now *purified* that the Priestly tradition might have a promise made. For the priests, *purification* is a pre-condition to *promise.*

c. These strange ritual experiences (35:1–4; 35:5–15) affirm the formation of an alternative community which will be faithful. The new community is found by *renunciation, renaming, reclothing,* and finally, *receiving a promise.* Indeed, all things are made new.

Jacob and His Three Generations

The miscellaneous materials of 35:16–29 touch upon the death of the father (vv. 27–29), the death of the wife (vv. 16–21), the birth of the son (vv. 16–21), the disobedience of the son (v. 22a), and the full listing of all the sons (vv. 22b–26).

1. The juxtaposition of the *birth* of treasured Benjamin and the *death* of the beloved Rachel is a significant one (vv. 16–21). The linking of the two events shows how intensely intergenerational is the faith and life of this family. Dying always happens in the midst of new life. Living always happens in the midst of death. There is, after all, a time to be born and a time to die (Eccles. 3:2). And this time, like every poignant time, is both times. Rachel has not been mentioned since the dramatic scene

283

of 33:1–7. But that scene is enough to show that she (with Joseph) is the treasure of Jacob's life. Benjamin is the son born late, as is clear in the later intrigues of Joseph (cf. 42:36). This late son is the most valued of Jacob, perhaps as his best, last link to Rachel. The life of this community is a life of sorrow and celebration. Because of the promise-keeping, life-giving God, sorrow does turn to joy (John 16:20–21). Death does move on to new life. The narrative is strikingly silent on emotions and on the statement of any implications. It is enough to state the data, for the rest is obvious. As though to stress the historical reality of this family, that it must face death and move on, the narrator ends with the brief report, "Israel journeyed on. . . ."

2. The second indication of the abrasion of the generations is the brief note on Reuben, Jacob's first-born (35:22). Scattered in the texts are hints of the disarray of the family at the end of Jacob's life. There is the sorry picture of Simeon and Levi (Gen. 34), of Judah (Gen. 38), and now of Reuben. Thus, the four oldest, the early sons of Leah (cf. 29:32–35), are less than models in this narrative. But this is how it is with the promise. It is always in jeopardy. The promise is not assured or dependent upon the quality of its bearers.

The action of Reuben is not to be evaluated simply as an issue of sexual morality, but as a political issue. The taking of the father's concubines is an attempt to seize power, claim the leadership and, in fact, announce that the old man is dead (cf. II Sam. 16:20–23). While there are important Davidic parallels, there is also evidence of affinity to the sordid stories of Judges 19—21. The old man (read "king") is dead. Everyone does "what is right in his own eyes" (Judg. 17:6; 18:1; 19:1; 21:25). Perhaps it is a measure of how fully syncretized this family had become in one generation. And perhaps there is even a grim contrast of 35:22 and chapter 34. Confronted by the challenge of Canaanite culture, Jacob's sons cannot find a way of fidelity. This one (Reuben) *yields* completely to the cultural forms of well-being. The other two brothers (Simeon and Levi) *resist* the culture and destroy (34). The texts together provide a way to consider the extremities as the faithful find themselves caught in a deathly culture. This cryptic note offers one more evidence of conflict in the life of Jacob, even at its close. The text only hints at the pathos of the old man.

3. At the close of the section, the death and burial of Isaac are reported (35:27–29). Three items may be noted.

a. Isaac has lived to fullness, a faithful keeper of the promise and fully blessed (cf. Gen. 26).

b. He is able to rest in Hebron, in the place secured by father Abraham (Gen. 23) and where Jacob will also be buried (50:12–14). There is calm and faithful closure to this life.

c. Most important, the burial is conducted by both sons, Esau and Jacob, even named in that order. When the brothers had separated (33:16–17), it was not clear whether this was a reconciliation or a truce. But this text makes clear that there was a reconciliation. Even in this Jacob-oriented tradition, the older brother is remarkably valued. The venom has been removed from the oracle of 25:23.

The Genealogy of Esau

The note in 35:29 prepares the way for the extended genealogy of Esau (36:1–43). The most remarkable feature of this genealogy is that it is here at all. It is stunning that the long conclusion of the Jacob tradition concerns Esau. Every listener to the whole story knows that we are ready to move to Joseph, to forget that older generation and move on to the new. But the tradition itself is not in such a hurry. The tradition finds it difficult to turn loose of Esau. And that raises important issues for a tradition undoubtedly shaped by the pressures and loyalties of the Jacob family.

1. As we have observed, Esau is handled carefully and respectfully all through this narrative. There is considerable information available to later generations. Esau is presented with touching feeling in chapter 27 at the time of the stolen birthright. He is presented nobly in the reconciliation of chapter 33. In 36:7, it is stated that the division of property between Esau and Jacob is not disputed but done practically and even irenically. As with Lot (13:6–8), the division is described without acrimony or any stigma attached to Esau. The overall impression is given that now, finally father Isaac can let go of his elder son. Only once (in the Priestly tradition of 28:1–5) does Isaac freely concede Jacob a blessing. And even where Esau is criticized (26:34–35), he is later reported as making amends (28:6–9). For this, the tradition implicitly commends him. Not once in the entire tradition is there a harsh word for Esau. Even his anger toward Jacob (27:34–41) is presented uncritically and not without justification.

2. This does not mean that primogeniture is still regnant or

285

that Esau is really the primal heir. Too much has been paid by Jacob to concede that. The free choice of Jacob by Yahweh (25:23) is sure and unchallenged in the narrative. But Esau is there, very much there. He is present in dignity at the death of Isaac and present with studied deference in these genealogical statements. Two ways are suggested to hold together the election of Jacob and the attractive reality of Esau.

a. We have likely divided the tradition too soon, presuming that the text rejects Esau for the sake of elect Jacob. We read it this way in order to trace the elect line of elect persons to Jesus. While the tradition does do some narrowing and does choose one son over another in the interest of the elect line, we have seen that with Ishmael and Esau, the tradition does not do so easily or quickly. Even in the Jacob circles of traditioning, the election of Jacob does not imply the rejection of Esau. Read with excessively Christian eyes, the temptation is to be too christological. Read with Jewish eyes, the temptation may be to be excessively Israelite.

Without one disclaimer, the Esau community belongs to Genesis. To be sure, beyond chapter 36 the Esau memory is not developed. But it is there. It is not rejected or closed. The Bible chooses to follow the Jacob line. But that makes the Esau story no less legitimate. We are required by this carefully placed text to recognize the large vision of Genesis. This book of gracious beginnings belongs to Muslims (children of Esau) as well as to Jews and Christians (children of Jacob). In Gen. 34:22 (cf. v. 16), it was the Shechemites who had shared the ecumenical vision of "one people." Genesis holds to that inclusive vision. It is only later, in the sixth and fifth centuries, that polemics against Edom begin to occur (Obad.; Mal. 1:2–5). It is important that in Genesis, even in the Priestly material from a later period, there is no hostile parting of the brothers. Even Luther, given as he is to polemics, can concede to Esau and his community that "they became participants not in the promise but in the mercy which the promise shows forth." Characteristically, negative dimensions are attributed to Jacob and not to Esau.

b. While the main thrust of our interpretation has been concerned with the claim of election, there is more here than the matter of election. There is an undeniable focus on that one line in the family. But Genesis does not pretend that that is all there is. The memory has not been purged or revised to exclude the others.

286

It is a problem to affirm the election of Jacob and yet to assert the legitimacy of the others. But that is what this tradition does. It is for that reason that Henning Graf Reventlow and others speak about *universalism* as well as *election* in Genesis ("'Internationalismus' in den Patriarchenüberlieferungen," in Donner, Hanhart, Smend, eds., *Beiträge zur Alttestamentliche Theologie*, 1977, pp. 354–70). The broad perspective of Genesis, of this God as the God of all peoples, is not limited to the "map" (Gen. 10) or the genealogies (Gen. 5; 11). It continues even through the militant Jacob narratives which most zealously insist on election.

c. This awareness has important implication for the *faith community* in the context of the *human community*. While God has a particular and precious relation to this chosen community, it is not the Lord's only commitment. In other ways and on other grounds, these others are also held in his care and kept in his promise. This genealogy does not waver from identifying in Esau a line of kings and princes whose legitimacy is not in question (36:31). No doubt the kings born here fulfill and share in something of the promise to Abraham and Sarah (17:16).

Such an inclusive vision places a check on over-zealous understandings of election. It affirms that there are "other sheep not of this fold" (John 10:16). Even Deuteronomy, which did not hesitate to claim the most for Israel (cf. Deut. 7:6–8), finally must recognize this reality in the economy of God: "You shall not abhor an Edomite, for he is your brother" (Deut. 23:7).

The narrative concerning Jacob moves a long way from the birth of the brothers in 25:19–26 to the death of the father (35:27–29). We have seen that the oracle of 25:23 did come to fruition (33:1–17) but in a strange and ironic form. The brother relation is resolved, albeit tenuously. Now the narrative turns from that brother relation (which has dominated the Jacob narrative) to the intergenerational problem which is resilient in the patriarchal narratives. As we shall see, *the sons of Jacob* pose issues more difficult to resolve than does *the brother of Jacob*.

PART FOUR

The Joseph Narrative: The Hidden Call of God

GENESIS 37:1—50:26

We know that in everything God works for good with those who love him, who are called according to his purpose. For those whom he foreknew he also predestined to be conformed to the image of his Son, in order that he might be the first-born among many brethren. And those whom he predestined he also called; and those whom he called he also justified; and those whom he justified, he also glorified (Rom. 8:28–30).

The Joseph narrative offers a kind of literature which is distinctive in Genesis. It is distinguished in every way from the narratives dealing with Abraham and Jacob. The intellectual world of this narrative has much more in common with the David story of II Sam. 9—20 than it does with the ancestral tales. While we cannot be sure, a plausible locus for the narrative is the royal, urban ethos of Solomon which imitated international ways and which sharply critiqued the claims of the old tribal traditions. Its presuppositions suggest a cool detachment from things religious that is contrasted with the much more direct religious affirmation of the Abraham and Jacob stories. This narrative appears to belong to a generation of believers in a cultural climate where old modes of faith were embarrassing. The old idiom of faith had become unconvincing. Thus, the narrative should be understood as a sophisticated literary response to a cultural, theological crisis. How does one speak about faith in a context where the older ways are found wanting? That is the issue in the Joseph narrative.

288

As one might expect, the theological claims of the narrator are subdued and mostly implicit. Nonetheless, the narrative has an identifiable and singular intention. It urges that in the contingencies of history, the purposes of God are at work in hidden and unnoticed ways. But the ways of God are nonetheless reliable and will come to fruition. This narrator does not express the passion of the Abraham narrative about the demand for radical trust. Nor is conflict so scandalously valued as in the Jacob narrative. Rather, this narrator is attentive to the mysterious ways of God's providence. The purposes of God are not wrought here by abrupt action or by intrusions, but by the ways of the world which seem to be natural and continuous. There is no appeal for faith or response, for the main point is that the ways of God are at work, regardless of human attitudes or actions. In a climate with doubts about the reality or effectiveness of God, this story takes a high view of God, so high that human action is declared irrelevant. Not only the brothers, but Joseph as well, are unaware until the very end of the ways of God in keeping the dream.

Critical Questions

Because this material moves in a different intellectual arena with a different style of faith, the critical questions have a different shape from those of the other ancestral material.

1. The Joseph narrative (in its main parts) is not a collection of unordered tribal memories which have come together in a relatively undisciplined way, as is the case with Gen. 12:1—36:43. Rather, the Joseph narrative is a sustained and artistically crafted statement of considerable literary finesse. The shaper of this narrative is not simply an arranger of old traditions, but a genuine creator who fashions a new statement with a programmatic theological intent.

In addition to that sustained story, we may identify other elements that are set alongside it:

    a. Gen. 38 a curious story, unrelated to its context. It must be treated independently.

    b. Gen. 46:1–7 a theophany concerning Jacob. In the primary Joseph story, there are no direct theophanies. This narrative has more in common with the older ancestral materials.

    c. Gen. 46:8–27 a genealogy inserted in the narrative.

289

      d. Gen. 47:28—48:22; 49:28–33; 50:1–14 diverse materials related to the death of Jacob.

      e. Gen. 49:1–27 a poem of tribal history in the mouth of Jacob.

      f. Gen. 50:15–26 a report on the death of Joseph.

      The main narrative consists of chapters 37; 39—45; 46:28—47:27. It is difficult to determine the ending of the main narrative, but we follow Coats (*From Canaan to Egypt,* 1976, pp.7–54) in seeing 47:27 as the end. The movement of this narrative is from the initial dream of Joseph (37:5–9) to the secure settlement of Israel in the land under the governance of Joseph (47:27). Exposition of the main narrative requires that it should be taken as a continuous unit, even though its length requires that it be handled in smaller parts.

      2. The literary shape of the main narrative may be observed from two different perspectives.

      a. Consistent with the structuring of the primary narrative (37:5–9—47:27), the power and validity of the dream in 37:5–9 emerge as a main issue. The dream functions in the Joseph narrative as the oracle of 25:23 does for the Jacob materials. The dream slowly works itself out in the narrative. The story is concerned that the *family* and the *empire* should "bow down." Beginning with the dream in 37:7–9, the story moves by progressive *bowing down.* (Note the use of "rule" and "dominion" in v. 8 between the two statements of "bow down.") Seen in this way, the dream stretches to 50:18, in which the brothers bow down fully. There are intermediate steps in the development of this theme in 42:6; 43:26, 28. The prevalance of the theme makes clear that the realization of the dream is a major question of the narrative.

      b. It is clear that the disclosure statements of 45:4–8 and 50:19–20 are the major theological statements which interpret the entire narrative. In these two places only does the narrator make obvious the programmatic claim that God's leadership, though hidden, is the real subject of the narrative.

      3. Egyptian influences are apparent in the narrative. This is evident in the use of words, social customs, and procedure. One conclusion from this may be that this is an older Egyptian narrative now used for Israelite purposes. Or it may be a story told in an actual Egyptian setting, perhaps framed by Israel. The argument of Egyptian influence can cut either way. It may lead to a conservative historical conclusion that the narrative

reflects genuine Israelite history. Here we conclude that the observation of Egyptian influences and parallels is illuminating in terms of the style of the narrative and the craft of the narrator. But it cannot help us make any historical judgment about the narrative.

4. It is commonly agreed that the Joseph narrative is a work of art designed to make a statement to Israel. For such expression, questions of historicity are inappropriate. The most that can be asked concerns the historical setting of the artist and not the historical setting of the purported events themselves. The proper question is not "When did this happen?" Rather, we may ask, "In what cultural, intellectual context might this kind of literary statement have been achieved?" There is no consensus about this question, either. Some scholars would date the narrative late in the monarchical period of Israel. The most influential hypothesis is that the narrative is part of a major literary attempt of the Solomonic period (tenth century B.C.) to provide a statement about the hidden rule of God in the affairs of persons and nations (followed by Von Rad, *Old Testament Theology* I, 1962, pp. 48–86). Though that hypothesis is under some attack, it helps to focus the important issue. In a general way, this exposition will follow Von Rad in assuming such an ethos, even if the connection to Solomon is held loosely. It frees interpretation from asking unanswerable historical questions and focuses on the literary and theological achievement of the work. In such a perspective, the *person* of Joseph as well as the *narrative* about Joseph becomes a literary means by which an important theological affirmation is offered in Israel. And it is offered with singular literary finesse and sensitivity.

5. George Coats has shown that the Joseph narrative is a literary device to link ancestral promises to the Exodus narrative of oppression and liberation. Before this narrative, there were older traditions about the *promise* to the forebearers and about the *deliverance* from Egypt. But no way was found to link the two memories, one of which is based in *Canaan* and the other in *Egypt.* To overcome that problem, Coats suggests, this narrative was constructed. The Joseph account, then, has no independent life or function. It never existed on its own but was formed after the other materials were fixed to make a narrative linkage. It serves to carry this family from Canaan to Egypt and oppression. So far as it goes, Coats is surely correct and will be presumed to be correct here. However, as Coats also recog-

291

nizes, the material is too rich and suggestive to be handled simply as a literary connector. The narrative also makes a subtle and evocative theological statement. The dream for rule on the part of Joseph is achieved. But it is short-lived (cf. Exod. 1:8). Though Joseph controlled the empire for a time, the tendency of imperial oppression is resilient. Against that power, the dream of freedom and dominion is fragile. But neither does the Joseph narrative simply end in oppression. It flows on toward the liberation of Moses. Thus, the Joseph text is an interlude between the oldest *promises* of Israel (Gen. 12:1–3, e.g.) and the *groans* of the slaves (Exod. 2:23–24), which anticipate freedom. But it is only an interlude. In a short time, the strategies of this competent man and the security of this people are reduced to groans. The power of the empire is enduring. Its memory of human commitments is brief. Competence quickly turns into impotence as the narrative moves from Joseph to Moses. In the full memory of Israel, too much importance must not be given to this interlude even though it affirms the persistent sovereignty of Yahweh.

Theological Affirmations and Possibilities

Based on the two explicit statements of 45:5–8 and 50:19–20, theological exposition is concerned with the providential ways of God's leadership. God's way will triumph without the contribution of any human actor, including even Joseph himself.

1. Though the exposition posed here is not dependent on dating, let us begin with Von Rad's placement of the narrative in the tenth century of Solomon because of the expositional keys it offers. That was a remarkable time in Israel's life, a time for flexing muscles and being secure in one's own strength (cf. I Kings 4:20–21; 10:6–10). It may have been a time of reasonableness in which wisdom teachers were at work discerning the order of the creation and seeking to harness the mysteries of life to royal programs.

In such a context, one may ask about the relationship of power and faith. In a time of knowing so much and doing so much competently, what does it mean to trust in God? The question addressed to that intellectual climate is certainly not remote from our own context. In our own climate of modernity, the issues are even more acute, for in that ancient world the gods had not completely fled. But there is enough of a comparison that we may sense the affinity we have with the issues alive in that day. Is God relevant to a social situation in which human control seems established and sufficient?

The theme of the Joseph narrative concerns God's hidden and decisive power which works in and through but also against human forms of power. A "soft" word for that reality is *providence.* A harder word for the same reality is *predestination.* Either way—providence or predestination—the theme is that God is working out his purpose through and in spite of Egypt, through and in spite of Joseph and his brothers.

The purpose of God is announced in the dream at the beginning of the narrative. Neither Joseph nor his family knows what they are dealing with. The narrator gives no hint that this is from God. The God of this narrative does not appear, speak, act, or intrude. But there is no doubt about his governing intent and capacity. It is God who guards the dream (and the dreamer) until the dream is public (45:5–8; 50:19–20). Perhaps only when he uttered those words of disclosure did Joseph see fully what was happening. But he did not need to see fully to receive the dream. It is an amazing story to address a time when to see and know and control were all important.

2. The narrative is also about the hiddenness of God. The narrator has found a mode of storytelling appropriate to the theme. The story hints and implies. Only very late does it make anything explicit. Only at the end are intentions discerned. Perhaps even the artist did not know until the end where it would come out. Perhaps even the artist is overwhelmed by this awesome central figure. In its completed form, the narrative is bracketed between the *dream* of 37:5 and the *doxological* affirmation of 50:20 which announces everything.

The listening community may be invited to live bracketed between the *hint of the dream* and the *doxology of the disclosure.* That is where Joseph lived, between hint and doxology. The narrative may be a call to the listening community to let the dream be at work, even when its outcome is less than clear. It is a dream of power gained and used. It is a dream of family saved when death was anticipated. It is a dream of empire fed when Israel need not have cared. It is a dream which dramatically transformed the empire and led to a vocation for this one born to rule. It is a dream come true. And Joseph is found faithful to the dream.

3. The task of the expositor is difficult here because the

293

possibilities are so readily polarized. At one extreme, one is tempted to say too much, to echo the old stories about a rescuing God who intrudes to make all things right. But this narrative addresses people who know too much and will not accept such a raw confession. At the other extreme, one is tempted to claim too little. Then one may urge a humanism which believes in a God who "has no hands but ours" to do the work. The narrative works its subtle way between a primitivism which believes too easily and a humanism which is embarrassed about faith. Like the narrator, the interpreter must speak about a transcendence which is quite concrete. The overriding power of God's rule is not a vacuous sovereignty. Its purpose is to feed a people. This hidden God has a quite identifiable historical purpose. And though that purpose is worked out with reference to imperial power and well-being, his goal is the creation of a community of liberation (cf. Exod. 1, immediately after Gen. 50).

The narrative concerns the hidden but sure way of God. For that reason, we have cited Rom. 8:28–30 as a point of entry into this narrative. In that statement, Paul affirms the same "good" that Joseph affirms to his brothers in 50:20. To be sure, the Pauline statement is christological. But the text may provide a clue to the reality of Joseph. He is surely "predestined" by God for rule. He is "in the image," born to rule. He is to be the "first-born among many brethren." He is the one finally "glorified." And all because "everything" worked toward his destiny.

The narrator of our text, no more than Paul, knows how this can be. The ways of this God are inscrutable. But they are nonetheless sure and reliable. That is something Joseph and his brothers learned only late. But it is foundational for faith. This narrator does not doubt that this affirmation of transcendent, concrete purpose can be embraced even by the wise and the strong of the earth.

4. At another level the story concerns the struggle of a family. It is a specific, concrete family. But it may illuminate the issues of power in any family. The crisis in the family is anticipated in the relation between the father and the son (37:3–4). That in turn sparks the quarrel among the brothers (37:19–20). The conflict of the brothers is persistent in the narrative. At the death of the father, fear evokes new tensions among the sons (50:15–21). The family is kept off-balance by the dream of Joseph. It looms over the entire family. The dream may be a blessing. But it disturbs the peace and at times seems

294

to be a curse. The family, like many others, would manage better without a dream to disturb and disrupt the normal "proper ordering."

5. The family issues tilt toward political realities. The narrative concerns the potential for life or death that is related to power.

a. The story is about the "given" problem of famine. It is a problem which besets all, Egyptian and Israelite. It is a problem for which no one is responsible. And yet if there is to be a future, it must be wrought in the midst of the famine. It is the famine which overrides the empire. And so the issue of power is posed: Is there anyone, Israelite or Egyptian, who can cope with the problem of famine which lies beyond the wisdom of the empire (41:33)?

b. The question of power focuses on the strange relation of mighty Egypt and unknown Israel. What an incongruity! Conventional wisdom would anticipate that Israel must depend on Egypt. Egypt would give life to Israel (42:1–2). It has always been the case that the strong nourish the weak. But here the realities of power have nothing to do with what has always been. Finally, the empire is dependent upon Israel (cf. 12:10–20). The narrator characteristically understates this incredible reality. But we are led to wonder about the distribution of public power in this narrative. Something is at work which violates common sense and *Realpolitik*. Egypt is presented as helpless and immobilized (41:8). What the empire cannot do for itself, one from this extraordinary family does for it.

The reversal of roles in which Israel dominates and Pharaoh is the suppliant is an anticipation of the reversal of the Exodus. The empire is destroyed (Exod. 14:30). The hopeless slaves dance the death of the empire (Exod. 15:1). This inversion in the Joseph narrative is a simple and personal one. In Exodus it becomes public. Both narratives point to this One who speaks about first and last (Matt. 19:30; 20:16; Mark 9:35; 10:31) and who causes inversions. Our narrative is a reflection on the mystery of power. We know less than we imagine we do about power. As Pharaoh discovered, power will not be reduced and managed as we might wish.

c. The issue of power is focused on the person of Joseph. Especially in Gen. 41, Joseph is the model for those who are born to rule. Perhaps (as Von Rad suggests) this is a didactic piece on success in politics. This narrative affirms that power is

295

a good thing. It celebrates the capacity to make tough decisions, to face crisis boldly, and to practice prudence so that the empire can be fed. At the same time, however, this is public power for the public good. Political power is defined as a faithful way to serve the community. That underlying assumption may be important in a time when faith and virtue might be distorted into passivity and privatism.

This narrative, then, suggests new ways to think about faith and power in relation to public realities. We have seen that the text approaches the question from three perspectives: (1) In terms of power to address large public problems not caused by human agent, (2) in terms of the interaction between imperial power and power of the "least," and (3) in terms of modeling prudent use of power for the public good. From each perspective, Joseph is the new paradigm for the dynamic of power and faith.

d. This narrative may have been formed in a time when the reality of God was not doubted but treated as irrelevant. In response, this narrative affirms that even in the face of the empire and in the presence of great human competence, God is God and will work his purposes through human persons or in spite of them:

> For my thoughts are not your thoughts,
> neither are your ways my ways, says the LORD.
> For as the heavens are higher than the earth,
> so are my ways higher than your ways
> and my thoughts than your thoughts (Isa. 55:8–9).

God has his ways. They are not vague and eternal. They are concrete and "timeful" (cf. Gal. 4:1–6). God may work through our ways. But his ways are not equated with nor derived from our ways. This narrative invites the listening community to explore the "good" that God intends in spite of us (50:20). Perhaps in this address to the brothers, the "good" that God had first discerned in creation (Gen. 1:31) is renewed and reasserted.

A Scheme for Exposition

296

The chart exhibits the accents of the following exposition. It suggests that the dream of chapter 37 governs all that follows. The units of 45:1–15; 50:15–21 receive major attention. They articulate fulfillment of the dream and the resolution of its ac-

GENESIS 37:1—50:26: THE JOSEPH NARRATIVE

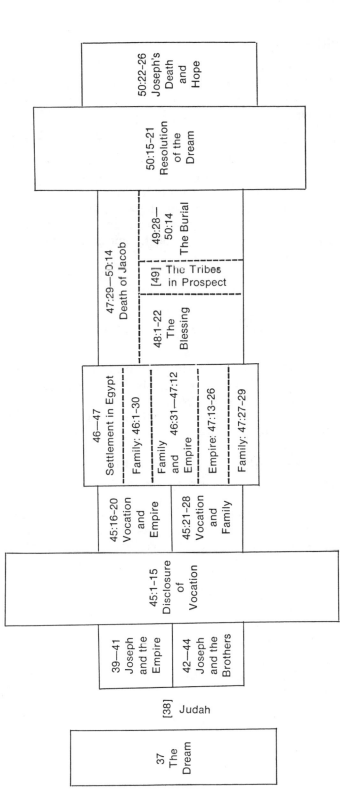

companying crises. In the units of 39—41; 45:16–28 and 46—47, an attempt is made to show that Joseph is continually confronted by the dual realities of his *family* and the *empire*. The dream must work its way midst these two powerful realities which stand in some tension with each other. In 47:29—50:14, there are reports of the deaths of Jacob and Joseph. The dreamer is dead by the end of our narrative. What remains is the dream. At the end, this community is on the brink of oppression (cf. Exod. 1). It waits for liberation with groaning. Indeed, after the commanding figure of Joseph, the community waits for the "first-born among many brothers" (Rom. 8:29). The narrative does not doubt the faithfulness nor the power of the Giver of dreams.

Genesis 37:1–36

This chapter marks the beginning of a new narrative which continues to the end of Genesis. It sets the main themes and issues which will dominate the entire Joseph narrative. Joseph, beloved son of Jacob's old age, is introduced abruptly. He now embodies the new history. The narrative reflects a sharp new beginning.

The chapter is easily divided into two parts. Verses 1–4 introduce the entire Joseph narrative and set the *family tensions* which trigger the action. Verses 5–36 announce the main theme, the *power of the dream* and its conflict with business as usual, embodied by the brothers. Already in this brief unit the theme of the entire narrative is clear. The battle is between the dream and the "Killers of the Dream." The dream seems nullified by the end of the chapter. The father believes the dreamer is dead (v. 33). The brothers believe the threat of the dream has been removed (v. 28). Only the single verse hints at another possibility (v. 36). The main character in the drama is Yahweh. Though hidden in the form of a dream, silent and not at all visible, the listener will understand that the dream is the unsettling work of Yahweh upon which everything else depends. Without the dream there would be no Joseph and no narrative. From the perspective of the brothers, without the dream there would be no trouble or conflict. For the father,

298

without the dream there would be no grief or loss. The dream sets its own course, the father-brothers-dreamer notwithstanding. And in the end, the dream prevails over the tensions of the family.

The Introductory Issue of Love/Hate

1. The narrator moves ancestral history to the new generation (vv. 1–4). All the promises of Abraham and the futures of Jacob are now lodged with this new one, Joseph, though his brothers will not concede it. Even though the Joseph narrative is very different from the preceding ancestral sequence, it now serves that history. Whether Joseph was originally a wisdom example or a royal courtier, he is now Jacob's son, pressed to serve a promise. His name is "add" (cf. Gen. 30:24–25). He is added, by the mercy of God. According to the brothers, he is added as an unwelcome afterthought. According to the narrative, he is added as a special gift which reshapes everything. He is added, by the mercy of God, because the family story depends on him, for his dream will save the whole family. Without Joseph, there is no future. He is the "last" one (cf. 33:2, 7), for little Benjamin does not figure here. The narrative presents the strange inversion whereby the "last" becomes the first one. The one who arrives very late in the family becomes the bearer of blessing and life for the others.

2. Quickly and skillfully, we are told everything. The narrator understands so much about human motivation but is restrained and forbids psychologizing. The story unfolds without analysis as the dream is born into a hopeless triangle: the boy, the father, and the brothers.

a. The boy is too young, not able to do much, confined to domestic chores. It is easy, then, to resent, to become a tattler. He and little Benjamin are a second family, fully spoiled and in turn scorned rivals. From the beginning, Joseph has been able to get by with everything which the older ones had not been permitted.

b. The father is the one who has made his own way ruthlessly. He kicked his way out of the womb and into the promise. He has been unscrupulous, never one for protocol or propriety. He, too, was a last one become first (25:23). Now, in his old age, he dotes on a son born late to him. This son is a sign that the promise still works in his life and in his body. And in this one, Jacob sees promises he himself has not lived. Nothing is to be

299

withheld from this special one added late. Out of this deep, arbitrary, almost embarrassing devotion, Jacob gives Joseph a special robe, a mark of regal status, and announces that this son is the wave of the future (v. 3). (The "coat of many colors" likely was a long robe with special sleeves. Its exact description is lost to us. But it clearly was luxurious and a sign of singular favor.) Bruce Dahlberg observes that the language for the coat is related to the clothes of the garden ("On Recognizing the Unity of Genesis," *Theology Digest* 24:360–67 [1977]; cf. Gen. 3:21). Perhaps this beloved son at last fulfills what is intended by God's gift of clothes in the garden.

c. The brothers are observant and sensitive. They see what the narrator concedes. Jacob is partial. His arbitrary love evokes their hatred. Trouble is sure to come in such a triangle of love and hate.

The promise of the fathers, if it is to live, must survive in such a turbulent triangle. The story contacts our life, for each of us lives at some point in such triangles—as one having been loved too much (Joseph), one loving too much (Jacob), or one feeling loved too little (the brothers). There is enough here to write about *The Politics of the Family* (R. D. Laing, 1971). But this family is a seedbed for promise which will shatter and break open the tense triangle.

The Politics of the Dream

The remainder of the unit of 37:1–36 (vv. 5–35) is divided into three clear scenes, each with different parts to play in the drama:

Scene 1	(vv. 5–11)	The dream is announced. Power relations and tension are indicated which will dominate the action.
Interlude	(vv. 12–17)	A curious interlude which does not visibly affect the action.
Scene 2	(vv. 18–31)	The brothers are dominant. This scene witnesses the violent action which links the tension of Scene 1 and the grief of Scene 3.
Scene 3	(vv. 32–35)	The grief of Jacob at the death of the dreamer son is enacted.

300

Thus, the three scenes move from *tension* (vv. 5–11) through *violence* (vv. 18–31) and, finally, to *grief* (vv. 32–35). Verse 36, as we will see, stands strangely outside the scenes. It is not expected after the drama reaches its closure (v. 35). But it is carefully placed there by the narrator to give a hint: There is more to come. There is more in the dream that the brothers cannot stop.

1. Scene 1. Joseph dreamed (vv. 5–11). Of course he dreams. It is what this people was called to do. This boy was born to dream—not to work, not to shepherd (cf. Luke 2:49). The narrator understands the dream as a gift from God. That is God's hidden way in this narrative. After the beginnings (vv. 1–9), we expect the dream to have its say. The father formed a son to dream. From his youth on, the father has nurtured in Joseph a bias toward dreaming. Jacob evoked in Joseph's life a sense of his being bound for something more and something better beyond the competence of his older brothers. The last one must dream, for those that came first have preempted all the visible places. The narrator sets a dream to guide the whole story. In the following episodes, all sorts of enemies of the dream try to resist: the brothers, the woman (chap. 39), the famine (chap. 41), all resist the dream and fail. They cannot! The boy is without guile. He presumes this "great expectation" in his body. But dreams cause conflict. They endanger the "pecking order." So the hatred mounts. The one called to dream is in peril because of this disruptive dream.

a. The story is not interested in the empty, formal process of dreams. It will do us little good to investigate the general phenomena of dreams. This particular dream has concrete substance. And we must attend to that substance. The substance of the dream is in the words *"reign"* and *"rule"* (v. 8). The dream is a vision of history being inverted against all the odds. "Reign" *(mlk)* is a royal word used in relation to the patriarchs only by the P tradition (17:6; 35:11). ("Rule" [*mšl*] is used only for Joseph among the fathers [cf. 24:2].) We have seen the word used only twice for persons (cf. 1:16–18) in the pre-history: in 3:16 concerning the perverted relation of the man and the woman; and in 4:7, in the ironic promise to Cain that he might control the power of sin. But it occurs nowhere before this in reference to political power. This is a first awareness in the text of genuine, responsible political power. With the dream of Joseph, something new enters the awareness of Israel. Historical hope appears which will wait until 45:8, 26 for its fulfillment. The narrative now has within it a drive toward power. We must follow the story to see its fruition.

301

b. The issue is set with a strange incongruity: dream and power. "Power" is so concrete and earthly. "Dream" appears to us so remote and hidden. We must ask about the power of dreams. But we must proceed as theologians, not in terms of depth psychology. We must see that in this presentation, the dream is a political power. In recent experiences of liberation, the political power of dreams is evident. A dream is a power which neither tradition nor force can finally resist. So for Joseph, the ways of God are utterly beyond his ways or the ways of his brother. Life in this family will not be reduced to what can be understood. And the vision within this family is not a private one about security or happiness. It is a public one about power. As we might expect, these dreams are dreamed especially by the powerless one in the family. Dreams permit the imagining of new political possibilities which immediately threaten the old and call it into question. So the dream threatens the brothers and the empire.

The narrator plays with the theme. For every ruler, there must be *bowing down.* The sheaves bow down (v. 7). The stars bow down (v. 9; cf. 1:16–18). The father wonders, "Shall I bow down" (v. 10)? There is dreaming and bowing down. And there is hatred. Already (v. 4), the love of the father has evoked the hatred of the brothers. Now the dream causes them to "hate him the more" (v. 5). And "yet more" (v. 8). After the second dream (v. 9), the tension is escalated to *jealousy* (v. 11). At that moment, the thought of murder is surely born. The brothers are not political theorists. But they know the threat of hope. They are the older ones. They have had things as they wanted them. Against their age and power, the boy is helpless. So he dreams. The dream is a way of hoping for a new arrangement very different from the present. Even as a dream, such hope is a threat. It anticipates the end of the present order. The issue is joined as it always is in this family. It is not just a petty quarrel but a life and death struggle. One voice in the struggle is for keeping life as it is, resistant to every hope and vision. The other voice, hopeless as things now stand, thinks revolutionary thoughts of another way. The issue is joined.

c. And Jacob. He is the proud father of twelve. He does not want to choose. He can dream with his precious son, for his old visions still stir. But he has wealth and would settle for peace in the family (cf. 34:30). Some resist, like the brothers, the dream. Others, like Jacob, just want it subdued for now. So the father

302

plays his public role. He chides the dreamer, identifies with the brothers in their resistance, and regards the dream as absurd (v. 10). But the narrator adds a note which permits some play. The old man sounds like the brothers in his indignation. But there is a difference. The brothers are jealous, unambiguously so. But the father "kept the event" and remembered the encounter (v. 11). He is mystified and confused, but hopeful, too, not fully ready to dismantle the dream. The dreamer is fortunate to have a father who thinks inversions are not altogether foolish. The father has bequeathed the dream to his son. And now he honors it discreetly. He allows for the possibility. His own hopes did not permit him to be closed to surprise. (This gingerly note is not unlike that of another parent. The linguistic parallel is worth noting in Luke 2:19. Mary also knew something was afoot. She did not know what. But she honored it in ways that the others missed.) Thus the narrator here concludes this triangular confrontation with a shrewd hint. There is more to come. The fearful brothers have missed it. But the father knows more than the brothers. "Israel" knows and waits.

2. Interlude. Verses 12–17 relate a curious encounter with an unnamed man. The incident is only a curiosity and has no bearing on the main development of the plot. The geographical range from Hebron to Shechem (v. 14) encompasses the primary arena of our forebearers in Palestine. This episode may reflect the unification of Abraham (Hebron) and Jacob (Shechem) traditions in the service of a unified monarchy. Dothan, likely located north of Shechem, has no special significance for the story. Its mention attests to the deeply rooted concreteness of the story.

3. Scene 2. After the interlude of verses 12–17 (which reflects a geographical shift of the action to a new setting) the ambivalent father is absent. Now there is only the *ruler* to be, meeting those destined to *bow down* (vv. 18–31). The narrative prefigures the relation of ruler and ruled. But none of the participants knows that now. Now there is only a meeting of the much loved one and those immersed in their hatred. For Joseph, the future is a prospect to be celebrated, a promise to be kept. For the brothers, the future is a deathly threat. But it can be resisted! They resolve to stop it.

a. Verse 5 has announced the theme of Scene 1 (vv. 5–11): "Joseph had a dream." So now verse 19 states the theme of the second scene (vv. 18–31): "Here comes the master of the dreams" (author's translation). The bearer of dreams is a threat.

303

Those who are well off as secure older brothers prefer what is to what may come by way of dreams. They conclude the way to deal with the dream is to kill it—kill the dreamer and thereby kill the dream. Scene 1 offered in the person of Joseph a glimpse of the *hopeful* humanity called by God. Scene 2 now lets us see humanity in its *resistant hopelessness.* In hopelessness, the brothers have resolved to kill the dream—but they cannot carry it out. The dream is stronger than their resolve. By the end of the scene, they leave in an appearance of triumph. But the narrative knows better.

b. In the second scene, the main conflict of dreamer and killers of the dream is presented (vv. 18–20, 31). Verses 21–30 offer a narrative delay with the ploys of two older brothers, Reuben and Judah. Their actions serve to heighten the suspense and underscore the gravity of resistance, as well as to mitigate the vengeance.

So there is Reuben, who engages in a deception to save his brother (vv. 22–24). (There is some conflation or confusion concerning the roles of Reuben [vv. 21–22, 29–32] and Judah [vv. 26–27]. This is conventionally explained as rival versions of the same story told by rival tribes, so that the two brothers compete for a positive role. However, the actions of both brothers are appropriate to the story.) Reuben is presented here as responsive but cowardly, and killers of the dream will not be restrained by a responsible coward. The Reuben episode (vv. 21–24) ends with a second mention of the special robe (v. 23). The giving of the robe has been equivalent to enthronement (v. 3). Jacob thereby designated his son as his special heir (cf. Isa. 47:2–3; Matt. 26:65; 27:27–31). Now the dream is in jeopardy as the robe serves a different function, now *de*thronement.

Then there is Judah—another coward, but at least respectful of the problem of guilt (vv. 26–28). As a result of his cowardice, the transition is accomplished. The family of promise is at last on its way to Egypt, in anticipation of the exodus.

Then Reuben appears again to find his feeble rescue foiled (vv. 29–30). Now is the time to deceive the old man. Deception upon deception, first a misjudgment, then a coverup. As with Macbeth, the blood will not be covered. And as with Lady Macbeth, the guilt will not vanish. Resistance to the dream requires endless deception. The brothers have believed, in their rage, that life could be administered against the dream.

But as Scene 1 ends with an equivocal hint in the mind of the father (v. 11), so Scene 2 ends with an ambiguity. Will the lie prevail? Is that the end? Can the dream be so readily nullified? What then of the source of the dream, the One who has not yet appeared? Does the family Israel deal with a God who will so easily abandon his dream? For now, that issue is muted by the narrator, but the whispered questions will resume with verse 36.

4. Scene 3. The third scene (vv. 32–35) begins again with the long robe (v. 32). First, it was used for *enthronement* (v. 3). Then it was an instrument of *dethronement* and symbolic death (v. 23). Now it is used as *evidence for the death* of the dream. The robe began in deep *love*. Then it was torn in deep *hate*. Now it is the main tool for a deep *deception*. Is history such a lie? It seems to work. The father believes. Unknowingly, he enters into the charade of his sons. He sees the body of the dreamer torn and ended by violence of unknown beasts. He does not know, as we do, that the beasts couch at the door of his other sons. (The themes of Cain and Abel [Gen. 4:1–16] reappear again among brothers not preferred in their offering.)

a. Because the deception was so large and the dream so precarious, the narrative ends in grief. The hate of the brothers has triumphed over the profound love of the father. The scene is a ritual of death, despair, hopelessness. Israel lives where dreaming causes grief. He goes through the motions. His children play their roles, keeping a proper public face, all the while knowing it is a facade (v. 35). Or perhaps only his sons know. His daughters weep, but they may be innocent. But how are people comforted when the beloved child is no more (cf. Jer. 31:15)? How do hopers hope when the dream is taken? In Israel, what of a father when the precious child is no longer? How do people cope? How do they endure in promise? There is something singular in the Old Testament about a father and a son. So much has been entrusted to that young body. The body torn by the beast carried the future of the people. The "added" one is irreplaceable. No ritual covers it. No other children can substitute. David offers evidence both ways. At one death (II Sam. 12:15–23), he has the courage to move past the death and the hurt. But at the other death (II Sam. 18:31—19:4) he grieves deeply. Here Jacob is like the second David. He refuses to be comforted (v. 35).

b. When we read this third scene, it is hard to tell what we

305

are treating. Is this only a boy lost to a family? Perhaps. But perhaps we also are grieving the loss of Israel from history. With deep knowing, the tradition has taken this scene of grief and refusal of comfort and made it the main metaphor for the death of Israel at the fall of Jerusalem. Israel is without a comforter (Lam. 1:2, 9, 16, 17, 21). And the answering poet begins the new history with the new speech: "Comfort, comfort my people" (Isa. 40:1). This poetry is an answer to Lamentations, perhaps also an answer to the ancient father Jacob. The poet of Isa. 40:1 gives a faithful answer to the reality of human loss. But it is not given in our chapter. Israel must wait. Comfort is slow and paced. It comes only late:

> "Truly, truly, I say to you, you will weep and lament, but the world will rejoice; you will be sorrowful, but your sorrow will turn into joy" (John 16:20).

The story of this family is about mourning and comfort. Comfort will be given (Matt. 5:4). But the mourning is deep and long. The loss is real. We are not dealing in our text with a mere life "passage," but with a death. The dream can disappear. It is fragile and precarious.

Jeremiah understood the inconsolability of the loss. Jacob, in Genesis 37, stands with mother Rachel in Jer. 31:15:

> "A voice is heard in Ramah,
>   lamentation and bitter weeping.
> Rachel is weeping for her children;
>   she refuses to be comforted for her children,
>   because they are not."

The grief of Rachel is deeper and more massive. But Jacob prefigures it. Scene 3 is about the incredible frailty of Israel and of Israel's faith. It is so fragile that the main character, the one who bears the dream, does not even appear. The bearer of the promise is gone as well. "They are not." Jacob remains, believing it really happened. In any case, the grief is real.

This narrative leaves us waiting for the words we know will come, but for Israel, only slowly:

306

> As one whom his mother comforts,
>   so I will comfort you;
> You shall be comforted in Jerusalem.
> You shall see, and your heart shall rejoice;
>   your bones shall flourish like the grass (Isa. 66:13–14).

While we are dealing with the story of one father and his grief (partly genuine, partly faked) this story cannot be heard without hearing in it the deep grief of Israel at exile, at holocaust, at every coming of death to damage the dream. That has now become the field in which this story must be heard. The listening community is permitted to face the power of uncomforted grief in any time. We are all children of grief—if not that of death, then of empty failure, of dreams dreamed but unlived. All kinds of tomorrows are crushed for the sake of tough, ruthless todays. There is ample ground for refusing to be comforted.

5. Scene 1 ends in a hint (v. 11). Scene 2 ends in a deception (v. 31). Scene 3 ends in a charade that takes on reality (v. 35). That would have been enough, for the movement is sure and draining. But the narrator takes our eyes at the last moment from the bereft old man and turns us to Egypt (v. 36). Egypt is now the locus of action. And we are left to question the odds of a *dream* vis-à-vis an *empire*. It is not much of a hope. It is, perhaps, only a change of venue for the killers of the dream. The status of Joseph is not unlike that of Jehoiachin in Babylon (II Kings 25:27–30). He is not free. But he also is not dead (cf. Eccles. 9:4). As long as he is not dead, the unfree one need not give up on the promise.

The listening community may be led by all of this to wonder. What dream is still dreamed over us? What promise is guarded on our behalf? In response to overwhelming dreams, we play many roles: Like Joseph, we sometimes dream; sometimes like the brothers, we deny the dream. And sometimes we are like Jacob to "keep the thing." We play all parts in the tense triangle. But clearly, the dream does not depend on the father or the brothers or even on Joseph. It is at work on its own (John 5:17; Phil. 2:13). Amazingly, even as Joseph sets out for Egypt as a slave (v. 36), God has not abandoned the dream.

Genesis 38:1–30

This peculiar chapter stands alone, without connection to its context. It is isolated in every way and is most enigmatic. It does not seem to belong with any of the identified sources of ancestral tradition. It is not evident that it provides any significant theological resource. It is difficult to know in what context it might be of value for theological exposition. For these reasons, our treatment of it may be brief.

1. The major problem in dealing with the chapter is that even close study does not make clear its intent.

a. It may be that the text serves to trace tribal history, that is, the development of the clans of the tribe of Judah (vv. 27–30). That, however, would seem an odd way to proceed.

b. It is clear that the text assumes a practice of Levirate marriage (cf. Deut. 25:5–10). This provided that if a married man dies without an heir, the next male kin is responsible to marry the widow so that she may bear a proper heir for the dead man. Such a custom may have been operative (cf. Ruth 3:1–13). But there is reluctance to implement it in this narrative, especially with the third son, for it was risky after the death judgment on two brothers (v. 11). It may be that the narrative is simply a presentation of the custom and the difficulties with it. However, that would apply only to the first part (vv. 1–11), whereas the interest of the narrative focuses on the interaction between Tamar and Judah in the middle part of the narrative (vv. 12–26).

c. An additional difficulty for interpretation is the role of Tamar. She is identified as a "sacred prostitute" (vv. 21–22) fulfilling a legitimate Canaanite social role (cf. Deut. 23:17–18). But on the other hand, she is described as a "harlot" as well (vv. 15, 24) with no claim of social legitimacy. These distinctions might make a difference in assessing the role of Judah. The use of the term "harlot" as distinct from "sacred prostitute" serves to introduce moral connotations which are essential to the plot of the story.

d. It is not impossible that the narrative serves primarily as a vehicle for the genealogy (vv. 27–30) which leads toward David, and ultimately, to Jesus (cf. Matt. 1:3). And yet that seems doubtful, for the genealogy is not intrinsically related to the narrative.

e. Because the narrative is so obscure in its intent, the theological expositor might be tempted in misleading directions. On the one hand, attention to historical questions of social practice (the Levirate marriage) or tribal history may be of some interest. But they are not likely to be helpful for our exposition. On the other hand, care must be taken not to moralize or to evaluate the conduct of either character on criteria

308

outside the narrative itself. The narrative makes no point at all of the adultery (cf. 19:30–38). It is the case that Judah has an intense moment of righteous indignation over the harlotry of Tamar (v. 24). But that is only an instrumental cause in the story. It is not the point of the narrative. Judah's concern is, in fact, for his proprietary interest in her as properly belonging to his third son Shelah (v. 11). This interest of Judah operates even though we are told he refused his third son out of fear. Thus *his indignation* (v. 24) is linked with *his refusal* (v. 11), which in turn triggered *her deception* (vv. 14–19). His indignation reflects on his own irresponsibility according to social expectation (cf. Matt. 7:1–5). Judah is caught in a web of his own actions, which involve several layers of social failure. Our interpretation must not introduce moral dimensions alien to the text itself.

2. The structure of the story is in three parts:

Verses 1–11 simply create the scene by showing the need of Tamar and the refusal of Judah to give his son as was expected. It is the fear (v.11) which later creates the problem for Judah (cf. v.26).

Verses 12–23 tell of Tamar's enticement of Judah, first the trick by Tamar (vv. 12–19) and then Judah's inability to locate her (vv. 20–23). It is worth noting that Judah has no concern about her retention of his pledge, nor is his sexual relation with her at issue at any point in the narrative (cf. Lev. 18:15).

Verses 24–26 report the confrontation in which Judah acknowledges his own involvement. Interpretation must take care that the issue of dispute turns on Judah's refusal of his son (v. 26) rather than on the act of adultery even though in verse 24 that is the cause of his initial indignation. Clearly, Judah judges Tamar's adulterous actions by a norm very different from the one he applies to himself.

Verses 27–30 appear to add a genealogical note unrelated to the main movement of the narrative.

3. It is clear that the interpretive payoffs are to be found in the third element (vv. 24–26). And within that section, exposition may most usefully focus on the remarkable verdict of Judah (v. 26): "She is more righteous than I." That concession on his part constitutes the main turn in the narrative. According to the mores of the time, Judah had only protected his interest (his son). But Tamar had engaged in a subterfuge which included violation of her betrothed and of the father of the betrothed.

309

That would be the norm by which a helpless widow might be assessed and executed (v. 24). Thus, a striking contrast is established between this man who has standing and status in the community and this woman who stands outside the law and is without legal recourse. It would be enough (and the end of the narrative) if in his pride he had condemned her and she, in her shame, had been executed. Then the narrative might have ended in verse 24.

But the narrative moves on. Judah's participation (in vv. 16–18) is now made public. A contrast is made between the minor offense of Tamar and the major violation of Judah. Judah's involvement in the indictment he speaks (v. 24) serves to deemphasize it. The narrative is now free to ignore verses 12–23 and focus on verse 11, which is the real point at issue. The result is a fresh definition of righteousness, an unexpected assessment of guilt and innocence (v. 26). Until this point, there had clearly been a double standard for the man and the woman. Now, there is a new norm. The new norm seems to be echoed later: "Every one to whom much is given, of him *much* will be required; and of him to whom men commit *much* they will demand the more" (Luke 12:48).

Not much, in fact nothing, has been given to Tamar. And she is not indicted for much. After verse 24, the narrative not only minimizes her wrong but vindicates her. The story ends without stigma attached to her. By contrast, Judah is the one to whom much has been given: sons, goods, standing. From him, more is asked. Even by the conventional canon of righteousness, more is asked, as seen in the criteria of righteousness in Job 31:9–23 on the care of widows. To be sure, a kind of risk is asked of Judah (with his son) that is not recognized by Job. But nonetheless, it is likely that the status of Judah in the community binds him to the same criteria as those of Job. Because he had security and status, he is expected to care in more responsible ways. What is asked of him is that he risk his son for the sake of the community, that he make his son, even his last son, available for the solidarity and future of the community now focused in the person of this defenseless widow. The offense of Judah is like that of Achan (cf. Josh 7:1; I Chron. 2:7) who in fact is Judah's great-great-grandson. It is the sin of looking after private interest at the expense of the community.

310

4. The narrative contains a radical critique of morality for those who will pursue it. The text makes a judgment about

relative guilts. Tamar has committed the kind of sin the "good people" prefer to condemn—engaging in deception and illicit sex and bringing damage to a good family. For a moment, until aware of his own involvement, Judah reacts on the basis of that sort of "morality" (v. 24). In ways apparently congruent with popular morality, Judah has spurned the claims of his daughter-in-law. By his indifference, he has violated her right to well-being and dignity in the community (v. 11). The narrative juxtaposes his prudent but self-serving withholding and her deceptive harlotry.

In that context, a new insight about righteousness comes out of the mouth of Judah (v. 26). He draws an unexpected conclusion. In the midst of this sordid story of sexuality, there is a new understanding of righteousness. The story may give us pause about the usual bourgeois dimensions of sin. What is taken most seriously is not a violation of sexual convention, but damage to the community which includes a poor, diminished female.

The dramatic turn in the narrative (from v. 24 to v. 26) is like that of Nathan and David (II Sam. 12:1–6). Judah is surprised in verse 25 by the data that indict him. In verse 24, Judah mouths the old righteousness of double standards and conventional morality. But the insight of verse 25 leads (v. 26) to a new radical perception of righteousness.

It goes only slightly beyond this text to turn to the "new righteousness" in the gospel (Matt. 5:17–20; Rom. 10:1–13). The new righteousness moves beyond the rules and calculated innocence to the free embrace of the gifts of the community. If Judah and Tamar be taken as models for faithfulness and unfaithfulness, it takes no imagination to know where in this story Jesus of Nazareth would have found "his folks" (cf. Mark 12:41–44). Such an interpretation has no desire to glorify Tamar or to make a virtue of her action. The story has no interest in her intrigue. But in contrast to Judah, in her worldly way, in her determination to see justice done, she may be used by the narrator as a foreshadowing of the One who taught and embodies a new righteousness. That other One also offers a dangerous criticism of the old righteousness which sanctioned oppression in the name of propriety.

In any case, it can hardly be irrelevant that Judah, this practitioner of dangerous righteousness, is named among the parents of Jesus (Matt. 1:3). It is perhaps ironic that from this same strange liaison came both Achan (cf. Josh. 7:1), the one

311

prepared to destroy the community for his own private interest, and Jesus of Nazareth, the one set to evoke a new community. That community of the new righteousness is already anticipated in the judgment of Judah (v. 26).

Genesis 39:1–23

Chapter 39 takes up the story of Joseph in Egypt. There is a connection between 39:1 and 37:36, so that chapter 38 is clearly an intrusion in the narrative. (R. Alter may be correct in suggesting a deliberate contrast in the role of sexuality in chapters 38 and 39 as they are presently placed ["A Literary Approach to the Bible," *Commentary* 60:70–77 (1975)].) Probably chapter 39 belongs to the larger unit of 39—41. The unit is distinguished from chapter 37 before it and 42 after it. Chapters 39—41 know nothing of Joseph's family, father, or brothers. They focus only on Joseph's rise in the Egyptian empire without reference to his Palestinian connections. Perhaps this narrative about the rise to imperial power comes from a circle of tradition quite different from that of Joseph and his brothers. It is clear that *prospering in the empire* is the theme of three continuous episodes: *(a) 39:1–23,* with Potiphar's wife; *(b) 40:1–23,* dreams in prison; and *(c) 41:1–45,* Pharaoh's dreams. In all three, Joseph is confronted with a dangerous possibility and in each case he succeeds. How he succeeds is the thrust of each story. Success of the *dream* in the *empire* must be reported without claiming too much or too little.

As part of that larger unit, we may take chapter 39 as a unit self-contained enough for an independent analysis. We may divide the chapter into three parts: *verses 1–6,* which describe the new situation of Joseph, *verses 7–20* which report the main action of seduction and escape, and *verses 21–23,* which describe Joseph's new situation at the end of the episode. It shows the dangerous way in which Joseph is moved from the first context of *power* to the last context of *imprisonment.* The opening and closing sections contain explicit theological statements which illuminate and frame the events of the middle section.

The large question faced in this narrative is, How does Joseph fare in Egypt? Or, put differently, How does the *dream-*

bearer succeed in the face of the *empire?* The interface between *the people of the dream* and *the rulers of the empire* is a delicate and mixed one that has no simple resolution. The dreamer serves and finally saves the empire. But it is equally clear that the resources and techniques of the empire matter decisively to the dream people. The presence of the dream in the empire is an ambivalent matter that must be treated with discernment and restraint. This chapter claims that there is something unique about Joseph which sustains and preserves him even in the face of the wiles of the empire.

Seduction and Refusal

Our exposition begins in the middle of things (vv. 7–20).

1. The narrator (and the listening Israelite community) is privy to information not given in the story itself.

a. We know (as the woman does not) that Joseph carries in his person the dream of the God of Israel (vv. 5–6). Because of that dream, he has power to bless the empire, but he will not be co-opted by it.

b. We know (as the woman also knows but misunderstands) that Joseph is born to rule, and here he does rule. He has everything in his charge from Pharaoh that can fill him with power (v. 4). Moreover, he is entrusted by "the Dream-Giver" to rule both Egypt and Israel, to govern Egypt and to care for Israel. But the woman misunderstands this and regards him as potent in other ways. She wants to sleep with him. He is indeed potent. But his potency, his being potentate, is laden with meanings that she does not understand. Perhaps the story is presented so that no Egyptian can ever understand what this power is about.

c. We know (and so does the woman) that he is attractive in every way (not unlike the boy David, destined to rule—I Sam. 16:18. Both are champions of the people, born to rule). Note that beauty runs in this royal family (Gen. 29:17). The woman is drawn to Joseph's beauty and desires him because of it.

Thus the woman *(a)* lacks some information, *(b)* has some information but misunderstands it, and *(c)* has some correct information but wrongly exploits it. Her action is based on a thorough misreading of this unseducible man. The incongruity   313
between how it is with Joseph and how the woman imagines it to be is essential to the narrative. The story enhances this incongruity at the expense of the Egyptian woman. Egypt will not

have its way even though the Israelite prince is attractive even in his steadfastness. He will concede nothing to the empire. The intimate maneuvering between the dream-bearer and the woman embody the risky interaction of the faithful and the empire. Joseph is prepared to live much of his life and conduct much of his business on the terms of the empire. But there are limits about which neither the woman nor, subsequently, the Pharaoh know. It is that hidden edge given to "the Hebrew" which the story sharpens.

2. It is, of course, not possible to identify the Egyptian officer, Potiphar. He is presented as a high official. But historical data are lacking. In any case, the narrative has no interest in him or in any historical connections. It is well known that the episode (vv. 7–20) has a close parallel in the "Story of Two Brothers," an Egyptian tale of the Late Bronze Period. Thus we have here a non-Israelite traditional narrative taken over as a way to present the way of the dream. Our exposition will observe the ways in which the *narrative* is used in the service of the *dream*.

3. The narrative contrasts the duplicity of the woman with the single-minded determination of the man. The duplicity and its pitiful failure are evident in two words.

a. First, the term *lie.* There is the command, "lie with me" (v.7). Then there is Joseph's refusal to "lie" (v.10). There is the repeated command (v.12), and the word is used to accuse him (v.14). Thus the word presents the entire interaction which moves from *command* and seduction through *refusal* to *accusation.* R. A. Carlson has suggested that the same verb, *lie (škb)* is structurally important to the story of David in II Sam. 10—20 and I Kings 1—2 (*David the Chosen King,* 1964, pp. 180–93). Carlson's analysis at one level speaks of "sleeping around" as a violation of the Torah (cf. Deut. 22:22–29). But it also suggests the characteristic imperial attempt to generate security and well-being in manipulative ways. The ones who have royal power are tempted to imagine they are beyond the reach either of the Torah or of common sense (wisdom). Thus, while the woman's self-seeking may be characteristic of the empire, it is recognized by Joseph as a sure way to destruction.

314

b. The second trigger word involved in the deception is *"hand,"* that is, power. Before this episode, Joseph is freed from the "hand" of the Ishmaelites (v. 1). (The word "hand" is in the

Hebrew text.) Yahweh prospers his hand (v. 3) and everything of Pharaoh is given into his hand (vv. 4, 6, 8). Verse 6 offers a subtle reservation which Joseph understands well even though the woman does not. The exception is the "bread" Pharaoh would eat. This is likely a euphemism for his wife, for "food" is here a cipher for sex. Thus, the incongruity of verse 1–6 and 7–20 is stronger. The one thing forbidden is the one thing sought by the woman. The woman miscalculates. Unaware of his power and his resolve (v. 8), she grasps him (v. 12). But the grasping does not reach Joseph. Only his clothes are left in her hand-power (vv. 12–13; cf. 37:27; cf. Mark 14:51–52). Her imperial, grasping ways are not as powerful as she presumed. Joseph has his own power and is not subject to hers. She ends her grasping, holding the form of power (his clothes) but in fact being empty-handed. It is not the first time Joseph has had to function without his royal clothes (37:23). The clothes do not make this man. It is the dream that makes this man and that the woman cannot take from him.

4. Like all the Joseph material, this narrative is shrewd and restrained. It does not want to say too much. With enormous skill and patience, the narrator offers variations on the themes of "lie" and "hand." Through it all, things are not what they seem. The woman has completely misunderstood. In her miscalculation about power, she brings her own humiliation. While the ostensible agenda is adultery (clearly a violation of the Torah), the narrative does not linger on sex. Adultery is a case in point about the destructive "normal" ways of the empire. It is also a way of manifesting the character and quality of this man who refuses. It is recognized in wisdom teaching (which lies behind the narrative) that seduction by the foreign woman will ruin both man and career:

> For the commandment is a lamp and the teaching a light, . . .
> to preserve you from the evil woman,
>> from the smooth tongue of the adventuress.
> Do not desire her beauty in your heart,
>> and do not let her capture you with her eyelashes;
> for a harlot may be hired for a loaf of bread,
>> but an adulteress stalks a man's very life (Prov. 6:23–26; cf. 7:10–20).

315

The refusal of Joseph is based in a characteristic combination of prudence and faith:

I am held accountable by my master and must not violate that trust. It would be a sin against God (v. 9, author's translation).

(It could also be suicide.) The story is not at all uncomfortable with the juxtaposition of faith and prudence. In this royal world, they come together. But Joseph's is a special kind of prudence. It is not a calculation about personal well-being. More likely, it is an understated sense of being a man of destiny, a destiny not to be squandered on a fling of passion. Joseph is not a passionless man. He has his passions, but they are of a very different kind.

5. The rest of verses 7–20 is predictable. The scorned woman turns accuser (cf. II Sam. 13:15). The framing of Joseph on false charges is capped by the pejorative name, "Hebrew" (v. 17). This use (cf. 40:15; 41:12; 43:32) reflects a low class, socially rejected person, undoubtedly scorned by the people around the throne. The framing is unexceptional except for one thing: The listening Israelite community knows what the future holds. They know about the power of the dream that the despicable Egyptian woman cannot suspect. This high-born woman is a prototype of the imperial mother, the mother of dead children (Exod. 11:5), whereas "the Hebrew" is the model father of many (Exod. 1:15–21). The narrative moves in a sequence of *seduction* (vv. 7–12a), *refusal* (v. 12b), and *accusation* (vv. 13–20). And all the while, Joseph keeps the *dream* free from accommodations to the empire.

The Theological Context of the Narrative

The narrative appears to be focused on the human interaction of lust and integrity. But that interaction is sandwiched between two remarkable theological assertions.

1. In verses 1–6 things happen quickly and decisively even though there is no real narrative of events. Within these few verses, the Hebrew slave is catapulted to the peak of the empire. The visible agent is his Egyptian master.

a. But the real cause is this other One: "The LORD was with Joseph" (v. 2). We will hear the name of the Lord in this narrative four times (vv. 2, 3, twice in 23,) in parallel formulae. The affirmation that the Lord is with Joseph is made twice at the beginning and twice at the end. Three times the result of the formula of accompaniment is prosperity, success (vv. 2, 3, 23). In those flat, undeveloped assertions, everything is said that needs to be said. This affirmation is the decisive claim of the entire narrative. So far as this narrative is concerned, every-thing is explained. It is not claimed that because of Yahweh everything will work out. Nor is it promised that the key actor will be easily saved from trouble. But the narrator offers an understanding of reality that is an alternative to every imperial presupposition of control. Such an alternative must have been problematic in royal Israel. It was the premise of the wisdom teachers in Israel. They observed and understood not only that there is an *abiding order* to life which no imperial ingenuity can ignore, but also that there is an *inscrutable power* for life at work in spite of everything human cleverness devises (cf. Prov. 21:31). The text witnesses to the hidden life-giving power of God at work in the midst of imperial death. This is not cheap grace. Nor is it a *deus ex machina.* But it is, nonetheless, the claim upon which everything hangs. It is that affirmation, be-fore and behind, which shapes the encounter of verses 7–20.

b. This inscrutable power for life in the midst of death is a theme present in many parts of the Bible. It is central to the inexplicable rise and power of David. For all his other virtues, this is the decisive factor from the beginning (I Sam. 16:18). It is decisive in his contest with Goliath (I Sam. 17:37), in his struggle with Saul (I Sam. 18:12, 14, 28; 20:13), in his building of an empire (I Sam. 15:10), and in his rise to the throne (II Sam. 7:3, 9). The formula is used to describe what has no rea-sonable explanation, the emergence of a real newness in human politics.

The formula, "the Lord is with him," may be royal in its origin, as the Davidic usage suggests. It designates those chosen by Yahweh. But it is then employed in a much more conflicted and tenuous life, that of Jeremiah. It is affirmed in his call (1:8). And it is affirmed in assurances of protection that are military in their nuance (1:19; 15:20; 42:11).

The formula, as we have seen, is prominent in Genesis. Here as much as anywhere, we have to do with a God who leads, abides and goes with. It is especially important in the Jacob cycle. (See the pivotal passage of 28:13–15.) It is also affirmed of Isaac (26:3).

We may note two other familiar passages which may be heard differently in the political, cultural context of Joseph. In Psalm 23, a song of trust, the promise, "I will be with you" is stated by the believer as the quintessence of faith: "You are with me" (v. 4). And in the Matthean version of Jesus' depar-

317

ture, this is Jesus' ultimate promise to the church: "I am with you always, to the close of the age" (Matt. 28:20).

c. Gen. 39:2–3 affirms the premise of biblical faith and sets the conduct of Joseph (vv. 7–20) in a new context. The narrative affirms that Yahweh is God, that Yahweh is Joseph's God. From this, the narrative derives two other assertions.

1) First, because this God is Joseph's God, Joseph prospers (vv. 2, 3, 23). Such a claim for faith in God must be handled carefully. Clearly Job and his friends found the evidence unconvincing. Too much must not be claimed for this story. It is enough to tell the story and let it make its own claim.

2) The second derivative claim is that Yahweh's blessing is in the empire for the sake of Joseph (v. 5; cf. 30:30). That is a remarkable claim to make. Because of this faithful man with whom Yahweh abides, the empire is blessed even though it neither knows nor serves Yahweh. The blessing is not autonomous. It is never fully in Joseph's hands. It is always in the power of this God "with us."

The cluster of themes—"being with," giving a blessing, causing prosperity, protecting and feeding (as in Ps. 23)—makes it possible to summarize the theological affirmation of this narrative in the words of Num. 6:24–26:

> The LORD bless you and keep you: The LORD make his face to shine upon you, and be gracious to you: The LORD lift up his countenance upon you, and give you peace.

The same elements are present. The use of the familiar blessing formula may help to see what a stunning claim is made in 39:1–6 and in all the Joseph narrative. Both the Joseph narrative and the classic benediction refute the ways of the empire. They call the listening community to disengage for another loyalty. In 39:7–20, two ways are in conflict with each other, the predictable way of the empire, which seeks to generate its own well-being, and the way of Immanuel ("God with us"). The way of Immanuel is the way of one who gives gifts, who evokes and fulfils dreams, who calls kings, who summons and saves, who prepares tables and lets cups run over. Like Joseph, the listening community is confronted with alternatives and needs to decide.

318

2. In the conclusion of verses 21–23, the same themes are repeated after the central incident. Again, Yahweh is with him (vv. 21, 23). Again Yahweh causes prosperity (v. 23). The narra-

tive has an unforeseen ending. Joseph should have been harshly treated. Every child of the empire knows one cannot violate royal persons without paying. One cannot even appear to violate. But Joseph is imprisoned only briefly. Very quickly this man of dream and destiny is again on the increase. The new motif is in verse 21, which explicates the gospel of verses 1–6. Yahweh shows Joseph *loyalty (hesed)*. Yahweh is abidingly loyal to his own. Yahweh makes his own judgment and does not accept the verdict of the empire. How very different Yahweh is from Egyptian expectations. He is loyal. His loyalty has the capacity to transform situations.

On Confidence (vv. 1–6, 21–23) and Concreteness (vv. 7–20)

As we have seen, this narrative in three parts is organized in a/b/á sequence. Verses 1–6 and verses 21–23 are much alike. They provide an envelope for the story of verses 7–20. The temptation of our exposition may be to focus on the episode in the middle, for that is where the dramatic action is. Or conversely, we may be tempted to stress the beginning and ending portions because that is where the theological claims are made. Faithful exposition requires holding these elements together. *Life must be lived at great risk,* as in verses 7–20. It must be lived in the face of deceit, temptation, and seduction. It must be lived in the empire where there appear to be ways to gain self-security. The episode of verses 7–20 is a complete, self-sufficient story, with action taken primarily on pragmatic grounds.

On the other hand, verses 1–6 and 21–23 are high theology. *Things are confidently settled.* There are no issues, no abrasions, no incongruities here. Our exposition must find a way of affirming together the high theological claims and the conflicted imperial episode. At the same time, it is true that *life is confidently settled* (vv. 1–6, 21–23) and that *life must be lived at great risk* (vv. 7–20). Both are true. Either taken by itself is false.

This narrative is not explicit kerygmatic theology. Nor is it mere pragmatism. It is, rather, a story that struggles with the contact of real life with real faith. It makes affirmations about both, convinced that they belong together. This narrative assumes an essential compatibility between *experience of Yahweh* and *experience of life.* It is tempting, either with excessive religiosity or as children of the world, to choose one at the

319

expense of the other. Those who are tilted toward religious affirmation may never make it beyond verse 6 to the realities of the empire. Those who are children of this age may assume (as did the royal woman) that the episode begins in verse 7. Either way alone misunderstands the text. But there are no easy formulae for having both. In the structure of this passage, the good news is that life is "sandwiched." To take only the filling of concrete action or only the container of theological affirmation does not provide the nourishment the narrative has in mind. It has in mind, rather, a kind of humanity which fully relies on God and which fully engages human experience. Joseph is a man who receives "loyalty" from God (v. 21) and who lives loyally in relation to his Egyptian master (vv. 8–9).

Genesis 40:1–23

In 39:7–20, Joseph has his first confrontation with the ways of the empire. He has resisted temptation from the seductive woman out of loyalty to his master and fear of God (vv. 8–9). Now in this chapter, he has his second encounter with the empire. If one follows conventional source division, chapter 40 and chapter 39 may belong, respectively, to J and E. However, they are not mutually exclusive. In important ways, chapter 40 is a parallel to chapter 39. Both add to the general theme of 39 —41, Joseph's rise and success in the empire.

Like chapter 39, chapter 40 must be heard in the total unit of 39—41. The primary movement of 39—41 comes in chapter 41. Chapters 39—40 appear to be only preparatory. In the present chapter, we are alerted to Joseph's gifts as a dream interpreter. But in terms of the actual advancement of Joseph, there is none. At the beginning, he is in the prison, even "in charge" (39:22). At the end (40:23), he is still there, but forgotten. This chapter serves primarily to pace the narrative and to build suspense toward the confrontation of chapter 41.

Also like 39, the chapter offers a clear and balanced structure. It begins with the two dreams of the baker and the butler (vv. 1–8). In this section, the dreams are uninterpreted. It concludes with closure to these events, with one royal servant (the butler) being given *life*, and the other royal servant (the baker) given over to *death* (vv. 20–23). Thus the chapter is nicely bound with *two dreams* (vv. 1–8) and *two fulfillments* (vv. 20–23). Between are the *two interpretations* of the dreams (vv. 9–15 and vv. 16–19). It is in the middle section that Joseph appears. Thus, Joseph is presented as the conduit, the way of movement from dream to fulfillment. Our attention is focused on Joseph. But he is rather incidental to the external events of this narrative which is concerned with the destinies of the two royal servants.

Much of the dramatic power of the narrative derives from the play on the phrase, "lift your head," used positively (v. 13) (cf. II Kings 25:27, which has the same phrase) and negatively (v. 19). The phrase is repeated (v. 20) with reference to both servants, so it is not until the last moment that we learn of their contrasting destinies. (Some commentators delete the phrase "from you" in v. 19, thus keeping the phrases completely symmetrical.)

The Meaning of the Dream

Interpretive issues in this chapter will necessarily focus on the reality of the dream.

1. It is well known that dreams are prominent in ancient literature and in Egyptian reports. The issue of dream interpretation is a crucial one in the ancient world. Thus the narrative has an authentic Egyptian coloring. But that understanding is not central to the theological claim of the text.

2. It is important in our exposition not to be distracted either by a history-of-religions approach to dreams, nor to rely on contemporary notions of the meaning of dreams. However, it may be helpful to dialogue briefly with three such notions in order to sharpen our perception of the distinctive biblical view of dreams. For example, out of analytic psychology, there is a widespread view that dreams help us relive and work through dimensions of the past which have been repressed. Dreams are said to be part of personal "archaeology" (Paul Ricoeur, *Freud and Philosophy*, 1970, pp. 521–25). But clearly, the dreams of our text are not oriented toward the past. They are aimed at a future God will grant. Or from a second perspective, current Jungian psychology treats dreams as data of a common unconscious which is shared by all persons. That is, dreams are a way of discerning an unknown and generalized field of reality. Against that, the dreams of Gen. 40 are not general but quite concrete

321

and specific. They do not reflect a field of reality that already exists, but instead, they assert a newness that is anticipated and yet to happen. Or, thirdly, in some quarters dreams are handled by a kind of psychological gnosticism. This perspective assumes that dreams can be interpeted by special techniques, used by persons with identifiable skills. In the ancient world, there were persons skilled in such techniques. But this narrative makes a different claim. The dream is a gift, and its interpretation is a gift, done not by a special skill or technique, but by the power of God freely given to this particular man.

3. The dreams of this chapter have no independent importance. They offer ways of presenting Joseph. The narrative has no interest in the butler or the baker, or even in the Pharaoh who has a birthday (v. 20). The interest is in the destiny of Joseph, his sorry lot and his unusual authority. From the beginning, even with his scornful brothers, Joseph is the "master of the dream" (37:19). The entire narrative is concerned with the large dream of chapter 37, the dream of rule. In chapter 40, we meet two subordinate dreams. But the narrator does not linger with them. They are only instruments of the larger dream. The question beneath the narrative is the future of Joseph's dream. Chapter 40 is to be seen as a step along the way as that dream comes to fulfillment.

The God of the Dreams

The dream and its interpretation need to be received as a theological statement.

1. An audacious claim is placed in the mouth of Joseph (v. 8). It is asserted that dream interpretation belongs to God and to God alone. The dreams are not to be handled by human wisdom, by imperial administration, or by analytical decoding. They are rather the in-breaking of other purposes known only in the mystery of God. Pharaoh, like every imperial master, presumes a monopoly on knowledge. But in these dreams, knowledge is of another kind. And Pharaoh has no part in it. We are confronted here with knowledge that lies outside the epistemology of the empire. The monopoly of knowledge in the empire is broken. Pharaoh knows many things. He knows how to manage and administer and control. As we may see in the Exodus narrative, he knows how to prosper and how to oppress. But he does not know how to discern the movement of God's way within his realm. Only God knows that. And only Joseph

322

does God's work in this situation. Joseph is the utterly free and authoritative man who operates by God's gift and who is not answerable to the empire. He need heed neither Egyptian restraints nor Egyptian ways of knowing. Thus, Joseph's monopoly of dream interpretation, of discerning the irresistible future, is subversive to the empire.

2. The dreams are not ends in themselves. They are means in the narrative to speak about a new understanding of the future. We are accustomed to think about the future as formed by effort and choice, or at least derived from the present. The narrative attests to another way of the future. It insists that the future lies beyond human competence either to bring or to halt. The future is inscrutably in God's hands and not human hands. God's ways ·bring underived newness. The men in Joseph's prison (it is Joseph's prison, not Pharaoh's) are not fated, as though all things were settled. Nor are they free, as though they could decide. The narrative moves beyond both imperial fatedness and human freedom to the mystery of God's way. God's inscrutable way will have its decisive say, even in the empire (cf. Prov. 19:21).

3. Thus, these dreams, as servants of the larger dream, may be characterized in terms of three crucial theological intents.

a. The dreams are *theonomous*. They have to do with God and God's rule. They tell what God will do, albeit in the rule of Pharaoh. They claim that only God knows the future and only God decides the future.

b. The dreams are *kerygmatic*. They are news about a new situation that cannot be derived from or predicted from the present. Neither the baker nor the butler could guess how their "heads would be lifted." The dreams announce a new situation.

c. The dreams are *eschatological*. They speak of God's coming resolution of human issues. It is clear that the story cannot be handled by a general phenomenology, but only by a very concrete concern for Joseph and for the theological intent of the narrator.

The implication (v. 8) is that God has a future which is to be worked out in the context of the empire. That "God is with Joseph" (39:2, 3, 21, 23) does not mean private comfort. Rather, it claims that even in Egypt, the dream dreamed over Joseph will move according to God's sovereign purposes.   323

4. The future is in the hand of God (and not Pharaoh). But the narrative, explicitly (v. 8) and implicitly throughout, assigns

this power of God to the historical person of Joseph. The theological claim of verse 8 is unambiguous: "Do not interpretations belong to God?" But this is immediately followed by and linked to the cruciality of Joseph: "Tell them to me, I pray." Joseph is God's man. He is in and with and for the empire. But he remains God's man. The narrative is not finally about dream interpretation. The dream is a vehicle for the strange sovereignty of God lodged in this specific man. There is entrusted to Joseph more than the master knew or intended in 39:6. There is now placed in Joseph's hand the power to handle the rise and fall of the empire.

The Role of Joseph

After the central claim (v. 8), the narrative moves now through the two dream narratives (vv. 9–11, 16–17) and two dream interpretations (vv. 12–13, 18–19). The resolution of the two dreams and, thus, the vindication of the two interpretations is told in verses 20–22. Of themselves, the dreams, the interpretations and the resolutions of them, are not of great interest to the narrator. The sequence is rather obvious and expected. The public role of Joseph is grand and sweeping. He speaks. And it happens as he has said. The inscrutable and authoritative way of God in the mouth of Joseph brings life and it brings death. The future is unfathomable. It can only be received.

The counter-theme does not focus on the grand truth of dreams nor on the strange way of God's hidden future. Rather, it focuses on the pathos of this man (vv. 14–15). Joseph steps outside his formidable public role. We are shown the personal struggle of a man still in prison. For all his ability to amaze others, he himself is still in great need (cf. Matt. 27:42). The counter-theme (vv. 14–15, 23) stands in stark contrast to the ostensible theme of verses 9–13 and 16–22. The man who seems to be quite in control is here needful. The pitiful plea of verses 14–15 is unexpected after his public performance. It is remarkable that this man nearly identified with God (v. 8) now is reduced to a plea. The powerful man born to rule is also a needful one, one of "the least" (Matt. 25:40, 45). In 39:21, it is affirmed that God shows him "loyalty" (ḥesed). But in 40:14, he asks for "kindness" (ḥesed), not from God, but from the imprisoned butler. The liberator of the butler is now himself dependent and in need of liberation. For all his reliance on God, Joseph must depend on the act of a covenantal neighbor.

324

The little speech of self-identification (vv. 14–15) embodies three motifs of the main theological tradition: *(a)* It awaits Exodus, even using the technical term, "bring me out." The entire Joseph narrative waits with Israel for Exodus. *(b)* He sees that his sorry lot is because of Torah violation (v. 15). The prohibition, "Thou shalt not steal," originally concerned kidnapping (cf. Deut. 24:7). Death comes where the Torah is ignored. *(c)* He asserts his innocence. He believes in the claims of innocence and therefore he has a right to be delivered. After the great imperial dreams are dreamed and the Pharaoh can "lift heads" and "lift heads off" (vv. 20–22), there is still Joseph, called by God but left in an untenable position.

The power of God is sure enough. But Joseph awaits a human act of solidarity upon which the history of this people now depends. The narrative ends tersely (v. 23). He asks for remembering (v. 14). He asks for remembering in the same way God remembered Abraham and qualified the brimstone (19:29). He asks for remembering the way his mother Rachel had been remembered and he had been born (30:22). He asks for remembering and perhaps God is remembering. But so far as this story goes, Joseph is forgotten (v.23).

The text brings us to an incongruity where faithful people must live. How may we reconcile the *grand claim* (v. 8) which seems utterly effective and the *unrelieved pathos* (vv. 14–15) which ends in dismay (v. 23)? It is in that incongruity that human faithfulness must be practiced. It is in that setting that the dream of God is tested. The dream of God for Joseph is not for times of obvious credibility. It is for times when the claims run against the evidence. And Joseph is left to wait even as father Abraham had. The butler forgets Joseph now, even as Egypt will forget him (cf. Exod. 1:8). Joseph is left with this question: Is there a *remembering* done by Yahweh beyond the forgetting of the empire? Joseph does not know. The butler does not care.

Genesis 41:1–57

This chapter completes the larger unit of chapters 39—41 concerning Joseph's destiny in the empire of Egypt. Chapters

39—40 function as preparation for this chapter, in which the narrative makes its major turn. In 39—40, nothing substantive has happened to Joseph. At the end of chapter 40, Joseph is not better off than at the end of chapter 37. He is still forgotten (40:23). The dramatic movement of the narrative has been delayed until this chapter. Only now the dream to rule from chapter 37 is given substance. The focus of this chapter is upon the inscrutable power of that dream, unrecognized by Pharaoh and even by Joseph.

The narrative is divided into three parts, structured as prologue (vv. 1–8) and epilogue (vv. 46–57) with the middle section (vv. 9–45) containing the main dramatic account about Joseph. To be able to face the powerful claim of the middle section, we will first consider the "before" and "after" parts so that the deep break in the story becomes evident.

The Failure of the Empire

The prologue (vv. 1–8) sets the problem of Pharaoh. We have seen Joseph's problem. People in prison are inclined to think kings do not have problems. But as it turns out, the problem of Pharaoh is more acute than that of Joseph. The dream takes initiative away from Pharaoh. The king is no longer the subject, but the object. He receives messages. He does not generate or authorize them. Kings are normally protected and screened from unwelcome messages. They hear mostly good news. But the dream penetrates the royal isolation. The loss of royal initiative is the back side of the rise of Joseph. This is intensified by the climax of verse 8. The best wisdom of the empire is dysfunctional. The empire is helpless before the inscrutable power of God which comes like a thief in the night (cf. I Thess. 5:4). It is like a thief, for it has robbed the king of his confidence, his control, and finally, of his expected future.

1. This episode is a refutation of the wisdom and technique of the empire. It is a challenge to the epistemology of Pharaoh. Egyptian ways of knowing are called into question. Knowledge is power. And now imperial knowledge has failed. And with that failure, authority is diminished. This ludicrous scene of Egypt's "the best and the brightest" has obvious parallels in Dan. 2, 5, where again the claims of the empire are contrasted with the innocent discernment of Israel. An even more dramatic parallel is in Exod. 7—8 in the plague cycle. In Exod. 7:22, the empire is competent. But then the stakes are upped. By

326

8:18, the competence of the empire is superseded. Foreshadowed here with Joseph, the narrative of Exodus invites Israel to marvel at its peculiar destiny in the face of the empire now become helpless. The power of this age is rendered helpless before the inscrutable purpose of God. The failure of the royal machinery is paralleled by the drought narrative in the Elijah-Ahab story of I Kings 17—18. (There also the king is helpless to guarantee life when the rule of God does not grant it.)

In Jesus of Nazareth, the same issue is twice dramatically presented. At the birth of Jesus, Herod is helpless because he does not have adequate knowledge and he cannot manage his future (Matt. 2:1–8). And at the end of his life, Jesus stands before Pilate. Or is Pilate before Jesus? The issue in Gen. 41, as in John 18:28—19:16, is a remarkable inversion of power. The one accustomed to presiding is now placed in the dock. With Pharaoh (as with Herod and Pilate) the power of the empire is put in question and refuted by the dream. The refutation of the empire creates the necessary opening for Joseph. The narrative reports the subtle but unambiguous delegitimation of Egypt's whole presumed reality. The dream presents the king with a new reality he cannot domesticate. No wonder he is "troubled" (v. 8, cf. Matt. 2:3). No wonder he is frantic to find out the intent of this message which has surprised him in the night when his screening apparatus was down. No untoward messages reached the king in the daytime. But the night belongs to the penetrating power of God.

2. The substance of the dream is as startling as the mode. It is enough of an affront that the message comes in such an "unauthorized version." But the content is even more troubling. We cannot grasp the trouble fully until we recall that the Nile River is not only a geographical referent. It is also an expression of the imperial power of fertility. It is administration of the Nile which permits the king to generate and guarantee life. The failure of the Nile and its life system means that the empire does not have in itself the power of life (cf. Ezek. 29:3). It is for that reason that the plague of the Nile is so crucial (Exod. 7:7–22). An assault on the Nile strikes at the heart of Pharaoh's claim to authority. Conversely, "famine" refers to the failure of self-generative powers and the helplessness of the empire in the face of death. The dream's juxtaposition of *Nile* and *famine* is an exposé of the futility of Egyptian ways of existence. The river is now characterized by death.

327

This opening unit is not a hidden code that is hard to understand. It is, rather, a subversive but intelligible announcement that unauthorized and unacceptable messages have penetrated the empire. The substance of those messages is that the claims of the empire are fraudulent. Egypt has become not a place of life, but of death. Joseph appears just as the presumed conventional world of the empire is placed in deep crisis.

The New Administration Gives Life

The epilogue of the narrative (vv. 46–57) portrays the newly empowered Joseph offering Egypt and the world an unexpected situation of prosperity and well-being. The narrative reflects the firm authority of Joseph. He is clearly in charge. None may resist or question (v. 55). As the story develops, there is a ruthlessness which makes survival possible. There is also remarkable *technical "know-how"* put at the service of imperial well-being. But most of all, there is the lonely figure of Joseph in his newly granted *sovereignty*. The Joseph of verses 46–55 is strongly legitimated in sharp contrast to the pitiful Pharaoh (vv. 1–8). Whereas that sorry Pharoah is destined to death, Joseph represents the new power of life for the empire and for the world.

1. This new sovereignty is evidenced in its effectiveness by the multiple use of *all*: . . .*all* the land of Egypt (v.46); . . . *all* the food (v. 48); . . . *all* my hardship, . . .*all* my father's house (v. 51); . . . *all* the lands, . . . *all* the land of Egypt (v. 54); . . *all* the land of Egypt, . . . *all* the Egyptians (v. 55); . . . *all* the land, . . . that was in them (storehouses; RSV has "storehouses," which Hebrew lacks) (v. 56); . . . *all* the earth, . . . *all* the earth (v. 57). The repeated emphasis on "all" is not accidental. We may linger for a moment with its repeated use. A helpful comparison may be made with Psalm 145, a stylized doxology of God's gracious protection and sustenance of all of creation. In that psalm, there is also a repeated use of "all": good to . . . *all*, . . . *all* that he has made (v.9); . . . *all* thy works, . . . *all* eons (RSV has "everlasting"), . . . *all* generations (v.13); . . . *all* who are failing, . . . *all* who are bowed down (v. 14); . . . *all* look to thee (v. 15); . . . *all* his ways, . . . *all* his doings (v. 17); . . . *all* who call upon him, . . . *all* who call upon him (v. 18); . . . *all* who love him, . . .*all* the wicked (v.20); . . .*all* flesh (v. 21).

Of course, there is no necessary link between this doxology and our narrative. But in both, the words make a broad claim.

328

The psalm credits life directly and completely to *God.* In our chapter, the mediation of *Joseph* is the key. What is claimed for God in the psalms is here assigned to Joseph. Either he acts for God or he usurps the life-giving function of God. Either way, he is the *immediate* source of life and well-being. The narrative does not sense any conflict between God's creative power and human management. But clearly we meet here a very different mode of faith. Joseph has preempted the usual claims of doxology. His administration functions so that the abundance may become visible. The narrative contrasts the futility of Egyptian technique and Joseph's capacity to turn the earth to life-giving possibility. Before Joseph (vv. 1–8), there is imperial death. After Joseph (vv. 46–57), there is life.

2. The reference to the two sons of Joseph (vv. 50–52) appears to be ill-placed here and imposed on the story. But they are an important anticipation of what comes later (chapter 48). The two etymologies reported here give an interesting turn to the story. "God has made me forget" (v. 51), means that the old life of persecution and misery has been put behind. A new era has begun. The name "Ephraim-fruitful" (v. 52) serves to contrast Joseph, bearer of promise and life, with the fruitless, hopeless reality of the empire. The first son affirms *discontinuity* of Joseph from the old troubled history of Jacob. The second name sharply contrasts this family of *blessing* with the kingdom of curse. The *fruitful* one has life even in the kingdom of *affliction* (cf. 29:32; 31:42). In the present form of this narrative, it is hinted that Joseph fulfills the charge to the first ones (1:28) to be fruitful.

Elevation of the Life-giver

The main action of 41 takes place in the middle section (vv. 9–45). Before this, there has been the *futility of Egypt* (vv. 1–8). After this, there is *well-being* even in the midst of famine (vv. 46–57). Between the futility and the well-being, there is Joseph (vv. 9–45). Something is going on in these verses that neither Pharaoh nor Joseph understands.

The verses of this center section are neatly divided into two parts by "Now therefore" (v. 33).

1. In verses 9–32 (before the "therefore"), Joseph and Pharaoh engage in an exploration of the dream. Joseph the forgotten one (40:23) is now remembered (41:9–13). He is remembered just at the right time. The butler had forgotten (40:23),

329

but now he remembers! The narrator claims that Joseph can do what Pharaoh cannot do. He can receive the future as God gives it. The narrative does not ask why Pharaoh could not receive this future from God. Perhaps Pharaoh is unable to discern the future because he is too enmeshed in his own present, with all the self-justification that goes with it.

Joseph, by contrast, is open to and resolute about the new future. This unit presents the retelling of the dream (vv. 17–24) and the interpretation (vv. 25–31). In his interpretation, Joseph stays consistently theocentric. He is not distracted by the interesting phenomena of the dream itself. The focus is turned toward God, the one with whom Pharaoh finally must deal. Joseph makes flat and unembarrassed statements to introduce the new reality to Pharaoh:

"God will give Pharaoh a favorable answer" (v. 16).

"God has revealed what to Pharaoh he is about to do" (v. 25).

"God has shown to Pharaoh what he is about to do" (v. 28).

"The thing is fixed by God, and God will shortly bring it to pass" (v. 32).

The rest of the words (vv. 9–32) are clear and predictable. The meaning of the dream flows easily. The explanation is not exceptional. But the theocentric casting of the narrative is remarkable.

a. The God is not named or identified. This may reflect the Elohist source. More likely, it shows the restraint of a court speech in which one is not expected or permitted to make theology concrete. Joseph clearly refers to the God of his family. But all this need not be made explicit for the king. It is enough to establish a transcendent referent beyond the empire which stands over-against the empire both as a principle of criticism and as an alternative source of life.

b. Note the confidence of the speech. It is not an occasion for excitement, persuasion, or argumentation. It is already done. It is established and decided without any particular reference to Pharaoh (cf. Isa. 14:24–27). The future in Egypt does not depend upon Pharaoh. He does not get to decide. In fact, Pharaoh is irrelevant and marginal to the future of the kingdom. No wonder a "cool" speech is made by Joseph. He has calmly announced to the lord of Egypt that the future is out of his hands (cf. Dan. 3:14–18). That much is implicit in the dream. In its mode and in its substance, the dream presents the coming real-

330

ity that is not conjured or willed by the king. It is settled and it will happen. The king is helpless in the face of God's coming future. This is a bold and risky message to deliver.

c. The power of God is contrasted with the feeble power of Pharaoh. The criterion of the true God (cf. Isa. 41:21–29) is that God is the one who can cause a future. In Gen. 41, it is clear that Pharaoh can cause no future. Nor can he resist the future that God will bring. The royal way is to think that the future must be derived from the present through careful planning and calculation.

But in this quiet, confident speech, Joseph ends that notion of the future. It is God, not royal power or imperial planning, who will cause the future. It is this God who will give life and bring death, who will cause the Nile to produce or cause famine to come (cf. Deut. 32:39; Isa. 45:7). Such a dream must have seemed nonsense to the Pharaoh.

In this enormous claim, we are not dealing with a marginal incident in the Bible. We are confronted here with the very premise of much of biblical faith: God has the capacity to work newness against every administered convention. That premise is fundamental to the Exodus, where the same Nile is used as a sign of God's intervention (Exod. 7:20–21). It is the basis of claims in the exilic literature that God is sovereign, even while other claimants appear to have power (cf. Isa. 46:1–4; Ezek. 37:1–4). That same premise is indispensable to the work of Jesus (cf. Luke 7:22) and to the disruption of Easter (Mark 16:6–8). The narrative announces the free, sovereign God is at work in the very center of Egyptian existence.

2. The narrative shifts in verse 33. Joseph is not only the dream interpreter. He is prepared with a concrete follow-up program. The fixed purpose of God is no occasion for human abdication. The firm purpose of God requires bold royal action. The intervention of God does not end royal responsibility, but sets it in a context where a new course of action is required. God's purpose is not the end of human planning but the ground for it. That God's "plan" is above human "plans" (Isa. 55:8–9) does not mean there should not be human planning. It means that it must be responsive and faithful to God's plan.

Joseph finishes the dream interpretation (v. 32). But note that after his interpretation, there is no response from Pharaoh. We are not told that he accepted the interpretation or agreed to it. Indeed, the narrative proceeds as though there were no question of this. The initiative is completely in God's hands.

331

Pharaoh listens to the interpretation. He does not speak. He listens very carefully. Joseph proceeds immediately with human plans for implementation. Pharaoh is still a receptive listener. He initiates nothing.

a. *Now therefore* (v. 33)! The purposes of God demand a human counterpart. In this juxtaposition of divine plan (vv. 9–32) and human action (vv. 33–45) is the seed of incarnational faith. The drama of *God's future* must be embodied and implemented by *human imagination.* There must be an imperial choice of someone to do it (v. 33). Pharaoh must now unwittingly choose the one whom God has already chosen. The *transcendent purpose of God* (vv. 25–32) is tied to *concrete historical action* (vv. 33–36). There could not have been the saving historical action (vv. 33–36) if there had not been the dream. But if there had been only the dream (vv. 17–24) and its interpretation (vv. 25–32) without historical response (vv. 33–36), there would have been no saving. Thus, verse 33 presents the hinge that is structurally important. The point is pivotal not only for this narrative but for the whole narrative faith of Israel. The situation of the narrative is not unlike the solemn resolutions passed in church meetings: Whereas . . . be it resolved. In this text, the "whereas" is the fixed dream of God which Pharaoh cannot escape (vv. 9–32). The "whereas" is the coming drought and famine. The "therefore be it resolved" is that the proper man must be found to act in response to the dream (vv. 33–45).

b. Joseph's concrete proposal (vv. 33–36) is without guile. There is no hint that Joseph refers to himself, though the narrator knows where the story will lead. While these verses offer a full strategy for the crisis, our focus is upon verse 33. A man is needed who is "discreet and wise," who bears the marks of discernment and shrewdness and who fears God, for "fear of God" is the ground of all discernment and shrewdness (cf. Prov. 1:7). This is not only a description of the right man, but an announcement of a new ruling agenda. The new ruler must act in the context of God's sovereign dream. Biblical faith has had enough of strong leaders who know everything except the power of God's sovereign dream (cf. Isa. 10:13–14; 47:10; Jer. 4:22; Ezek. 28:2–10). This tradition within the Bible presents a consistent critique of those who practice the "wisdom of the world" (I Cor. 1:20). They deploy royal power subject to none. But they are obtuse about the dream of God for well-being which is fixed and will have its way.

332

c. Joseph describes one who bears the marks of royalty (v. 33). But the royalty envisioned here is not the royalty valued in Egypt. Solomon becomes an embodiment of the ruthless self-serving way of Egyptian royalty, but he is also the one characterized by the very gifts Joseph identifies (I Kings 3:12; cf. Ezek. 34:1–10). What Joseph urges is royalty measured by Israelite norms. There is a striking parallel between these marks ("discreet and wise," v. 33) urged by Joseph and those of the expected king of Isa. 11:2–3:

> And the spirit of the LORD shall rest upon him,
>   the spirit of *wisdom and understanding,*
>   the spirit of counsel and might,
>   the spirit of knowledge and the fear of the LORD.
> And his delight shall be in the fear of the LORD.

The one expected by Isaiah is the one who is attentive to the poor and the meek, who practices righteousness and faithfulness, who rules toward peace. If Isa. 11:1–9 be permitted to interpret our verse, then the urging of Joseph is for a royal person who may be under Pharaoh but who has a very different perception of reality.

3. The story moves from the sagacious counsel of Joseph (vv. 33–36) to the immediate implementation of Pharaoh (vv. 37–45). There is no evidence that Pharaoh understands Joseph as making a reference to himself. The thing is wrought by God who will bring to fulfillment his personal dream to Joseph (37:7, 9) and his public dream to Pharaoh (41:2–7, 17–24). Pharaoh does no special persuading of Joseph. Joseph neither resists nor needs to be persuaded. The words have all been spoken. The implementation of Joseph's plan is treated by the narrative as a foregone conclusion and not as something suspenseful or very interesting. It happens quickly. We may surmise it happens because the Giver of dreams is at work. This mysteriously sanctioned dreamer is wise by the best standards of the world (Prov. 11:26).

a. Then follows the enthronement of the one designated in the dream to rule: (1) the royal proclamation (v. 41; cf. Ps. 2:6); (2) the insignia of office (v. 42; cf. Luke 15:22–23); (3) public acclamation (v. 43; I Kings 1:25, 39; II Kings 9:13; Phil. 2:9–11); (4) a royal name (v. 45; cf. Matt. 16:17–18; Phil. 2:9–11); (5) legitimacy by marriage (v. 45; I Sam. 18:20–29).

The cry of acclamation rendered "bow the knee" (RSV)

333

(v. 43) appears to derive from an Egyptian word. Its meaning is now lost to us. So also the Egyptian names are obscure (vv. 45, 50). At best, only guesses can be made either about the meaning of the names or of their historical identity.

The entire procedure (vv. 41–45) appears to be a proper Egyptian litany of installation. Joseph is now completely encapsulated in Egyptian reality. That is the intent of Pharaoh. The narrator does not raise any question about it. He is fully Egyptian, easily accepting the role and authority of his new office. But Joseph has many faces. Soon enough, he will make appeal to the God of his tradition. For now, the narrative provides a delicate blend of fidelity and enculturation, of faith and reason. The influence of Israel's faith tradition is subdued. But it shapes the man, the narrative, and we may suspect, even the empire.

b. The episode ends with this beloved son of Jacob now the beloved son of the empire. Pharaoh does not understand God's ways. The one who is accustomed to *knowing* what is going on in fact understands nothing. The one who appears to have *power* has none at all. The hidden way of the dream outflanks both the *power* and the *wisdom* of the empire (cf. I Cor. 1:25). This understated attack on the dominant rule and epistemology is echoed by the one who also brings a new rule:

> I thank thee, Father, Lord of heaven and earth, that thou hast hidden these things from the wise and understanding [*sophôn kai sunetôn*] and revealed them to babes. Yea, Father, for such was thy gracious will. . . . Blessed are the eyes which see what you see! For I tell you that many prophets and kings desired to see what you see, and did not see it, and to hear what you hear, and did not hear it (Luke 10:21–24).

(The Greek terms for "discreet" and "wise" of Gen. 41:33 are *phronim* and *sunetôn*. Only the second of these is used in Luke 10:21. But the parallel is surely worth noting.) Joseph is the "babe" who sees and hears and knows and trusts. Egypt understood nothing of all that.

The entire unit (39—41) has come a considerable distance. It begins with the mere survival of a boy who dreamed a dangerous dream. It ends with this boy having become a public man with power of life and death (41:44). Those killers of the dream at Shechem had not killed a dream (37:20). Unknowingly, they had advanced the cause of the dream. Joseph and the narrative have gotten along without the brothers all this time. It is time for their reappearance. But now, their strident way will become humble supplication. By 42:1, everything is inverted. Now the brothers hope only to survive. But they must deal with this one for whom the dream has become reality.

Genesis 42:1—44:34

These three chapters (42—44) form a balanced counterpart to chapters 39—41. In 37:6-9, Joseph dreams two dreams. The first was about the "bowing down" of the sheaves. The second was about the "bowing down" of the sun, moon and stars. It may be that both dreams refer to rule over his family. But after chapter 37, the narrative is developed in two quite distinct directions. Chapters 39—41 concern Joseph's rise in the empire of Egypt and his *rule over Egypt.* Parallel to that, chapters 42 —44 concern his *rule over his brothers and his father.* Thus, the present chapters more directly concern the fulfillment of the dreams over the family. And yet, the *rule over his brothers* could only happen as a result of his *rule over Egypt.* Chapter 42 returns to the theme of the brothers in 37, which was not mentioned in 39—41. In 42—44, Joseph's dominant role in Egypt is necessary and presumed. But nothing is made of it except as a condition for dealing with the brothers.

The drama of the narrative moves from the dream of 37 to chapter 45, where the fulfillment becomes visible.

37 Dreams of rule

         39—41 rule over the empire

         42—44 rule over the family

45 Open fulfillment of the dreams.

Chapters 37 and 45 provide the focal points for theological interpretation. The two intervening sections of 39—41 and 42—44 develop and enhance the plot, heighten the suspense, and retard the action. In 39—41, the development is external and public. In 42—44, the interplay is primarily relational and even psychological. Externally, not much happens here. At the end of chapter 44, things are still unresolved. The listener is left

335

waiting. The wait is developed with consummate art. By 44:34, expectations are built to a remarkable intensity.

The Structure of the Passage

The three chapters (which we treat as a unit) are structured in two parts, each part containing two encounters as well as an introduction and two interludes:

Introduction (42:1–5) The famine as life/death issue for Israel

a 42:6–25 *First meeting between Joseph and brothers*
(Interlude in 42:26–28: departure and trick)

      b 42:29–38 *First meeting of Jacob and sons*

      b́ 43:1–15 *Second meeting of Jacob and sons*
(It is not simple continuation of the proceeding. There is discontinuity caused by the severity of famine.)

á 43:16—44:34 *Second meeting between Joseph and brothers*
(Interlude in 44:1–5: trick motif).

The unit is developed in terms of a chiasmus, with the first sequence Joseph and then Jacob; the second sequence is reversed, with the sequence of Jacob and then Joseph. The encounters in a/b/b́/á, that is, Joseph/Jacob/Jacob/Joseph, provide the framework for the drama.

The Players in the Drama

Joseph is the son who knows what is happening and has all the power. By contrast, Jacob is the father who knows nothing but cares and grieves his loss. The external agenda is the prince of the empire giving food to this helpless family. The internal agenda is the control of Benjamin. The dramatic power is in the unequal struggle between father and son, with the brothers as intermediaries. In that struggle, the son is bound to win. He will win because he controls the food and because he has the necessary knowledge. He will win because he has had a dream dreamed over him. By the end of this unit, we will wait only a little longer for the disclosure of his full triumph and his assertion of rule.

336   The dramatic contest between father and son presents to us a Joseph very different from the one we have previously encountered. In chapter 37, he is a naïve and guileless boy. In chapters 39—41, he is a noble and effective man of integrity who is not intimidated by the royal woman (39), the royal offi-

cers (40), nor even the Pharaoh (41). But in 42—44, he is now a ruthless and calculating governor. He understands the potential of his enormous office and exploits his capacity fully. He not only manipulates the scene but seems to relish his power to intimidate and threaten. Perhaps we have here the result of a very different process of tradition. Or perhaps the new situation simply evokes a changed portrait.

The famine is only the occasion for the narrative (42—44). The agenda of this narrative concerns members of this family coming to terms with each other, with the past, and with the dream. In addition to food, this family struggles for survival at several levels. The *struggle for survival* is at the same time a *struggle for faith,* a struggle to trust in a promise, and a struggle to believe in the power of a dream. The intricacies of family relations become the mode in which faithfulness is at issue and in which the future must be received. We are concerned with a specific family battling with a specific dream. *Survival* and *faithfulness* are demanding issues in the empire. But they are no less so in the family.

Dealing with "the politics of the family," this shrewd narrator has observed that every interaction is a power move which at the same time is a move of faith and a move of desperation. The life of this family is a game with many players. None of the players knows all the rules because the Key Player is always less than visible.

1. Let us begin with *the brothers.* This undifferentiated group is bound by their initial act against Joseph (cf. 37:20–31). The resulting deception of their father (vv. 32–35) lies at the bottom of everything. The brothers have no room in which to act, no energy for imagination, and no possibility of freedom. They are bound by the power of an unforgiven past, immobilized by guilt, and driven by anxiety. Their guilt and anxiety can surface neither in the presence of the father nor in the presence of Joseph. Now they seek to act effectively, honestly, and openly. Their speeches to Joseph are genuine. They mean what they say. But they are not free enough to make them effective.

a. The guilt of the brothers has an enormous power: "In truth we are guilty concerning our brother" (42:21). "How can we clear ourselves? God has found out the guilt of your servants" (44:16). They are not free enough to have faith. They are harnessed to the past. As a result, the brothers are excessively concerned for the safety and well-being of their father and Benjamin. Having falsely grieved their father, they must be on

337

continual guard that they do not add to his grief (44:30–34). Because they could not believe the dream, they are forced to treat father Jacob as though he were the last generation who must be kept alive and unharmed for perpetuity. They cannot see themselves as a generation of promise-bearers. They certainly have no clue about their brother Joseph. They are unable to think of any generation after themselves. They are fated, locked to a past moment. They cannot be open to any new possibility, either as a new gift from God or as fresh work of Joseph.

b. But the flow of the narrative has its own life in spite of the brothers' fearful enslavement. The dream of chapter 37 does move forward. It includes them, even though they do not know it. Three times the brothers play their unwitting part in the dream they think they have avoided:

[They] *bowed themselves* before him with their faces to the ground (42:6).

They *bowed* their heads and made obeisance (43:28).

They *fell* before him to the ground (44:14).

The dream is happening. The future is at work toward life. But in their fearfulness, the brothers do not notice it.

c. Their sense of fatedness touches their understanding of God. In 44:16, they link their guilt to God. In 42:28, they express their desperate faithless posture more directly: "What is this that God has done to us?" Their limited view of God requires a *quid pro quo* response to their own guilt. They see their guilt as the definitive factor in human and divine relations. They are unable to believe in any promissory God who might break beyond their hopeless mendacity. As a result, the brothers must live in a world where no new thing can be anticipated.

d. For the most part, the brothers are an undifferentiated lot. But we may note several times when individual brothers do become identified. This includes the self-serving rebuke of Reuben (42:22), the passionate promise of Reuben (42:37), the pledge of Judah (43:8–10) and, above all, the speech of appeal by Judah (44:18–34). Though the final speech of Judah comes closest, none of these genuinely caring acts is an act of faithful freedom. Every time, the brothers act as if compelled by the fatedness they have already embraced in chapter 37. They seek to compensate for their other deception. But they remain

338

trapped, unable to extricate themselves from their hopeless fear.

2. The second actor in this poignant interplay is *the father.* In both 42:2 and 43:2, it is Jacob who initiates the trip to Egypt. He, too, plays a part in serving the dream. But his life is defined by the deception his sons have worked on him. All his words reflect the heavy loss of Joseph. Jacob is resolved to risk no more, certainly not beloved Benjamin. Jacob's last appearance in the narrative (37:35) was his refusal to be comforted. He resolved to go to death in his grief.

a. The issue of grief is decisive for Jacob. In 42:38, it is actual grief for Joseph and anticipated grief for Benjamin which block any new action. In 44:29–34, it is the same grief of Jacob (articulated by Judah) which creates a dramatic pause in the narrative. But in 43:11–14, there is a break in the grief which must be closely scrutinized. In a final resolve for bread, Jacob releases his cherished Benjamin in a stylized speech: "Take some of the choice fruits . . . . Take double the money. . . . Take also your brother." And then this basis for sending the young one: "May El Shaddai grant you mercy before the man." The father invokes this old name for God and hopes for mercy. Everything is staked on that one name. Injured Jacob believes more than his sons. He dares to think of a new possibility. In his boldness, he breaks the cycle of his own grief and loss. And at the same time, he breaks the sons' spiral of betrayal and deception. Jacob is a picture of faithfulness that permits newness. He is able to care and grieve and therefore to hope.

b. In his old age, he is still a man of more faithful passion than his sons. It is troubled but still believing passion. He knows it is only mercy that can break the cycle.

His faith, however, carries a tone of resignation in the next line: "If I am bereaved of my children, I am bereaved" (v. 14). It is difficult to know where faith leaves off and cynical resignation sets in. The line is echoed in the noble resignation of Esther (Esther 4:16). Jacob has a passionate faith in El Shaddai. On that faith he will risk his beloved son. But that faith is mixed with a desperate hope and even cynical resignation. And with it all, there is Jacob's realistic need for bread. As a younger man, he gave the pottage for a birthright (25:29–34). Now the pottage looms a bit larger for him. In this text, Jacob offers a picture of faithfulness which is richly textured with human passion.

339

3. The third actor is *Joseph*. He is the one whom the others think dead but who holds in his hand the power of life. He knows more than the others. But he does not know everything. He is not an innocent bystander in these strange turns. Joseph's sense of his own interest is keen. He is cast by the narrator in his public role as a benevolent administrator. And in that role, he expresses what can pass for civil religion: "I fear God" (42:18). That statement may indeed be one of devoutness. But the narrative gives no support for such a reading. There is no clue of any special commitment. From his public disclosure, Joseph seems a governor void of passion. He is a cool practitioner of civil religion. Beneath that cool front, there are two further facets of Joseph's person which are important for this narrative.

a. He is presented as ruthless, cunning, and vengeful. He is prepared to return to his brothers some of the grief caused him. He has forgotten nothing. There is nothing noble about him. There is no hint that he has any awareness of a larger vocation. The God-fearing cliché of 42:18 does not touch much of what follows. He remembers the dream (cf. 42:9), but he sees it only in terms of power, not vocation or fidelity.

b. But he is not a man without passion. His passion is not for his brothers, not for the well-being of his family, not even for his father. His overriding passion is for Benjamin (42:15–16; 43:30). He wants to know if Benjamin is alive, and he wants to see him. That yearning sets Joseph on a collision course with his father, who cannot bear to release the beloved son of his old age. The hungry father wants to keep Benjamin; the ruling son wants to see him. The brothers are placed in a dilemma by their guilt, between the father they have deceived and the brother who owns the food.

The meeting of the two sons of Rachel is a moving moment (43:29–34). Joseph is "warm" for Benjamin (43:30). The term *kmr* (RSV, "yearned") is used in a parallel way only in Hos. 11:8 referring to Yahweh's passion for Israel. (The only other use is Lam. 5:10.) The phrases of Gen. 43:30 and Hos. 11:8 are close parallels and may be used to interpret each other. What is said here of Joseph, Hosea dares to say of God. The deep yearning and profound emotional response are parallel in the two dramatic portrayals. Joseph is moved with a passion he cannot resist. He is moved to tears. He tips his hand by being noticeably

340

generous to the young one (v. 34). He utters a special blessing over him (v. 29). The public facade of passionlessness is penetrated.

The narrative gives no hint of why Joseph experiences this special yearning. The question does not occur. We have no report in previous narrative for a special relation. Benjamin is utterly passive. Perhaps he is only a device for the movement of the drama. Perhaps the story could be taken at face value. These are the two valued sons, all that remain from Rachel (46:19). A relation between them might be anticipated on that basis alone. But it is also plausible to suggest that unlike the other brothers, Joseph is not totally fixed on the past. He can think of the future, of the younger one, of the next generation. He is not finally preoccupied with the hurt of his father or even with revenge toward his brothers. He can be attentive to what is yet to come. In subsequent history, as these brothers become tribes, it is Benjamin and Joseph (Ephraim and Mannasseh) (Gen. 49:22–27) who are the new Israel. It is they who shape the memory and receive the future. Perhaps Joseph is presented here as the one who still waits for what God is yet to give.

c. Two speeches transfer Benjamin from Jacob to Joseph, from Palestine to Egypt:

The release of Jacob: El Shaddai grant you mercy *(raḥᵃmîm)* (43:14).

The welcome of Joseph: God be gracious *(ḥānan)* to you, my son (43:29). These are not lines taken at random. The father wishes God's mercy *(raḥᵃmîm)*. The brother wishes that God would be gracious *(ḥānan)*. The two lines together frame the movement of Benjamin from one generation to the next. It is worth noting that the two blessings together, *raḥôm* and *ḥanôn*, comprise a fundamental formula as Israel speaks of Yahweh and his purposes (cf. Exod. 34:6; Neh. 9:17, 31; Pss. 86:15; 103:8; 111:4; 112:4; 145:8; Joel 2:13; Jon. 4:2). Together, these two speeches bestow upon Benjamin the most profound blessing Israel has in its power to give. Together, they anticipate for Benjamin a new history.

4. All of these facets of the family drama are at work as we approach the climax of the narrative. Each facet acts and interacts with the others:

The brothers are *fated,* expecting only retribution from God.

341

The father is deep in *grief,* able to release his young son in faith, but partly in resignation.

The ruling brother is a *cool* practitioner of civil religion, yet he *yearns* for his brother.

And little Benjamin is like a *pawn,* but a pawn with great blessings spoken over him.

The poignancy of this interaction will not be lost on the listening community. Every person and every family knows about these extremities of pain and estrangement in which humanness is at issue. Where yearning and hurt, deception and grief, hope and ruthlessness come together is where this special family moves toward dream fulfillment. But by the end of our verses, *nothing is fully resolved.* The father knows nothing about how it is in Egypt. The brothers know nothing, missing even the hints given in their strange treatment. Benjamin gives no signal that he knows, even though he is especially well treated. And even Joseph cares only that Benjamin is here. He has won a provisional triumph. He gives no hint yet of seeing any larger picture.

The unit ends with everything open. The speech of Judah (44:18–34) is unanswered. The family has gone deeper and deeper into its deathly game. Now Benjamin, the focus of the brothers, of the father and of Joseph, is in jeopardy. The brothers are terrified. The father must wait at a distance. With everything unsettled, only a fear of the evil all this may bring is present at this point in the scene (44:34).

The narrative has its own way. The narrator plots the moves without the consent of the players. The narrative is a proper mode for the movement of the hidden call. The narrator knows that the hidden God moves without the assent or knowledge of any of the players. Thus, there is a congruity between the shrewd way of the narrator and the free way of God who moves behind the scene. God moves on to keep the dream. The human actors make their choices and have freedom in their ways. But through and in spite of such freedom, God is at work. The listening community can only wait, along with the narrator, to see how it will end with the inscrutable way of God and the determined ways of human actors. Waiting must be done, for it is not yet time for disclosure and recognition.

Genesis 45:1–28

The narrative reaches its culmination in 45:1–15. We have waited since chapter 37 to find out about the power of the dream. The dream indirectly has concerned *rule over Egypt.* That has been established in chapters 39—41. The dream has concerned the *rule over father and brothers.* That has been advanced in 42–44. But none of the players is yet aware of the linkage of dream and fruition. In this chapter, we come to the primary resolution of the entire Joseph narrative. Everything before this has pointed to this chapter. After this, everything is derivative. In the chapter itself, our main attention is on verses 1–15. In the remainder of the chapter, the twin themes of *empire* and *family* are played out respectively (vv. 16–20 and vv. 21–28). But these derive from the stunning disclosure of verses 1–15.

The moving appeal of Judah (44:18–34) triggers the disclosure scene. The abrupt disclosure follows appropriately after the eloquent plea. But seen in larger context, not only the speech of Judah but the entire narrative moves toward this moment. The narrative has held off this pivotal disclosure until the last possible instant. Those who have entered into the pathos of this family, a family driven by a dream to conflict and fear, are now prepared for the turn. In a single artistic moment, the entire plot is made visible. In this scene, the plot is larger than every player, including Joseph.

The Crucial Disclosure

We may first consider the particular rhetorical cast of verses 1–8, the key verses of this chapter. In this critical scene, the disclosure is for the family, not the empire. The controlling agenda is the way this family is governed by a dream and the way this family chafes against that dream (cf. Acts 26:14–19). What is revealed here is not for the eyes of the empire. The listening community is not asked by the narrator to leave the room with the empire (45:1) but is invited to stay with the family. We are permitted to witness a gospel disclosure: The

343

dead one is alive! The abandoned one has returned in power! The dream has had its way!

1. Three rhetorical matters shape the disclosure.

a. First in verse 3 and more fully in verse 4, the dead-one-now-alive discloses his identity: "I am Joseph." This is a standard formula of self-disclosure used even by God (cf. Isa. 41:4; 44:6; 45:6). Perhaps it is a royal form of self-proclamation. It is obviously more than an introduction. It is a self-assertion which serves to reshape and redefine the entire situation. The key fact in the life of this family is that they must live now with the reality of a live, powerful, ruling Joseph. There is something going on which the brothers had long since disposed of (or so they thought). The terror and astonishment of the brothers (v. 3) is not unlike that of the early church with the disclosure of the live Jesus (Mark 16:8). The family is suddenly set in a new context. Their presumed world has been irreversibly shattered.

They had yet to discover that this assertion was a complete break with the past. They feared that the live Joseph would exploit and act out the past. (Joseph's trickery in chapters 42—44 would support such an expectation.) But Joseph does not. He breaks with that past. He invites his brothers to put that pitiful past behind them. (In 50:17, it is evident that they have not been able to do so.) Joseph opens to them another future. His self-announcement in regal language is a beginning with new possibility. The new possibility does not come from anything done by the brothers. It is, rather, a gift wrapped in the speech of their brother.

b. The second rhetorical device (vv. 3b-5) derives from the juxtaposition of lament and salvation oracle. That form consists in a first statement of trouble (here "dismay"), which is followed by a response. And the response characteristically begins, "do not fear," followed by an announcement of graciousness. The form begins (v. 3) as the brothers are "alarmed," as well they might be. Their past puts them in grave danger. The wrath of their now powerful brother is imminent. But the response of Joseph is not the expected one. Instead of a response that depends on the past estrangement, his fresh speech concerns something new: Do not be dismayed, ... Do not be angry with yourselves (cf. Deut. 20:3; Isa. 41:10, 13, 14). . . . for God sent me. . . . There is nothing explicit here about forgiveness or reconciliation. The narrative is too terse for that.

The substance matches the artistic power of the story. The narrative asserts that Joseph can speak a word which creates newness. That is why 45:1–15 is structurally at the center of the entire Joseph narrative. In this speech of Joseph, the power of the conspiracy of chapter 37 is broken. The break with that awful deed comes in this lordly speech. But this regal speech is based on the flood of passion discerned in 44:30; 45:1, 14–15. Joseph's speech is filled with passion. There is as much at stake for him as for the brothers and the father.

In his power to speak a future, Joseph does not abandon his royal role. This speaker is not the typical Egyptian court figure. He is portrayed as a deeply human person who is impacted and transformed by his brothers. The family bond is deep for Joseph, deeper than Egyptian success. Clearly, Joseph cannot resolve the family brokenness by a regal Egyptian act of *sovereignty*. It requires an act of Israelite *passion*, an act of *salvation*. Luther has observed that when this brother announces himself, he uses no Egyptian throne name (cf. 41: 45) but his own family name. He identifies himself as Joseph, the one "added" by God, the surplus of meaning and joy and hope given to this family of faith. The point is a central one in biblical faith: The power to create newness does not come from detachment, but from risky, self-disclosing engagement. Joseph's speech pattern echoes the speech of Yahweh elsewhere, as in the salvation oracles of II Isaiah (cf. Isa. 41:9–13; 44:1–5).

c. But it is the third element which is crucial. The announcement of verses 5*b*–8 provides a basis for the salvation assurance (v. 5*a*). The basis is characteristically introduced with "for" and a motivational clause (cf. Jer. 31:1–11; Isa. 43:-1). Now the narrator has Joseph make the main point. He makes it three times in a formula of commission: (1) "God sent me to preserve life" (v. 5*b*). (2) "God sent me before you to preserve for you a remnant" (v. 7). (3) "It was not you who sent me, but God; and he has made me father . . . and lord . . . and ruler . . ." (v. 8). This is the key speech in the entire Joseph narrative. Perhaps Joseph has kept this to himself until now. More likely, Joseph did not know either. We have not had a hint before now that Joseph had any notion of being a part of God's purpose. The revelation breaks as news upon the entire family. The news is abrupt in a narrative that has been shaped in a quite secular way. This speech completely redefines the situation for all parties. Now the *guilty fear* of the brothers is superseded. The *grief* of the father is resolved. He had grieved unnecessarily, for what seemed death was God's

345

way to life. The *revengeful cunning* of the successful brother is superseded. He has no need to triumph over his family. The *guilt* of the brothers, the *grief* of the father, and the *revenge* of Joseph are all used as means for this disclosure of the hidden call of God. None of that matters now, for the whole family is now brought to a new moment.

The purposes of God have been at work "in, with, and under" these sordid human actions. In this threefold statement of God's purposes (vv. 5–8), the first two concern a future for Israel. They announce unambiguously that God wills and works life for this people. The technical terms "remnant" and "survivors" are an assurance of a future against heavy odds. The third statement (v. 8) turns to the empire. Again, the twin themes of family and empire have been brought together. And the culminating word is "ruler." It has been the crucial word since the dream (37:8). The use of the word marks an arc of continuity from 37:7–10 until 45:8. Joseph was dreamed to be a ruler. Now he is a "ruler-lord-father," not just over the family, but over the empire. And it is the work of God. No one could stop it. And no one else can be credited with it. Although critical data suggest that this is a secular story, a wisdom tale or the account of a royal courtier, here the story is claimed for explicit theological purposes. The secular narrative of Israel is a context in which the God of Israel works out his purpose.

2. The narrative now hinges on the conviction that God is free. He is at work for his purpose in spite of, through, and against every human effort. Such a reading collides with any easy *humanism.* It also collides with a kind of *supernaturalism* which wants to distinguish between God's work and human work. Against such humanism which separates God's work and ours, this narrative affirms that the arena of human choice is precisely where God's saving work is done. Barth has articulated the mystery in this way:

> God accompanies the creature. This means that He affirms and approves and recognizes and respects the autonomous actuality and therefore the autonomous activity of the creature as such. He does not play the part of a tyrant toward it. . . . He loves the creature, that He genuinely recognizes and affirms it for what it is in itself and what it does by itself, that He does not annihilate it for the first time reveals its true nature. . . . It is not, then, the creature which works in God's working, but God himself who works on and in His own working (Barth, *Church Dogmatics,* III, pp. 3, 92, 94, 111).

Thus Barth states the dialectical reality that God does his own work and at the same time fully honors the work of his creatures. So it is with Joseph and his brothers. They did their free work. But in the end, it was God at work in their work who brought life (cf. Phil. 2:12–13). On this point, Barth appeals to Rom. 11:36:

> For from him and through him and to him are all things. To him be glory for ever. Amen.

In Joseph's self-disclosure (vv. 5–8), we are at the center of a great faith affirmation. Neither the *freedom of the creature* nor the *gracious sovereignty of God* is canceled. They are not in conflict, nor are they to be equated. God's will makes use of all human action but is domesticated or limited by no human choice.

Earlier reference (p. 292) has been made to Von Rad's disputed placement of the Solomonic achievement in ancient Israel in a context of human success, security, and achievement. While that cannot be demonstrated, such a possibility suggests that the narrative intends to refute the proud notion that human persons can autonomously choose and manage their own futures. It asserts that in the face of arrogant and strident ingenuity, the Eternal Spirit has his own purpose. And even if delayed, that purpose will not be defeated.

3. Such claims of God's sovereignty are alien to the mood and ethos of our culture. The main claims of this text are a scandal:

a. The narrative asserts that God's purpose is *finally sovereign.* It will not be questioned or altered. It may be held in abeyance, but it works with and through every human action. It makes use even of the dark side of human action and planning.

b. The sovereign character of God's purpose can *create a real newness,* a Genesis, an unextrapolated freshness which negates the past, redefines the present, and opens futures. It is that sovereign quality which permits the family of Jacob to begin again. In our time, where conflicts have raged so deeply, so long (e.g., Northern Ireland, Palestine, South Africa), we find it hard to believe in the possibility of newness. The future seems only a replay of the past. But this narrative makes a tenacious counter-affirmation.

c. The narrative asserts that God's purpose is *utterly gra-*

347

cious. The commission formula of verses 5, 7 affirms "for life" (cf. John 10:10). The premise of Israel's faith is that Yahweh wills life for his people. God is remarkably resourceful against every threat of death (cf. Amos 5:4, 6; Ezek. 18:32). No more than Joseph may the listening community abandon our role in life-giving. But our efforts to seek, clutch, and even "create" life too often ignore God's gracious, singular, and sovereign way with life.

d. The narrative affirms that God's purpose is *hidden and mysterious.* It is hidden so that no participant in the story has a clue about it until now. The purpose does not depend on human resolve or willingness. There is no hint about how it happens. At the crucial turns, the narrative moves abruptly and tersely, refusing to reflect on cause or method. That is why *story* is the proper mode for this faith. It never lingers to explain but only recites and retells for the wonder found in the telling. It does not linger in Gen. 1—2 over the miracle of creation. It does not linger in Gen. 18:1–15 over the way of the new birth. It does not linger over the gift of rain (I Kings 18:41–46). It does not linger over the way a blind man sees (John 9). It does not linger over the amazement of Easter (Mark 16:1–8). Biblical faith affirms and moves on, even when we would pause to analyze and explain. It will linger to relish and discern the wonder, but never to explain.

e. The narrative affirms, at the same time, that God's purposes are worked out *in concrete history* through the actions of identifiable persons. The giving of life to the family may have been willed from eternity by God. But it is in the life of Joseph, spoiled boy become ruler, that the way of God is accomplished.

4. This text (and derivatively, the entire Joseph narrative) presses our exposition toward the theme of divine providence. The ways of God in this narrative are subdued and invisible. Yet they are decisive. The decisiveness of God is not expressed here with active verbs or in terms of great interventions. It is a mode of faith which is more delicate to articulate and not as blatantly satisfying as "mighty deeds." And yet it is an important dimension of the biblical claim. The same mode of faith is especially evident in the Isaiah tradition.

348

a. In Isa. 9:7, after the visionary promise of a new king and a new power arrangement, perhaps dismantling the Assyrians, the poem ends defiantly: "The zeal of the LORD of hosts will do this!" Yet God does not act. He only proposes.

b. More programmatically, Isa. 14:24–27 asserts God's will and ends with a note of near stridency:

The LORD of hosts has sworn:
"As I have planned, so shall it be,
and as I have purposed, so shall it stand, ...
For the Lord of hosts has purposed,
and who will annul it?
His hand is stretched out,
and who will turn it back?"

c. More familiarly, Isa. 55:8–9 affirms the ways of God which fit none of our preconceptions:

For my thoughts are not your thoughts,
neither are your ways my ways, says the LORD . . .
so are my ways higher than your ways
and my thoughts than your thoughts.

An affirmation like that is not for understanding—by Joseph who speaks it, the brothers who hear it, or the listening community which now claims it. It is a new context in which to live. It is not for understanding but for doxology. The narrative is offered so that the listening community can sing with the generations:

The love of God planned my salvation,
before I saw the light of day,
And took away the law's damnation,
of him whose feet had gone astray;
God's love is mine, O blessed mortal!
It opens wide the heavenly portal
("I Sing the Praise," Gerhard Tersteegen).

The main decisions were made "before I saw the light of day." Yet this disclosure of the sovereign, gracious purpose of God for life does not lead to inactivity or abdication on the part of Joseph. It leads to action.

5. And so this man who is sent by God issues commands (vv. 9–13). His commands have the tone of one who has become "father-lord-ruler" of the empire. His command is enveloped by "make haste" (v. 9) at the beginning and by the same verb (v. 13) at the end. The well-being of Egypt is available to this family. The family which has been on the brink of starving has its fortunes sharply reversed. Now it has a royal provider (v. 11). The family can count on this one who is "glorified" in Egypt (v. 13). Joseph fills the role of provider, for that is the way of the story. But it is known by all parties that the real provider is the

349

hidden One (cf. 22:8, 14). The family is bound to this discreetly providential life-giver.

The Empire Mobilized; the Father Summoned

The remainder of this chapter (vv. 16–20, 21–28) explores the implications of the new world made available to this family.

1. Joseph's plan receives imperial sanction (vv. 16–20). It is more than we might have expected. The storehouses and abundance of Egypt are placed at the disposal of Israel.

The *empire* has been opened for the sake of this *family*. For now the last ones have become the first ones. How could it be that the empire should give so much to these nobodies? As recently as 43:32, they could not even eat at the same table. We are not told why this shift comes in Egyptian treatment. We only know that the "best" of the land is now for Israel (v. 20). The poverty-stricken, hunger-ridden people now are richly blessed. This is a startling fulfillment of the gospel promise about feeding:

> Blessed are you that hunger now, for you shall be satisfied (Luke 6:21).

> Therefore I tell you, do not be anxious about your life, what you shall eat or what you shall drink, nor about your body . . . (Matt. 6:25).

> He has filled the hungry with good things,
>   and the rich he has sent empty away (Luke 1:53).

Such an eventuality is not to be explained. Undoubtedly, reasons of imperial policy could be found to justify such actions by Pharaoh. But that misses the point. It is a gift from God. That God has chosen to bless this family is the single ground for the new imperial posture (cf. 12:2–3).

2. The other development from verses 1–15 is the report back to father Jacob (vv. 21–28). Jacob is as moved and passionate in his reception of good news as he has been in grief (cf. 37:32–35; 42:36–38; 44:31–32). Initially, the news is too abrupt for the old man. He cannot believe the impossibility of death become life. But then he does believe. His own life threatened by heart attack (v. 26), Jacob is transformed to new vitality as he grasps the news. For what other word does a father ever want to hear except, "My son is alive"? In Jesus' most telling parable (Luke 15:11–32), the supreme cause for a party in heaven or on earth is the inversion that celebrates the new life

350

of the dead son. Jacob's news concerning Joseph is a paradigm for the resurrection faith of the New Testament. It is only by the power of God that Joseph is alive. The gospel announcement (45:21–28) is that the dead one lives. By God's grace, Jacob's deep sorrow turns now to still deeper joy (cf. John 16:21–22).

Jacob speaks as a father. But he is not just any father. He speaks as the voice of the whole family of promise (v. 28). He has been waiting all this time in grief and anxiety. He has waited to know how his lost son could bear his promise. But he speaks now as one assured that the promise is intact, that the future is assured to a new generation. The family dimension of the disclosure is completed with the words: "It is enough" (v. 28). The word *rab* (RSV "enough") could be rendered "sufficient" or "abundant." What a word to end on! This old man has hungered all his life for an heir, for none of the other eleven can substitute for Joseph. And he has been a victim of deathly deception. But now he has this crowning moment: Abundance! He has not yet seen and touched. But he knows. His "cup runs over" (Ps. 23:5). And his world is changed. He knows what it means to affirm that "our sufficiency is from God" (II Cor. 3:5). The listening community is invited to share in the unqualified joy of this father for whom the future is now open. Jacob's joy lets this powerful scene of disclosure end as a doxology. The scene gives moving witness that

> The LORD upholds all who are falling,
> and raises up all who are bowed down (Ps. 145:14).

The journey Jacob now undertakes is like that of the shepherds who must also go to "see this thing that has happened, which the Lord has made known to us" (Luke 2:15). Like them (Luke 2:16), Jacob also goes "in haste." And like them, he sees for himself the "birth" of a son. God's hidden, determined work not only assures food from Pharaoh to the family. It also brings life to this hopeless father.

Genesis 46:1—47:31

351

The primary dramatic conclusion of the Joseph narrative is reached in 45:1–8. The remaining materials of chapters 46—50 settle issues between the generations. Thus with a look to the *past,* there must be the settlement of Jacob in Egypt, with his death and burial. In a look to the *future,* there must be blessing for the generations to come. Chapters 46—47 address those outstanding matters. These chapters contain a collection of diverse materials reflecting on the two themes, *Joseph and his family* and *Joseph and the empire.* The materials have a miscellaneous quality about them. There does not seem to be any artistic effort at coherence. The power of sustained narrative is largely exhausted by the end of chapter 45. Because these verses seem to be a collection of incidental elements, there may not be any intentional overall structure. Thus we will deal with it according to three themes: *(a)* The *family theme* concerned with Jacob (46:1–7; 47:7–12; 47:27–31); *(b)* The *imperial theme* (47:13–26); *(c)* The *tension* between the family and the empire (46:28—47:6). In relation to these three themes, we shall see, respectively, that *Jacob* functions as the mouthpiece for the promise tradition, *Joseph* demonstrates again his mastery of the Egyptian enterprise, and that *the brothers* are thrust into a dilemma between the faith of the fathers and the success of the "dream brother" with the accompanying temptations of the empire.

(Our discussion will not be concerned with the genealogy of 46:8–27 which presents a list of all of those who went down into Egypt. A few brief remarks here will suffice. The list in vv. 8–25 has a highly structured and stylized view of Israel, organizing the sons of Jacob into tribes [cf. 35:22*b*–26]. Two matters are worth noting in the section. First, Rachel's two sons are listed as a separate entity [v. 19]. Second, the number of seventy persons is taken as a concrete number with specific factors noted [vv. 26–27]. Elsewhere, the number is treated in a more stylized fashion to indicate that the vast people ["as many as the sands of the sea," "as the stars of the heavens"] came from a small group, by the mercies of God [Deut. 10:22; cf. Ezek. 33:24; Acts 7:14]. But that theological function of the number seems to be operative here.)

Family Narratives Concerning Jacob

352

The narratives concerning Jacob form the framework of these two chapters. At the beginning (46:1–7), there is a theophany authorizing his sojourn into Egypt. At the end

(47:27–31), there is closure to his life with provision for his burial. Set between these is one other Jacob episode, the encounter with Pharaoh (47:7–12). In contrast to the narrative of chapters 37—45, these chapters are little concerned with Joseph and focus on Israel (=Jacob) in Egypt. They seem already to be looking toward the Book of Exodus.

1. The theophany (46:1–4) and the corresponding sojourn narrative (46:5–7) turn the focus from Joseph to Israel.

a. The report of the theophany follows the stylized form of summons (v. 2*a*), answer (v. 2*b*), and assurance (vv. 3–4). As is characteristic of such reports, the emphasis of the report is not on the *appearance* of the deity but on the *promise* made (cf. 35:9–12). This narrative is placed here to assert that the old promises of Genesis 12—36 are still operative. God still vouches for them. Going to Egypt, that is, leaving the land of promise, does not jeopardize the promise. John Skinner sees this permission to leave the land as an intentional counterpart to 12:1f. and the permission to reenter it (cf. 31:13; *A Critical and Exegetical Commentary on Genesis,* 1930, p. 491).

b. The specific language of "great nation" (v. 3) of course echoes the earlier promise (12:2; 18:18). The Joseph narrative (which, as we have said [p. 289] no doubt had a very different kind of origin in tradition) is here claimed for and pressed into the service of the old promises. While the passage is brief and laconic, it serves to stamp the narrative as one of promise. The call of God to this people, hidden as it is with Joseph, is a call to trust the promise. It is for a blessed future of well-being that everything in the present must be faced. It is the promise of God which circumscribes the fears of Jacob and sanctions the journey.

c. It may be an important expository point that the only report of theophany and promise in the Joseph narrative is made this late and then not at all to Joseph. At no point in the narrative is Joseph confronted in such a way. Two expository possibilities arise from that observation.

1) It is likely that the difference reflects the different types of *literature.* The Jacob stories, including this one, belong to the old saga tradition in which theophanies and explicit promises from God are not unusual. In contrast, the Joseph material reflects a much more urbane and sophisticated religious perspective (which is not to say superior) in which nothing so direct

353

ever happens. The dream report is as close as the Joseph narrative comes to theophany. But even that is not explicitly linked to God.

2) The texture of the two men presented in the two traditions is very different. As the artist portrays him, Joseph is most characteristically a cool, reserved person of power from whom religious passion is remote. This is in contrast to his father, who has lived a passion-filled life. The placement of 46:1–7 in the midst of the Joseph narrative suggests a theological incongruity. Perhaps the contrast intends to show the discontinuity between the generations and yet suggests that the old tradition of *passion* and the newer mode of *coolness* both testify to the same realities.

d. The subsequent journey (vv. 5–7) is one of triumph and well-being. The movement is presented as a public procession as guests of Pharaoh. The narrative is not explicit but hints that Egypt is mobilized for the comfort and safety of Israel.

2. The second Jacob episode in this unit is 47:7–12. Jacob is presented to Pharaoh. The text offers a dramatic meeting between *the Lord of Egypt* and *the father of promise*. The two have only Joseph in common. The confrontation is between two ways of life: one embodies what is secure, royal and condescending; the other a way that is precarious, unstable and perhaps supplicating. Though we are generations away from the Exodus reckoned by the memory of Israel, in the shaping of the literature, the meeting of Pharaoh and Jacob is only three pages away from the Exodus. Any Israelite who hears this story will not be unaware of the realities of oppression and liberation which are soon to come. This narrative is skillfully set so that Jacob quietly has the better part. At the beginning (v. 7) and at the end (v. 10), it is Jacob who blesses Pharaoh. Israel blesses Egypt. This could be no more than a conventional, *pro forma* greeting. Or it could be deference to an old man. But in this context, neither is likely. The reference is surely to the powerful gift entrusted to this family which the empire needs and does not have (cf. 39:5). As Wolff has shown, the narrative affirms that every other people waits on the blessing entrusted to this family ("The Kerygma of the Yahwist," *Interpretation* 20:131–58 [1966]). The empire has need of Jacob and his family. This claim is not lost on the later generations who hear this story through the prism of the Exodus (cf. Exod. 12:32).

The exchange between the father and the Pharaoh is telling. Pharaoh is engaged in chitchat. But Jacob seizes his casual question to characterize his existence as one of sojourning (v. 9). He does not mean a noble religious pilgrimage but a precarious landless existence (cf. Deut. 26:5). His family has lacked land to call its own. But it has never doubted the promise of land to come (cf. 17:8; 28:4; 37:1; Heb. 11:8–22). The posture of the two men is sharply contrasted. Pharaoh has land. He is settled, safe, and prosperous. Jacob has none. But he believes the promise far beyond any Egyptian realities. Now Jacob is before Pharaoh. But in fact, it is the promise-bearer who holds court. As a result, the land of Pharoah is at the disposal of Jacob (vv. 11–12). The promise is at work for this family, in Egypt as in Canaan.

3. The third Jacob section of this unit concerns the death of Jacob and the transmission of the promise to the coming generation (47:27–31). The text affirms Israel has been blessed (v. 27). Jacob's age is given (v. 28; cf. v. 9). Though he earlier says his days are few, the longevity of Jacob is surely a measure of blessing. The main point is the promise evoked from Joseph that Jacob will be properly buried in Hebron (cf. 25:9–10; 35:27–29). This may be simply a burial note. And yet the narrator is especially attentive to it. The paragraph balances 46:1–4. In that unit, Jacob did not want to jeopardize the promise by leaving the land. He does not leave without the sanction given in the theophany. Now (47:27–31), he wants to embody his ultimate commitment to the land of promise even in his death. Jacob is doggedly fixed on the land. He knows he is a child of the promise. And he will not permit any imperial attractions in Goshen to turn his head from the promise. He will not be seduced into Egypt. He will be *in* Egypt, but not *of* Egypt (cf. John 17:16–17). He can wait. He has waited a lifetime. Now he can wait in the time of his death, for he knows his heirs. He is not of some "now-generation" which cannot wait. The absence of such faithful patience renders persons more open to seduction, more likely to be turned to the attractions of Egypt. Faithful waiting, even beyond a lifetime, provides standing ground for the true promise against all the false alternatives.

4. The theme of *Joseph's family* is expressed in three units centered on father Jacob. The intent is to make clear that Goshen is not Israel's home and can never be. While Goshen may provide a resting place, it is not the end of the story. It is a place for a "genesis" but not a fulfillment. True sojourners must be prepared, after the well-being of Genesis, to look to the

355

oppression and liberation of Exodus. The three Jacob incidents look beyond the patriarchs to Moses.

Joseph and the Empire

The other major motif in these chapters is Joseph and the empire. The narrative of 47:13–26 is interwoven with the Jacob materials but has no relation to them. The family theme is absent in these verses. Attention is given to the shrewdness of Joseph and his devotion to the cause of Pharaoh. Joseph is ready to exploit the family in order to enhance the holdings of the crown (cf. 41:46–49, 53–57). The text originally may have reflected a revision of the tax and tenant system. But now its function is to show the prowess of Joseph the administrator. The theme is picked up from chapter 41. As always, Joseph is not a disinterested person.

Joseph's shrewdness shows that entering the world of the empire brings dangers with it. The Egyptian empire offers food and therefore life. But it is never far from exploitation, oppression, and slavery. As though to set the stage for the Exodus, the result of Joseph's tax reform is that citizens sell their persons to the throne (contrast Lev. 25:35–55). They become bond servants and forfeit their freedom. Joseph may be credited with shrewdness. But for a tradition looking to the Exodus, it is a doubtful credit. Joseph plays both sides of the street, family and empire. Perhaps he is not always clear on which side of the street he belongs. It is enough to note that the *reserves of food* are also potential *sources of oppression* (cf. Exod. 16:2–3; Deut. 8:3; I Kings 4:20–28; Mark 8:15). The tightly administered program of this text is not far removed from the imperial policies of Exod. 5:5–19. Questions might usefully be raised about the ways in which a vast economic apparatus keeps its promises and what the costs and hazards are. The people of promise might ask if there are alternatives to imperial modes of nourishment (cf. Mark 8:15; John 6:35).

Empire and Family

The interface of family and empire is a delicate one. That is evident in the remaining portion of these chapters (46:28– 47:6). In this text, Joseph plays the other side of the street. He helps his brothers engage in a subterfuge against Pharaoh. (There is an odd confusion in the matter. In 46:33–34, the brothers are explicitly advised to avoid the mention of shepherds before Pharaoh, for shepherds are anathema to the Egyptians. Yet when asked [47:3], they respond directly with the very information against which they had been warned. The text makes nothing of this strange behavior by the brothers, nor can we.) The deception urged by Joseph is not pursued by the brothers. For whatever reason, the conclusion is a happy one. They receive the best land and an offer to occupy positions of influence in Egypt (47:6). But even in that generous grant, there is an urging to join the throne, to be "princes of cattle" (v. 6). The grant has a price. It is to join the royal world. It is an irony worth noting that Egyptians suffer in their survival as slaves, Israel pays for its royal position. Either way, economics puts persons in danger. While the narrative moves to this satisfying conclusion, there is within the settlement a deep tension. The brothers are not children of the empire. They are left to deal with the relation of the promise to Israel and to the royal power (cf. Mark 12:13–17).

The Unresolved Dilemma of Joseph's Family

This section of the text (46:1—47:31) is disjointed and probably not too much should be made of the material. Nonetheless, the presentation seems to offer a model for how it is with the faith of this family. Joseph is placed in a most problematic situation, between the deep hopes of his father and the heavy demands of Pharaoh, that is, between the buoyancy of the tradition and the pressure of the empire. And that is where he must live his life.

Joseph plays his royal role, administering land and preempting more, even granting to Israel a *possession* (47:11). The family called to *sojourn* now *possesses!* Jacob is a contrast to his son. He yearns not for land but for his son (46:28–30), and that is enough. He is not a man of *possession* but of *promise*. His land-yearning is that the promise should be honored in death as in life. The father stands as a reminder against the sons concerning the attraction of Egypt. Perhaps Jacob could have benefited more fully from the gifts of Egypt, but only at the price of the promise. So the contrast is sharply set. *Pharaoh* is the one who possesses everything and assigns possessions (47:6). *Jacob* had earlier sought possessions in the world of Laban. But in his seasoned old age, he trusts the promise more. And *Joseph* continues his characteristic juggling act, trying to have it both ways. Before this text (45) and after this text (48—50), he is

357

faithful to father Jacob. But in this unit of 46—47, he faces both ways. His game is a chancy one. How far can one play the imperial game, for the sake of the promise, before the promise is crushed by the force of the empire?

From that question, it is interesting to speculate on the move from Genesis to Exodus. What all is hidden in the phrase, "a new king who did not know Joseph" (Exod. 1:8)? Was the fault in the new Pharaoh who could not discern Joseph's peculiar identity? Or might it be that the colors of Joseph had become so unclear and ambiguous that to the new Pharaoh he looked like every other royal administrator?

Perhaps the turn toward oppression reflected in Exod. 1 can be credited not only to Pharaoh, as is conventional. Perhaps the turn is partly based on the compromising way of Israel after the lead of Joseph, who played the royal game and forgot the promise. Pharaoh could hardly be expected to honor a peculiar identity if Israel itself did not take it with singular seriousness. We do not know. But it is clear that Joseph's Israel lived dangerously near the brink of Egyptianization. As the narrative approaches its conclusion, the promise remains intact. But it is in jeopardy from compromise. The old man died steady in the promise. Yet the son has experienced something of the imperial alternative. The choices are subtle and not made all at once. The outcome is uncertain. Could it be that the subtle tempting of Gen. 3:1-7 is again at work on God's special creature?

Genesis 48:1—50:14

The drama of the ancestral story moves to its completion. After the primary disclosure of 45:1-8, we have given attention to the tradition which tells of Jacob and his sons being securely settled in Egypt (46:1—47:31). There the focus was on new life —Jacob is found; the family is fed. Now it is death time. This section also contains diverse materials. But they are all narratives about Jacob and his family facing death.

358

These materials may be useful to the listening community of our own time in facing the problem of death. Modernity would rob us of the capacity to face death faithfully. The collapse of tradition and memory, of community and hope, has made death an acutely private crisis for which individual persons lack resources. As Robert J. Lifton has shown, we have experienced a collapse of faithful language *(Living and Dying,* 1974, pp. 31f., 97, 137 and *passim).* We have no symbols sufficient for our experiences. The power-laden words of religious tradition have been flattened or replaced by one-dimensional profane language. As a result, we have no symbols with which to speak about transcendent meaning related to the reality of death. These materials in 48:1—50:14 indicate how death is faced in this sojourning family which trusts the promise.

As we have grouped the materials, there are three unrelated texts connected only by the common theme of Jacob's death: *(a)* a prose account of the blessing for the next generation (48:1–22); *(b)* a general blessing in poetry for all the songs of Jacob (49:1–27); and *(c)* a narrative about the provisions for the death and burial of Jacob (49:28—50:14). We will deal with each of these in turn.

A Blessing for the Coming Generation (48:1–22)

Jacob's death raises questions about continuity between the generations.

1. A programmatic restatement of the blessing which binds this moment to Abraham and Isaac before him is offered in Gen. 48:3–4. Every generation in this family has had to depend on the promise. But Jacob more than any other has relied on the promise during his life of conflict. He has found the promise did not fail. This review (vv. 3–4) looks back especially to 35:11–12. It contains *(a)* an appeal to the God of the Israelite tradition who is an outsider in Egypt (48:3); *(b)* reference to blessing as the characteristic way of this God's action (v. 3); *(c)* the substance of the blessing as fruitfulness and multiplication (v. 4); and *(d)* the assurance of an enduring land (v. 4). That is the rootage from which Jacob comes as he turns back to his fathers. On that statement, everything hangs for this family. Nothing may be added to it. And one cannot get behind it to any other assurance. Each new generation must decide to trust in this promise.

Jacob offers this statement at a crucial juncture in the history of the people. It is placed just between Genesis and Exodus. Joseph has been tilted toward Egypt, but the blessing serves to separate sharply Israel's inheritance from all things Egyptian. The father will have no limping along on both opinions, as

Joseph may be inclined to do (I Kings 18:21). The next generation cannot for very long hold both to Egyptian land and yearn for another. Calvin states it well in suggesting that the family is called to "bid farewell to Egypt" because they "could not be reckoned among the progeny of Abraham without rendering themselves detested by the Egyptians" (cf. John 15:19; Exod. 1:8). Jacob calls his son to trust the promise and only the promise. Jacob's insistence was prefigured in his meeting with Pharaoh when he reasserted his destiny as a sojourner (47:7–12). In the same way, the blessing may be embraced by the next generation. But it requires a decision, a disengagement (cf. Josh. 24:14–15). The embrace requires a renunciation (cf. 35:1–4), for the promise will have no "half-heirs."

2. Jacob's purpose is to claim the next generation for this way of life and this reading of reality (vv. 5–6). The purpose of these verses is to turn the *memory* of verses 3–4 into a *hope*. The focus is not on the word already spoken but on a promise still to be kept. It is the way of Egypt (and of every kingdom of this world) to abolish the future for an uncriticized present. But Jacob and his faithful children will not abandon the future. They insist on *God's future* which places every *Egyptian present* into question. Perhaps the coming generations will value the Egyptian present. But the old man still hopes. His head has not been turned. He continues to grieve over Rachel (v. 7; cf. 35:16–21), and it is that very grief which becomes the source of hope. He grieves enough to expect something new. His final task before death is to see that hope continues to be the main business of his family. For Jacob, the capacity to hope has made him persistently a man of conflict. That is the nature of this promise. He wishes nothing other than this for his heirs. He knows that when they believe the promise, they will be in conflict with present reality, even as they are blessed with hope.

3. The blessing is a baptism into hope. Jacob is a man continually surprised by the power the blessing has for him. He has lived so many years with the mistaken notion of Joseph's death. And now, at the last moment, he is not only with Joseph (cf. 45:28; 46:28–29) but with the sons of Joseph as well. These young sons mark the culmination of this life of pathos and hope. Jacob can imagine no one-generational existence. From the beginning, he has lived for the generation to come. His task now is not only to bind the generations together. It is not enough that the young ones be bound to and loyal to Jacob. For he will

360

die. He intends to bind the generation to the promise. The promise is more powerful and enduring than any generation. The role of this parent and every parent in this family is to keep the promise visible and articulate for the young ones. In baptism, we speak almost glibly of becoming "children of the promise." But that is who we are. The promise is not a fuzzy, optimistic feeling about the future. It is a concrete assurance about being heirs to a new kingdom yet to be given (cf. Rev. 11:15). Thus far, the family has had hints and foretastes of blessing. But full blessing in the land is still to come.

a. This family has begun in blessing (12:1–3). Now, the blessing is on the move again (vv. 8–14). The blessing has been kept alive for such focal moments as this. It is a high and solemn moment. The words have not grown wooden or mechanical. The solemnity is for those moments when memories are turned to hope. The laden moment depends on a powerful touch, on hands laid on, on transmission from bone to bone, from flesh to flesh. The scene is one of high drama. Joseph seems to let go of his sons as if he were saying good-bye to them (v. 10). Jacob is deeply moved. The grandsons are a sign of how richly he is blessed beyond every expectation (v. 11). If there were any Egyptians watching, it must have seemed ludicrous. Such sacramental, symbolic acts must always appear absurd to the empire. Egypt is accustomed to *grasping* land and having it quickly. But when one *waits* for the land as Israel does, there is no way to force the issue. One must only wait. Blessings are for waiting. Laying on of hands is for hoping. The grandsons cannot receive more than that. The grandfather cannot give more than that. And it does not matter if the empire cannot understand.

b. The substance of the blessing (vv. 15–16, 20) provides a crowning summary of ancestral faith. It may well be a quite old statement. Its content is as close to a credo as this tradition comes. It is completely focused on God. Thus, four times:

> The God before whom . . . (v. 15)
> The God who . . . (v. 15)
> The angel who . . . (v. 16)
> God make you . . . (v. 20).

361

The One who is the subject of this sacrament of hope is the One who has been with and for this family and has never been found wanting. Jacob may allude to Abraham and Isaac. But even that depends on and is sanctioned only by trust in this God. The blessing given here concerns the One on whom Jacob relied, with whom he has wrestled and by whom he has been kept and surprised (28:15; 32:25–30).

1) The verbs describing God's actions are decisive: "walked," "led," "redeemed," and "make." Jacob affirms this one who has *led.* The word covers so much. The metaphor is that of shepherd, who has protected him "through many trials and snares." But the word can also be rendered as the one who "fed" me, who nourished. We have seen this motif in the narrative (pp. 349–350). The term "redeem," of course serves as an anticipation of the Exodus narrative.

2) The third mention of God (v. 16) is by way of angel, an alternative way to refer to God. The angel is the one who came strangely to Sarah and Abraham about an "heir" (18:1–15). Perhaps it is the one with whom Jacob wrestled, God come near (32:22–32). It may be that this line of the blessing is best interpreted by Ps. 103, for the son as well as the father understands, "he redeems my life from the pit" (Ps. 103:4; cf. Gen. 37:29).

3) The words tumble out of the mouth of the old man. The metaphors move swiftly. The blessing summarizes the whole story of the God who endures and intrudes, who sustains and inverts, who makes the whole way of Israel a way of life. At this point in the strange venture now spanning three generations, Jacob's last act is to bind his grandsons to the precious promised way of reality. It is a way about which Joseph has vacillated, a way of which Egypt understands nothing. But now a fourth and fifth generation have been blessed into the way of promise.

The young boys may have wondered about this strange act. Does it matter? Could it possibly matter in the context of the empire? And the narrative simply affirms: Of course it matters. It has always made a difference for this family. For this family at this time, there are only these words and gestures. That is all there is to keep this family in the way of hope. Such words and gestures are naïve and fragile, precarious against the empire. But this history of hope is always precarious. The old man has learned that it is enough (cf. 45:28). The listening community will find it enough as well, if we attend to it.

362   4. Finally, we come to the center of the narrative (vv. 17–19). Only now is the intent of the episode apparent. In the midst of this remarkably solemn drama, Joseph spots an incredible mistake. It is like using the wrong name at a baptism or

having the wrong grave at the cemetery. Joseph must violate protocol and interrupt his father. Joseph had carefully arranged his two sons to get the proper blessings. He had placed Manasseh on his left so that, facing the other way, the old man would put his right hand on the son on the left. And conversely, the left hand was for the boy on the right, the younger one.

a. But the text says, "crossing his hands" (v. 14)! Why had Jacob done that? Because he was old and could not see better? Because he was an unredeemable trickster who remembered his own blessing (27:18–40) and only continued the scandal? Or is the narrative this way because of an *ex post facto* awareness of the domination of the other tribe in the history of all the tribes? All these reasons have some cogency to the detached observer who seeks an explanation. But the expositor is not permitted to explain things. The narrative itself refuses to explain. It only tells and leaves it there. In the bounds of the story itself, there is no reasonable explanation given. The story refuses to speculate. As it stands, the act is inexplicable, as has been every major turn in the life of this family.

b. Jacob is not startled by the interruption of Joseph. He is not angry or upset or impatient. It appears even that Joseph's statement is not new information to him: "I know, my son, I know" (v. 19). It is as if the old man is also chagrined but self-assured at this arbitrary act that was not his own doing. It is as though this strangely assigned blessing is not his to decide, as though he were helpless before the power of the blessing to have its own way (cf. Num. 23:11–12; 24:10–13). Or is the response to his son one of condescension, as though Joseph has no chance to understand, so Jacob will not waste an explanation? In any case, as the narrator has it, all three generations must bow before this inscrutable act which is irreversible. As in all parts of this narrative, the initiative belongs to the One who is never quite visible. What happens is the mysterious way of God. Jacob honors that mystery. And Israel dares to believe that a future is set, not by an old man making an error, but by the power of God. The pathos of the old man is not unlike that of his father Isaac long before (27:33–38). Only the old man is Jacob, not Esau. Jacob must have recalled that event with a mixture of feelings. But the blessing will work its own way, and none can resist it. Isaac knew that. And so does Jacob. And now Joseph must face that reality.

363

The expositor must permit the listening community to

sense the sharp arbitrariness of the act, the same arbitrariness we have seen in the oracle of 25:23. Here, it is an arbitrariness against which Joseph protests and before which Jacob is help-less. To those who like their religion reasonable and their Bible respectable, this will hardly do. But it is not an arbitrariness to be solved like a problem. It is a reality which redefines life. We are not dealing with a modest act of capriciousness confined to chapter 48. That same freedom on God's part runs throughout this narrative. Even as with Ishmael and with Esau and with Jacob's other sons, God has ignored the claims of primogeni-ture. The rights of the elder son are here disregarded again with Manasseh. It may be that Jacob remembers the pain of his long history with Esau. He might wish to pull his hand back and save the conflict. But he refuses. He refuses because it is not his to pull back. And so the right hand, the one with the power, the one which holds the future, remains in its place on the head of the younger (cf. Exod. 15:6, 12; Pss. 17:7; 18:35; 20:6; 48:10; 60:5; Isa. 41:10, 13; 48:13).

c. Jacob refuses. He refuses because this is the God who chooses midwives of Israel against the claims of the empire (Exod. 1:15–22). He refuses because this God walks with David in the face of Saul (I Sam. 16:1–13), in the face of Goliath (I Sam. 17:41–54), and even in the face of David's brothers (I Sam. 17:28). Jacob refuses because at the last this God accompanies the crucified One (Acts 2:32) who leads the band of the lame, blind, poor, and lepers (Luke 7:22). That band includes all those excluded by the claims of primogeniture, merit, and reason. And Jacob refuses because his own life has been a surprise given by God. He would not, as an old man, resist that surprise for the next generation. Our exposition must leave things as the narra-tor does, assured that we are not dealing with the capriciousness or carelessness of an old man. Rather, we are faced with the hidden power of God, who reshapes history.

d. When the old man refuses, Joseph is silent. He does not argue. Perhaps he understands. Perhaps he does not. But the blessing continues (v. 20). It is a blessing for both sons. There are no words which discriminate for the one brother against the other as there were for Isaac over Ishmael and Jacob over Esau. The words leave things equal. The shocking difference rests in the silent power of the hand. After the poetry of the blessing, the narrator adds a simple statement about consequence: "Thus he put Ephraim before Manasseh" (v. 20). The narrator does not understand how or why anymore than the participants in the drama. And beyond that, there can only be wonderment and silence.

5. The unit concludes (vv. 21–22) with one more restatement of the land promise. Here the promise is not directed to all-Israel as is usual, but specifically to the tribes of Ephraim and Manasseh. These two were to become the core elements of pre-monarchical Israel. The statement of verse 22 is enigmatic. The mountain "slope" is the "shoulder" *(Shechem).* Thus, there is an allusion to Shechem which becomes a key point of reference for the tribes (cf. Gen. 34; Judg. 9 and Josh. 24). These two verses appear to be an etiological addendum to the narrative, the dramatic end of which comes in verse 20.

A Blessing to the Sons

In this collection of materials dealing with the death of Jacob, the second element is the poem of 49:2–47. The poem very probably is early. But its placement here is secondary. It has no evident connection with the context and no bearing on the larger narrative. It is customary to have a blessing recital inserted in the narrative at the death of a great leader (cf. Deut. 33). However, while this poem is placed as a blessing, it is not introduced as a blessing (v. 1) and is not. Only the transitional comment of verse 28 regards it as a blessing. It is, rather, a schematic presentation of the twelve sons/tribes with anticipation of their futures (cf. 35:22–26). Of the biblical materials, the genre of the poem has most in common with Deut. 33. It might better be termed a "testimony." While it poses as an anticipation, it is surely descriptive of a situation of a later time of history, at the time of its composition. Thus, it is of primary interest for the historical data it supplies. Probably, it intends to be political propaganda to advance some tribal claims at the expense of others.

1. The poem has a curious function in relation to the blessing of chapter 48. It is clear that the two chapters serve quite different purposes with very different kinds of literature. As we have seen, chapter 48 has appropriate connections to the narrative and advances the plot. By contrast, the poem of chapter 49 seems to have no important connection with its context. It is inserted here to serve different purposes. The function of the narrative of 48:1–22 is to deal with the issue of transition in the narrative itself. It confines itself to the Joseph tribes which are

365

the core of early Israel. Chapter 49, by contrast, ignores the dramatic movement of the narrative and presents an unrelated statement on the power relations of the tribes (sons?) at a later time when Judah-David is preeminent.

Johannes Lindblom has observed that for the twelve sons/tribes, there are two kinds of materials ("The Political Background of the Shiloh Oracle," VTS 1:78–87 [1953]): *(a)* There are *epigrammatic statements* which offer a brief characterization or stereotype of a tribe in the form of an aphorism. In this poem, examples are Zebulon (v. 13), Issachar (vv. 14–15), Dan (vv. 16–17), Gad (v. 19), Asher (v. 20), Naphtali (v. 21), and strangely enough, Benjamin (v. 27). *(b)* There are *oracles* of a more extensive kind which concern the relative power, influence or favor of a tribe. In this poem, these concern Reuben (vv. 3–4), Simeon and Levi (vv. 5–7), Judah (vv. 8–12), and Joseph (vv. 22–26). Presumably, the poem reflects a time when these tribes were the more important.

2. The poem is probably dated not later than the tenth century. Its interpretation is not likely to serve a theological expositor very richly. At best, attention might be given to the Davidic development of Judah which hints at Messianic dimensions, and to Joseph (vv. 22–26), which refers to the preeminence of the central northern tribes (cf. 48:15–16, 20). It is curious that the reference is still to Joseph after chapter 48 and not to Ephraim and Manasseh. This is yet another evidence that the poem is only secondary in this context. And with Joseph being given such extended consideration, it is striking that Benjamin receives only a mention. One would expect more, on the basis of the valuing of Benjamin in the Joseph narrative *and* on the basis of the importance of the tribe during the time of Saul.

3. The characterization of Joseph is more intimately and intentionally linked to the preceding narratives than any of the other tribal references. We may note this at three points: *(a)* Verses 22–23 attest to the fruitful well-being of Joseph, an assertion that in him the promises are being kept. *(b)* Verses 24–25 provide a full statement about the God of this tradition. In brief scope, God is variously referred to by the metaphors of shepherd and rock, and by the three titles, "Mighty One of Jacob," "God Almighty" (=El Shaddai), and "God of your father." The verses offer nearly a catalog on the ancestral ways of characterizing God. *(c)* Verses 25–26 overflow with reference to blessing, the word used no less than six times. While the poem as a whole

presents difficult points of interpretation, the Joseph section bears testimony to the power of this God to keep his promises and turn the riches of creation toward his chosen. While not too much should be made of it, there may be cautious links between the blessings of creation (Gen. 1—2) and this oracle. Now at last the gifts of creation have been assigned to this special object of God's electing love. Such a scheme might give some overarching order to the entire Book of Genesis. It may also suggest how the cosmic hopes of God for his creation are actualized and made concrete in this particular people.

The Death of the Father

The first task of the dying father was to bind the coming heirs to the promise. This is the function of chapter 48 and, in a secondary way, the poem of chapter 49. The second task for the dying man is to provide for his own burial and resting place. This is the subject of 49:28—50:15. The narrative is presented with majesty and serenity, befitting the death of one confident in the promise. The narrative divides into two parts: *(a)* 49: 28–33 is the last *speech* of Jacob instructing his sons; *(b)* 50:1–14 is the *implementation* of his request by Joseph. It is clear that the narrative is problematic. Two literary complications are evident. First, the charge in the first part is made to all the brothers. But in the implementation, the matter is solely the responsibility of Joseph with the brothers only incidentally mentioned (50:8, 14). The first part attempts a connection with the poem of 49:1–27, whereas the second part still carries out the Joseph narrative. Second, Jacob is kept dying by the narrator for quite awhile until the business is cared for. Thus, 50:1 has connections to 47:30, which is itself an appropriate ending to the life. The overlap makes literary space for the content of chapters 48 and 49.

1. Jacob's last charge (49:28–33) is that he be buried *(a)* in the land of promise and *(b)* with his fathers. The text alludes to Genesis 23 in which the purchased and legally secured plot functions as an earnest of the land yet to be given (cf. 25:7–11; 35:27–28). While our text appears simply to specify the proper land, reference to this inalienable property right is also a reference to the promise. It is as though the dying Jacob wishes to go ahead to be on hand in the land when it is fully given.

367

2. The last scene in the life of Jacob again juxtaposes the family and the empire (50:1–14). To be sure, Joseph mourns his

father as a proper son should (v.1). He attends to his father in a careful and loyal way, but in this report he also acts fully like an Egyptian.

a. Perhaps the conclusion should be drawn that the significant part of Jacob's dying is concluded in chapter 48. In 50:1–14, all that remains is to give public and ceremonial closure of an obviously Egyptian variety. Everything is now done Egyptian-style, the embalming (v. 3), the journey by Egyptian permit (vv. 4–9), the lamenting (vv. 10–11). But even in that context, Jacob dies an honored man. The one who had kicked his way out of the womb (25:22–26) and "conned" his way into God's promise (25:29–34; 27:22–29) is at rest in the plot of promise and is honored even by the empire. In an understated way, the narrative speaks of a complete inversion. The "last one," the one desperately hungry and grieving and so often hopeless, has become the "first one," honored in his death even by the Pharaoh.

b. But the narrative would not have our heads turned by the Egyptian honor. He does not die an Egyptian. He does not want to die an Egyptian. He most fears he will be buried in the wrong place as a son of the empire (v. 5). Both his acts, the binding of his heirs (chapter 48) and the provision for burial (49:28–33), are militantly Israelite acts. They reject and resist any accommodation to Egypt. The acts are intended to place the narrative and the family squarely in the current of the promise. The Joseph narrative can be read as an independent story without intrinsic connection to the promise of the ancestors. Probably, it was originally unrelated to the fathers. But it is the persistent dominant presence of Jacob which insists that the Joseph story be genuinely Israelite. It is almost as though the matter keeps coming up in spite of the narrator. It is as powerful as the force that crossed the old man's hands in 48:14.

3. It is the story of the *promise* that gives shape to the *dying*. There is nothing here of any life after death. Jacob goes not to *heaven*, but to *Hebron*. Going to Hebron at death suggests an important and distinctive attitude toward death. Jacob continues to hope in his death. But his hope is not that immortality is to be remembered by his children, one often held by Jews. Nor is his hope one that is often held by Christians in a stereotyped "life after death." Rather, Jacob does his dying as he does his living, in terms of a promise that is not doubted. And

368

that is enough, even though he does not know the form of the fulfillment (48:3; cf. Heb. 11:17–22).

The fulfillments of well-being and land do not depend on historical indications of success, upon survival of specific human agents, nor upon the political capacity to capture. They depend only on the faithfulness of God. And that is guaranteed by nothing other than the word of the trusted promise-maker. It is that and only that which gives peace and well-being to Jacob in death. There is certitude that the promise is alive and at work. It is dependent upon and limited to no human or historical agent, because it is of God himself. Both the binding of the heirs (48) and the burial provision (49:28–33) are grounded in the promise. The heirs are to trust that promise. The burial is to anticipate it. Fulfillments are not evident here, but they are fervently hoped for. The affirmation of the text is unmistakable. This man who has been so deeply in conflict all his life can die appropriately. All his conflicts have been in the presence of the promise-keeper. His is a troubled faith, but it is a robust faith. The listening community can learn from this old man about living and about dying. This is not resignation to a blind fate. It is not possible to know what the Egyptians thought as they watched this regal procession. But the man of conflict knows that,

> The strife is o'er, the battle done;
> The victory of life is won;
> The song of triumph has begun.
> Alleluia! (Palestrina, 1591).

Genesis 50:15–26

The narrative now comes to a conclusion. But Genesis is not an ending. It is a beginning. The narrator must look ahead toward the exodus. More immediately, with the death of father Jacob, the politics of the family are scrambled. New possibilities and new dangers arise among the brothers in the absence of the father.

The narrative is divided into two parts. There is the settlement of matters between Joseph and his brothers (vv. 15–21).

369

This is a dialog shaped as a stylized exchange between lord and subjects. The second part is a narrative report of the death of Joseph (vv. 22–26). Most interesting is the charge Joseph gives to his brothers concerning his death and their future. In part, the charge of the second part parallels that of Jacob just before (49:29–32). But the additional feature is a forward look to the liberation to come.

The Settlement with the Brothers (vv. 15–21)

The politics of the family are not the major concern of the narrator. But they are always present. Characteristically, the politics of the family are subordinated to the power of the dream. And even in this penultimate scene (vv. 15–21), the dream still works its way. We have seen that the dramatic structure of the larger narrative runs from the dream in chapter 37 until its fruition in 45:1–8. In important ways, this unit offers a reprise of the dream statement, reaffirming the claims made there.

The brothers are not yet rid of their guilt (vv. 15–17). Even though 45:1–15 has already given assurance on this score, the brothers do not know whether the assurances will hold. Now Jacob is dead. Perhaps Joseph will now unleash his long-restrained resentment. The brothers face a new circumstance requiring new assurances. The enduring power of guilt and its resultant fear is a matter about which every family knows. Like every family, these brothers know that the only one who can break the cycle and banish the guilt is the wronged party, the one whom they most fear.

1. So the brothers make a candid plea for forgiveness (v. 17). The plea is the conventional formula used in the tradition of Moses (Exod. 32:32; cf. 34:7). It is the stylized form addressed to God in the lament tradition of the psalms (Pss. 25:18; 32:5). While the formula often has a theonomous reference, it is also used for appeal to human persons (cf. Exod. 10:17). Forgiveness in our verses is treated as a human, political agenda. The prime minister is the only one who can do what must be done. All parties know it. Without his action, the brothers are fated to the old history of fear and anxiety.

370

2. In verse 18, the narrator slows the action with a striking narrative comment: The brothers "came and fell down before him and said, 'Behold, we are your servants.' " The verb *fall down* brings the encounter into relation with the dream of

chapter 37. By this statement, the dramatic arc of the whole is extended from chapter 37 to chapter 50. The dream which Joseph dreamed is now unwittingly fulfilled by the brothers. There is no straight line of plot through all of these chapters. There is only a weaving together of "accidents" and "fortuitous" events that are not the doing of the father or the brothers or even of Joseph. There is something dark and deep going on in the story that shapes it in spite of all the actors. The plea of the brothers and the enigmatic response of the prime minister are set in a new context. The relationship between them is now exactly as had been anticipated and rejected in chapter 37. The brothers do "fall down." They are "servants." And Joseph holds all the initiative.

The narrator is not interested in the matter of guilt. It is not the issue to be resolved. The brothers are preoccupied with it only because they are unknowing about the larger agenda of the dream. Guilt operates for them only because the dream is not fully embraced or trusted. The expositor thus may reflect upon the relative significance of *guilt* and *dreams.* There is a large vocation accessible to this family. But the brothers miss it because they are busy with their betrayals which have such destructive staying power. The text permits us to penetrate beneath the ethical restrictiveness of the brothers for the sake of the dream. What the narrator knows (that the brothers miss) is that the dream has been at work all along, not diminished by their morality. The change of agenda from *guilt which restricts* to *dreams which liberate* is the same struggle Paul has in his battle for the promise against the law (Gal. 3—4). The power of the promise leads people past such fearful paralysis to a new life. Thus, the dream fulfillment (v. 18) leads us to the response of Joseph (v. 19). Joseph is not really interested in the guilt question. For him (in this unit) it is the dream which counts. That is now fully visible even though Joseph has vacillated along the way.

3. The response of Joseph is enigmatic (v. 19). It could hardly have satisfied or reassured the brothers. The rhetorical question is rather like a rebuke. Joseph echoes the impatient, indignant speech of his father to Rachel (30:2). Like Jacob before him, Joseph is adept at sorting out which things belong to God (things like forgiveness and the birthing of children) and the things which are properly human (cf. Mark 12:13–17). Joseph is portrayed here somewhat differently than elsewhere.

371

The narrator exercises great freedom in tracing the lead character. In chapter 45, in the first disclosure, Joseph claims everything, including the capacity to forgive his brothers. But now things are sobered, perhaps more realistic. Joseph now seems aware of the limits of his authority. The brothers had been "rendering" to Joseph what did not belong to him. Perhaps his response shows a high theological sensitivity in which he refuses to transgress the things of God (cf. the response of Jesus, Luke 12:14).

But what does the enigmatic response of Joseph mean? If we assume Joseph's good faith, it means that the cycle may be broken. But is his counter-question an act of good faith? His posture in 45:1–5 leads us to think so. Or is it another playful parrying so that when it is finished the brothers do not know where they stand? Is it rather a resentful refusal to forgive? Forgiveness is as deep as human relations can go. This narrator permits an exploration of the danger, trickery, and potential duplicity in such human affairs.

It is probable that the narrator intends the rhetorical question of Joseph to be ambiguous to the brothers and to us. It may be a ploy so that Joseph tells them they will have to deal with God. But his question may be a more direct and personal statement. In that case, perhaps the narrator returns to the question of Cain: "Am I my brother's keeper" (Gen. 4:9)? Paul Riemann suggests that this is a serious question on the part of Cain ("Am I My Brother's Keeper," *Interpretation* 24:482–91 [1970]). He argues it is God and not Cain who keeps brother. Thus Joseph may be asserting that the guilt of his brothers is no proper concern of his. He is prepared to deal with other matters that are his business. Such a shrewd distinction is in character for the Joseph given us here. But such a response is provisional. Betrayals and hurts in the family are not easily overcome. They have a lingering power. That lingering is evident here. Till the very last, the narrator is subtle. Neither we nor the brothers know how Joseph is disposed toward them. It is like waiting for the other shoe to drop.

4. The rhetorical question of Joseph is at best a parenthetical remark, at most an incidental ploy. His real speech is an assurance, "fear not," and a new affirmation that takes the brothers quite by surprise (v. 20). The response "fear not" is the primary way in the Bible of giving assurance to those who are frightened or endangered (cf. pp. 344–345). We have heard it

with Abraham in 15:1. It is characteristically used in the oracles of II Isaiah in exile (41:10, 13, 14; 43:1; 44:2; cf. Jer. 30:10). And it is used at the birth of Jesus (Luke 2:10) and in his resurrection (Matt. 28:10). This "salvation oracle" has the power to invert situations. It is spoken in order to announce that the purposes of God are much larger and more powerful than the grip of guilt. Joseph has authority to speak this word and so make things new for his brothers (see 45:5–8). The speech transcends their preoccupation with guilt and turns them to a fresh way of understanding what has happened.

5. That affirmation now prepares the brothers and the listening community for the formidable announcement of verse 20. This verse, as Von Rad and many others have seen (cf. "The Joseph Narrative and Ancient Wisdom," *The Problem of the Hexateuch and Other Essays,* 1966, pp. 296–300), is a summary of the entire Joseph narrative. The conventional translation "meant" is illuminated by the alternative rendering of *ḥāšab* as *plan.* Thus, "you planned it for evil, but God planned it for good." The verse asserts that the brothers have been too much concerned with their plan, that is, their plot to eliminate Joseph. So great was their concern that they could not see that in the midst of their scheme was another plan about which none of them knew, a plan hidden but sure in its work. That plan from God is evident only now. It intends that the family of Jacob, by the hand of Joseph, should be brought to a time of well-being and a place of "good" in the Egyptian empire. The plan is that this family is destined for life in a world of death. And none of the ways of either Pharaoh or the brothers could keep that plan from happening.

a. This verse can be used as entry into a major strain of Old Testament faith. This way of thinking is reflected in the psalmic tradition of laments. There, the speaker in trouble is aware of being victimized by those with evil plans. Those critiqued in these psalms sound very much like the brothers of Joseph:

Let them be turned back and confounded
    who *plan* evil against me (Ps. 35:4; cf. v. 20).

He *plans* mischief while on his bed,
    he sets himself in a way that is not good (Ps. 36:4).

All day long they seek to injure my cause,
    all their *plans* are against me for evil (Ps. 56:5)

373

But the psalmist, so endangered by these hostile thoughts and plans, is sure that God will override these plans:

Thou hast multiplied . . .
 thy wondrous deeds and thy *plans* toward us; . . .
As for me, I am poor and needy,
 but the Lord *plans* for me (Ps. 40:5, 17).

The psalmist's prayer is caught between the power of evil plans and the counter-plan of God. That is where the psalmist, like Joseph, must live and pray:

The LORD brings the counsel of the nations to nought;
 he frustrates the *plans* of the peoples.
The counsel of the LORD stands for ever,
 the *plans* of his heart to all generations (Ps. 33:10–11).
Deliver me, O LORD, from evil men,
 preserve me from violent men,
who *plan* evil things in their heart, . . .
Guard me, O LORD, from the hands of the wicked;
 preserve me from violent men
 who have *planned* to trip up my feet (Ps. 140:1, 4).

(In these psalms, I have followed the RSV except to make clear the use of *hāšab* by consistently rendering it as "plan." The Joseph statement reflects that entire prayer tradition).

These bold prayers reflect the conviction that it is enough to trust the plan of God to refute the deathly plans of others. In God's world, we are not helpless in the face of such devices. One can suggest that the narrator of our text has taken this tradition of piety as the basis for a dramatic story. The story embodies in practice the faith of these psalms.

The listening community may here reflect on the inscrutable way in which the purposes of God supersede the best human plans. On the one hand, that is an assurance that we may trust ourselves to God's transcendent purposes. On the other hand, it warns us that our plans are provisional and "subject to review." The deepest of human intentions are set in the context of God's unyielding intent.

b. A second useful field of interpretation, as Von Rad has shown, is the wisdom teaching which juxtaposes the plans of evildoers and the transcendent power of God *(Old Testament Theology* I, 1962, pp. 439):

374

There are six things which the LORD hates, . . .
a heart that devises wicked *plans* (Prov. 6:16, 18).

Commit your work to the LORD,
   and your *plans* will be established (Prov. 16:3).

A man's mind *plans* his way,
   but the LORD directs his steps (Prov. 16:9).

Many are the *plans* in the mind of a man,
   but it is the purpose of the LORD that will
      be established (Prov. 19:21).

He who *plans* to do evil
   will be called a mischief-maker (Prov. 24:8).

Joseph is here an embodiment of what is most honorable in the *wisdom tradition* of Proverbs. He is an expression of what is most passionate in the *lament tradition.* His statement to his brothers is candid and knowing. He is clear that his life has been cast between competing plans, plans for death and for life.

But Joseph is also sure that God's plans for life will triumph. He does not know how, nor does the narrator say how. It is enough to have this testimony at the conclusion of the work.

c. These two dimensions belong together in the affirmation of this narrative:

1) *Realism* about our human place of jeopardy.

2) *Certitude* about its outcome, by the faithfulness of God. *Realism* taken alone leads to despair, for then we only know about the danger but not about the outcome. *Certitude* taken alone leads to romanticism, for then we only know the victory but imagine we are immune from the battle. But the narrative is unflinching in realism and undoubting about the outcome.

The note of *realism* is urgent for the listening community, for we are inclined to be romantic about piety. It is precisely this gospel which understands the place of jeopardy in which we are called to live. At the same time, the narrative invites the listening community to participate in the faithful *certitude* of the wisdom teachers. They do not doubt that God will triumph. And the narrative invites sharing in the great *passion* of the psalms which are sure of God's attentiveness. The listening community, like Joseph, can say with the psalmist, ". . . I have not seen the righteous forsaken" (Ps. 37:25).

d. Joseph's affirmation (vv. 20–21) has a special affinity to the experience of Jeremiah. In chapter 18, the prophet is clear that Yahweh's plan for his wayward people is punishment (v. 11). He observes that Israel will not take the plan of God seri-

375

ously. They propose their own stubborn alternative (vv. 12, 18). But the striking assertion of the prophet is that Yahweh in his sovereign way may change his plan and give life (v. 8). So what, then, is Yahweh's plan? In neither the Joseph narrative nor the Jeremiah passage is it an immutable plan which is always and everywhere the same. Rather, we are dealing with Yahweh's intent for his people to which Yahweh may be faithful in a variety of ways. No more than the narrator in our text does Jeremiah doubt that Yahweh has a resilient purpose for his people. From another part of the Jeremiah tradition come these words, strikingly congenial to the Joseph narrative: "I will visit you, and I will fulfil to you my promise and bring you back to this place. For I know the *plans* I have for you, says the LORD, *plans* for welfare and not for evil, to give you a future and a hope" (Jer. 29:10–11). The situations of Joseph and Jeremiah are parallel. Jeremiah's Judah in the seventh-sixth centuries is in exile in Babylon. Joseph's family in Egypt is now entering its servitude. Both times are filled with evil plans which lead to servitude and displacement. Jacob's sons will end in the pit of hopelessness where the dreamer had been sent (37:24; Exod. 2:23–25). But the gospel proclamation on both occasions is uncompromising: There is another purpose powerfully at work. No scheming brothers and no imperial power can resist that other purpose. God has a plan for his people, and that plan will not be defeated.

e. That same conviction about the sure purpose of God for his people is given lyrical expression by Paul:

> We know that in everything God works for good with those who love him, who are called according to his purpose (Rom. 8:28).

Paul echoes Joseph. God means it for good. Paul echoes Jeremiah. God's plan is for welfare. And that plan works through everything. Thus in 50:20, we do not have simply a climax to the story. We have a programmatic affirmation of the gospel which has governed the entire story. The evil plans of human folks do not defeat God's purpose. Instead, they unwittingly become ways in which God's plan is furthered.

The plan of God is for *good*. The narrative has been hinting at the outcome. Thus, in 45:20 and 47:6, the phrase the "best land" is a rendering of *"good"* land. And the Pauline parallel of Rom. 8:28 is a promise for "good." But most importantly, the usage here has connections to God's verdict on creation in 1:31.

376

"Very good" is how the creation is envisioned by the creator. And that purpose to give such "good" to his creatures has been at work all through the narratives of Genesis. It may or may not be intentional, but the use of this word in 50:20 serves to bind the entire text of Genesis into one sweeping statement. From the beginning (1:31) until the death of Joseph (50:20), the God of creation and of Israel has been about only one thing. And God has used even the ways of Joseph's brothers to bring his creation to its rich fulfillment. That is God's overriding purpose.

6. It is no wonder that Joseph now announces the substance of the overriding purpose of God (vv. 20–21). It is for life. It is for life that the empire cannot give (cf. John 14:27). Only the God of Israel can guarantee this kind of life. The speech affirms that the plan of life for Israel receives concrete implementation in the work of Joseph who provides. In chapter 41 Joseph had already understood that the plans (dreams) of God are sure (vv. 25–32). And he had understood with equal clarity that they require concrete historical implementation (vv. 33–35).

Joseph's recognition of God's sure plan for Israel does not lead to abdicating trust. It leads to a vocation. There is a perfect correlation between God's will for life and Joseph's work of providing (cf. 45:11; 47:12). This way of presenting Israel's faith is at the same time deeply believing and radically secular. It does not doubt the plan of God in the least. But at the same time, it accepts responsibility for the plan. Joseph does not "leave it all in God's hands." But he also does not believe that "God has no hands but ours." He accepts his vocation.

7. The encounter with the brothers is concluded with "comfort" (v. 21). The issue of guilt has been completely overcome. The agenda has moved beyond any concern for *retribution* to the larger issue of *vocation*. Twice now he has said to them, "fear not" (vv. 19, 21). Their alienation, fear, and grief are overcome. As is evident in Isa. 40:1–2, "comfort" is an exile-ending word. In our text as in Isa. 40:1–2, "comfort" is paralleled by "speak to the heart" (v. 21). The translation in the RSV is misleading, for it does not indicate the precise parallel to Isa. 40:1–2. But the parallel can hardly be incidental:

Verse 21: "he reassured them" *(nhm)* = "Comfort, comfort" *(nhm)* (Isa. 40:1).
"he comforted them" *(yᵉdabbēr 'al-libbām)* = "speak tenderly to the heart" *(dabbᵉrû 'al-lēb)* (Isa. 40:1).

377

The word of comfort in both contexts is speech which penetrates to the deepest dimensions of existence, where homelessness can be dealt with. The brothers have been homeless and ill-at-ease since their actions in chapter 37. They introduced the agenda of death into the family. But the vocation of Joseph, by the plan of God, is to give life to that family.

The comfort has been long in coming. The use of the word "comfort" *(nhm)* here may be a conscious reference to 37:35. At the beginning of our narrative Jacob refused to be comforted *(nhm)*. Now the comfort denied in 37:35 has come to fulfillment. Thus the linkage of 37:35 to 50:21 suggests another evidence of the artistic coherence of the story. The comfort had to wait a generation. But it has come. The brothers' plan grieved the father and put the whole family in exile. The persistent good plan of God finally has given comfort and promised homecoming.

The Death of Joseph (50:22–26)

Now that the story has told of its resolution to the crisis of chapter 37 (50:15–21), we are prepared for the death of Joseph (vv. 22–26). Joseph in death is as inscrutable as he was in life. He is fully Israelite, yet partly Egyptian. This final report is given as a chiasmus:

    a) full years *in Egypt* (v. 22)
        b) a claiming of heirs for the *land* (v. 23)
            c) the land *promise* (v. 24)
        b) an oath to the *land* (v. 25)
    a) embalming in *Egypt* (v. 26).

1. The story is framed by Egyptian claims. In verses 22 and 26, the first and last words are "in Egypt." Joseph dwelt in Egypt (v. 22). He was put in a coffin in Egypt (v. 26). The report begins with the dating of one hundred and ten years, a proper and blessed age in Egypt. In verse 26, it is concluded with embalming, honored like his father Jacob (50:2) with an honor befitting a Pharaoh. He died as he dreamed, a well-regarded ruler.

2. But the heart of this narrative (vv. 23–25) and perhaps the heart of the man are fully Israelite. That is announced in three ways.

a. Joseph is securely placed in the generations of Israel (v. 23). He held his great-grandchildren on his knees. He claims them as his heirs.

b. Like father Jacob, he knows that his real place of rest is the land of promise, not Egypt (v. 25). For all the well-being of Egypt, it is not home. Egypt can for a time be a place of good fortune. But it is not the land of promise. Joseph's wish in death is like that of Jacob (49:28–33). He wishes to be present in the land for the fulfillment of the promise which he does not doubt. There is to be a long waiting (cf. Exod. 13:19; Josh. 24:32), but Israelites do not weary of waiting for land. Joseph is more fully Israelite here than anywhere else in the entire narrative. Here he fully embraces the promise yet to be kept.

c. At the center of these five verses (v. 24), Joseph reasserts the land promise, appealing to the oath of the fathers. This is the only time the promise is on his lips. One can argue that the narrator has finally made his lead character into a genuinely Israelite figure. Or if one stays within the narrative itself, one may conclude that only at death has Joseph come to understand fully who he is. The last words of Joseph are neither reminiscences nor grudges. *They are hopes.* His last words are the last words of every Israelite who receives a genesis from God. The use of the word "visit" in verses 24–25 (in both cases used with an absolute infinitive for emphasis) is the same word of Jeremiah to the exiles (Jer. 29:10). The visit of God is an *exile-ending intrusion.* That is the hope of sixth-century exiles in Babylon. It is the last, best hope of Joseph. Joseph knew that the way of his people would be like his own way with God—visited, interrupted, intruded upon—according to God's dream. In God's way and in God's time, that visit is Israel's source of hope. An unvisited history is no history at all. But Joseph knows Israel's history is visited in powerful and irresistible ways.

So the narrative ends in Egypt, awaiting the visit. The narrator is sure of the visit. That is the Genesis. The visit of God creates possibility for another beginning. By 50:26, we are still at the beginning, still at Genesis awaiting God's newness. The prime minister dies, not reviewing old troops or remembering old visits, but hopeful of a new Genesis. God has sworn his word. God keeps his word. And so there is a waiting.

From the speech of creation until the affirmation of Joseph at death, we have been attentive to God's call. We have attended to the *sovereign* call by which "God calls the worlds into being." We have also considered the way in which God calls us into his church. That call has been *embraced* by Abraham and Sarah, has set Jacob into many *conflicts* and has worked its

379

hidden way through the life of Joseph. The beginning made in Genesis moves toward the oppression and liberation of Exodus. The promise of a good land (=earth) continues on its way. The listening community waits with Israel. And while waiting, it, too, must decide about the call.

BIBLIOGRAPHY

1. For further study

CALVIN, JOHN. *Commentaries on the First Book of Moses Called Genesis,* translated by John King (Grand Rapids: Eerdmans, 1948).

DELITZSCH, FRANZ. *A New Commentary on Genesis,* 2 vols., 5th ed. (Edinburgh: T. & T. Clark, 1899).

DILLMAN, AUGUST. *Genesis: Critically and Exegetically Expounded,* 2 vols. (Edinburgh: T. & T. Clark, 1897).

DRIVER, SAMUEL ROLLES. *The Book of Genesis,* WESTMINSTER COMMENTARIES (London: Methuen & Co., Ltd., 1904).

GUNKEL, HERMANN. *Genesis,* GÖTTINGER HANDKOMMENTAR ZUM ALTEN TESTAMENT, 4th ed. (Göttingen: Vandenhoeck & Ruprecht, 1917).

LUTHER, MARTIN. *Lectures on Genesis,* edited by Jaroslav Pelikan, 8 vols. (St. Louis: Concordia Publishing House, 1958-1965).

_____. *Luther's Works,* vols. 1-8 (St. Louis: Concordia Publishing House, 1958-1966).

RAD, GERHARD VON. *Genesis,* OLD TESTAMENT LIBRARY, 1st ed. 1961, rev. ed. 1973 (Philadelphia: Westminster, 1961).

SKINNER, JOHN. *A Critical and Exegetical Commentary on the Book of Genesis,* INTERNATIONAL CRITICAL COMMENTARY, 1st ed. 1910, rev. ed. 1930 (Edinburgh: T. & T. Clark, 1910).

SPEISER, EPHRAIM AVIGDON. *Genesis,* ANCHOR BIBLE (New York: Doubleday, 1876).

WESTERMANN, CLAUS. *Genesis 1—11,* BIBLISCHER KOMMENTAR: ALTES TESTAMENT (Neukirchen-Vluyn: Neukirchener Verlag, 1974).

2. Literature cited

ALTER, ROBERT. "A Literary Approach to the Bible," *Commentary* 60, No. 6: 71-79 (1975).

ANDERSON, BERNHARD W. "From Analysis to Synthesis: The Interpretation of Genesis 1—11," *Journal of Biblical Literature* 97: 230-39 (1978).

AUERBACH, ERICH. *Mimesis* (Princeton: Princeton University Press, 1965).

BARTH, KARL. *Church Dogmatics* III, 1,2,3 (Edinburgh: T. and T. Clark, 1958-60).

_____. *The Humanity of God* (Richmond: John Knox Press, 1960).

BLENKINSOPP, JOSEPH. *Prophecy and Canon* (South Bend, Indiana: University of Notre Dame Press, 1977).

BUECHNER, FREDERICK. *The Magnificent Defeat* (New York: Seabury Press, 1966).

CARLSON, R.A. *David, the Chosen King* (Stockholm: Almquist and Wiksell, 1964).

CARRINGTON, PHILLIP. *The Primitive Christian Catechism* (Cambridge: Cambridge University Press, 1940).

CLARK, MALCOLM. "The Flood and the Structure of the Pre-Patriarchal History," *Zeitschrift für die Alttestamentliche Wissenschaft* 83: 204-10 (1971).

_____."A Legal Background of the Yahwist's Use of 'Good and Evil' in Genesis 2—3, *"Journal of Biblical Literature* 88: 266-78 (1969).

CLINES, DAVID. *The Theme of the Pentateuch, Journal for the Study of Old Testament,* Supplement 10 (Sheffield, University of Sheffield, Dept. of Biblical Studies, 1978).

COATS, GEORGE. *From Canaan to Egypt* (Washington, D.C.: Catholic Biblical Association of America, 1976).

CROSS, FRANK M. *Canaanite Myth and Hebrew Epic* (Cambridge: Harvard University Press, 1973).

DAHLBERG, BRUCE T. "On Recognizing the Unity of Genesis," *Theology Digest* 24: 360-67 (1976).

DAUBE, DAVID. *Studies in Biblical Law* (Cambridge: Cambridge University Press, 1947).

GESE, HARMUT. *Lehre und Wirklichkeit in der Alten Weisheit* (Tübingen: J.C.B. Mohr, 1958).

HABEL, NORMAN C. "Yahweh, Maker of Heaven and Earth," *Journal of Biblical Literature* 91: 321-37 (1972).

HANSON, PAUL. *Dynamic Transcendence* (Philadelphia: Fortress Press, 1978).

HELD, H.J. with Günther Bornkamm and Gerhard Barth. *Tradition and Interpretation in Matthew* (London: SCM Press, 1963).

LAING, R.D. *The Politics of the Family and Other Essays* (New York: Pantheon Books, 1971).

LIFTON, J. ROBERT. *Living and Dying* (New York: Praeger, 1974).

MCEVENUE, SEAN E. *The Narrative Style of the Priestly Writer*, ANALECTA BIBLICA 50 (Rome: Biblical Institute Press, 1971).

MENDENHALL, GEORGE. "The Shady Side of Wisdom: The Date and Purpose of Genesis 3," *A Light unto My Path*, H.N. Bream, Ralph D. Heim, C.A. Moore (Philadelphia: Temple University Press, 1974), pp. 319-34.

_____. *The Tenth Generation* (Baltimore: Johns Hopkins University Press, 1973).

MINEAR, PAUL S. *To Heal and to Reveal* (New York: Seabury Press, 1976).

NEAL, MARIE AUGUSTA. *A Socio-Theology of Letting Go* (New York: Paulist Press, 1977).

NIEBUHR, H. RICHARD. *Christ and Culture* (New York: Harper, 1951).

VON RAD, GERHARD. *Old Testament Theology I* (New York: Harper and Brothers, 1962).

_____. *The Problem of the Hexateuch and Other Essays* (New York: McGraw-Hill, 1966).

RENDTORFF, ROLF. "Genesis 8, 21 und die Urgeschichte des Jahwisten," *Kerygma und Dogma* 7: 69-78 (1961).

_____. *Das Überlieferungsgeschichtliche Problem des Pentateuch* (Berlin: Walter de Gruyter, 1976).

REVENTLOW, H. GRAF. "'Internationalismus' in den Patriarchenüberlieferungen," *Beitrage Zur alttestamentlichen Theologie*, ed. by H. Donner, R. Hanhart, R. Smend (Göttingen: Vandenhoeck and Ruprecht, 1977) 354-70.

RICOEUR, PAUL. *Freud and Philosophy* (New Haven: Yale University Press, 1970).

_____. *The Symbolism of Evil* (New York: Harper, 1967).

RIEMANN, PAUL A. "Am I My Brother's Keeper?" *Interpretation* 24: 482-91 (1970).

ROTH, WOLFGANG M. "The Wooing of Rebekah," *Catholic Biblical Quarterly* 35: 177-187 (1972).

SCHMIDT, H.H. "Rechtfertigung als Schöpfungsgeschehen," *Rechtfertigung*, J. Friedrich, W. Pohlmann, P. Stuhlmacher (Göttingen: Vandenhoeck and Ruprecht, 1976) 403-14.

_____. Der Sogenannte Jahwist; Beobachtungen und Fragen zur Pentateuchforschung (Zurich: Theologischer Verlag, 1976).

SCHMIDT, LUDWIG. "De Deo," *Beihefte zur Zeitschrift für die alttestamentliche Wissenschaft* 143 (Berlin: Walter de Gruyter, 1976).

SEGUNDO, JUAN LUIS. *Our Idea of God* (Maryknoll, N.Y.: Orbis Books, 1974).

VON SETERS, JOHN. *Abraham in History and Tradition* (New Haven: Yale University, Press, 1975).

STEINBECK, JOHN. *East of Eden* (New York: Bantam Books, 1976).

TERRIEN, SAMUEL. *The Elusive Presence* (New York: Harper and Row, 1978).

THOMPSON, THOMAS L. *The Historicity of the Patriarchal Narratives, Beihefte zur Zeitschrift für die alttestamentliche Wissenschaft* 133 (Berlin: Walter de Gruyter, 1974).

TILLICH, PAUL. *The Eternal New* (New York: Scribner, 1963).

TRIBLE, PHYLLIS. *God and the Rhetoric of Sexuality* (Philadelphia: Fortress Press, 1978).

WALSH, JEROME T. "Genesis 2:46—3:24: A Synchronic Approach," *Journal of Biblical Literature* 96: 161-77 (1977).

WEIMAR, PETERS. *Untersuchungen zur Priestenschriftlichen Exodusgeschichte, Beihefte zur Zeitschrift für die alttestamentliche Wissenschaft* 146 (Berlin: Walter de Gruyter, 1977).

WESTERMANN, CLAUS. *"Arten der Erzählungen in der Gesesis," Forschung am alten Testament,* Theologische Bucherei 24 (Munich: Chr. Kaiser Verlag, 1964) 9-91. Now printed in translation as Part A of *The Promises to the Fathers* (Philadelphia: Fortress Press, 1980).

——————. *Blessing in the Bible and the Life of the Church* (Philadelphia: Fortress Press, 1978).

WHITE, LYNN J. "The Historical Roots of Our Ecological Crisis," *Science* 133:1203-07 (1967).

WOLFF, HANS WALTER. "Jonah—The Messenger Who Gambled," *Currents in Theology and Mission* 3 (1976).

WÜRTHWEIN, ERNST. *Wort und Existenz* (Göttingen: Vandenhoeck and Ruprecht, 1970).